THE CRITICAL HERITAGE

The Critical Heritage Series

GENERAL EDITOR: B. C. SOUTHAM, M.A., B.LITT. (OXON.)
Formerly Department of English, Westfield College, University of London

For list of books in the series see back end paper

CLOUGH

THE CRITICAL HERITAGE

Edited by
MICHAEL THORPE
Associate Professor of English University of Calgary

BARNES & NOBLE PUBLISHERS
NEW YORK

Published
in Great Britain 1972

Published in the United States of America 1972
by Barnes & Noble Publishers
© Michael Thorpe 1972

ISBN 0 389 04508 X

Printed in Great Britain

General Editor's Preface

The reception given to a writer by his contemporaries and near-contemporaries is evidence of considerable value to the student of literature. On one side we learn a great deal about the state of criticism at large and in particular about the development of critical attitudes towards a single writer; at the same time, through private comments in letters, journals or marginalia, we gain an insight upon the tastes and literary thought of individual readers of the period. Evidence of this kind helps us to understand the writer's historical situation, the nature of his immediate reading-public, and his response to these pressures.

The separate volumes in the *Critical Heritage Series* present a record of this early criticism. Clearly, for many of the highly productive and lengthily reviewed nineteenth- and twentieth-century writers, there exists an enormous body of material; and in these cases the volume editors have made a selection of the most important views, significant for their intrinsic critical worth or for their representative quality—perhaps even registering incomprehension!

For earlier writers, notably pre-eighteenth century, the materials are much scarcer and the historical period has been extended, sometimes far beyond the writer's lifetime, in order to show the inception and growth of critical views which were initially slow to appear.

In each volume the documents are headed by an Introduction, discussing the material assembled and relating the early stages of the author's reception to what we have come to identify as the critical tradition. The volumes will make available much material which would otherwise be difficult of access and it is hoped that the modern reader will be thereby helped towards an informed understanding of the ways in which literature has been read and judged.

B. C. S.

Contents

CONTENTS

Poems by Arthur Hugh Clough (1862)
(including *Amours de Voyage*, 1858)

Letters and Remains of Arthur Hugh Clough (1865)

The Poems and Prose Remains (1869)

Later estimates (to 1920)

CONTENTS

ix

Acknowledgments

My thanks are due to the following for permission to use some of the items reprinted below: to G. Bell & Sons Ltd, for a chapter from *New Essays Towards a Critical Method* by J. M. Robertson; to Constable & Co. Ltd, and Greenwood Press, Inc, Westport, Conn., for an extract from *Arthur Hugh Clough*, by James Insley Osborne; to the Clarendon Press, Oxford, for extracts from *Letters of Matthew Arnold to Arthur Hugh Clough* (ed. H. F. Lowry) and *The Correspondence of Arthur Hugh Clough* (ed. F. L. Mulhauser); to Macmillan & Co. Ltd, for an extract from *A History of Nineteenth Century Literature*, by George Saintsbury; to *The Times Literary Supplement* for the review by A. S. MacDowall and to the *Sewanee Review* for the article by Martha Hale Shackford.

For help in tracing certain quotations I am thankful to Dr P. G. van der Nat of the University of Leiden and to Mr Adolf Höfer. Professor Leonard Kriegel kindly obtained copies of some of the American material. For the saving of much time and effort I owe my largest debt to the timely publication of the *Descriptive Catalogue* compiled by Messrs Houghton, Timko and Gollin.

Preface

The main text of this volume consists of sixty-one essays, reviews and extracts from books and letters which have been selected with the object of giving a fair impression of the contemporary and near-contemporary response to the work of Arthur Hugh Clough. The period covered by the pieces I have chosen is 1848, the year in which *The Bothie of Tober-na-Vuolich* appeared, to 1920. The terminal date was not easy to decide. Clough died early, in 1861, leaving much of his best work unpublished. In 1862 two selections appeared: *The Poems of Arthur Hugh Clough*, edited by his friend C. E. Norton and published in Boston, and in England *Poems by Arthur Hugh Clough*, with a Memoir by F. T. Palgrave. The contents of these were very similar and both excluded many readily available poems. Though a few new items were added by Palgrave to the second edition of his selection in 1863, the important poems 'Easter Day' and *Dipsychus* were not allowed in print by the reluctant Mrs Clough until 1865, and then only in a small edition, *Letters and Remains of Arthur Hugh Clough*, 'for private circulation only'. Mere fragments from *Dipsychus* had been included in the previous volumes. Mrs Clough's fear that the poem was 'too unfinished' and liable to mislead readers as to her husband's true beliefs still led her to censor it severely, both in 1865 and again in 1869, when *The Poems and Prose Remains of Arthur Hugh Clough, with a Selection from his Letters* was at last allowed to brave the public eye. Mrs Clough herself provided a Memoir for this, having also edited it with the doubtless indispensable aid of John Addington Symonds. Not before 1869, then, was a fairly substantial edition of Clough's poetry generally accessible.

The 1869 edition continued in use throughout the remainder of the nineteenth century and supplied the source for several other editions of the poems, large and small. Its text was only challenged once before the appearance of the modern *The Poems of Arthur Hugh Clough*, edited by H. F. Lowry, A. L. P. Norrington and F. L. Mulhauser (Oxford, 1951). This was by *Poems of Clough* (1910), for which the editor, H. S. Milford, collated the *Poems* (1862) with the original edition of *Ambarvalia* (1849) and a copy of *The Bothie* which Clough had himself corrected. The editors of 1951 extended this treatment to the whole of Clough's work, returning to the original manuscripts for their texts and supplying copious notes on variants. Their edition includes many additional lines to previously published poems, particularly *Dipsychus*, though in this case they exceed their editorial function by consigning to the notes those parts they think poorly executed.

So we see that in Clough's case a collection of this kind conspicuously lacks the advantages of acquaintance with the whole corpus of his work. Nevertheless, an assessment of the bulk of his output could fairly be made in 1869, a year which produced three substantial essays by R. H. Hutton, Henry Sidgwick and J. A. Symonds. I did not draw the line at that point because I thought that if there must be a dividing line it should be defined, not by date, but by opinion, sentiment and attitude. This selection shows that, during the late nineteenth century a strong body of opinion regarded Clough as one of the most representative and noteworthy Victorian writers. Symonds had written in 1869 of the debt felt towards Clough by a generation then in their twenties, while one of the strongest pro-Clough articles of the later period came from a critic, J. M. Robertson, who belonged to a generation unborn when Clough died. If Thyrsis fell by the wayside early, his work marched on abreast at least of his friend and elegist's, fit to be mentioned often enough in the same breath as Tennyson's and Browning's.

As one of the things I thought this book might do was to throw light on Clough's sharp decline from favour in the twentieth century, I decided to set my limits to include chiefly what I will call his reputation in his own time, which I define not by the limits of his short life, but by what may be called Victorian sentiment, rounding this off with symptomatic examples of reaction against him. Conveniently, this period could be seen as culminating with the relative indifference shown towards the centenary of his birth in 1919.

In editing the material printed below, it has been assumed that it will be read in conjunction with *The Poems of Arthur Hugh Clough* (1951). For this reason, and to save space, it has seemed best to omit very long quotations from articles and reviews and to substitute instead a clear brief reference to the texts as given in *The Poems*. (If quotations in full were included, this book would have been twice the length: the attitude of the Victorian critic to the function of quotation, for which there seems to have been almost unlimited space, may be represented by these words from the *Rambler* (No. 20): 'Of their poetical merit it is needless to speak, for the quotations we have given will enable readers to judge for themselves.') To facilitate reading, shorter quotations of verse, up to ten lines approximately, have been printed entire. Quotations made from Clough's prose have generally been printed in full, as the prose is likely to be less readily accessible to readers. It seemed undesirable to clutter the text with notes indicating where early critics' quotations differ in detail from later, revised texts, as, for example, with *The Bothie* and *Amours de Voyage*; *Poems* (1951) provides this service. Where early critics' quotations from *The Bothie* differ markedly from those of the corrected version (most of which appeared in *Poems*, 1862) I have left them as they stand and added notes to facilitate the reader's comparisons. In the case of *Dipsychus* I have occasionally supplied notes to indicate where a reference to the version of 1869 may be found in the greatly differing scheme of the modern edition.

In general I have printed only those parts of the comments on *Ambarvalia* which are concerned with Clough's contribution to the joint volume, but occasionally I have retained those on Burbidge's in order to keep the tone and judgments of reviewers in their original perspective (see Nos. 16, 18, 19).

Where the authors of anonymous pieces have been traced, their names have been included in the headnotes of the relevant items. Footnotes have been kept to a minimum: unless otherwise indicated, they are my own. I have supplied translations, where I could, for quotations that may need it, but I have not included tags among these. I have silently corrected obvious printing, spelling or punctuation errors and omitted the page references to early editions which some reviewers supplied.

Each item has been headed with a paragraph supplying a brief 'placing' comment on the piece itself and, where it seemed useful, on the critic. The chronological arrangement of items has been determined, first, by the dates of publication of the various collections of Clough's work; second, for the period after 1869, by the date when the item was first published. Readers who wish to trace the history of comment upon any particular work will find full references in the Index.

MICHAEL THORPE
Leiden/Calgary

Chronological table

Abbreviations

A.H.C., Descr. Cat.: Arthur Hugh Clough, a Descriptive Catalogue, ed. Richard M. Gollin, Walter E. Houghton and Michael Timko, New York Public Library, 1966–7

Corr. I or *II: The Correspondence of Arthur Hugh Clough*, Volumes I and II, ed. F. L. Mulhauser, Oxford: Clarendon Press, 1957.

Poems (1951): The Poems of Arthur Hugh Clough, ed. H. F. Lowry, A. L. P. Norrington and F. L. Mulhauser, Oxford: Clarendon Press, 1951

PPR I or *II: The Poems and Prose Remains of Arthur Hugh Clough* (1869), with a selection from his letters and a Memoir, edited by his wife. Vol. I: Life, Letters, Prose Remains. Vol. II: Poems.

SPW: Selected Prose Works of Arthur Hugh Clough, ed. Buckner B. Trawick, University of Alabama Press, 1964

Introduction

I

There was ample contemporary response to Clough's work, so much so that the present volume can lay no claims to being exhaustive. I have, however, printed virtually all the reviews of the volumes published during Clough's lifetime, *The Bothie of Tober-na-Vuolich* (1848) and *Ambarvalia* (1849), while in the later period I have concentrated on giving space to the most substantial essays and reviews. These have been reinforced with extracts from letters written to Clough or about him by a number of important Victorians who were themselves creative writers, with several of whom, such as Matthew Arnold, Emerson and J. A. Froude, Clough had a close personal relationship. If a few of the earlier reviews were somewhat cursory and ill-natured, reflecting a Philistine prejudice against bright young Oxford men, this is amply compensated for by the thorough and often very favourable articles and reviews of the 1860s, written in response to the posthumous collections of Clough's work published in 1862 and 1869. In these first twenty years Clough probably received at least as much critical attention from the reputable critics of the day as did Matthew Arnold or, in an earlier period, Tennyson. In fact, the volume and kind of the initial response to Clough's volumes of 1848–9 compares very favourably with the reception given to the early Tennyson as represented in Professor J. D. Jump's *Tennyson: the Critical Heritage*. In comparison with his friend Arnold, whose first volume, *The Strayed Reveller and Other Poems*, came out one month after *Ambarvalia*, in February 1849, Clough seems to have got off to a far better start. A later reviewer of Arnold's *Poems* (1853) reports that his early work was received with 'general indifference' (*Westminster Review*, xxv, April 1853, 146). If this is true, it may have been partly owing to its anonymous publication—under the initial 'A'—but in one case *The Strayed Reveller* was reviewed together with *Ambarvalia*. This was in the *Guardian* (No. 17) and there it is interesting to see that both were welcomed, with inevitable reservations on the score of immaturity, as worthy potential successors to Tennyson. This was only the first of several comparisons between the two—and these were not always to

Arnold's advantage. As late as 1869, we find the High Churchman J. B. Mozley, going to this extreme in the course of an article in which he discusses Clough and Arnold in turn: 'To pass from Clough to Mr. Matthew Arnold, is to pass from one who poured out his whole soul in verse to one with whom verse is a pleasant recreation' (*Quarterly Review*, cxxvi, April 1869, 348). At that time, while he had the whole of Arnold's poetry before him, including the *New Poems* of 1867, Mozley's comparisons were limited to Clough's *Poems*, 1863. Readers today who have lost the Victorian habit of thinking of Clough as being in the same company as Arnold, Tennyson and Browning, may feel the need in the course of reading this volume to reconsider their comparative judgments.

The solid core of Victorian appreciation of Clough is in the typically expansive essays and reviews of the 1860s and little except repetitious biographical information has been cut from these. Since Clough died before the bulk of his work was either published or commented upon, we can only guess at what his response to his critics would have been, though his reactions to his friend J. C. Shairp's adverse criticisms of *Amours de Voyage* (No. 25) and his review in 1853 of Arnold and others—the crucial part of which is quoted in the extract from Waddington's biography (No. 46)—show that Clough knew very well what he was doing and what he wished to do. But his failure to complete anything substantial after about 1851, ten years before his death, naturally led critics, from Palgrave (No. 24) onwards, to look for explanation and extenuation in his life. Unfortunately, they seized upon him as being pre-eminently 'one of those' Victorians, 'whose memoirs should be written when they died,' to quote Mrs Bulstrode upon her sainted husband (*Middlemarch*; Chapter 36). Their biographical preoccupation tended to deflect their concern from evaluation of what Clough did achieve: in bulk at least his collected poems compare closely with those of Arnold, who also wrote most of his poetry in the space of a few years in his late twenties and early thirties.

Some two-thirds of the collection printed below covers virtually all the valuable comment, English and American, up to 1869, the year when *The Poems and Prose Remains of Arthur Hugh Clough* appeared, the most complete collection of Clough's work accessible in the nineteenth century. After this date, I have had to be more selective. While making sure that the better and more influential critics are represented, I have tried also to provide a reliable cross-section of the varying views. I have excluded many pieces which seemed either wholly derivative in their critical comment or concerned exclusively with Clough's 'philosophy' rather than his literary achievement; for the latter reason especially I have not included any of the relatively scanty European comment during the period, which is chiefly of German origin. One might have thought that Clough would be a tempting quarry for Taine or Ste Beuve, but they left him alone. In addition to the numbered items, many shorter comments will be found in the introductory survey which follows. I feel confident that this collection plots faithfully the intriguing rise and fall of Clough's reputation up to the centenary of his birth.

II

DURING CLOUGH'S LIFETIME

Clough's early works, *Ambarvalia* (January 1849) and *The Bothie of Toper-na-Fuosich* (November 1848), received quite as much favourable attention as a new writer could expect, including long notices by such outstanding men as Charles Kingsley at home (No. 7) and R. W. Emerson in America (No. 8). Owing to its rare vitality, *The Bothie* made the stronger impression: Kingsley acclaimed the 'genial life' of 'a man who seeing things as they are, and believing that God and not "taste" or the devil settles things, was not ashamed to describe what he saw, even to Hobbes's kilt, and the "hizzies' " bare legs'.[1] It is striking that several of those who enthused should have been writers who felt the oppressions of the Mrs Grundys of the time: Kingsley and Emerson, Thackeray (No. 2) and Froude (No. 6). The anonymous reviewers were less welcoming. In the *Literary Gazette* (No. 9) and the *Spectator* (No. 3) there is a tone of crusty animus against uppish young Oxford men; despite this, the former magazine's airy debunking of *The Bothie* does seem to have influenced Clough in his later revisions. There was, of course, some excuse for irritation with *The Bothie*'s 'in-group' appeal, but by no means the whole of Oxford was as delirious as Matthew Arnold somewhat churlishly suggests in his letter to Clough soon after the poem came out (No. 1). And Clough reported to Emerson in February 1849 that 'in Oxford though there has been a fair sale and much talk of it, the verdict is that it is "indecent and profane, immoral and (!) Communistic".'[2] That same month Clough received a chilly letter from Provost Hawkins of Oriel, of which he was then Fellow—but not for much longer—informing him that 'there are parts of it [*The Bothie*] rather indelicate; and I very much regretted to

3

find also that there were frequent allusions to Scripture, which you should not have put forth. You will never be secure from misbelief, if you allow yourself liberties of this kind.'[3]

With one important exception, we may regard the detractors as members of the old guard in matters literary and religious. But the exception, Matthew Arnold, Clough's close friend and correspondent, destined to shadow him throughout all future criticisms and histories, must have been hard to take. While Thomas Arnold the younger, Clough's model for the radical Hewson, enthused from New Zealand over 'an action, I truly think, among the boldest and purest that I have known',[4] his brother, who was to have no great success with *The Strayed Reveller* (February 1849), supplied the dash of cold water that chastens most when it comes from a friend. What to J. R. Lowell, one of Clough's first and most faithful American supporters, was one of the poem's great virtues, is dismissed by Arnold as merely factitious. Lowell did 'not know a poem more impregnated with the nineteenth century or fuller of tender force and shy, delicate humour':[5] to Arnold this fresh modernity was 'plunging and bellowing' in the 'Time Stream'—a typically 'American' fault, in fact (No. 1). His rigid standards of classical restraint, his preference for the 'great action' left no room for Clough's exuberant mock epic. Yet he was capable of greater generosity in the memorial tribute he paid Clough at Oxford shortly after receiving news of his death (No. 23): by then he was himself the more securely established poet, no longer Clough's tetchy and impatient rival.

If Arnold failed to do *The Bothie* justice, he nevertheless made a genuinely friendly and shrewdly critical effort over *Ambarvalia*. His letters (No. 14), prompted by reading some of the *Ambarvalia* pieces in manuscript, pinpoint a recurrent and still live issue in Clough criticism: is he, though a notable truth-teller, no 'artist'? Does he offer Truth, but not Beauty? Today's reader will wish to consider whether what Arnold means by beauty can be made an exclusive test of poetic achievement; Clough, we may be sure, had his distinctive views on this, but unfortunately his side of the correspondence has not survived. A glance at the by no means adulatory reviews of *Ambarvalia* will reveal how completely out of fashion he was. His knotty poems were almost all concerned with what the reviewer in the *Rambler*, who did find them congenial, called the 'inward life' (No. 20): in Clough's own words, 'the questing and the guessing/Of the soul's own soul within'. Others found 'obscurity', thought rather than poetry, and a want of finished craftsmanship. Several actually prefer the sub-Tennysonian echoes of Clough's now forgotten fellow-poet, Thomas Burbidge. With Burbidge they knew where they were: 'he speaks far more intelligibly' (No. 16), shows 'more promise . . . of taking a high place among the lyrists of the day' (No. 19) and has a 'more decidedly poetical temperament' (No. 21).

Some impression of Clough's own critical viewpoint may be gained from 'Recent English Poetry', his review of several volumes of poems by Alexander Smith, Matthew Arnold and others, printed in the *North American Review* in July 1853.[6] There he gets his own back, somewhat sweepingly, it must be admitted, on Arnold and the beauty-mongers. Much later in Clough criticism this article was turned to account by Samuel Waddington, who gives a long extract from it to help define what he sees as two schools of poetry, 'of form and manner, on the one hand, and of thought and subject-matter, on the other' (No. 46). He places Clough, of course, in the latter school, but to little critical purpose—except to perpetuate a practice which may be attributed largely to Arnold's influence, of suggesting that in poetry 'beauty' excludes 'thought' and 'thought' 'beauty'. It certainly did not occur to Arnold, or any of the earlier critics, where Clough's pre-Romantic roots lay, nor in any case would one who could safely, in 1880, dismiss Dryden and Pope as 'classics of our prose' have been impressed by Clough's affinity for them.[7]

It was in an American magazine that Clough's review appeared and it was America—and has been, to the present day—where he was most warmly received. He found, when he went there himself, that 'people here put it [*The Bothie*] on the drawing room tables . . . and find it innocent enough, which indeed, believe me my dear child [he is writing to his fiancée, who may have had some doubts on this score] it really is—a little boyish of course—but really childishly innocent.'[8] The encouragement of Emerson and Lowell has already been mentioned: it was their friend and fellow Brahmin, Longfellow, whose example in *Evangeline* (1847) had, in fact, combined with Homer's to inspire *The Bothie*. In the second of his 'Letters of Parepidemus', published in *Putnam's Magazine* (August 1853), Clough paid tribute to Longfellow for acclimatizing English, 'our forward-rushing, consonant-crushing, Anglo-savage enunciation', to hexameters.[9] Opinion was, and always has been, divided, as to whether Clough also was successful in this: according to William Rossetti, Tennyson found *The Bothie* 'execrable English',[10] while, on the other hand, Palgrave could report to Clough that the Laureate 'frequently reads *Ambarvalia* (1st division) and spoke the other day of "Qui laborat orat" in language of high admiration and sympathy'.[11] *Ambarvalia*, 'the casualties of at least ten years',[12] had more surface polish; *The Bothie*, dashed off in a bare two months, was bound to fall foul of those who, less responsive to its spirit, looked more coldly at what they considered to be its stylistic faults.

It was in the country of Emily Dickinson and Walt Whitman, not in an England dominated by formalist criticism or characterized by the straitened feeling of even so good a friend as J. C. Shairp (No. 25), that Clough could expect to prosper or at least get a sympathetic hearing. Lowell persuaded him to let *Amours de Voyage*, written in 1849 but bottom-drawered for fear of the Mrs Grundys at home, appear in his new *Atlantic Monthly*. After seeing the manuscript, Lowell wrote in December 1857: 'I like it more than *The Bothie* . . . the same exquisite shading of character and refined force of expression which the wise found in that, they will find in this. Mrs. Grundy has her eye so turned to scene painting and the Hercules-and-Lichas style of displaying power that she is quite unable to feel your quiet Art: her torpid nerves need grosser excitements: but the Atlantic has readers who will feel and love you.'[13] This may have been so, but Clough still preferred to let it come out anonymously in 1858. We can only guess at the wider American response, on which the testimonies of Emerson (No. 26) and C. E. Norton (No. 27) differ. In his correspondence about the poem and reactions to it Clough goes increasingly on the defensive. Writing to F. J. Child on 16 April 1858, in the month when Canto III of the serialized '5 act epistolary tragi-comedy or comi-tragedy' appeared in the *Atlantic*, he thinks 'no one will find much natural pleasure' in it.[14] Evidently he was anticipating the 'natural' disappointment with the ending which came from even so favourably disposed a reader as Emerson (No. 26). Already, the *Ambarvalia* poems had given warning that, in seemingly endorsing in *The Bothie* the popular dictum of Carlyle—'The end of man is an action, and not a thought'—Clough was voicing only a passing impulse of yea-saying. In the *Amours* Carlyle's dictum is turned on its head:

> *Action will furnish belief;* but will that belief be the true one?

'Doubt,' warned the *Guardian*, striking, if we may judge from similar reactions to Arnold's early volumes, the approved contemporary note, 'is not a poet's mood' (No. 17). The *Guardian* was complaining conservatively of *Ambarvalia*, but it was depressing for Clough to be told off in similar terms by the previously sympathetic Emerson because unpleasant endings are 'inadmissable in poetry'. Clough protested in vain that the poem was to be read as fiction and that the ending was consistent with Claude's character, but he was so far shaken by Emerson's objections as to confess to the more sympathetic C. E. Norton: 'my defence can only be that I always meant it to be so and began it with the full intention of its ending so—but very likely I was wrong all the same. . . .'[15]

It seems worthwhile to speculate here on another possible American connection. If *The Bothie* was partly inspired by *Evangeline*, might Clough not also have had Longfellow's tale in mind when writing the *Amours*, for which it could have served as anti-model? The separation of lovers and the quest are common to both, Longfellow's being the 'positive' to Clough's 'negative'. *Evangeline* is a tragic tale in the romantic tradition, of love crossed by cruel circumstance: like Tristan and Iseult, Gabriel and Evangeline are re-united after a lifelong quest, only for one to witness the other's death. Clough gives us instead a mock epic of modern love, with a tragi-comic issue brought about by the unheroic inadequacy of the lovers to measure up to the high claims of Romantic Love. It does, however, mar this speculation a little to find William Whewell in his 'English Hexameters' (from which an extract is given here, No. 12) complaining of the 'sad' and 'aimless' 'course of events' of *Evangeline* and regretting, like Emerson on the *Amours*, the want of a 'satisfactory' (i.e. happy?) ending. If even Longfellow could concede too much to 'reality' for some palates Clough had good reason to fear for his poem's reception.

III

RESPONSE TO THE 'POEMS' OF 1862

Like Keats's, Clough's reputation had for some years after his death to contend with the well-meant extenuations of his friends. Also like Keats, he suffered from the fact that by no means all his best work was in the reader's hands when he died a premature death. It was, in any case, inevitable that the negative impression made by the sceptical poems in *Ambarvalia* and by the misunderstood *Amours de Voyage* (though this was hardly known in England when Clough died) should have reinforced the feeling that he had left all too little accomplished. His friend Dean Stanley's obituary notice can only be called defeatist:

'Those who knew him well know that in him a genius and character of no common order has passed away, but they will scarcely be able to justify their knowledge to a doubting world.'[16] The tone of the obituaries, described by George Eliot, who was 'deeply touched' by the quotation of 'Qua Cursum Ventus' (a favourite poem with critics) in the *Spectator*'s contribution, as one of 'affectionate respect',[17] was echoed and given general currency by that of Palgrave's 'Memoir' to the first Clough selection which appeared in 1862 (No. 24).

Palgrave set a pattern for admiration of the man combined with diffident praise of the honest and upright content of the works, which was to reach its peak when Goldie Levy found at the end of her *Arthur Hugh Clough; 1819–1861* (1938) that 'Clough is more interesting than his poetry.' This was the ultimate endorsement of Palgrave's first give-away: 'he rather lived than wrote his poem'. Palgrave's apologetics invited ripostes like Henry Fothergill Chorley's (No. 29) and G. H. Lewes's (No. 31), who accused him of 'rhetorical evasion'. An anonymous reviewer in the *Saturday Review* declared roundly that 'published poems must be taken for what they are worth in themselves, and not for what they may be worth in connexion with certain elements of a dead man's character' (No. 28).

Clough's most sympathetic critics at this stage devoted their energies to bracing up the rather feeble, though virtuous, character sketched by Palgrave. W. L. Collins saw the poems as 'only the leisure fancies of a mind that was always active, which never shrank from the harder and more prosaic work of life, and which, under different circumstances, might have left for itself a more enduring record'.[18] Trying to build a more substantial case for the defence, David Masson (No. 30) concentrates upon bringing out 'the peculiar cast of his philosophy' by means of a painstaking examination of Clough's self-searchings. Masson finds that no simple generalizations can be made, that Clough is a tough and flexible thinker, but he does not examine the works closely. While he justly insists that in the *Amours* some part of Claude's speculations must be the poet's, he concludes that 'the interest and power of the poem lie in the passages of general thought and feeling . . . and in the historical notes and allusions it contains'. Closer critical comment comes from W. Y. Sellar (No. 34) who asserts that no reader is entitled to expect 'immediate perspicuity' of the shorter poems, but instead of pursuing this insight he concludes by emphasizing the separation between the 'artistic accomplishment' and 'the thought'. He, too, though more appreciative, regrets the unpleasantness of *Amours de Voyage*. With Bagehot (No. 33), who had early shown a strong interest in Clough personally and who complains with admirable forthrightness of the too frequent publication of 'the dreadful remains of nice young persons', we are in more positive company. He stresses the toughness of Clough's '*straining*, inquisitive, critical mind' and shrewdly considers whether the *Amours* can be related to the currently influential views on 'great actions' which Arnold had expressed in the Preface to his *Poems* (1853). Another positive voice was that of R. H. Hutton, who had been at least part-author of the *Spectator* obituary referred to above and who contributed an admiring but, as yet, tentative evaluation of the *Poems* to the *Spectator* of 12 July 1862. This has not been printed in full here, to avoid repetition; its main points are more maturely argued in his later articles on Clough (see especially No. 39 below). It shows Hutton hesitating to applaud outright what he will later defend as Clough's true strength. Regretting that 'suspense of mind is antagonistic to poetry', he isolates for praise those poems, such as 'Qua Cursum Ventus' and 'Say Not the Struggle Naught Availeth', in which he finds 'the unity of lyrical passion' that is forged through the mastery of doubt. Returning to Clough in 1869, Hutton will become one of his most perceptive champions in a climate in which doubt was still a dirty word.

IV

RESPONSE TO THE MORE COMPLETE EDITIONS, 1865, 1869

During the sixties Clough's widow devotedly applied herself to the task of sorting his remains with a view to representing his memory more fairly than she had dared to do at the time when the 1862 *Poems* was being prepared. Then, though she had written to C. E. Norton that it would be 'a pity to leave out anything truly individual', she had, fearing that certain pieces would cause misunderstanding, at length omitted, among other things, 'Easter Day' and all but a few innocuous fragments of *Dipsychus*. She tried to make good these omissions in the privately circulated *Letters and Remains* (1865), but it was not until 1869, in the two-volume *Poems and Prose Remains*, that critics and the general public had access to this material and more *Dipsychus* was still heavily bowdlerized *pro pudore*, as was to be expected of an editor who, like some early reviewers, found that innocent, but suggestive, poem 'Natura Naturans' 'abhorrent'.[19] Though it had been in *Ambarvalia*, it was dropped in 1862, but restored to favour in 1869. *Dipsychus* worried her more; it was 'too unfinished', not only in composition, but also in attitude. Writing to the Rev. Percival Graves before publishing to ask him about the advisability of printing the whole, she wonders which passages he would favour selecting and speculates about her husband's unfinished intentions:

I believe . . . that the end was left indistinct because it was so in his own mind. I cannot think he meant the feeling of religion in one sort or other to succumb but that he did think there must be a time of dearth so to speak in practical life, especially to a mind somewhat overfed in youth. I [regret?] so much that he did not live to do more, because I think he would have done differently later. He did change enough to make me think he would have gone farther and this also makes me shrink from giving out anything which might *look* as if it was the final result at which he had attained.[20]

Though she omitted some 400 lines from the manuscript, including almost the whole of one scene (Scene IIA in *Poems* (1951)), she nevertheless printed what she recognized to be a very inferior sequel, 'Dipsychus Continued: a Fragment', which she described to Graves as being 'most unsatisfactory . . . a sort of citing of commonplace views as having a degree of truth in them'.[21] The chief effect of her censorship of *Dipsychus* was to tone down those parts concerned with Dipsychus' sexual inclinations and temptations. Not without reason had Clough warned her, when he left the manuscript of *Dipsychus* in her care during his stay in America, not to look into it. She had peeped (who wouldn't?), but she confessed to him, struggling bravely with her distaste:

It is strange those peeps and reminders of your old times and thoughts and your other sides always upset me—I believe I am unjust. Now I am writing to you, it seems to come back to a more usual state, but it is horrid—they seem to me full of honest coarse strength and perception. I don't mean to blame but I don't like it. I don't like men in general; I like women—why was not the world made of women—*can* there not be strength without losing delicacy. . . . I did hardly know that good men were so tough and coarse. I mean not that they prefer evil, but they consider of it so much—I do not mean anything about you—you always give me the impression of being good, very good.[22]

No doubt she was typical of the sheltered ladies of her time. We may think it unfortunate for Clough that it fell to such a person to edit his poetry, though in her collaborator, John Addington Symonds, she had someone who was hardly squeamish. They both had, in any case, to consult the taste of the time.[23]

Symonds was the first English critic of some creative pretensions himself to attempt sustained criticism of Clough. His two long essays, of which the second, published shortly before the volumes of 1869 appeared, is printed here (No. 38), show a writer of a new generation deliberately taking stock of existing opinion and enhancing it with his own. In one of the letters by which he made contact with Mrs Clough in 1867 he felt able to inform her that there were several of his genera-tion 'at Cambridge and Oxford who look on Mr. Clough's poems as the expression of their deepest convictions'. Among these were Henry Sidgwick (No. 41) and W. J. Courthope, whom Symonds described as

one of Mr. Clough's most warm admirers. The *Amours de Voyage* are always in his mind and on his lips. He believes in him as one of the true artists, as one of the greatest masters in language, of this century. Nor is Courthope lavish of admiration. On the contrary: he has few good words to say for Browning or Swinburne or even Wordsworth.[24]

An extended appreciation on these lines by Courthope would have been a unique contribution to Clough studies, but unfortunately he failed to carry his *History of English Poetry* (1895-1920) beyond the Romantics. It seems likely that he and Sidgwick had a considerable influence on what Symonds wrote.

Since he belonged to a new generation and had no intimate connec-tion with Clough's circle—or any strong reason for prejudice against it—Symonds was able to take up a totally fresh standpoint. By the late 1860s it was becoming possible to turn a cooler eye upon such topics as the German Higher Criticism and the Tractarian and Dar-winian controversies. Symonds could make a more objective analysis of Clough's religious position, substantiating his views with much previously unquoted evidence from the letters, looking back on Clough as one who 'happened to live during a period of transition in the history of human thought'. He offers the most constructive criticism of *Amours de Voyage* to date, drawing attention to its novelistic qualities, a point which both Hutton (No. 39) and Sidgwick (No. 41) pick up and which is most strongly developed later by J. M. Robertson (No. 54); he finds, unlike earlier critics, that 'we cannot mistake the irony'. He vindicates Clough in terms which only critics who have the advantage of hindsight can confidently use: 'it is the poet's function to hold up a mirror to his age, as well as lead it . . . we still admire Hamlet and Faust'. An allied point, in terms of artistic perspective, is Symonds's passing comparison with Wordsworth's revolution in the direction of simplicity and directness, which he sets implicitly in his last paragraph in opposition to the poetry of the 'present age', by which we may suppose he means, from hints dropped earlier in the essay, the poetry of Tennyson, Swinburne and their imitators.[25] (With Tennyson Symonds is, however, at one in his admiration for the *Mari Magno* tales. Symonds thinks them likely to be 'the most popular of his works'; Tennyson's son reports his father's opinion that 'Clough . . . had great poetic feeling: he read me then his *In Mari Magno* and cried like a child over it.'[26]

Symonds's essay is also distinguished for some shrewd comparative comments—not 'analysis', which, for him as for most Victorian critics, signifies copious quotation interlaced with sketchy commentary on subject-matter and plot. Nevertheless, in pointing out how Clough's mind works characteristically by 'thesis and antithesis' without reaching a synthesis, he puts his finger on an important aspect of the poetry's metaphysical quality. This, however, had to await fuller development in Walter E. Houghton's analysis of Clough's 'poetry of structures' (*The Poetry of Clough*, 1963).

R. H. Hutton (No. 39), in a typically shrewd and humane essay on the 1869 volumes, pursued the comparison with Arnold more constructively than had been done before, a comparison which becomes, from now on, a fairly constant feature in Clough criticism. It was natural in the nineteenth century to think of them together, whereas in the twentieth, until recently, Clough has been little more than a footnote to Arnold. Lowell was sadly wrong when he prophesied in 1866:

. . . we have a foreboding that Clough, imperfect as he was in many respects, and dying before he had subdued his sensitive temperament to the sterner requirements of his art, will be thought a hundred years hence to have been the truest expression in verse of the moral and intellectual tendencies, the doubt and struggle towards settled convictions, of the period in which he lived.[27]

(J. M. Robertson (No. 54) points out that this differs subtly from Lowell's conjecture elsewhere that in the future Clough's poetry may be considered 'the best utterance in verse of this generation',[28] from which he concludes that Lowell 'gives up the point' of Clough's 'strictly poetic success'; actually, he does not, as the second quotation, from an article published in January 1869, is the later.) It is interesting that Lowell, too, shares in the reaction against Tennyson: in 'Swinburne's Tragedies' he complains that 'the dainty trick of Tennyson cloys' and also regrets Browning's 'difficult' writing.

Another of Clough's faithful Americans, C. E. Norton, enthused over the 1865 volume, praising Clough's 'liberal temper, his questioning habit of mind, his absolute devotion to truth, and his sense of many sidedness',[29] but his article is largely biographical and too similar in viewpoint to Norton's earlier piece in the *Atlantic Monthly* (No. 27) to need printing here.

When we turn to Sidgwick (No. 41) we find a more sustained and confident attempt to indicate the subtlety and maturity of Clough's thought, setting it, as Symonds does, in the movement of mind of the mid-nineteenth century. It was time Clough, an advanced thinker, had his turn: like him, 'we are growing [generally] more sceptical in the proper sense of the word'. If anyone amongst contemporary poets deserves the name 'philosophic poet' it is not Tennyson or Browning, but Clough, who more often than they has the intensity of feeling necessary to make the expression of ideas in verse a genuine poetry, not a versified prose. Sidgwick's comments on the originality of Clough's 'scientific' scrutinizing of Love are suggestive, but they lack the necessary dimension of comparative criticism: it was, perhaps, natural for a mid-Victorian critic to forget Donne—and even Shakespeare—but he should not have forgotten Browning.

I should, perhaps, conclude this section with a reminder to the reader of the appearance in 1866-7 of Matthew Arnold's 'Thyrsis, A Monody, to commemorate the author's friend, Arthur Hugh Clough', whose superficial sense, at least, probably did more to shape the Clough Myth than any item in this volume except Palgrave's 'Memoir'. Extracted from the conventional context of the pastoral elegy phrases like 'too quick despairer' rapidly became too facile a means in the text-books of neatly distinguishing the pale flower from the accomplished mandarin.

V

LATER ESTIMATES (TO 1920)

If the opinions discussed in the previous section are a reliable guide, it seems that in 1869 the prospects for the reputation of Clough's poetry were more than fair: he was holding his own with the other great Victorians in a climate of positive response which seemed likely to strengthen. Symonds had chosen to advertise him as one whose cast of mind was especially congenial to a younger generation less inhibited than their fathers by disabling doubt, a generation, as

Sidgwick points out, more freely capable of scepticism. Edward Dowden, following on in 1877, responds strongly to the fact that 'Clough wrote almost always with the consciousness of two or more conflicting feelings' (No. 43). It is less the doctrine than what we have come today to think of as the poet's attitude to his experience that matters. It is striking that this characteristic should also have been singled out by so different a critic as Bishop Lyttelton (No. 44), though in his desire to see Clough's 'humorous irony' as covering an essentially sound viewpoint he makes rather light of the negative side; yet in this very attempt he pays unconscious tribute to Clough's antithetical power.

Nevertheless, the Clough Myth lingered on, warping much of the later comment. Clough was unlucky in his first biographer, Samuel Waddington (No. 46), a plodding commentator devoid of literary insight: he confines himself almost entirely to the content of the poetry, perpetuating the 'thinker' versus 'singer' theory (this time linking Clough with Browning) and burying Clough deeper by using his 'purity' as a stick to beat contemporary decadence. Some years later, it was appropriate, but no more constructive, that Lionel Johnson should have diagnosed 'decay' in Clough (No. 51), contrasting him with the lofty humanism and more refined artistry of Arnold (who had some vogue among the aesthetes). The Arnold-Clough comparison continues to crop up frequently. Unfortunately, this is more often to play them off against each other for the sake of glib contrast than to bring out their affinities. Yet it must be admitted that in what they said of each other Arnold and Clough invited as much. Reviewing Waddington's biography in 1882, R. H. Hutton follows Clough's own line of criticism of Arnold's poetry in the article 'Recent English Poetry', taking his cue from Waddington's extensive quotation from it (see below, pp. 313-15). He opposes Clough the 'realist' to one who 'frames his pictures . . . in golden margins of felicitous fancy' (No. 47), implying that the reason for Clough's 'relative neglect' is that he deals with realities which most readers seek to escape when they turn to poetry.

Yet how much truth is there in Hutton's assumption of 'unpopularity', plausible though it sounds? A writer in the Saturday Review was to note in 1888 that since 1877 'only three years have passed without a fresh impression of the Poems and Prose Remains' (No. 49).[30] The Review's polemic against the 'Cloughomaniacs' is hardly the sort of fire one would expect Hutton's 'unpopular' hero to draw. The

Saturday Review goes out of its way to disparage the hallowed favourites, surprisingly exempting for praise 'The Latest Decalogue' and commenting that 'if Clough had had a healthier mind, he might have been more considerable as a satirist than he ever could have been as a serious poet'; it is, instead, the 'second-rate sensitive minds' and 'morbid egoists' who find in him their soul-mate and model. Writing at the same time, Coventry Patmore voices a similar opinion, though more temperately, and wonders at 'the considerable figure he stands for in the estimation of the present generation' (No. 50). Patmore is, however, with that majority who, whatever their valuation of the rest of Clough, exempt *The Bothie* from displeasure for its 'healthy', 'human' and 'natural' appeal (an appeal, incidentally, which Clough found in Patmore, whose example helped to inspire *Mari Magno*). If we add to the dissentient voices that murderous limerick by Swinburne (No. 52) which, as we may infer from Saintsbury (No. 53), must have had a deflating effect utterly out of proportion to its length, we have a bewildering range of response: Clough is dull, humorous; morbid, healthy; a realist, a second-rate sensitive; he is unjustly neglected and, by the young, extravagantly overrated. If to arouse such sharp divisions of opinion as these is, as some think, a mark of greatness, then it is a distinction that Clough has never lacked.

Into this confusion of critical opinion bedevilled by the affective fallacy, J. M. Robertson injected the most thorough attempt since Symonds to make an objective, rounded evaluation of Clough's work (No. 54). His chapter on Clough from *New Essays Towards a Critical Method* (1897) is a fair sample of the work of a now forgotten Victorian critic who, in a period clotted with historical and impressionistic criticism, made a brave attempt to give criticism a scientific underpinning. Robertson's essay shifts the critical ground efficiently from the sentimental tendencies, on the one hand, of the 'Oxonicules and Bostonicules' Swinburne sneers at, and from the sour-intentioned disparagement these provoked, to an analysis of the literary quality of Clough's work based on his own threefold 'aesthetic', 'psychologic' and 'sociological' approach. Viewing Clough's 'analytic fiction' in verse form in historical perspective, he argues persuasively that it was composed at a time, in 1848–50, when English fiction was 'on the whole . . . imperfectly intellectual'. To see Clough's work in this light, it was especially important to point out how much more original was *Amours de Voyage* in 1849, when it was composed, than it was in 1858—or 1862, when it reached the wider English public. Robertson penetrates the journalistic concern of much earlier criticism of *The Bothie*, showing how this deflected critics from their real task which was to appraise the 'delicately humorous parody' Clough achieved by using Virgilian and Homeric metre and other technical devices. His 'psychologic' and 'sociological' approaches enable him to appraise also the insight which has gone into the handling in *The Bothie* of a 'youthful Radical' and the delicate touches which make up a Jamesian portrait (or rather sketch) of a lady in the *Amours*. Here, no doubt, he overstates his case when he exclaims 'how much more real is the lady than some of that artist's [James's] presentments!'—but the comparison remains acute.

Yet, if the writer of 'Clough and his Defender' (No. 55) is to be believed, Robertson launched his critique just as the tide was running out: Clough's reputation had 'so waned and dwindled during the last twenty years among all classes of readers that it might seem . . . to have well nigh reached its vanishing point'. 'Twenty years' is evidently an exaggeration in the light of what we see was being written around 1888, but from then onwards (Robertson's essay, he claims, was actually written in 1887) there is a dearth of noteworthy pro-Clough criticism, a want of strong voices raised in his favour, which lasts, with a few exceptions, well into the twentieth century.[31] We may find one explanation for this in the tone of F. R. Statham's long essay, published in 1897 in three magazines, *National Review*, *Eclectic Magazine* and *Living Age*. This provides a sentence that neatly sums up the fatal trend that began with Palgrave: 'Clough,' writes Statham, 'was one of the very few men of the present century who can claim to be studied, not for what they did, but for what they were' (*National Review*, April 1897, 201). Statham's article, as so often is the case, puts the life before the work, and Clough is canonized as a shining example of faith and fortitude in a materialistic world. Such praise may make a man, but it will break a poet: Swinburne's limerick is directed as much against such admirers as against the poetry (if, indeed, he had read it).

To return for a moment to Robertson's more critical defence, besides shrewdly probing Robertson's weak point—his seeming defence of Clough's poetry as prose fiction—the *Academy* reviewer throws criticism back into the hexametrical morass. It was, of course, inevitable that generations subjected to metrical drill on public-school parade grounds should have been so little capable of seeing beyond it—a limitation which Clough himself shared to some extent when he took the risk of parodying it for humorous purposes. Even so favourable a late defender as E. Forster (No. 56) cannot find a good word for the hexameters, while Charles Whibley, one of Clough's early twentieth-century editors, felt bound to devote most of his Introduction to an apology for them. It should be added, however, that one authoritative and forward-looking discussion of Clough's handling of the accentual hexameter did appear at the turn of the century, in Robert Bridges' *Milton's Prosody*. It has not been included here because Bridges' technical discussion of extracts from Clough can be adequately appreciated only in the light of the laws of stress-prosody which Bridges lays down in his book as a whole. It is worth noting that he singles out Clough's poetry as more deserving of notice than any of the English accentual hexameters he has 'tried to read'.

My quotations [he notes] are from Clough because I have found him an exception, and am charmed with the sympathetic spirit of his *Bothie* and *Amours*, in which he has handled aspects of life, the romance of which is very untractable to the Muse, and chosen for them a fairly satisfactory though not a perfected form. If Clough did not quite know what he was doing in the versification (and if he had known, he could have used some of his liberties more freely, and others more sparingly), yet he knew very well what he was not doing.

'What he was not doing', in particular, was writing classical hexameters, but instead, as was appropriately pointed out by the editor of Hopkins, substituting 'six stresses or speech accents, with their complements, for the six quantitative feet of the classic hexameter'.[32] (Bridges might have found a more 'sparing' use of the rhythm of the accentual hexameter in T. S. Eliot's *Four Quartets*, though, as Helen Gardner has noted in her *The Art of T. S. Eliot*, Eliot's heritage would have been *Evangeline*, not the more experimental Clough.)

We may regard the Rev. Stopford Brooke's chapter published in 1908 (No. 57) as the last of the thoroughly Victorian estimates, treating the poems primarily as a means to understanding Clough, conceding their artlessness but entering a special plea for 'a gentle and charming talent'.

In 1909, the year after Brooke's *Four Poets*, the 'New Revised Edition' of the 1869 volumes, first printed in 1888, was reprinted for the last time. This was followed by H. S. Milford's *Poems of Clough* (1910), a valuable re-editing of the 1862 *Poems*. The *Poems*, published in Oxford Plain Texts in 1912 and re-issued in 1914, was probably occasioned by the fact that Clough was just out of copyright: this was only a selection of the more popular pieces with extracts from *The Bothie* and the *Amours*, almost nothing from *Dipsychus*. In 1913 the 1888 edition of the poems was superseded by *Poems of Arthur Hugh Clough*, identical in content with the former volume except for Charles Whibley's apologetic Introduction, which might well have been omitted for all it could do for Clough's reputation. A representative quotation from Whibley may be found in the *Contemporary Review*'s rejoinder (No. 58); yet this, strongly pro-Clough though it is, is evidently a rearguard action in the face of the early Georgian poets' realistic innovations—'these current writers, who supply incapacity for form and absence of scholarship by vigour that is not unattractive and coarseness that vainly calls itself virile . . .' Similarly, W. K. Gill, taking Whibley to task in the *Spectator* (28 February 1914, 346) for undue emphasis on Clough's 'intellectual weaknesses', defends Clough in fatally old-fashioned terms. He praises the 'admirable melody' of *Mari Magno* and firmly [believes] not only that certain of his lyrics and elegies will last as long as the English language, and that his un-rhymed verses, whether we call them English hexameters or blank dactylics, are destined to play a real part in the evolution of English poetry'. It is ironical to reflect what these reviewers might have said if they could have seen 'Land of Empire' or the lines Mrs Clough had excised from *Dipsychus*; more so to reflect how those Georgians and Futurists, hot in their rejection of the Victorians and their bloodless sons, the Decadents, would have reacted to Clough if only they had paused for a moment to read at least the Clough that was accessible to them. Though the 'coarser' elements were not printed till the *Poems* of 1951, wit, realism, humour, a deliberate 'artlessness' where nice art would muffle sense and feeling, all these 'modern' qualities could have been discovered by the patient and unprejudiced reader of even those editions available in 1910. Instead, the Romantic–Victorian tradition suffered a blanket dismissal:

Poetry, it was assumed, must be the direct expression of simple emotions, and these of a limited class: the tender, the exalted, the poignant, and, in general, the sympathetic . . . Wit, play of intellect, stress of cerebral muscle had no place: they could only hinder the reader's being 'moved'—the correct poetical response.

So F. R. Leavis, sweepingly summarizing early twentieth-century reactions against the Victorians in *New Bearings in English Poetry* (1932), a 'seminal' book in which, incidentally, Clough is not even mentioned

—yet how thoroughly in sympathy with this indictment of so much that is bad in Victorian poetry Clough would have been himself!

Somehow Clough was lost sight of around 1910, though, as our items from the *Contemporary Review* (1914) and *The Times Literary Supplement* (1920) show, this does not mean he was absolutely ignored, or, when he was noticed, treated unfavourably. He was virtually obliterated in the general eclipse of the great Victorians, whether poets, politicians or pukka sahibs, which set in during and after the Great War. The mood of this eclipse reached its extreme in Lytton Strachey's brilliantly biased caricatures; of Clough he writes:

This earnest adolescent, with the weak ankles and the solemn face, lived entirely with the highest ends in view. He thought of nothing but moral good, moral evil, moral influence, and moral responsibility. . . . Perhaps it is not surprising that a young man brought up in such an atmosphere should have fallen a prey, at Oxford, to the frenzies of religious controversy; that he should have been driven almost out of his wits by the ratiocinations of W. G. Ward; that he should have lost his faith; that he should have spent the rest of his existence lamenting that loss, both in prose and verse; and that he should have eventually succumbed, conscientiously doing up brown paper parcels for Florence Nightingale.[33]

As with the Swinburne epigram (No. 52), a grain of brilliant distortion can outweigh a mass of earnest sympathy. For the brighter members of the new generation, to whom Strachey was a voice refreshingly free of cant (as Clough had been to Symonds and his contemporaries), these few words alone must have ensured that, if they had not already read Clough—and 1914–18 left little time for that—they certainly need not do so now, Clough was with the priggish Dr Arnold, Strachey's favourite Aunt Sally, a lesser waxwork among the Guilty Victorians.

So when Clough's centenary came round, in November 1919, it was unlikely that he would find a new champion among young and influential writers and critics. Though he did get one biographer, he was again, as in 1883, unlucky enough to be landed with an apologist, not a champion. An extract from J. I. Osborne's *Arthur Hugh Clough* has been given below for interest (No. 60). It was calculated to do little more than perpetuate the Myth of the Interesting Failure. More bracing than the biography itself is A. S. McDowall's sympathetic and generous review in *The Times Literary Supplement* (No. 61). Even this, however, has the bias and limitation of so much Clough criticism: as MacDowall says, 'everyone who writes of Clough's poetry quickly begins talking of the man'. Not that this should, or could, be avoided, but such a discussion should always lead us back to the work. This is one of the virtues of Martha Hale Shackford's 'Clough's Centenary: His *Dipsychus*' (No. 59). Her comments on the life have been retained here for the sake of comparison with both Victorian and Stracheyan approaches. She neither apologizes for Clough nor sentimentalizes about him, but concentrates on bringing out those 'traits that we admire especially: flexibility and shrewdness of intelligence joined with an invincible idealism'. By stressing the intelligence and the part it plays in the work as strongly as the idealism she tried to direct interpretation back on to the high road laid down by Clough's best Victorian critics. It is fitting that it should have been an American who spoke up most strongly for Clough in 1919 (though it must be admitted that another American, reviewing Osborne, spoils this impression a little by taking the biographical line and lamenting, 'it was the tragedy of his life that while he wished to pray with the faithful, his keen intelligence forced him to scoff with the scornful'[34]). As Miss Shackford notes at the beginning of her essay, Clough was probably most at home in America, and, with such champions as Lowell, Emerson and C. E. Norton he had good reason to be. A writer in the *Boston Review*, in 1862, thought 'We are more in sympathy with such earnest, searching minds, than the mass of Englishmen' (No. 35); while a later American critic, who admired Clough for being his own man—'his fine original nature took no tinge of the prevailing influences about him'—had gone so far as to speculate that, 'If he could have remained in the liberal American atmosphere, and have been spared his untimely taking-off, he might have come to greatness.'[35] This may well be just, though the New England Brahmins he fell among had their own limitations.

VI

THE CRITICAL TRADITION AFTER 1920

Though the positive revaluation of Clough cannot be dated earlier than 1951, when Lowry, Norrington and Mulhauser's edition of *The Poems of Arthur Hugh Clough* appeared, he was not totally neglected, for good or ill, during the previous thirty years. Ironically, since Clough was the Victorian poet whom modern taste might have found most congenial, it was during this period of relative indifference that modernism was becoming consolidated. Clough was kept down with the rest of the Victorians, including Arnold, who was also roughly handled by Strachey, as well as by the Bloomsberries, the Sitwells and T. S. Eliot: their revival, in the past twenty years, more or less coincides with his. If he has lagged behind Arnold, as well as Tennyson, Browning and others, it is largely because of the recurrent, debilitating preoccupation with his seductively discussable personality.

It is not the task of this book to treat the modern fortunes of Clough's reputation in detail, which would be superfluous in any case since excellent surveys already exist.[36] I shall confine myself to mentioning some of the most interesting criticisms and indicating the main lines of development.

It was unfortunate for Clough, as for other Victorians, that one of his few notable critics in the 1920s was F. L. Lucas. Lucas's 'Thyrsis', first published in *Life and Letters Today* (II, May 1929), reprinted in *Eight Victorian Poets* (1930) and again in *Ten Victorian Poets* (1940), is a singularly destructive exercise in Stracheyesque disparagement. Clough is peppered with mnemonic phrases, 'Rugbeian elephantiasis of the conscience', 'Hamlet with a touch of Polonius', and dismissed as 'the impersonation of an age when religious doubt was not, as now, a rare and mild greensickness, but a crippling, even a fatal malady'. In a brief essay in *Portraits* (1931) Desmond MacCarthy tries to correct the distortions of Strachey and Swinburne, especially as to Clough's personal weaknesses. His insights into the importance of the poetry are suggestive but sketchy: 'He preferred truth to beauty, which spoilt his chance of being a great poet; but he became in consequence a unique poet. We ought to be thankful he did not ride off like his contemporaries on the high horse of some prophetic cause, or even on Pegasus.'[37] (In this latter respect MacCarthy neatly turns the tables on Swinburne's 'torrents of unreadable ecstasy'.)

The next important positive contribution was H. F. Lowry's Introduction to his edition of *The Letters of Matthew Arnold to Arthur Hugh Clough* (1932). This includes a strong reappraisal of Clough's real, as opposed to the 'ideal', side represented in Arnold's 'Thyrsis': his intellectual sharpness, humour and imagination. But Lowry's main quarry was Arnold; though he takes care to stress the younger Arnold's debt to Clough, he only had Arnold's side of the correspondence. In the same year the minor satirist Humbert Wolfe, in *The Eighteen Sixties* (ed. John Drinkwater), seized on what might have been a more profitable line of approach, but his thesis that Clough was less a frustrated believer than a frustrated satirist muffled by 'the swaddling clothes of Arnoldism' is vitiated by his assumption that Clough remained nevertheless a case of unfulfilled promise. This hard-dying myth is perpetuated by both the next biography of Clough, Goldie Levy's *Arthur Hugh Clough; 1819–1861* (1938), which concludes self-defeatingly 'Clough is more interesting than his poetry', and the widely-read, excellent biography of Clough's Corydon, *Matthew Arnold*, by Lionel Trilling (1949), where Clough is treated throughout as an interesting footnote for contrast, not an important poet in his own right.

The distinction of publishing the first modern revaluation of Clough's poetry, brief though it is, probably belongs to Michael Roberts, who comments in his Introduction to *The Faber Book of Modern Verse* (1936) on its affinities of tone and intention with the poetry of Eliot and Pound. Roberts, however, is still anxious to stress Clough's Victorian limitations. Yet in the past twenty years a growing number of critics have drawn attention to Clough's modernity: John R. A. Yeoman finds an affinity of tone between MacNeice's *Autumn Journal* and *The Bothie*;[38] John Heath-Stubbs sees Clough as both 'the Victorian forerunner of that school of poets who have attempted "social-realist" poetry in our own century' and 'the wistful unbeliever . . . fundamentally inconsistent and sentimental';[39] both V. S. Pritchett[40] and J. D. Jump[41] single out *Amours de Voyage*, the latter calling it 'a minor masterpiece' and commending the serio-comic tone so rare in decorous Victorian poetry, yet so vitally appealing to us; the reviewer of the 1951 *Poems* in *The Times Literary Supplement* lays more emphasis on the modernity of *Dipsychus* and *Mari Magno* and suggests fresh approaches by treating the 'prose' elements of Clough's poetry as serving a deliberate artistic purpose,[42] an example followed by J. M. S. Tomkins, reviewing the *Poems*.[43] A more influential voice was that of Stephen Spender who wrote up Clough as one of the 'Great Writers Rediscovered' for the *Sunday Times*,[44] appraising in particular his use of a language that 'exactly conveys his temperament and his meaning, and which is idiomatically modern' (this tribute comes from one whose modern poetry somewhat reverses Clough's approach in conceding too much, Clough might think, to Arnoldian 'beauty').

The centenary biography, *Arthur Hugh Clough; the Uncommitted Mind*, by Katharine Chorley (1962), is more positive than its predecessors, making full use of the modern additions to the Clough canon, but it is marred by a psychoanalytical theory, encouraged perhaps by the old *a priori* assumption of Clough's inadequacy for life, that he laboured under an unconscious childish desire for 'complete and exclusive possession of his mother'. Lady Chorley gives this theory more emphasis than her highly selective reading of the poems seems to warrant. While it is certainly an approach valid in a biographical study, it is a pity that its tendency is primarily to add a sophisticated modern underlay to the myth of maimed genius.[45] Also, though this is far from being his intention, one must object on similar grounds to the unfortunate title of Michael Timko's *Innocent Victorian* (1966), especially since the word 'innocent' defies Timko's capacity to explain it. Nevertheless, Timko's book is critically very constructive, elucidating Clough's thought as it emerges from his prose and interpreting the poetry freshly in its light. Timko points a suggestive parallel with E. M. Forster, in terms of a shared awareness of 'good-and-evil', but in his anxiety to stress Clough's commitment to 'positive naturalism' which he believes springs from this he gives the impression of an almost saintly consistency of attitude. He makes no allowance for the possibility that Clough might have expressed different feelings and thoughts in poetry. His excessive emphasis on Clough's prose thought is partly explained by his desire to correct what he regards as Walter E. Houghton's 'undue emphasis' in *The Poetry of Clough* 'on technique'. Houghton's work is indeed somewhat unbalanced in this respect, the result, perhaps, of his desire to resurrect Clough and 'sell' him for his modernity. To this end Houghton provides several illuminating close analyses of individual poems aimed primarily at bringing out affinities with the poetry we admire today, but these are related more often than Timko concedes to Clough's religious and philosophical thinking and contrasted with the prevailing Victorian attitudes. Where Timko and Houghton differ chiefly is in their interpretation of the man. Both books deserve careful reading and are worthy additions to American appreciation of Clough, but neither seems definitive.

Two cogently argued recent English contributions may be found in *The Major Victorian Poets: Reconsiderations* (ed. Isobel Armstrong, 1969), a book whose very title is gratifying to devotees of Clough. Though they differ in mode of argument, both Barbara Hardy's comprehensive 'Clough's Self-Consciousness' and John Goode's close discussion of '*Amours de Voyage*: the Aqueous Poem' direct our attention back to Clough's individual qualities of thought and expression, from which, they think, excessive preoccupations with him as verse-novelist, solitary Victorian satirist or forerunner of Eliot, have deflected us. Mrs Hardy delicately defines the Cloughian quality which evades

Houghton's and Timko's more precise formulations: 'Clough is too impassioned,' she maintains, 'and too uncertain to be praised as an ironist. To call him an "intellectual poet" is as misleading as to call him a verse-novelist. He is a feeling analyst, a writer of lyrical narrative, an ironist who moves beyond irony, an intellectual both sensuous and passionate.'[46] This indicates another concern Mrs Hardy and Mr Goode share, to enable us to see Clough himself and his emotional concerns in a fresh light, as productive of subjective poetry as valuable in its own way as the 'satirical' or 'intellectual'. In fact, they remind us to use such terms warily; and Mrs Hardy calls us back to a recognition of Clough's essential complexity when she writes, 'He gives us in his art what he was tormented by in life, the endless impositions of thought-and-feeling which is within the experience of most average sensual intellectuals.'[47] For comparison she turns, like Timko, to Forster rather than Eliot, but with what seems a truer accent upon their subtly non-committal stance.

Verse-novelist, lyricist; ironist, satirist; sensuous, bare and dry; intellectual, emotional; positive, non-committal; humorous, solemn. One could multiply the contrasts or seeming contradictions: if a controversial variousness is an essential mark of greatness, at least Clough has that. And for a poet to be acclaimed increasingly as modern, over a hundred years after his death, is another mark of distinction. Appreciation of Clough is steadily broadening, but the many-sided work that will enable us to see his poetry whole, embracing these contradictory possibilities, has yet to be written. At present, critics are correcting and supplementing each other, intent upon restoring the image. In doing so, they will need to bear in mind that Clough, however modern we would have him be, remains for ever a mid-Victorian and that in some respects he may have been seen in a clearer light by his contemporaries than by us. Certainly such men as Bagehot and Sidgwick or R. H. Hutton transcend the destructive stereotype put about by the Stracheys and the Lucases, whom they surpass in justice and sanity. Clough's best Victorian critics, especially those of the 1860s, tried to set a 'real' (in Arnold's sense) standard of judgment to which, where the Victorians are concerned, we have only returned in recent years. If less analytical than ourselves, they have a keen eye for comparative values, not turned only on the English tradition. This collection enables us, I hope, to judge how that standard was eroded in the course of time by prejudice and circumstance; it may serve, too, as a critical object-lesson in the making and breaking of one writer's reputation.

NOTES

1 Charles Kingsley, *His Letters and Memories of his Life* (1877), ed. by his wife, *I.* 191.
2 *Corr. I.* 240.
3 *Corr. I.* 247–8, 28 February 1849.
4 *Corr. I.* 272, 24 September 1849.
5 J. R. Lowell, *Letters*, I. 224; ed. C. E. Norton, 1894.
6 *North American Review*, LXXVII, July 1853; reprinted, with some deletions, in *Prose Remains* (1865) and *Poems and Prose Remains* (1869); full text in *SPW*, 143–71.
7 Matthew Arnold, *The Study of Poetry* (1880). Cf. in *SPW* Clough's Lecture VI, on Dryden; though he sees the period 1650–1700 as one 'rather of the senses and the understanding than of the spirit and the imagination', he believes, nevertheless that no later writer can 'outdo' Dryden 'in vigour of mere writing, in manliness and force of style' (pp. 105–6).
8 *Corr. II.* 338, 26 November 1852.
9 *Poems* (1951), 582.
10 *Pre-Raphaelite Letters and Diaries* (1900), 239.
11 *Corr. II.* 412, 7 April 1853.
12 *Corr. I.* 240, Clough to Emerson, 10 February 1849.
13 *Corr. II.* 537, 21 December 1857.
14 *Corr. II.* 546.
15 *Corr. II.* 551, June 1858. Some years after Clough's death Carlyle complained to Emerson in terms such as, with more confidence, Clough might have used in his own defence—that Emerson took 'so little heed of the frightful quantities of *friction* and perverse *impediment* there everywhere are' (Carlyle to Emerson, 6 April 1870, *The Correspondence of Carlyle and Emerson*, Boston, 1894, II. 360).
16 *Daily News*, 9 January 1862.
17 George Eliot to Mrs Richard Congreve, *Letters*, ed. G. S. Haight (1954–1955), 23 February 1862, V, 67.
18 'Clough's *Poems*', *Blackwood's Edinburgh Magazine*, XCII, November 1862, 586. The review is assigned to Collins in *Blackwood's Contributors Book*, National Library of Scotland (see *A.H.C. Descr. Cat.* 76).
19 Letter to C. E. Norton, 25 April 1862, quoted Chorley, *Arthur Hugh Clough* (1962), 263.
20 Quoted from MSS., *A.H.C. Descr. Cat.* 35.
21 *Ibid.*
22 *Corr. II.* 402.
23 On the 'otherness' of sexual experience in Victorian England, see Steven Marcus, *The Other Victorians* (1966); the author of *My Secret Life*, which Marcus discusses in detail, who was in Naples at about the same time as Clough, writes in terms very different from those of the parts of *Dipsychus*

Mrs Clough excised *pro pudore:* 'I went abroad again early in December
to Naples with a friend, and had women there of course' (*My Secret Life*,
ed. G. Legman, Grove Press Abridged Edition, 1966, 307).

24 *The Letters of John Addington Symonds*, ed. Schueller and Peters, I. 771-2,
9 November 1867.

25 For other adverse contemporary criticisms of Tennyson, for his artificiality
and failure to treat subjects close to contemporary interests, see John D.
Jump, *Tennyson: The Critical Heritage* (1967), Introduction.

26 Hallam Tennyson, *A Memoir*, I. 480: Tennyson's emotional reaction may
have been due less to the quality of the poetry than to his recollections of
meeting Clough on his ill-fated 'recuperative' travels in France only a few
months before his death; Clough had then read to him some of the Tales,
which he was writing *en route*.

27 'Swinburne's Tragedies', *My Study Windows* (1871), 192.

28 'On a Certain Condescension in Foreigners', reprinted in *My Study Windows, op. cit.*

29 'Arthur Hugh Clough', *North American Review*, October 1867.

30 *Poems and Prose Remains* was reissued in 1871, 1874, 1877, 1878, 1879, 1880,
1882, 1883 and 1885 (*A.H.C. Descr. Cat.* 38).

31 W. H. Hudson's 'Arthur Hugh Clough', in *Studies in Interpretation* (1896),
is a painstaking exposition of Clough's thought, but of no critical importance; the same limitation applies to Edouard Guyot's *Essai sur la Formation
Philosophique du Poète Arthur Hugh Clough: Pragmatisme et Intellectualisme*
(1913).

32 *Milton's Prosody* (1901–1921), 106–10.

33 *Eminent Victorians* (1918), 216–17.

34 Joseph Wood Krutch, 'Log of a Spiritual Voyage', *The Bookman*, li,
August 1920, 687–9.

35 *Victorian Poets* (1876), 244.

36 See Walter E. Houghton's (somewhat misleadingly entitled) 'Arthur Hugh
Clough: A Hundred Years of Disparagement', *Studies in English Literature*,
Autumn 1961, 30–61, substantially reprinted as the first chapter of *The
Poetry of Clough* (1963); *A.H.C. Descr. Cat.*, whose listing of 87 major and
minor entries in biography and criticism for the years 1921–50 and 134 for
1951–66 indicates the growth of interest in recent years; and the selective
annotated bibliography in *Innocent Victorian: the Satiric Poetry of Arthur
Hugh Clough* (1966), by Michael Timko.

37 'Clough', *Portraits* (1931), 65.

38 'Mr. MacNeice's Poems', *TLS*, 18 November 1949, 751.

39 *The Darkling Plain* (1950), 108–11.

40 'Books in General', *New Statesman*, 6 January 1951.

41 'Clough's *Amours de Voyage*', *English*, ix, Summer 1953.

42 'The Poetry of Clough', *TLS*, 23 November 1951, 748.

43 *Modern Language Review*, xlviii, April 1953.

44 *The Sunday Times*, 3 November 1957.

45 Two other recent biographies perpetuate, on the whole, the Failure Myth: *Arthur Hugh Clough (1819–1861)*, by Paul Veyriras (Paris 1964), places Clough very firmly in the Victorian context, but like Goldie Levy and others M. Veyriras finds the man more interesting than his work; David Williams's *Too Quick Despairer* (1969)—another unfortunate title—is a vigorous and racy brief introduction which, though it offers the uninitiated reader some keenly suggestive pointers to Clough's 'modernity', forfeits the opportunity to stress his individual strength.

46 *The Major Victorian Poets: Reconsiderations*, 273.

47 *Ibid.* 266.

THE BOTHIE OF TOPER-NA-FUOSICH,
A LONG-VACATION PASTORAL

November 1848

(Re-titled *The Bothie of Tober-na-Vuolich*, 1855)

1. Matthew Arnold to Clough

From a letter 15, 22 or 29 November 1848 (*The Letters of Matthew Arnold to Arthur Hugh Clough*, ed. H. F. Lowry, 95).

Three years older than Matthew Arnold, Clough came to Rugby at the beginning of Dr Thomas Arnold's reforming headship. He became the Doctor's prize pupil and was welcomed into the Arnold family circle, but his relationship with Matthew did not become close until the latter followed him to Oxford as a Balliol Scholar in 1841. Clough, by then Fellow of Oriel, was naturally cast for the role of Matthew's mentor, but the relationship rapidly developed, as may be judged from the letters quoted in this volume, into one between equals. Despite considerable differences of temperament and outlook, they remained firmly attached to each other in later life (see also Nos. 13 and 23 below).

... I have been at Oxford the last two days and hearing Sellar[1] and the rest of that clique who know neither life nor themselves rave about your poem gave me a strong almost bitter feeling with respect to them, the age, the poem, even you. Yes I said to myself something tells me I can, if need be, at last dispense with them all, even with him: better that, than be sucked for an hour even into the Time Stream in which they and he plunge and bellow. I became calm in spirit, but uncompromising, almost stern. More English than European, I said finally, more American than English; and took up my Obermann,[2] and refuged myself with him in his forest against your *Zeit Geist*.

[1] For Sellar see No. 34
[2] *Obermann* (1804), by Etienne Pivert de Senancour.

—But in another way I am glad to be able to say that Macpherson[3] gave a very good account of the sale: and that, though opinions differed, I found what I thought the best such as Riddell's[4] and Blackett's in favour of the metre strongly: the opinion of the first has a scientific, that of the second an aesthetic value. Stanley[5] thought him the best hexameter he had seen in the modern languages. My people at home could not manage the metre, but thought there was humour and pathos enough in the poem to stock a dozen ordinary poems.

[3] The Oxford publisher of *The Bothie*.

[4] James Riddell (1923–66), then Fellow and Tutor at Balliol; he had been Arnold and Clough's contemporary there in student days.

[5] A. P. Stanley, another contemporary, later Dean of Westminster and author of *The Life of Dr. Arnold*.

2. Thackeray to Clough

1848

From a letter 26 November 1948 (*Corr. I*, 228).

Clough had sent Thackeray a complimentary copy of *The Bothie*. They had already met at Oxford, and Thackeray had extended to Clough his instinctive sympathy for rebels against the established order. He praised him for throwing up his Fellowship on religious scruples and linked him with Francis Newman in a letter written in 1849 as 'thinking men, who I daresay will begin to speak out before many years are over, and protest against Gothic Xtianity' (*Letters*, II, 581, ed. G. N. Ray) (Thackeray refers here, of course, to the 'Romanizing' influence of the Oxford Movement). Thackeray and Clough travelled to America on the same ship in 1852.

. . . I have been reading the *Bothy* all the morning and am charmed with it. I have never been there but I think it must be like Scotland—Scotland hexametrically laid out that is . . . and it seems to me to give one the proper Idyllic feeling which is $\frac{1}{2}$ sensual and $\frac{1}{2}$ spiritual I take it—serene beauty awakening pleasant meditation—what is it?—your description of the sky and the landscape—and that figure of the young fellow bathing shapely with shining limbs and the blue blue sky for a background—are delightful to me. . . . I have been going over some of the same ground (of youth) in this present number of Pendennis; which I fear will be considered rather warm by the Puritans: but I think you'll understand it. . . .

3. Unsigned notice, *Spectator*

1848

In 'Publications Received', xxi, 2 December 1848, 1166.

In a letter to R. W. Emerson, expressing thanks for Emerson's praise (see No. 5) and that of his American friends, Clough comments that 'in England I shall not be troubled with a very onerous weight of celebrity'; he had then seen only Kingsley's 'cordial eulogistic article' (No. 7) and this 'contemptuous' piece in the *Spectator* (*Corr. I*, 240, 10 February 1849).

A long story of some Oxford students, who went to the Highlands of Scotland to combine relaxation and study; but one of them falls in love with a Scotch lassie, whom he finally marries. As a tale, the piece has little interest; and the school-like incidents and persons by which it is sought to be varied are of an unattractive kind, intended to be natural, but only trivial. In prose, such a story, treated in such a way, would scarcely have been ventured upon; and it seems difficult to understand why plain prose should be thought the better for being turned into prosaic verse. At first view *The Bothie of Toper-na-Fuosich* looked like some Oxford satire; but if it does cover any occult meaning, it is confined to the initiated.

4. Edward Quillinan to Henry Crabb Robinson

1849

From a letter dated 12 January 1849 (Henry Crabb Robinson, *Diary, Reminiscences, & Correspondence*, II. 303).

Edward Quillinan (1791–1851) was a minor poet and critic and a devotee of Wordsworth (whose daughter he married). Arnold describes him in his elegy upon him as 'a man unspoil'd, sweet, generous, and humane'. (Robinson, 1775–1867, best known for his *Diary*, was a founder of University College, London, where Clough became Professor of English in 1851.)

. . . I was very unwilling to commence it [*The Bothie*], for I detest English hexameters, from Surrey's to Southey's; and Mr. Clough's spondaic lines are, to my ear, detestable too—that is to begin with. Yet I am really charmed with this poem. There is a great deal of mere prose in it, and the worse, to my taste, for being prose on stilts; but, take it all in all, there is more freshness of heart and soul and sense in it than it has been my chance to find and feel in any poem of recent date—perhaps I ought to say than in any recent poem of which the author is not yet very much known; for I have no mind to depreciate Alfred Tennyson, nor any other man who has fairly won his laurel.

5. R. W. Emerson to Clough

1849

From a letter dated 10 January 1849 (*Corr. I*, 232–3).

The free-thinking Ralph Waldo Emerson (1803–82), the American transcendentalist philosopher, who had in 1832 left the ministry in reaction against the dogmatism of the Church and the formalization of religion, appealed strongly to Clough. When Emerson visited England in 1847 on a lecture tour, Clough wrote inviting him to visit Oxford where 'amongst the [less orthodox] juniors there are many that have read and studied your books, and not a few that have largely learnt from them'; Emerson came and 'everybody liked him'. Clough saw much of him in Paris at the time of the '1848' and later Emerson strongly influenced Clough's decision to try his luck in America.

I cannot tell you how great a joy to me is your poem. . . . This poem is a high gift from angels that are very rare in our mortal state. It delights and surprises me from beginning to end. . . . I knew you were good and wise, stout of heart and truly kind, learned in Greek, and of excellent sense, but how could I know or guess that you had all this wealth of expression, this wealth of imagery, this joyful heart of youth, this temperate continuity, that belongs only to high masters. It is a noble poem. Tennyson must look to his laurels. . . . Longfellow I sent it to, and he writes moderately enough, yet I will transcribe his note, as Longfellow is prized on your side of the water.

Altogether fascinating and in part very admirable is the poem of Mr. Clough. Tom Appleton read it aloud to us the other evening ['us' included 'Lowell, the poet']. . . . All were much delighted with the genial wit, the truth to nature, and the extreme beauty of various passages and figures; all agreed that it was a poem of a very high order of merit; no one criticised. . . .

then he praises 'the fine delineation of the passion of love,' and congratulates himself on the hexameters, etc., etc.

6. Froude to Clough

1849

From two letters 21 January 1849 (W. H. Dunn, *James Anthony Froude*, Vol. 1, 224–5) and 29 January 1849 (*Corr. I*, 234).

James Anthony Froude (1818–94), the historian and biographer of Thomas Carlyle, was, like Clough, having a difficult time at Oxford. He had taken Deacon's orders as part of the requirements of a Fellow of Exeter College, but soon after he wrote these letters to Clough he was to resign his Fellowship rather than continue with a divided mind. At the same time, in February 1849, his novel *The Nemesis of Faith*, a highly subjective book designed to illustrate how 'too exact a credulity' in religious matters was 'again bringing a nemesis behind it', was execrated by conservatives in the University, one of whom, the Rector of Exeter College, burnt a copy of it before the undergraduates.

From the letter of 21 January 1849;

I am sorry very sorry that you did not wait and let the *Ambarvalia* come first, to secure more respectful attention to what certainly wants it to bring out its merits. People don't expect philosophy in a thing coming out in the shape and with the *tone* of a sketchy poem; and won't look for it, and won't believe it is there when it seems to be, particularly when you set off so inauspiciously as I think you do in the *whole* of the first section. I think the last two lines of Hewson's speech there quite unnatural, at least no *good* fellow could have dragged them in in so unprovoked a fashion, and yet they are important and are made to strike, and so through the whole (except the fourth section, which is uniformly most excellent and worthy of anybody) I was forever falling upon lines which gave me uneasy twitchings; for example, the end of the love scene.

And he fell at her feet and buried his face in her *apron*.

I dare say the head would fall there, but what an image! It chimes in with your notion of the attractiveness of the *working* business, but our undisciplined ears have divided the ideas too long to bear to have them so abruptly shaken together.

Love is an idle sort of a god and comes in other hours than the working ones; at least I have always found it so. I don't think of it in my working time, and when I see a person I do love working (at whatever it may be) I have quite another set of thoughts about her. (This goes for the potato digging as well, of course.) It would do excellently well for married affection, for it is the element in which it lives. But I don't think young love gets born then. I only speak for myself, and from a very limited experience.

As to the story, I don't the least object to it on the *Spectator*'s ground. I think it would not have done in prose. Verse was wanted to give it dignity. But if we find it trivial, the fault is in our own varnished selves. We have been polished up so bright that we forget the stuff we are made of. Yet I have objections again here, for I don't believe in your Elspie. If any girl in her position was ever so highly cultivated, she is an exception, and so the moral would be false. I like all orders to keep among themselves, only I would take Nature's divisions, not ours. Her lordly souls should be as real lords as any we have now, and live as like them (in all except their beastliness). I dislike dirt in all its shapes, and dirty humanities are made on purpose to do the dirty work. If they are born into life in the queen's own bedchamber, I would have them taken out and put about it. Let those who are made fit for other matters keep their hands clean, and choose their mates among their like. But while things are as they are, I disbelieve in the mixing classes *bred*, if not *born*, *distinct*, and I think the Lord of Burleigh has the truer moral. I asked Emerson how he got on with the practice of the digging business while he preached, and he confessed with a blush (and that was something for a Yankee) that it wouldn't do. The theory seemed right but somehow he found it was wrong. He must take the outside life on the inside; they wouldn't assimilate.

And now you may think me a beastly aristocrat or what you please. I have said my say. But if I go to colonies I have told myself that I must have done with books and thinking and reading if I am to be good for more there than I have been here, and that I have got my stock which must last me out till the end. Finally, I don't like the metre, and in spite of the fourth section, I think the next volume will have to lift this as well as float itself. If all is like what I saw it will do it easy.

From the letter of 29 January 1849;

. . . Two days ago I read the *Bothie* aloud to a lady in whose judgment I place much reliance. I myself found it far more perfect read aloud than read silently, and between my own convictions and hers, I begin to allow I was in a heresy about it. Still she agreed with me that Elspie had too great a command of language and metaphor, and that very few women and no young girls did talk in finished simile, however clever they were. As to *Ambarvalia* I like them better and better, though here and there I find things which look like spots of ink on a beautiful engraving. *Singly sing* bothers me. The words look too much alike, and have a jingle about them. I don't like 'odour into *stench*.' I did not like 'of the brain and of the *belly*,' but I do like it now. But really the depth of thought in them all is quite wonderful. Mind I do not think them perfect. They will take a deal of shaping and polishing, and they are such hard stone that they will bear it. . . .

7. Charles Kingsley on *The Bothie*

1849

From an unsigned review in *Fraser's Magazine*, January 1849, xxxix, 103–10.

Kingsley (1819–75), Anglican clergyman, novelist, poet and Cambridge Professor of Modern History (1860–9), was prominent among writers concerned with social reform in the mid-century; he was a Christian Socialist and sympathetic towards Chartist aims. He bitterly opposed Tractarianism for its accent on celibacy and preached a full-blooded virility, including passionate—but godly —marriage.

'And when I tell ye I saw a glazier,' writes Thomas Hood's Irish footman from Mont Blanc, 'ye'll be thinking I mane a fine boy walking about wid putty and glass at his back, and ye'll be mightily mistaken; that's just what a glazier isn't like at all. And so I've described it to yees.'

Even so say we of Mr. Clough's *Bothie*. When our readers hear of an Oxford poem, written, too, by a college fellow and tutor, they will naturally expect, as usual, some pale and sickly bantling of the *Lyra Apostolica*[1] school; all Mr. Keble's defects caricatured, without any of his excellences—another deluge of milk-and-water from that perennial fount of bad verses, which, if quantity would but make up for quality, would be by this time world-famous,—and that is just what *The Bothie* is not like, 'at all, at all.'

Mr. Clough's poetic *début* would have been certainly an easier one had he followed in the track of the reigning Oxford school. The only conditions of initiation into that guild have been, lately, that a man should be thorough bigot; that his conceptions should be sufficiently confused, and his style likewise; and, above all, that he should be

---

[1] *Lyra Apostolica* (1836): poems by Newman, Keble, R. H. Froude, I. W. Bowden, Isaac Williams and Samuel Wilberforce.

melancholy. Werterism, now expelled from all other grades of society, has taken refuge, alas! in the institution which ought to be leading the age, not dragged grumbling in its rear; and thus has arisen a second and, we hope, last 'poetry of despair,' on strictly Church principles. To extract tears from sunshine; to hear the wailings of remorse in the song of a skylark; and prove the eternal perdition of Dissenters from the down on a dandelion—is, with these gentlemen, to see into the deepest spiritual symbolism of nature. But the thing is past a jest.

As for style, the prevailing problem with the Oxford poets has seemed to be, how best to hide the farthing rushlight of bigotry under the bushel of mystification; how an author, having no definite meaning, or, if he have one, being frightened at it, may so jumble his words as to mean nothing, or anything except what is cheerful, or manly, or expressive of real faith that God has anything to do with the world, or, indeed, has had since Astraea and the Stuarts vanished together in 1688.

Now, as we said before, the best possible way of describing Mr. Clough's poem, is to say, that all this is just what it is *not*.

But this negative method of description, *per modum tollendi*, as the schoolmen would have said, though pleasantly compendious for the reader, is hardly fair on the critic, to whom it gives no chance of displaying his aesthetic acumen at the author's expense: we shall, therefore, proceed to say something about what the *Bothie* is.

The poem sets forth, in playful earnestness, how a party from Oxford with their tutor, went to read in the Highlands for the long vacation; 'how they bathed, read, and roamed, all in the joy of their life and glory of shooting jackets;' and how, there and then, 'the eager, impetuous Hewson,' poet and ultra-ultra-radical, realized his theories of the nothingness of rank, and the dignity of dirty work, by flirting with Highland lassies—casting himself, in a sudden revulsion of feeling, at the delicate feet of 'Lady Maria'—and finally falling in love with 'Elspie Mackaye.' The incidents and arguments which flow out of Hewson's strange sayings and doings, together with his most deep and truly poetical 'love-story', make up the staple of the poem.

And here we must notice, first of all, the author's vivid and versatile faculty for drawing individual character. Adam, the tutor; Hobbes, 'contemplative, corpulent, witty;' Lindsay, 'clever, brilliant, do-nothing;' even the characters of whom little but the names appear— Arthur, Hope, and Airlie, Sir Hector, the old chieftain, David Mack-aye, the old army farrier, are each and every one of them living, individual persons—you could swear to them if you met them in the

street. Hewson the poet is more a type of a class than an individual—
so far right. But the women are as vividly sketched as the men. 'Katie',
the open-hearted child of nature, who thinks no shame to commence a
fresh innocent flirtation with every fresh acquaintance, and, like a
butterfly,—

> ... Takes pleasure in all, as in beautiful weather,
> Sorry to lose it, but just as we would be to lose fine weather.
> And she is strong to return to herself, and to feel undeserted,
> For she always keeps burning a cheerful fire inside her,

might pass for a type of the Celtic girl, such as you will meet with in
every village in Wales and Ireland, as well as the Highlands. And as a
contrast, Elspie Mackaye, really a noble ideal of the true Scotch-
woman, with all her rich Norse character, her wild Dantesque imagination, her shrewd, 'canny' insight, her deep and strong affections,
yet all crushed into order by that calm self-restraint which indicates,
not coldness, but intense and victorious energy—we must say, that
we know no recent fiction of a female character so genial, so original,
and yet so natural. But let Elspie speak for herself, in a scene of exquisite pathos and purity:

[Quotes VII. 109–36: 'When, you remember, you took my hand' to
'quite afraid and unwilling'.]

Mr. Clough has all the advantage of a novel subject, and one, too,
which abounds in fantastic scenery and combinations, as it were,
ready-made to his hands. On such ground he need only be truthful
to be interesting. The strange jumble of society which the Highlands
would present in the summer to such a party—marquises and gillies,
shooters and tourists—the luxuries and fopperies of modern London
amid the wildest scenery and a primitive people—Aristotle over Scotch
whisky—embroidered satin waistcoats dancing with bare-legged
hizzies—Chartist poets pledging kilted clansmen—Mr. Clough was
quite right in determining to treat so odd a subject in a correspondingly
odd manner. Such a cockney-savage Walpurgisdance does exist. It
may be seen, we are informed, every summer in the ancient haunts of
Rob Roy and 'the Children of the Mist.' It is a 'great fact of the age;'
and in our judgment, a very significant and not unpleasing one, and,
because it exists, Mr. Clough was quite right in telling us all about it;
and quite right, also, in telling his story in his own way, and in no one

39

else's. What possible model could he have followed? An Oxford colony in cockneyized Highlands! Conceive writing a pastoral thereon, after the manner of Theocritus, or Bion, or Virgil, or anybody else! Would Catullus' *Atys* have done? or Apuleius? or Aristophanes with modifications? or the *Pastor Fido*? or Sidney's *Arcadia*, perhaps? or *Comus*? or *Tristram Shandy*? or *Don Quixote*? or *The Vicar of Wakefield*? or Gray's *Elegy*? or Mr. Wordsworth's *Ruth*? or Mr. Tennyson's *Gardener's Daughter*? or Goethe's *Hermann and Dorothea*? or, perhaps, Mr. Gresley's *Bernard Leslie*?[1]

All which classic models considered, we confess our opinion that Mr. Clough could not have well embodied his conceptions in a form more thoroughly natural to them. He found the sublime and the ridiculous hand-in-hand, as they usually are, not only in cockneyized Highlands, but everywhere else, we suspect, on this earth; and, like greater men than himself, he has not been ashamed to draw them into the same picture. He has dared to set down honestly just what he saw, never caring whether it happens to be the fashion just now to talk of such things, or to skip them, and then fancy they don't exist; and he has been rewarded. There runs all through the poem a general honesty, a reverence for facts and nature—a belief, that if things are here, they are here by God's will or the devil's, to be faced manfully, and not to be blinked cowardly; in short, a true faith in God—which makes Mr. Clough's poem, light as may seem the subject and style, and coming just now, as it does, from noble old Oxford, anything but unimportant, because they indicate a more genial and manly, and therefore a more poetic and more godly spirit, than any verses which have come out of Oxford for a long time past.

How shamefully we have wandered! and we had just conceived the most gracefully turned period, now, alas! resolved into its mother element, to set forth how the *bizarrerie* of the subject was so charmingly expressed in the *bizarrerie* of the style; how a playful, mock-heroic key gave scope for all sorts of variations into the bucolic, sentimental, broad-farce, pathetic, Hebrew-prophetic, whatnot. Seriously, it is almost refreshing, in turning over page after page at random, to tumble, in these mannerist days, on such a variety as this. First, by way of a pastoral, or rather 'faunal,' sketch:

[Quotes V. 9–12, 20–37:'What if autumnal shower ...' and '... looked no more for Philip'.]

1 Reverend William Gresley (1801–76), *Bernard Leslie*, a tale in two parts, 1842–59.

And then, by way of a contrast:—

> Yes, I could find in my heart to cry, in spite of my Elspie,
> Oh, that the armies were arrayed, oh, joy of the onset,
> Sound, thou trumpet of God, come forth, Great Cause, to array us!
> King and leader appear, Thy soldiers sorrowing seek Thee.
> Would that the armies, indeed, were arrayed. Oh, where is the battle?
> Neither battle I see, nor arraying, nor King in Israel,
> Only infinite jumble and mess and dislocation,
> Backed by a solemn appeal, 'For God's sake do not stir, there!'

Or again, this scrap from the mouth of the gentle and philosophic tutor:—

> Women are weak as you say, and love of all things to be passive;
> Passive, patient, receptive, yea even of wrong and misdoing,
> Even to force and misdoing with joy and victorious feeling,
> Passive, patient, receptive; for that is the strength of their being,
> Like to the earth taking all things, and all to good converting.

We might go on forever quoting fresh, sparkling contrasts in matter and style. We will finish, however, with Mr. Hope's ecstasies at the prospect of three weeks' idleness and deer-stalking with his uncle at Balloch:—

> Fare ye well, meantime, forgotten, unnamed, undreamt of,
> History, science, and poets! lo, deep in dustiest cupboard,
> Thookydid, Oloros' son, Halimoosian, here lieth buried!
> Slumber in Liddell-and-Scott,[1] O musical chaff of old Athens,
> Dishes, and fishes, bird, beast, and sesquipedalian blackguard!
> Sleep, weary ghosts, be at peace, and abide in your lexicon-limbo!
> Sleep, as in lava for ages your Herculanean kindred!
> Sleep, and for aught that I care, 'the sleep that knows no waking';
> Æschylus, Sophocles, Homer, Herodotus, Pindar and Plato;
> Three weeks hence be it time to exhume our dreary classics.

What a quatrain of melodious hexameters in the middle of the last quotation! *O si sic omnia!*—the worshippers of *Hermann and Dorothea*, and pure classic form, will cry; and not without a show of reason, for indeed Mr. Clough has fully justified the warning which is given to readers in his introductory note, to 'expect every kind of irregularity in these modern hexameters;' 'spondaic lines,' he says, 'are almost the rule;' and, as we humbly think, a very good rule. But a large proportion of his hexameters are, to use the very mildest word, abnormal. The

[1] A fashionable Oxford lexicon [Kingsley's note].

scandalized scansionist stumbles on occasional trochees in every foot in a verse, to stop at last, horror of horrors! at a line which will not scan at all—forward, backward, or sideways. We will not quote an instance, we will spare the nerves of classical readers; their existence we must mention, if only to fulfil the reviewer's eleventh command-ment—'Thou shalt find every possible fault with thy neighbour, and more too;' and to move, as bound, our own aesthetic talents. How shocking, if readers should suspect from a critic's silence that he did not know a mistake when he saw it!

Mr. Clough may demand, not beg, pardon for these slips, sown rarely, as they are, up and down among some of the most perfect hexameters, in our humble opinion, which we have yet seen in the English language. When the author has given himself fair play, he has shown a complete mastery over the metre, and a faculty as yet, we fancy, all but unique, not of Graecizing or Germanizing his English, as most hexameter-writers have to do, but of Anglicizing the metre, of harmonizing not English to it, but it to English. For instance, in almost the first lines that come to hand:

> But, O Muse, that encompassest earth like the ambient ether,
> Swifter than steamer, or railway, or magic missive electric,
> Belting, like Ariel, the sphere with the star-like trail of thy travel,
> Thou, with thy Poet, to mortals mere post-office second-hand knowledge
> Leaving, wilt seek in the moorland of Rannoch the wandering hero.

Yet, after all, we do not think that Mr. Clough has been quite fair to himself in this respect. A high artistic finish is important for more reasons than for the mere pleasure which it gives to readers. There is something sacramental in perfect metre and rhythm. They are out-ward and visible signs (most seriously we speak as we say it) of an inward and spiritual grace, namely, of the self-possessed and victorious temper of one who has so far subdued nature as to be able to hear that universal sphere-music of hers, speaking of which, Mr. Carlyle says somewhere, 'that all deepest thoughts instinctively vent themselves in song.' And an author is, therefore, unfair to himself, who leaves any lines which may give a perverse and evil-speaking generation a handle for imputing to him, not want of skill, which in this case they cannot, but confusion of thought or haste of expression.

Thus much in our reviewer's right of taking our betters to task; to all which, if Mr. Clough should answer, that he does not care; that he left the said lines as a testimony that an author has a right to say his own say in his own way; that metre was made for thoughts, not thoughts for metre; that he has as much right to put in spondees where he likes, as Aristophanes had; that trochees fit a great deal better into English hexameters than anapaests ever did into Greek iambics; that his verses are not properly hexameters at all, but a fire-new discovery of his own genius, to be christened henceforth, Bothiaics; that as somebody, some time or other, must have invented each new metre, he has as good a right as his neighbors to make one, provided his manufacture be worthy: if he shall gently protest against the popular belief that the devil is, and has been, the only inventor since the beginning (when everything made itself;) if he shall denounce once for all the pedantry of metre-mongers, and call them in grimmest earnest scribes and pharisees, letting the spirit of verse starve while they haggle for the letter; if he shall assert boldly his belief that old Homer wrote by ear, and not by *Gradus*, and cared no more for 'longs and shorts' than Shakespeare and Burns did; and that, while Hermann was wasting his wits over his great unreadable *De Metris*, the ghost of Aristophanes stood behind his chair watching the bewildered German's *Bacchics* and *Brachycatalectics, Graidiocolosyrtics*, too, with thumb on nose, and grindings of Elysian coffee-mills;—to all this we can only answer—that we most thoroughly agree with him.

The author entitles his poem, *A Pastoral*; a classic title, from which we expect a classic poem, and, as we think, have one, in the spirit rather than in the letter. He has wisely tried to write, not as old Greeks wrote, but as they would have written now in this place; and there is a truly Greek, and, what is better, a truly English tone, all through the poem; a healthy, simple admiration of what is simple and beautiful wherever he finds it. He rejoices, like Homer or Theocritus himself, in eatings and drinkings, in sunshine, in bathing and dancing, in kissings and innocent flirtations, and in a good racy joke, too, now and then—some of which last, as we hear, have roused much pious horror at Oxford, a place where prudery is tolerably rampant, as it generally is wherever a good many young men get together. It is remarkable, by the bye, and we have verified it too, in the matter of this very poem, how the first person to discover any supposed impropriety in a book is sure to be an unmarried man, and the very last a married woman; whether from the superior pure-mindedness of the former class, the public may judge. It is a pity that men will not remember that the vulture's powers of scent, which could wind a dead sparrow among all the rose-gardens of Damascus, are not indicative of cleanliness in that most

43

useful bird. Would that they bore in mind the too-often-forgotten dictum of Dean Swift, who had had experience enough, certainly, in that time, 'that the nicest man has the nastiest thoughts',[1] and, moreover, that *Honi soit qui mal y pense* is the motto not only of English chivalry, but, as we had almost said, of Protestantism itself; and that those who wish just now to be true Englishmen, would do well to abide by it.

But to return. The poem evinces also a truly Greek spirit in its sense of the dignity of the everyday relations, and the humblest employments of life, a truth which is cleverly separated from the absurdities which are often jumbled with it, by occasional sly caricatures of the school which consecrates potato-forks and wash-tubs, and which, in its disgust of the evils of luxury, conceives itself bound to fall in love with the merely accidental vulgarities of poverty. The question of what is, or is not, truly dignified, runs through the whole poem, and helps to raise it gradually above mere Greek animalism into the region of the Christian nineteenth century, into disquisitions on rank and marriage, man and Providence, often of great vigor, depth and pathos. The author indulges, too, in those frequent repetitions of the same line, or part of a line, which are so common in the Greek poets, both epic and pastoral; and, we think, with a very pleasing effect. These repetitions act like the burden of a song, or the recurrence of the original air in music, after wandering variations. They make one feel, as in the old Greek poets, that the author is in earnest, and enjoys his conception, and likes to take it up, and look at it, and play with it again and again, lingering over it almost reverently, as if conscious that there was something more in it than he could bring out in words—an infinite hidden under the most trivial finite, which must be felt for again and again, ere it reveal itself. As an instance:

[Quotes VI. 1-15: 'Bright October was come' to 'the Bothie of Toper-na-Fuosich'.]

This allusion to autumn, as another instance of our meaning, is several times repeated towards the end of the poem, and each time with some fresh delicate addition to the charming miniature painting:

> The soft, misty mornings, and long dusky eves.

And then how

> The brackens are changed, and heather blooms are faded,
> And amid russet of heather and fern, green trees are bonnie;

---

[1] 'A nice man is a man of nasty ideas': Swift, *Thoughts on Various Subjects.*

making us recollect the stealing on of the swift, long, northern winter, and the breaking up of the party, with a sobered, and almost a saddened feeling, which harmonizes, too, very artistically, with a more serious tone, both of thought and of verse, which takes gradually, towards the end of the poem, the place of the genial frolic of its commencement.

The exclusively Oxonian allusions and phrases may be objected to, and certainly a glossary of a dozen words or so would have been a convenient appendage. But we think the author perfectly right in having introduced his Oxford slang. The thing existed—it was an integral part of his subject. Oxford men have peculiar phrases, peculiar modes of life and thought—he had no right to omit them. For ourselves, we cannot sympathize in the modern cosmopolitan spirit, which cries down all local customs, phrases, and costume; and wants to substitute a dead level uniformity for that true unity which is only to be found in variety; which prefers, as Archdeacon Hare well instances, the dead blank regularity of a modern street, to the rich and harmonious variety of a pile of old Gothic buildings; which would civilize Highlanders by making them abjure kilts and take to paletots, and is merciless to all peculiarities—except its own.

We recommend this whole story, as a fair and characteristic specimen of Oxford life, to those whose whole notions of the universities are drawn from the shallow cockney cavillers of the day. We are no more contented than they are with the present state of the universities. No more, for that matter, are the rising generation of the university men themselves, both masters and bachelors; they are as clamorous for reform as the mob can be, with, as we think, rather better notions of what reform ought to be. But though Oxford is not our Alma Mater, we must in her defence assert, once and for all, that the young men there, and in Cambridge, too, taken *en masse*, will be found far superior in intellect, earnestness, and morality—not to mention that most noble and necessary part of manhood, much sneered at in these cockney days, physical *pluck*—to any other class of young men in England. Compare them with the army, with the navy, the medical students. Compare them with the general run of shopkeepers' sons in town or country; compare them with the rising generation of young men in London, with their prurience, their effeminacy, their quill-driving commercialism, joining (we speak from experience) too often the *morale* of an old rake with the *physique* of a puling girl. Again we may recommend our readers to look at this picture of what an Oxford tutor, and an Oxford reading party, in most cases, are. And even if it should prove a little too favorably drawn to hold good in every case, it may serve as a fair set-off against the exaggerations on the opposite side of the question.

Let them remember that it is the evil, and not the good, of every institution and class which becomes notorious; that while they hear of the book-worms who ruin their intellects by pedantry and their health by morbid ambition, of the profligates who destroy themselves and their families too often by reckless extravagance, that these things are the exception and not the rule—that if they were not the exception, the universities could not hold together for twelve months—that their own members would pull the colleges about each others' ears. No doubt there are abuses and absurdities; none feel them so sorely as university men themselves. When an honest and earnest satirist, like Mr. Thackeray, will attack them, gownsmen will be the first to cry 'hear,' to thank him for laughing at them, for showing them where to laugh at themselves; while as for the crowd of whipper-snappers, who seem to fancy just now that the universities are fair game for every ignorant and inexperienced quill-driver who gets his living by reëchoing, cuckoo-like, the vulgar out-cry whether right or wrong, and who bear as much likeness to Mr. Thackeray and *Punch* as a tom-tit does to a trained falcon, university men simply despise them, and will, when their turn comes to lead the age, (a period which we fancy is not very far off,) show what their much-despised 'musty Latin and Greek' has taught them, and prove, as we hope, that they too appreciate 'the cause of the people,' and 'the spirit of the age;' and with the intention, not of getting their bread, like some, by ignorant declamation about them, but rather of serving God and man by patiently realizing them.

'But what, after all, is the purpose of Mr. Clough's poem?'

This, at least, is its purpose—'*To make people do their duty in that state of life to which God has called them.*' Whether the author attaches exactly the same meaning to those words as his readers do, remains to be proved. Further, we shall say nothing, for the author has said nothing; and he, doubtless, knows a great deal better than we what effects he intends, and we have no wish, or right either, to interfere with him. He seems to think, as indeed, we do, that it is far better to give facts and opinions on different sides, and let the reader draw his own conclusions from them, than to tack a written moral to the last page of his poem, as you sew a direction-card on a little boy's back when you send him off to school. Let the reader try to crack the nut himself; and not, as is usual in these lazy days, expect reviewers to do it for him. It will be wholesome exercise; and we will warrant the kernel worth the trouble.

8. R. W. Emerson, a review in the *Massachusetts Quarterly Review*

March 1849, ii, 249–52

Reprinted in *Uncollected Writings*, New York, 1912, 23–5.

See also No. 5, R. W. Emerson to Clough.

Here is a new English poem which we heartily recommend to all classes of readers. It is an account of one of those Oxford reading-parties which, at the beginning of a long vacation, are made up by a tutor with five or six undergraduates, who wish to bring up arrears of study, or to *cram* for examination and honors, and who betake themselves with their guide to some romantic spot in Wales or Scotland, where are good bathing and shooting, read six hours a day, and kill the other eighteen in sport, smoking, and sleep. The poem is as jocund and buoyant as the party, and so joyful a picture of college life and manners, with such good strokes of revenge on the old tormentors, Pindar, Thucydides, Aristotle, and the logical Aldrich, that one wonders that this ground has not been broken up before. Six young men have read three weeks with their tutor, and after joining in a country dinner and a dance in a barn, four of them decide to give up books for three weeks, and make a tour of the Highlands, leaving the other two partners with the tutor in the cottage, to their *matutive*, or morning bath, six hours' reading, and mutton at seven. The portraits of the young party are briefly but masterly sketched. Adam the tutor,

Lindsay the dialectician, Hope, Hobbes, Airlie, Arthur, who, from his thirty feet diving, is the 'glory of headers,' and Hewson. Philip Hewson, the hero of the poem, the radical poet, in this excursion falls in love with the golden-haired Katie at the farm of Rannoch, and is left behind by his returning fellows. The poet follows his hero into the mountains, wherever the restless Philip wanders, brooding on his passion.

Whilst the tutor anxiously, and his companions more joyously, are speculating on this dubious adventure of their comrade, a letter arrives at the cottage from Hope, who travelled with Philip, announcing that Philip and Katie have parted, and that Philip is staying at Castle Balloch, in assiduous attendance on the beautiful 'Lady Maria.' In an earnest letter to his friend the tutor, Philip explains himself; and the free-winged sweep of speculation to which his new life at the Castle gives occasion, is in a truly modern spirit, and sufficiently embarrassing, one can see, to the friendliest of tutors. Great is the mirth of the Oxford party at this new phase of the ardent Philip, but it is suddenly checked again by a new letter from Philip to Adam, entreating him to come immediately to the *bothie* or hut of Toper-na-Fuosich, to bring him counsel and sanction, since he has already found rest and home in the heart of—Elspie!

We are now introduced to Elspie, the right Anteros, hitherto pursued in vain under deceiving masks, and are made with Adam the tutor to acquiesce in Philip's final choice. The story leads naturally into a bold hypothetical discussion of the most serious questions that bubble up at this very hour in London, Paris, and Boston, and, whilst these are met and honestly and even profoundly treated, the dialogue charms us by perfect good breeding and exuberant animal spirits. We shall not say that the rapid and bold execution has the finish and the intimate music we demand in modern poetry; but the subject-matter is so solid, and the figures so real and lifelike, that the poem is justified, and would be good in spite of much ruder execution than we here find. Yet the poem has great literary merits. The author has a true eye for nature, and expresses himself through the justest images. The Homeric iteration has a singular charm, half-comic, half-poetic, in the piece, and there is a wealth of expression, a power of description and of portrait-painting, which excels our best romancers. Even the hexameter, which with all our envy of its beauty in Latin and in Greek, we think not agreeable to the genius of English poetry, is here in place to heighten the humor of college conversation.

9. 'English Hexameters', an unsigned review, *Literary Gazette*

18 August 1849, lxvi, 606–7

A journal which boasts of its *Horae Celticae* cannot pass this most extraordinary title-page without observing that the author ought to have been more guarded against the malicious Gael who imposed it on the inquisitive Sassenach.

> But as the doorway they quitted, a thin man clad as the Saxon,
> Trouser and cap and jacket of home-spun blue, hand-woven,
> Singled out, and said with determined accent to Hewson,
> Resting his hand on his shoulder, while each with eyes dilating
> Firmly scanned each: Young man, if ye pass through the Braes o'
> Lochaber,
>   See by the loch-side ye come to the Bothie of Toper-na-fuosich.

It is a vile jest, and it is lucky that it can only be understood by a few Highland worthies, who will no doubt enjoy a hearty guffaw over poor deluded Mr. Clough and his long-vacation pastoral near Lochaber, and (when rightly spelled) the Bothie of Tobair na Feosag, so well known in that country.[1]

The poem itself is a curiosity of irregular hexameters, whose spondaic lines run into each other like grooves. The poet sings of his vacation in the North, whither he retired with half-a-dozen of his pupils from Oxford (if we include Adam), to read and seek healthful recreation. These young gentlemen are described, and figure in the lay as Mr. Hope, a relation of the Earl of Hay's, a white-tied neighbour, nick-

---

[1] Elsewhere, to heighten the fun, we read—

> Finally too, from the Kilt and the sofa, said Hobbes in conclusion,
> Finally Philip must hunt for that home of the probable poacher,
> Hid in the braes of Lochaber, the bothie of What-did-he-call-it.
> Hopeless of you and of us, of gillies and marquisses hopeless,
> Weary of Ethic and Logic, of Rhetoric yet more weary,
> There shall he, smit by the charm of a lovely potato-uprooter,
> Study the question of sex in the Bothie of What-did-he-call-it.

[Reviewer's note]. This seems to have been the first published suggestion that the title was open to embarrassing interpretation—though she makes no reference to this review, see Katharine Chorley's otherwise full discussion, *op. cit.* 168–9.

named Adam the Tutor, Mr. Lindsay well befitting the liveliness of
the race of that name, Mr. Hewson aforesaid, Mr. Hobbes, and Mr.
Airlie, an exquisite of the first water. Highland games are strangely
spoken of, where

> Noble ladies their prizes adjudged for costume that was perfect,
> Turning the clansmen about, who stood with upraised elbows;
> Bowing their eye-glassed brows, and fingering kilt and sporran.

Poor Mr. Clough is at his bamboozlements again; but we cannot
comment in Earse, and it would be unfit to do so in English. A
public banquet follows, and the report thereof, differing so entirely
from what we are accustomed to in the newspapers on similar occasions, may be quoted as an example of the verse:

[Quotes *The Bothie*, I. 82–105; 'Spare me' to 'flattering nobles'.]

Of such materials is the whole composed, and often beautiful idea
made almost ludicrous by affectations, absurd terms, and ridiculous
versifying. We will quote some lines and passages in proof:

> Morn, in yellow and white, came broadening out from the mountains,
> Long ere music and reel were hushed in the barn of the dancers.

★   ★   ★

> Breakfast commencing at nine lingered lazily on to noonday.
> Tea and coffee was there; a jug of water for Hewson;
> Tea and coffee, and four cold grouse upon the sideboard;
> Cranberry-jam was reserved for tea, and for festive occasions;
> Gaily they talked, as they sat, some late and lazy at breakfast,
> Some professing a book, some smoking outside at the window,
> 'Neath an aura soft-pouring a still sheeny tide to the zenith.

Hewson, 'the Chartist, the poet, the eloquent speaker,' *loquitur*:

[Quotes *The Bothie*, II. 25–48: 'Oh, if our high-born girls' to 'hard
question!']

This sudden potato-disease reminds us of the rhyme,

> Did you ever see the D——l,
> With his wooden spade and shovel,
> Digging 'tatoes by the bushel,
> With his tail cocked up?

We cannot decide which is the best. While they are bepraising the attitudes and natural gracefulness of various labours, the lively Lindsay breaks in with his form,

> Or—high-kilted perhaps, cried Lindsay, at last successful,
> Lindsay, this long time swelling with scorn and pent-up fury.
> Or high-kilted perhaps, as once at Dundee.

And again, on a fresh topic:

> Aye, cried the Piper,
> That's the sore place, that confounded Egalité, French manufacture,
> He is the same as the Chartist who made an address in Ireland,
> *What, and is not one man, fellow-men, as good as another?*
> *Faith,* replied Pat, *and a deal better too*! so rattled the Piper.

Here are more extracts in the way of specimen:

> And from his seat and cigar spoke the Piper, the Cloud-compeller.
> Hope with the uncle abideth for shooting. Ah me, were I with him!
> Ah, good boy that I am, to have stuck to my word and my reading!
> Good, good boy to be here, far away, who might be at Balloch!
> Only one day to have staid who might have been welcome for seven,
> Seven whole days in castle and forest—gay in the mazy
> Moving, imbibing the rosy, and pointing a gun at the horny![1]

[Quotes III. 114–23: 'For it was told' to 'and had not a *brown* [copper] remaining'.]

Rowan and Ash are mentioned as two different trees; and Philip's flirtations with a highland lass are rather broadly painted, but prettily done towards the close:

[Quotes IV. 40–73: 'Spirits escaped from the body' to 'so I could go and uphold her'.]

The same ideas prevail in the joint volume of poems by Mr. Clough and Mr. Burbidge reviewed in the *Literary Gazette*, No. 1683, which see for our opinion [see No. 18]. There are strange notions as strangely expressed:

> You will not think that I soberly look for such things for sweet Katie,
> Contemplate really, as possible even, a thing that would make one
> Think death luxury, seek death, to get at damnation beyond it.[2]

---

[1] Cf. final version, III. 100ff. (*Poems*, 1951).
[2] Cf. final version, IV. 166ff. (*Poems*, 1951).

Thither also at times of cold and of possible gutters
Careless, unmindful, unconscious, would Hobbes, or e'er they departed,
Come, in a heavy pea-coat his trouserless trunk unwrapping,
Come under coat over-brief those lusty legs displaying,
All from the shirt to the slipper the natural man revealing.

                I shall not go at all, said
He, if you call me Mr. Thank Heaven! that's well over.
  No, but it's not, she said, it is not over, nor will be.
Was it not then, she asked, the name I called you first by?
No, Mr. Philip, no—you have kissed me enough for two nights,
No—come, Philip, come, or I'll go myself without you.
  You never call me Philip, he answered, until I kiss you.

It is beautiful only to do the thing we are meant for.
But they will marry, have husbands, and children, and guests, and households—
Are there then so many trades for a man, for women one only,
First to look out for a husband and then to preside at his table?
Learning to dance, then dancing, then breeding, and entertaining?
Breeding and rearing of children at any rate the poor do

Easier, say the doctors, and better, with all their slaving.
How many, too, disappointed, not being this, can be nothing!
How many more are spoilt for wives by the means to become so,
Spoilt for wives and mothers, and everything else moreover![1]

The plot ends with Philip winning his Highland lassie, and, oh!
laughable conclusion!—

[Quotes IX. 192–200: 'They are married' to the end of the poem.]

[1] Of these ten lines, which originally closed Philip's letter to Adam in IX (before
l. 40), Clough deleted all but the first when he revised the poem. Since he also altered two
of the other passages ridiculed here, it seems likely that this review influenced his judgment. Perhaps he felt that in this latter quotation Philip's distaste for the 'modern-fine-
lady' (II. 153) and the bourgeois marriage market was too harshly expressed.

10. Elizabeth Barrett Browning, to Miss Mitford

1849

From a letter dated 1 December 1849 (*Letters*, I. 429).

... We have had the sight of Clough and Burbidge, at last [she refers to *Ambarvalia*]. Clough has more thought, Burbidge more music; but I am disappointed in the book on the whole. What I like infinitely better is Clough's *Bothie of Toper-na-fuosich*, a 'long-vacation pastoral,' written in loose and more-than-need-be unmusical hexameters, but full of vigour and freshness, and with passages and indeed whole scenes of great beauty and eloquence. It seems to have been written before the other poems. ... I feel certain you will like it and think all the higher of the poet. Oh, it strikes both Robert and me as being worth twenty of the other little book, with its fragmentary, dislocated, inartistic character. Arnold's volume has two good poems in it: 'The Sick King of Bokhara' and 'The Deserted [*sic*] Merman'. I like them both. But none of these writers are *artists*, whatever they may be in future days.

11. W. M. Rossetti on *The Bothie,* review in the *Germ*

1850

W. M. Rossetti's review in the *Germ*, No. 1, January 1850, 34–46.

William Michael Rossetti (1829–1919), brother of Dante Gabriel and Christina, whose collected works he edited, was editor of the Pre-Raphaelite magazine the *Germ* which ran for four issues only in 1850. It is difficult to estimate how significant to the 'Brotherhood' was the singling out of *The Bothie* for the only poetry review in the first issue of a magazine dedicated to 'Nature' in literature and art, since W. M. Rossetti himself in a Preface to a facsimile reprint of the *Germ* (1901) notes: 'The only remark which I need make on this somewhat ponderous article is that I, as editor of the *Germ*, was more or less expected to do the sort of work for which other "proprietors" had little inclination.' Later, in *Some Reminiscences* (London, 1906), he comments that he had treated *The Bothie* 'from a very admiring point of view' (I. 102). But his taste was good: in No. 2 he noticed *The Strayed Reveller,* and in No. 4 *Christmas Eve and Easter Day.* Rossetti was only twenty when he wrote this review.

The critic who should undertake to speak of all the poetry which issues from the press of these present days, what is so called by courtesy as well as that which may claim the title as of right, would impose on himself a task demanding no little labor, and entailing no little disgust and weariness. Nor is the trouble well repaid. More profit will not accrue to him who studies, if the word can be used, fifty of a certain class of versifiers, than to him who glances over one: and, while a successful effort to warn such that poetry is not their proper sphere, and that they must seek elsewhere for a vocation to work out, might embolden a philanthropist to assume the position of scare-crow, and drive away the unclean birds from the flowers and the green leaves;

on the other hand, the small results which appear to have hitherto attended such endeavors are calculated rather to induce those who have yet made, to relinquish them, than to lead others to follow in the same track. It is truly a disheartening task. To the critic himself no good, though some amusement occasionally, can be expected: to the criticised, good but rarely, for he is seldom convinced, and annoyance and rancour almost of course; and, even in those few cases where the voice crying 'in the wilderness' produces its effect, the one thistle that abandons the attempt at bearing figs sees its neighbours still believing in their success, and soon has its own place filled up. The sentence of those who do not read is the best criticism on those who will not think.

It is acting on these considerations that we propose not to take count of any works that do not either show a purpose achieved or give promise of a worthy event; while of such we hope to overlook none.

We believe it may safely be assumed that at no previous period has the public been more buzzed round by triviality and common-place; but we hold firm, at the same time, that at none other has there been a greater or a grander body of genius, or so honorable a display of well cultivated taste and talent. Certainly the public do not seem to know this: certainly the critics deny it, or rather speak as though they never contemplated that such a position would be advanced: but, if the fact be so, it will make itself known, and the poets of this day will assert themselves, and take their places.

Of these it is our desire to speak truthfully, indeed, and without compromise, but always as bearing in mind that the inventor is more than the commentator, and the book more than the notes; and that, if it is we who speak, we do so not for ourselves, nor as of ourselves.

The work of Arthur Hugh Clough now before us, (we feel warranted in dropping the *Mr.* even at his first work,) unites the most enduring forms of nature, and the most unsophisticated conditions of life and character, with the technicalities of speech, of manners, and of persons of an Oxford reading party in the long vacation. His hero is

> Philip Hewson, the poet,
> Hewson, the radical hot, hating lords and scorning ladies;

and his heroine is no heroine, but a woman, 'Elspie, the quiet, the brave.'

The metre he has chosen, the hexametral, harmonises with the spirit of primitive simplicity in which the poem is conceived; is itself a background, as much as are 'Knoydart, Croydart, Moydart, Morrer, and Ardnamurchan;' and gives a new individuality to the passages of familiar narrative and every day conversation. It has an intrinsic appropriateness; although, at first thought of the subject, this will, perhaps, be scarcely admitted of so old and so stately a rhythmical form.

As regards execution, however, there may be noted, in qualification of much pliancy and vigour, a certain air of experiment in occasional passages, and a license in versification, which more than warrants a warning 'to expect every kind of irregularity in these modern hexameters.' The following lines defy all efforts at reading in dactyls or spondees, and require an almost complete transposition of accent.

There was a point which I forgot, which our gallant Highland homes have;
While the little drunken Piper came across to shake hands with Lindsay:
Something of the world, of men and women: you will not refuse me.

In the first of these lines, the omission of the former 'which', would remove all objection; and there are others where a final syllable appears clearly deficient; as thus:—

Only the road and larches and ruinous millstead between [them]:
Always welcome the stranger: I may say, delighted to see [such]
Fine young men:
Nay, never talk: listen now. What I say you can't apprehend [yet]:
Laid her hand on her lap. Philip took it. She did not resist [him]:

Yet the following would be scarcely improved by greater exactness:

Roaring after their prey, do seek their meat from God;

Nor, perhaps, ought this to be made correct:

Close as the bodies and intertwining limbs of athletic wrestlers.

The aspect of *fact* pervading *The Bothie of Toper-na-fuosich* (in English, 'the hut of the bearded well,' a somewhat singular title, to say the least,) is so strong and complete as to render necessary the few words of dedication, where, in inscribing the poem, (or, as the author terms it, 'trifle,') to his 'long-vacation pupils,' he expresses a hope, that they 'will not be displeased, if in a fiction, purely fiction, they are here and there reminded of times enjoyed together.'

As the story opens, the Oxford party are about to proceed to dinner at 'the place of the Clansmen's meeting.' Their characters, discriminated with the nicest taste, and perfectly worked out, are thus introduced:

[Quotes I. ll. 12–44: 'Be it recorded in song' to 'ample Olympian chamber'.]

A peculiar point of style in this poem, and one which gives a certain classic character to some of its more familiar aspects, is the frequent recurrence of the same line, and the repeated definition of a personage by the same attributes. Thus, Lindsay is 'the Piper, the Dialectician,' Arthur Audley 'the glory of headers,' and the tutor 'the grave man nick-named Adam,' from the beginning to end; and so also of the others.

Omitting the after-dinner speeches, with their

> Long constructions strange and plusquam-Thucydidean,

that only of 'Sir Hector, the Chief and the Chairman;' in honor of the Oxonians, than which nothing could be more unpoetically truthful, is preserved, with the acknowledgment, ending in a sarcasm at the game laws, by Hewson, who, as he is leaving the room, is accosted by 'a thin man, clad as the Saxon:'

> 'Young man, if ye pass thro' the Braes o'Lochaber,
> See by the Loch-side ye come to the Bothie of Toper-na-fuosich.'

Throughout this scene, as through the whole book, no opportunity is overlooked for giving individuality to the persons introduced: Sir Hector, of whom we lose sight henceforward, the attaché, the Guardsman, are not mere names, but characters: it is not enough to say that two tables were set apart 'for keeper and gillie and peasant:' there is something to be added yet; and with others assembled around them were

> Pipers five or six; *among them the young one, the drunkard.*

The morrow's conversation of the reading party turns on 'noble ladies and rustic girls, their partners.' And here speaks out Hewson the chartist:

> 'Never (of course you will laugh, but of course all the same I shall say it,)
> Never, believe me, revealed itself to me the sexual glory,
> Till, in some village fields, in holidays now getting stupid,
> One day sauntering long and listless, as Tennyson has it,
> Long and listless strolling, ungainly in hobbadiboyhood,
> Chanced it my eye fell aside on a capless bonnetless maiden,
> Bending with three-pronged fork in a garden uprooting potatoes.
> Was it the air? who can say? or herself? or the charm of the labor?
> But a new thing was in me, and longing delicious possessed me,
> Longing to take her and lift her, and put her away from her slaving.
> Was it to clasp her in lifting, or was it to lift her by clasping,

Was it embracing or aiding was most in my mind? Hard question.
But a new thing was in me: I too was a youth among maidens.
Was it the air? who can say? But, in part, 'twas the charm of the labor.'

And he proceeds in a rapture of talk on the beauty of household service. Hereat Arthur remarks:

'Is not all this just the same that one hears at common room breakfasts,
Or perhaps Trinity-wines, about Gothic buildings and beauty?'

The character of Hobbes, called into energy by this observation, is perfectly developed in the lines succeeding:

And with a start from the sofa came Hobbes; with a cry from the sofa,
There where he lay, the great Hobbes, contemplative, corpulent, witty;
Author forgotten and silent of currentest phrase and fancy;
Mute and exuberant by turns, a fountain at intervals playing,
Mute and abstracted, or strong and abundant as rain in the tropics;
Studious; careless of dress; inobservant; by smooth persuasions
Lately decoyed into kilt on example of Hope and the Piper,
Hope an Antinous mere, Hyperion of calves the Piper. . . .
'Ah! could they only be taught,' he resumed, 'by a Pugin of women
How even churning and washing, the dairy, the scullery duties,
Wait but a touch to redeem and convert them to charms and attractions;
Scrubbing requires for true grace but frank and artistical handling,
And the removal of slops to be ornamentally treated!

Here, in the tutor's answer to Hewson, we come on the moral of the poem, a moral to be pursued through commonplace lowliness of station and through high rank, into the habit of life which would be, in the one, not petty,—in the other, not overweening,—in any, calm and dignified.

'You are a boy; when you grow a man, you'll find things alter.
You will learn to seek the good, to scorn the attractive,
Scorn all mere cosmetics, as now of rank and fashion,
Delicate hands, and wealth, so then of poverty also,
Poverty truly attractive, more truly, I bear you witness.
Good, wherever found, you will choose, be it humble or stately,
Happy if only you find, and, finding, do not lose it.'

When the discussion is ended, the party propose to separate, some proceeding on their tour; and Philip Hewson will be of these.

'Finally, too,' from the kilt and the sofa said Hobbes in conclusion,
'Finally Philip must hunt for that home of the probable poacher,
Hid in the Braes of Lochaber, the Bothie of what-did-he-call-it.

Hopeless of you and of us, of gillies and marquises hopeless,
Weary of ethic and logic, of rhetoric yet more weary,
There shall he, smit by the charm of a lovely potatoe-uprooter,
Study the question of sex in the Bothie of what-did-he-call-it.'

The action here becomes divided; and, omitting points of detail, we must confine ourselves to tracing the development of the idea in which the subject of the poem consists.

Philip and his companions, losing their road, are received at a farm, where they stay for three days: and his experience of himself begins. He comes prepared; and, if he seems to love the 'golden-haired Katie,' it is less that she is 'the youngest and comeliest daughter' than because of her position, and that in which she realises his preconceived wishes. For three days he is with her and about her; and he remains when his friends leave the farm-house. But his love is no more than the consequence of his principles; it is his own will unconsidered and but half understood. And a letter to Adam tells how it had an end:

[Quotes IV. ll. 125–35, and 141–7: 'I was walking along' to 'in his fancy' and 'Doesn't yet see' to 'the arrow within me'.]

Philip Hewson has been going on

Even as cloud passing subtly unseen from mountain to mountain,
Leaving the crest of Benmore to be palpable next on Benvohrlich,
Or like to hawk of the hill, which ranges and soars in its hunting,
Seen and unseen by turns. . . .
                    And these are his words in the mountains: . . .
'Surely the force that here sweeps me along in its violent impulse,
Surely my strength shall be in her, my help and protection about her,
Surely in inner-sweet gladness and vigor of joy shall sustain her;
Till, the brief winter o'erpast, her own true sap in the springtide
Rise, and the tree I have bared be verdurous e'en as aforetime:
Surely it may be, it should be, it must be. Yet, ever and ever,
'Would I were dead,' I keep saying, 'that so I could go and uphold her.'

And, meanwhile, Katie, among the others, is dancing and smiling still on some one who is to her all that Philip had ever been.

When Hewson writes next, his experience has reached its second stage. He is at Balloch, with the aunt and the cousin of his friend Hope; and the lady Maria has made his beliefs begin to fail and totter, and he feels for something to hold firmly. He seems to think, at one moment, that the mere knowledge of the existence of such an one ought to compensate for lives of drudgery hemmed in with want; then he turns

59

round on himself with, 'How shall that be?' And, at length, he appeases his questions, saying that it must and should be so, if it is.

After this, come scraps of letters, crossed and recrossed, from the Bothie of Toper-na-fuosich. In his travelling towards home, a horse cast a shoe, and they were directed to David Mackaye. Hewson is still in the clachan hard by when he urges his friend to come to him: and he comes.

> There on the blank hill-side, looking down through the loch to the ocean;
> There, with a runnel beside, and pine-trees twain before it,
> There, with the road underneath, and in sight of coaches and steamers,
> Dwelling of David Mackaye and his daughters, Elspie and Bella,
> Sends up a column of smoke the Bothie of Toper-na-fuosich. . . .

> So on the road they walk, by the shore of the salt sea-water,
> Silent a youth and maid, and elders twain conversing.

> Ten more days, with Adam, did Philip abide at the changehouse;
> Ten more nights they met, they walked with father and daughter.
> Ten more nights; and, night by night, more distant away were
> Philip and she; every night less heedful, by habit, the father.

From this point we must give ourselves up to quotation; and the narrow space remaining to us is our only apology to the reader for making any omission whatever in these extracts.

[Quotes most of VII. ll. 1–15, 26–37, 47–59, 67–9, 74–102, 137–52, 166 to end.]

We may spare criticism here, for what reader will not have felt such poetry? There is something in this of the very tenderness of tenderness; this is true delicacy, fearless and unembarrassed. Here it seems almost captious to object: perhaps, indeed, it is rather personal whim than legitimate criticism which makes us take some exception at 'the curl on his forehead;' yet somehow there seems a hint in it of the pet curate.

Elspie's doubts now return upon her with increased force; and it is not till after many conversations with the 'teacher' that she allows her resolve to be fixed. So, at last,

> There, upon Saturday eve, in the gorgeous bright October,
> Under the alders knitting, gave Elspie her troth to Philip.

And, after their talk, she feels strong again, and fit to be his.—Then
they rise.

> 'But we must go, Mr. Philip.'
>   'I shall not go at all,' said
> He, 'if you call me *Mr.* Thank Heaven! that's well over!'
> 'No, but it's not,' she said; 'it is not over, nor will be.
> Was it not, then,' she asked, 'the name I called you first by?
> No, Mr. Philip, no. You have kissed me enough for two nights.
> No.—Come, Philip, come, or I'll go myself without you.'
> 'You never call me Philip,' he answered, 'until I kiss you.'

David Mackaye gives his consent; but first Hewson must return to
College, and study for a year.

His views have not been stationary. To his old scorn for the idle of
the earth had succeeded the surprise that overtook him at Balloch:
and he would now hold to his creed, yet not as rejecting his experience.
Some, he says, were made for use; others for ornament; but let these
be so *made*, of a truth, and not such as find themselves merely thrust
into examination from labor. Let each know his place, and take it,

> For it is beautiful only to do the thing we are meant for

And of his friend urging Providence he can only, while answering that doubtless he must be in the right, ask where the limit comes
between circumstance and Providence, and can but wish for a great
cause, and the trumpet that should call him to God's battle, whereas
he sees

> Only infinite jumble and mess and dislocation,
> Backed by a solemn appeal, 'For God's sake, do not stir there.'

and the year is now out.

> Philip returned to his books, but returned to his Highlands after. . . .
> There in the bright October, the gorgeous bright October,
> When the brackens are changed, and heather blooms are faded,
> And, amid russet of heather and fern, green trees are bonnie,
> There, when shearing had ended, and barley-stooks were garnered,
> David gave Philip to wife his daughter, his darling Elspie;
> Elspie, the quiet, the brave, was wedded to Philip, the poet. . . .
> So won Philip his bride. They are married, and gone to New Zealand.
> Five hundred pounds in pocket, with books and two or three pictures,
> Tool-box, plough, and the rest, they rounded the sphere to New Zealand.
> There he hewed and dug; subdued the earth and his spirit.

Among the prominent attributes of this poem is its completeness. The elaboration, not only of character and of mental discipline, but of incident also, is unbroken. The absence of all mention of Elspie in the opening scene and again at the dance at Rannoch may at first seem to be a failure in this respect; but second thoughts will show it to be far otherwise: for, in the former case, her presence would not have had any significance for Hewson, and, in the latter, would have been overlooked by him save so far as might warrant a future vague recollection, pre-occupied as his eyes and thoughts were by another. There is one condition still under which we have as yet had little opportunity of displaying this quality; but it will be found to be as fully carried out in the description of nature. In the first of our extracts the words are few, but stand for many.

> Meäly glen, the heart of Lochiel's fair forest,
> Where Scotch hrs are darkest and amplest, and intermingle
> Grandly with rowan and ash; —in Mar you have no ashes;
> There the pine is alone or relieved by birch and alder.

In the next the mere sound and the names go far towards the entire effect; but not so far as to induce any negligence in essential details:

> As, at return of tide, the total weight of ocean,
> Drawn by moon and sun from Labrador and Greenland,
> Sets in amain in the open space betwixt Mull and Scarfa,
> Heaving, swelling, spreading, the might of the mighty Atlantic;
> There into cranny and slit of the rocky cavernous bottom
> Settles down; and with dimples huge the smooth sea-surface
> Eddies, coils, and whirls, by dangerous Corryvreckan.

Two more passages, and they must suffice as examples. Here the isolation is perfect; but it is the isolation, not of the place and the actors only; it is, as it were, almost our own in an equal degree;

> Ourselves too seeming
> Not as spectators, accepted into it, immingled, as truly
> Part of it as are the kine in the field lying there by the birches.

[Quotes III. ll. 30–45: 'There, across the great rocky wharves', to 'the goddess of bathing'.]

> So they bathed, they read, they roamed in glen and forest;
> Far amid blackest pines to the waterfall they shadow,
> Far up the long long glen to the loch, and the loch beyond it
> Deep under huge red cliffs, a secret.

In many of the images of this poem, as also in the volume *Ambarvalia*, the joint production of Clough and Thomas Burbidge, there is a peculiar modernness, a reference distinctly to the means and habits of society in these days, a recognition of every-day fact, and a willingness to believe it as capable of poetry as that which, but for having once been fact, would not now be tradition. There is a certain special character in passages like the following, the familiarity of the matter blending with the remoteness of the form of metre, such as should not be overlooked in attempting to estimate the author's mind and views of art:

> Still, as before (and as now), balls, dances, and evening parties, . . .
> Seemed like a sort of unnatural up-in-the-air balloon work, . . .
> As mere gratuitous trifling in presence of business and duty
> As does the turning aside of the tourist to look at a landscape
> Seem in the steamer or coach to the merchant in haste for the city.
>
> I was one that sleeps on the railway; one who, dreaming,
> Hears thro' his dream the name of his home shouted out, —hears, and
>   hears not,
> Faint, and louder again, and less loud, dying in distance,—
> Dimly conscious, with something of inward debate and choice, and
> Sense of |present| claim and reality present; relapses,
> Nevertheless, and continues the dream and fancy, while forward,
> Swiftly, remorseless, the ear presses on, he knows not whither.

Indeed, the general adaptation of the style to the immediate matter, the alternation of the poetic and the familiar, with a certain mixture even of classical phrase and allusion, is highly appropriate, and may almost be termed constant, except in occasional instances where more poetry, and especially more conception and working out of images, is introduced than squares with a strict observance of nature. Thus the lines quoted where Elspie applies to herself the incident of 'the high new bridge' and 'the great key-stone in the middle' are succeeded by others (omitted in our extract) where the idea is followed into its details; and there is another passage in which, through no less than seventeen lines, she compares herself to an inland stream disturbed and hurried on by the mingling with it of the sea's tide. Thus also one of the most elaborate descriptions in the poem,—an episode in itself of the extremest beauty and finish, but, as we think, clearly misplaced,—is a picture of the dawn over a great city, introduced into a letter of Philip's, and that, too, simply as an image of his own mental condition. There are but few poets for whom it would be superfluous to reflect whether pieces of such-like mere poetry might not more properly form part of the descriptive groundwork, and be altogether banished from discourse and conversation, where the greater amount of their intrinsic care and excellence becomes, by its position, a proportionally increasing load of disregard for truthfulness.

For a specimen of a peculiarly noble spirit which pervades the whole work, we would refer the reader to the character of Arthur Audley, unnecessary to the story, but most important to the sentiment; for a comprehensive instance of minute feeling for individuality, to the narrative of Lindsay and the corrections of Arthur on returning from their tour.

> He to the great *might have been* upsoaring, sublime and ideal;
> He to the merest *it was* restricting, diminishing, dwarfing;

For pleasant ingenuity, involving, too, a point of character, to the final letter of Hobbes to Philip, wherein, in a manner made up of playful subtlety and real poetical feeling, he proves how 'this Rachel and Leah is marriage.'

The Bothie of Toper-na-fuosich will not, it is to be feared, be extensively read; its length combined with the metre in which it is written, or indeed a first hasty glance at the contents, does not allure the majority even of poetical readers; but it will not be left or forgotten by such as fairly enter upon it. This is a poem essentially thought and studied, if not while in the act of writing, at least as the result of a condition of mind; and the author owes it to the appreciations of all into whose hands it shall come, and who are willing to judge for themselves, to call it, should a second edition appear, by its true name; —not a trifle, but a work.

That public attention should have been so little engaged by this poem is a fact in one respect somewhat remarkable, as contrasting with the notice which the *Ambarvalia* has received. Nevertheless, independently of the greater importance of *The Bothie* in length and development, it must, we think, be admitted to be written on sounder and more matured principles of taste,—the style being sufficiently characterised and distinctive without special prominence, whereas not a few of the poems in the other volume are examples rather of style than of thought, and might be held in recollection on account of the former quality alone.

12. From William Whewell's review 'English Hexameters', in *North British Review*

In this review Whewell chiefly discusses Cochrane's translation of *Herman and Dorothea*, Longfellow's *Evangeline* and *The Bothie*, finding in these cases especially, as he says of the Goethe translation, that hexameters are better fitted than 'ordinary couplets' to convey 'homely reality'. In the remainder of the review he tries to establish rules for the dactylic hexameter, but without referring to *The Bothie* for his illustrations. It has been preferred here to Whewell's earlier 'Dialogues on English Hexameters', *Fraser's Magazine*, January 1849, xxxix.

Whewell (1794–1866) was Master of Trinity College, Cambridge, a mathematician and natural scientist; he also wrote on philosophical, theological and literary subjects. This article is ascribed to him by his biographer, Isaac Todhunter (see *A.H.C. Descr. Cat.* 68).

We have been unfortunate, in recent as well as in ancient times, in the original attempts which have been made at hexameters in England. Southey's *Vision of Judgment* combined almost every fault which can repel the lover of poetry. Politics and political intolerance, religious images and expressions bordering upon profaneness, machinery strange and yet mean, a multitude of personages and no drama, with the utter want of poetical interest, would have weighed down the most musical lines. But besides these faults, the Laureate's hexameters were, we are obliged to declare, tainted with the most shocking heresies in the article of versification, of which we may hereafter have a word to say. Passing over several minor essays in the same measure, all of which were more or less sportive, and therefore tended to diffuse a persuasion that hexameters could not be earnest, we may notice a little production which, though partly tinged by the same spirit, has still some remarkable characters in its composition. We speak of

Mr. Clough's *Bothie of Toper-na-Fuosich*. The strange name by which this composition is designated belongs, it seems, to a rude dwelling which stands in some region of the *Scotch Highlands*, and which is connected with the history of an Oxford reading party who spend the summer in its neighbourhood. In its versification, Mr. Clough's *Long Vacation Pastoral* is so uncouth and licentious as often to repel the most indulgent reader; for it is often impossible to know how the author intended his lines should read as hexameters, and not unfrequently, as appears to us, impossible so to read them by any force of false accent. Indeed, Mr. Clough seems to have regarded his performance mainly in the light of a good joke, and to have retained extravagancies of accent, phraseology, and imagery, as part of the jest. Yet, in spite of these blemishes, there is a tone of reality, culture, humour, and vivacity in the poem, which give it a considerable charm. The character of the several Oxonians, their eager colloquial discussions of the widest subjects, their several nicknames, and other fragments of a special language, which, after the manner of such young men, they have constructed for themselves during their season of domestic intimacy, their amusements, and their mode of treating their studies, are given with a truth which any one who has taken part in such an adventure cannot fail to be struck by. This kind of domestic life, as well as that of the family of the Pastor of Grünau and the Host of the Golden Lion, could only be faithfully given in the measure of the Odyssee. The main action here consists, first, in the colloquial speculations of the party concerning the place of women in society, and afterwards in the practical application of these by Philip Hewson, one of the party; who marries a Scotch lassie who dwells in the Bothie of Toper-na-Fuosich, and then goes out to New Zealand as a settler. Hewson is a democrat.

> Philip Hewson the poet,
> Hewson, the radical hot, hating lords and scorning ladies,
> Silent mostly, but often reviling in fire and fury
> Feudal tenures, mercantile lords, competition, and bishops.

Hewson is in the habit of declaiming to his friends against the helpless, artificial character which is imposed upon women by modern habits, and the trifling of modern gallantry.

> Still as before (and as now) balls, dances, and evening parties,
> Shooting with bows, going shopping together, and hearing them singing,
> Dangling beside them, and turning the leaves on the dreary piano,

Offering unneeded arms, performing dull farces of escort,
Seemed like a sort of unnatural up-in-the-air balloon work,
(or what to me is as hateful, a riding about in a carriage,)
Utter divorcement from work, mother earth, and objects of living,
As mere gratuitous trifling in presence of business and duty,
As does the turning aside of the tourist to look at the landscape,
Seem in the steamer or coach to the merchant in haste for the city.
Hungry and fainting for food, you ask me to join you in snapping—
What but a pink paper comfit with motto romantic inside it.
Wishing to stock me a garden, I'm sent to a table of nosegays;
Pretty, I see it, and sweet; but they hardly would grow in my borders.
Better a crust of black bread than a mountain of paper confections;
Better a daisy in earth than a dahlia cut and gathered;
Better a cowslip with root than a foreign carnation without it.[1]

The tutor of the party, 'the grave man, nicknamed Adam,' attempts
to answer this doctrine of the equality of women; and, among other
matters, to retort the illustration.

However noble the dream of equality—mark you, Philip,
Nowhere equality reigns in God's sublime creation.
Star is not equal to star, nor blossom the same as blossom,
Herb is not equal to herb any more than planet to planet.
True, that the plant should be rooted in earth I grant you wholly,
And that the daisy in earth surpasses the cut carnation,
Only the rooted carnation surpasses the rooted daisy.
There is one glory of daisies, another of carnations.

We might go on, for the discussion continues in an amusing and
spirited manner. But, as we have said, Hewson does not confine himself to speculative discussion. Having determined in his own mind that
women must do something and be something, not a mere doll, he
finds enough of his ideal to engage his thoughts in more than one case.
First, he says, in earlier youth,

Chanced it my eye fell aside on a capless, bonnetless maiden,
Bending with three-pronged fork in a garden uprooting potatoes,

who produces a movement in his heart. Now, in the course of a
holiday which the youths give themselves from their studies, to ramble
in the mountains, he comes to a farm by the loch-side of Rannoch,
where he is 'smitten by golden-haired Katie, the youngest and comeliest daughter.' But from her he tears himself, in consequence of the

---

[1] Cf. final version, ll. 55–67 (Poems, 1951).

passing glance of another damsel; and soon after, his companions hear of his falling away from his republican sternness. One of them

Came and revealed the contents of a missive that brought strange tidings;
Came and announced to the friends, in a voice that was husky with wonder,
Philip was staying at Balloch, was there in the room with the Countess,
Philip to Balloch had come, and was dancing with Lady Maria.

This whirling in the vortex of aristocracy does not, however, long continue. Soon after, Philip is heard of at the Bothie of Toper-na-Fuosich. He writes thence to his tutor concerning his having found Elspie Mackaye—

> She whose glance at Rannoch
> Turned me in that mysterious way; yes, angels conspiring
> Slowly drew me, conducted me, home, to herself; the needle
> Quivering, poises to north.

His tutor goes to him; approves his choice. We have the wooing, the father's consent; and, after a certain interval, during which he takes his degree at Oxford, and after a continuation of his discussions with his tutor on the object of human life, we have his wedding and his emigration.

We have dwelt the longer on this poem, because, notwithstanding its great, and indeed, wanton rudeness of execution, it seems to shew that the measure in which it is written may be made the vehicle of a representation of the realities of life, better than any more familiar form; more real and true, and yet not destitute, when managed by a poet, of poetical grace and ideal elevation. The conversation pieces in this, as in Herman and in Louisa, have more of the spirit of conversation than Cowper's *Table Talk*, Pope's *Satires*, Crabbe's *Tales*, or any versified attempts at familiar and argumentative dialogue in the language. And as we have already said, the very novelty of the measure makes us willingly accept a style in which the usual conventional phrases and dim generalities of poetical description are replaced by the idioms and pictures of common life.

13. Arnold's more objective view of
The Bothie

1861

From Oxford lectures *On Translating Homer* (1860–1); printed in
The Complete Prose Works of Matthew Arnold, Vol. I, *On the Classical Tradition*, Section III, 150–1.

Matthew Arnold (1822–88) was Professor of Poetry at Oxford
from 1857 to 1867. The passage quoted here is taken from the last
of three lectures *On Translating Homer* (1860–1) in which Arnold
compared the merits of various English versions of Homer and
considered whether their appropriate measure should be the
rhymed ten-syllable couplet, blank verse or the hexameter; it is
in speaking of his preference for the Homeric 'movement' of the
last that he digresses to praise his friend's efforts:

. . . Most of you, probably, have some knowledge of a poem by Mr.
Clough, *The Bothie of Toper-na-fuosich*, a long-vacation pastoral, in
hexameters. The general merits of that poem I am not going to discuss: it is a serio-comic poem, and, therefore, of essentially different
nature from the *Iliad*. Still, in two things it is, more than any other
English poem which I can call to mind, like the *Iliad*: in the rapidity
of its movement, and the plainness and directness of its style. The
thought in this poem is often curious and subtle, and that is not
Homeric; the diction is often grotesque, and that is not Homeric.
Still, by its rapidity of movement, and plain and direct manner of
presenting the thought however curious in itself, this poem, which,
being as I say a serio-comic poem, has a right to be grotesque, is
grotesque *truly*, not, like Mr. Newman's version of the *Iliad*, falsely.[1]
Mr. Clough's odd epithets, 'The grave man nicknamed Adam,' 'The
hairy Aldrich,' and so on, grow vitally and appear naturally in their
place; while Mr. Newman's 'dapper-greaved Achaians,' and 'motley-

[1] F. W. Newman's verse translation of the *Iliad* appeared in 1856.

helmed Hector,' have all the air of being mechanically elaborated and artificially stuck in. Mr. Clough's hexameters are excessively, needlessly rough; still, owing to the native rapidity of this measure, and to the directness of style which so well allies itself with it, his composition produces a sense in the reader which Homer's composition also produces, and which Homer's translator ought to *reproduce*,—the sense of having, within short limits of time, a large portion of human life presented to him, instead of a small portion.

Mr. Clough's hexameters are, as I have said, too rough and irregular; and indeed a good model, on any considerable scale, of this metre, the English translator will nowhere find. He must not follow the model offered by Mr. Longfellow in his pleasing and popular poem of *Evangeline*; for the merit of the manner and movement of *Evangeline*, when they are at their best, is to be tenderly elegant; and their fault, when they are at their worst, is to be lumbering; but Homer's defect is not lumberingness, neither is tender elegance his excellence. The lumbering effect of most English hexameters is caused by their being much too dactylic; the translator must learn to use spondees freely. Mr. Clough has done this, but he has not sufficiently observed another rule which the translator cannot follow too strictly; and that is, to have no lines which will not, as it is familiarly said, *read themselves*. This is of the last importance for rhythms with which the ear of the English public is not thoroughly acquainted. . . .

AMBARVALIA

January 1849

(A joint publication, with Thomas Burbidge)

14. Arnold, from various letters to Clough

1847-9

The extracts given below have been taken from *The Letters of Matthew Arnold to Arthur Hugh Clough*, ed. H. F. Lowry. Though only the last of these was written after *Ambarvalia* was published, they are all related to the contents of that volume, most of which Clough showed his friend in MSS.

i) The following extract from a letter Lowry dates 'early December 1847' is Arnold's reaction to reading in MSS. some of the poems Clough later included in *Ambarvalia*:

. . . I have had so much reluctance to read these, which I now return, that I surely must be destined to receive some good from them.—I have never been reminded of Wordsworth in reading them by rhythms or expressions: but of Tennyson sometimes and repeatedly of Milton— Little hast thou bested etc, e.g., [from 'In a Lecture-Room'] sounds to me Miltonically thought and expressed.

I have abstained from all general criticism, but here and there put a word against an expression: but it was done at a first reading, these are to be very slightly attended to.—It would amuse you to see how treatments differ, if you saw some things in which I have come on the same topics as you: those of your 4th poem. 1st vol. e.g. [The 4th poem in the copybook is an earlier version of 'Like a child/In some strange garden left awhile, alone' (Lowry)].

—The 2nd poem in the 1st volume [A poem which begins 'Enough, small Room: tho' all too true/Much ill in thee I daily do.' Clough never printed it.] I do not think—valuable—worthy of you—what is the word?

—And as a metrical curiosity the one about 2 musics does not seem to me happy ['The Music of the World and of the Soul'].

But on the whole I think they stand very grandly, with Burbidge's 'barbaric ruins' smiling around them. I think too that they will give the warmest satisfaction to your friends who want to see something of yours. Stanley[1] will have the 'calf' one ['The New Sinai'] by heart the day it appears.

(Letters, 61)

ii) . . . rare as individuality is you have to be on your guard against it —you particularly:—tho: indeed I do not really know that I think so. Shakespeare says that if imagination would apprehend some joy it comprehends some bringer of that joy: and this latter operation which makes palatable the bitterest or most arbitrary original apprehension you seem to me to despise. Yet to *solve* the Universe as you try to do is as irritating as Tennyson's dawdling with its painted shell is fatiguing for me to witness: and yet I own that to *reconstruct* the Universe is not a satisfactory attempt either—I keep saying, Shakspeare [*sic*], Shakspeare, you are as obscure as life is: yet this unsatisfactoriness goes against the poetic office in general: for this must I think certainly be its end. But have I been inside you, or Shakspeare? Never. Therefore heed me not, but come to what you can.

(Early December 1847, Letters, 63)

iii) A growing sense of the deficiency of the *beautiful* in your poems, and of this alone being properly *poetical* as distinguished from rhetorical, devotional, or metaphysical, made me speak as I did. But your line is a line: and you have most of the promising English verse-writers with you now: Festus for instance.[2] Still, problem as the production of the beautiful remains still to me, I will die protesting against the world that the other is false and JARRING.

No—I doubt your being an *artist*: but have you read Novalis? He certainly is not one either: but in the way of direct communication, insight, and report, his tendency has often reminded me of yours,

---

[1] A. P. Stanley, Arnold's contemporary at Rugby and Oxford, later Dean of Westminster and Dr Arnold's first biographer.

[2] *Festus* (1839) by Philip James Bailey.

though tenderer and less systematic than you. And there are the
sciences: in which I think the passion for truth, not special curiosities
about birds and beasts, makes the great professor—.

(About 24 February 1848, *Letters*, 66)

iv) . . . while I confess that productions like your Adam and Eve
[an incomplete poem in MSS., first published in *The Poems and Prose
Remains*, 1869, under the title 'Fragments of the Mystery of the Fall']
are not suited to me at present, yet [I] feel no confidence that they
may not be quite right and calculated to suit others. The good feature
in all your poems is the sincerity that is evident in them: which always
produces a powerful effect on the reader—and which most people
with the best intentions lose totally when they sit down to write. The
spectacle of a writer striving evidently to get breast to breast with
reality is always full of instruction and very invigorating—and here I
always feel you have the advantage of me: 'much may be seen, tho:
nothing can be solved'—weighs upon me in writing.

(20 July [1848], *Letters*, 86)

v) This letter is headed 'Friday' and Lowry ascribes it to the early part
of February 1849; *Ambarvalia* had appeared in January:

. . . If I were to say the real truth as to your poems in general, as they
impress me—it would be this—that they are not *natural*.

Many persons with far lower gifts than yours yet seem to find their
natural mode of expression in poetry, and tho: the contents may not
be very valuable they appeal with justice from the judgement of the
mere thinker to the world's general appreciation of naturalness—i.e.
—an absolute propriety—of form, as the sole *necessary* of Poetry as
such: whereas the greatest wealth and depth of matter is merely a
superfluity in the Poet *as such*.

—Form of Conception comes by nature certainly, but is generally
developed late: but this lower form, of expression, is found from the
beginning amongst all born poets, even feeble thinkers, and in an
unpoetical age: as Collins, Green and fifty more, in England only.

The question is not of congruity between conception and expression:
which when both are poetical, is the poet's highest result:—you say
what you mean to say: but in such a way as to leave it doubtful whether
your mode of expression is not quite arbitrarily adopted.

I often think that even a slight gift of poetical expression which in a common person might have developed itself easily and naturally, is overlaid and crushed in a profound thinker so as to be of no use to him to help him to express himself.—The trying to go into and to the bottom of an object instead of grouping *objects* is as fatal to the sensuousness of poetry as the mere painting, (for, *in Poetry*, this is not *grouping*) is to its airy and rapidly moving life.

'Not deep the poet sees, but wide' [Arnold quotes from his own 'Resignation']:—think of this as you gaze from Cumner Hill toward Cirencester and Cheltenham.—You succeed best you see, in fact, in the hymn, where man, his deepest personal feelings being in play, finds poetical expression as *man* only, not as artist:—but consider whether you attain the *beautiful*, and whether your product gives PLEASURE, not excites curiosity and reflexion. Forgive me all this: but I am always prepared to give up the attempt, on conviction: and so, I know, are you: and I only urge you to reflect whether you are advancing. Reflect too, as I cannot but do here more and more, in spite of all the nonsense some people talk, how deeply *unpoetical* the age and all one's surroundings are. Not unprofound, not ungrand, not unmoving:—but *unpoetical*.

(*Letters*, 98–9)

15. From an unsigned review of *Ambarvalia* in *Spectator*

20 January 1849, 65

The passage given below is only that part of the review which relates to Clough's contribution to the volume.

Although full of the faults that spring from the greenness and sufficiency of youth, there is more promise in *Ambarvalia* than in the great mass of verses that continually come before us. Whether this promise is to run wild and waste itself in wordy nothings, or be taught by study and self-cultivation to flow in a clear deep stream of poetry, is a question for the future to resolve.

The cast of mind and taste of Arthur H. Clough and Thomas Burbidge have sufficient generic resemblance to allow their poems to stand together; though we suppose it was college friendship, and the associations of the 'idem velle atque nolle,'[1] that induced their joint publication, rather than any critical reason. The characteristic of each writer is a sort of crude poetical power, which probably seems greater than it really is, from the vagueness both of subject and thought in which it is shrouded. Purpose, ideas, and frequently images, are seen as through a glass dimly; and possibly the reader is induced to ascribe a greater power to what he does not clearly perceive, on the principle of 'omne ignotum pro magnifico.'[2] This careless obscurity, this throwing of fragments as it were to the reader, is more visible in the poems of Mr. Clough; many of whose pieces are unnamed bits, as if he poured forth thoughts in verse without plan or purpose, and would not when done even be at the trouble of finding a title, but left the reader to infer that he had finished and begun anew, by some change of metre, or some apparent change of subject. Horace warns the poetical aspirant against the usual source of a poet's faults, being misled 'specie recti':[3] he never deemed it necessary to warn the candidate against the consequences of affectation, laziness, or contempt of his reader.

[1] *Idem velle atque idem nolle, ea demum firma amicitia est*—'Friendship is this—to desire, and to dislike, the same thing' (Sallust, *Catiline*, 20).

[2] 'The unknown is always thought grand', Tacitus, *De Vita Iulii Agricolae*, 30. 3.

[3] *Maxima pars vatum . . . decipimur specie recti*—'Most of us poets . . . deceive ourselves by the semblance of the truth', Horace, *Ars Poetica*, 24–5.

16. From an unsigned review in *Athenaeum*

10 February 1849, 135–6

The reviewer's quotation in full of Burbidge's 'To an Idiot Child' has been included here for comparison.

Ambarvalia, Poems by Thomas Burbidge and Arthur H. Clough, is a somewhat remarkable volume. Mr. Clough's portion is noticeable rather for its indications of what the writer might do than for what he has there done. Quaintness of thinking and of expression are alike marred by the effort to be too quaint. The straining after originality carries the author to the verge—and sometimes quite into the shadow —of obscurity. Take the following example of his manner.—

[Quotes 'The human spirits saw I on a day' entire.]

All through, Mr. Clough's share of the volume is full of the suggestions of a poetical power which these faults continually disappoint. The fol-lowing is more simple.—

> My wind is turned to bitter north,
>   That was so soft a south before;
> My sky that shone so sunny bright,
>   With foggy gloom is clouded o'er:
> My gay green leaves are yellow-black,
>   Upon the dank autumnal floor;
> For love, departed once, comes back
>   No more again, no more.
>
> A roofless ruin lies my home,
>   For winds to blow and rains to pour;
> One frosty night befell, and lo,
>   I find my summer days are o'er:
> The heart bereaved, of why and how
>   Unknowing knows that yet before
> It had what e'en to Memory now
>   Returns no more, no more.

Mr. Burbidge, a thinker of the same class, thinks yet more finely and speaks far more intelligibly. Still, he has the same tendency as his fellow minstrel to the curious in thought and form. If this be kept in due subordination, a new poet is born to us—and Mr. Burbidge will do far better things than he has here done. Even of what is here we have reasons for not presenting our readers with the best:—but the following poem will at least convey his manner—and something of his power.

To an Idiot Child

Sweet child, what light is in those eyes!
Like islands bright in sunset skies,
Ablaze with glory overweening
Yet cold—alive, yet dead of meaning!
Two goats upon the rocks at play
Nor wilder as they climb and leap;
Yet torpid in their sense are they
As awful mountain lakes that sleep
Far deepening downward from the day
To caves a thousand fathoms deep!

O Child of love, what hath become
Of thy sweet tongue?—would it were dumb!
—That now doth boisterously climb
Along the fragmentary rhyme,
Years back within thine infant ear
Lodged lightly—thus to re-appear,
Thus, as a vague, deceitful Muse
Its melody may re-infuse
Into a heart that hath declined
From the pure guidance of the mind.
O limbs, whose life is it ye live?
Which now no more your service give
To a considerant human soul!
Is it the wind which doth control
This graceful twining of your play?
Or do mild spirits, gently gay,
Thus prompt your motions to obey
The self-same impulse which persuades
The woodbine deep in oaken shades,
Her sturdy pillar to embrace
With movements of such matchless grace;
Or bids the skylark, of pure sound
Extracted from the dewy ground

While morning yet is all divine,
About the fleeing stars entwine,
In modulations soft as strong,
The bright inevitable line
Of its elastic song?

Poor Child! when Fancy's all is said,
What art thou but a creature dead,—
Dead to the real life of life,
The spiritual stir—the strife
Ineffable of soul and sense!
Yet mayst thou live without offence;
And thou, poor Child, in memory
A monument shalt stand to me
(With many a gem and many a flower,
And many a cloudlet of the sky)
Of God's surpassing love and power,
Who, speaking only to the eye,
Can carry with an inward smart
A voiceless meaning to the heart.

17. From an unsigned review of *Ambarvalia* and *The Strayed Reveller and Other Poems* by 'A' [Matthew Arnold] in the *Guardian*

28 March 1849, iv, 208–9

To say nothing of Mr. Tennyson's own creations, we owe him something for being, as we conceive, the indirect cause of such poetry as that of Mr. Clough and 'A'. In himself he seems to us to unite in no small measure the metaphysical depth of S. T. Coleridge, with the objective sensuousness of an old ballad; the quiet thoughtfulness of our Poet Laureate, with the sweetness and smoothness of Mr. Moore;

the outwardness of Homer with the inner life of our modern poets; but he is far more successful in embodying the merely intellectual element in the language of the passions; in investing the bare anatomy with living flesh and blood, and a graceful drapery, which shows the beauties which it half conceals; hence the peculiar charm of his love poetry, blending a semi-platonic purity with the glow of more human affection. This we take to be his special praise; and of this we are much reminded in 'A', and the first part of *Ambarvalia*. If the writer of the latter has more of that deep insight into things as they really are, of which some of his most thoughtful poems prove him to be possessed, the former has more of his pictorial power; both, like him, are eminent in the melody of rhythm, and in masterly selection, seemingly by instinct, of pregnant expressive epithets.

Mr. Clough is already known to our Oxford readers as the author of a *Long Vacation Pastoral*, not very intelligible, and hardly to be recommended, beyond the walls of the University. His present work, if less witty and amusing, is far more powerful, even in its fragmentary nature, more profound, more interesting, more rich in 'the thoughts that shake mankind'. Scintillations, as the abrupt little pieces are, they shed a light around, deep and wide, on human nature. Rarely relieved as the book is, by the boldly yet finely traced characters that stand out in such roundness from the *Pastoral*, yet is their loss atoned for by glimpses into those mysterious cells of the heart, which, as they lie deepest, so are most common to mankind at large. Mr. Clough must be content with 'fit audience, though few'. Those readers who are fond of 'poetry made easy',—who like the even tenor of superficial faultiness, the tinsel of glittering diction, and a 'false gallop' of thought —such we warn not to run the risk of bewilderment and a headache over these pages. Besides, the book is even more tantalising than it need be—there are very few headings to enable one to stand at the writer's view-point, and thence gaze around with him; no obvious arrangement, if any; not even marked pauses to prevent the shock of plunging from a Polkish love song into a metaphysical reverie (sometimes both are combined into one piece) with the versatility of a barrel-organ; and, at times, an hieroglyphical abruptness of expression which better suits the *déshabille* of an author's note-book than his appearance in public.

The first poem is a good specimen of the whole. There is in it a silvery melody, very dependent on due emphasis, and hence linked closely to the sense, as in old English poets, and a plaintive sweetness,

D

79

both worthy of Tennyson. It well represents, too, the tone of anxious heartfelt inquiry after truth which pervades the book, soothed, however, and calmed here, as in other places, by allusions to the only remedy, fulfilment of immediate duties:

[Quotes 'The human spirits saw I on a day' entire.]

Perhaps it might be objected that the question—What duty is? is left untouched in this poem; but Poetry is not bound to teach explicitly: she neither can nor ought to do more than point the way. Other passages, however, in his poems, must, we fear, make us add that the complaint from which Mr. Clough is thus sheltered as a poet, might be made with but too much truth against him as a thinker.

In almost every line of the poems there is great power and promise. A finished work they are not, as a whole, nor yet singly. They are the wild sad outpourings of an Aeolian harp, or the broken murmurings of a brook over rough places. Metaphors are said to be the test of a true poet. Here is one, beautiful and original:—

> Ah love, high love, she said and sighed,
> She said, the poet's love;
> A star upon a turbid tide,
> Reflected from above;
> A marvel here, a glory there;
> But clouds will intervene,
> And garish earthly noon outglare
> The purity serene.

Here are some thoughts not without their value, surely, for many, in these times of uncertainty and division:—

[Quotes 'Qua Cursum Ventus' entire.]

'When Israel came out of Egypt', is one of the least incomplete and grandest things in the book; but its apparent moral, that scepticism is the road to faith, is rather a strange one, and, though true in a certain sense, dangerous and unreasonable at a time, when, among persons likely to be readers, there is more liability to morbid restlessness than to apathetic quietism. Also, it is a slight inaccuracy, but one bearing on the subject, and so very tempting, to call Aaron the brother-*priest* at the time of the golden calf. The 'Silver Wedding' sadly wants explanation, without which its drift is hard to understand. Many are not acquainted with the custom of styling the twenty-fifth anniversary of the wedding-day, the silver, and its venerable successor in the fiftieth year, the golden wedding. But the poem is one of the most beautiful in the volume, and we heartily wish we had room to quote it. We must console ourselves with the very affecting stanzas in another page; very terse and nervous also, as though by one of our old poets:—

[Quotes 'My wind is turned to bitter north': for text see No. 16.]

Mr. Clough's style is very racy. He uses single words with peculiar aptness, and this, if done by impulse, is a sure mark of the true poet. And yet the words do not glare with a too prominent consciousness, like those in Coleridge's prose, nor give the idea of petty precision. Altogether the author seems to have a vigorous grasp on the English language,[1] wielding it, with the boldness and ease of a master-hand, to great and little things; and skilfully enriching it now and then with adventitious idioms, terse and new. In a word, the style, although slip-shod here and there, is well suited for the utterance of free original thoughts.

But, with all these merits, there are grave liabilities to censure, aesthetical and moral. Doubt, it may be urged, is not a Poet's mood. At all events, states of minds and feelings, however interesting, want to be associated with outward realities, or rather to be expressed in and by them. In this Mr. Clough falls very far short of the author of *Locksley Hall*. It is true that all real poetry must emanate from the heart; but also it must fasten its tendrils on the outer world; its business is to wed the material of the one to the living spirit of the other. Lastly, he is guilty often of too didactic an exposé of abstract truth—e.g. in the recipe for love, as it might be called:—

> Let Reason first her office ply;
> Esteem and Admiration high, &c. &c.

[from 'When panting sighs the bosom fill']

There is a want of substance, shape, and colour, for the imagination to feed upon.

Morally, the charge is similar, but, of course, more serious. The danger of autobiographical revelations is notorious, especially for minds of a certain constitution. We have no right to attach, definitely, autobiographical character to these poems—for certain positions of mind may be transient, though genuine while they last—however strong the appearance of it which they wear. In that light they would

---

[1] All who have read a pamphlet by Mr. Clough, published (1847) in Oxford, about the Irish, will readily allow this. [The critic's note.]

be as sacred from criticism as a published work can be. We are speaking of likely effects from reading them. The disgust at shams—the weariness of unmeaning conventionalities—the ardent longing for truth, and sense of duty—generous sympathy with fellow workers in the great cause of truth, whose conscience forces them to a different path from the writer's own—the noble elevation of sentiment over the Fetish worship of money or pleasure into a contemplation of the awful meaning of life—all this is truly grand and good. But through the book there runs a morbid self-consciousness, a critical and sensitive distrust of self, which are the very opposite of action, and direct hindrance to it:—

> Unless above himself he can
> Erect himself, how mean a thing is man!

Always to be mapping out the foundations on too vast a scale, and with an eye too curious and fastidious, is not the way to rear a goodly superstructure. Nor is it for human intellect to set about analysing and proving the ultimate principles—facts they are, and nothing more or less—of the reason or emotions. Weariness and vexation can only ensue. Nor is it for man to reject this or that system because it is not faultless. Better for us, perhaps, that we must put up with imperfection. In this world we must work: if we wait for symmetrical theories, whose beauty is marred by no troublesome incongruities, there is danger of evaporating in sentimentality, or stagnating in indifference:—

> The fruit of dreary hoping,
> Is waking blank despair.

The poems bear far more decided traces of thinking, than of reading—a fault, if any, on the right side. But is not this, insufficiently qualified by the other, apt to destroy the balance of the mind? Above all, of course, we who are firmly convinced that what we see so often alluded to, by thinkers of that class to which Mr. Clough belongs, as *mere* forms—worthy of the greatest hatred if they were so—are in reality the channels of important verities, in some instances effete in appearance from neglect or misuse, must be excused if we warn our readers against the bad philosophy which now-a-days ministers with so much subtilty and success to intellectual pride. Moreover, it may be asked, whether it be not merely a more subtle and elevated form of selfishness, that amiable and genial weakness which lays bare to the inspection of others the melancholy workings of its own breast—troubles not peculiar to the complainer—as if leaning helpless on their support and sympathy? Then, too, the excess of self-distrust is almost equally a want of faith with excess of self-confidence. That self-distrust alone has humility for its parent, which leans, for the support it cannot find in itself, upon something external, worthy of being the prop of the human soul. If it be said, that it is possible for men, without any fault of their own, never to have met with this 'something external', we answer, that indeed it is so, but it is equally possible, and far more usual, for men to reject the true prop, having constituted themselves the judges of its unworthiness. Great, indeed, is the sympathy due both to the voluntary and the involuntary wanderer: but the latter only has any excuse—the sufferings of the latter alone can be contemplated without danger by others. *Qui laborat, orat*, is a beautiful thought concerning one who has never been taught to pray, a pernicious falsehood about one who has rejected the practice. With such a one it will soon be *Qui non orat, nec laborat!* We are not, in these remarks, treating these poems so much as autobiographical revelations, as thoughts thrown before the minds of many readers not unlikely, from the fashion that now prevails among men of intellect and cultivation—especially those who have come under the influence of a popular writer lately deceased, as remarkable for self-reliance as for moral honesty and straightforwardness—to awaken echoes that may, in some cases, deepen into the knell of faith and religion. Byronian mawkishness is no longer in vogue: the fresh upright morality of the teaching of which we speak would dissipate in a moment such unhealthy exhalations. A mixture of misanthropy and debauchery is no longer the obvious way to be thought interesting: nor, when sensuality links itself with opposition to religion instead of hatred of mankind, is it much more popular. The vice now is to fancy oneself 'one of no common intellect, no common feelings,' and to reject, because men of less fine natures have abused them, the means of happiness with which Nature and Providence have furnished the humble as well as the intellectual of mankind. We are very far from hinting that this is applicable to the causes which have produced the painfully real traces of morbid struggling before us: but considering the probable effect upon some of the readers of these poems,—given to the world, we venture to say, without the slightest thought of influencing any one either way,—and remembering also the number of minds that are hampered by too much self-consciousness from fresh impulsive action, we cannot doubt that their indiscriminate circulation will do far more harm than good.

If we might suggest a new arrangement, we would advise our readers to bind up 'A' with Mr. Clough, in spite of that gentleman's present, we cannot say, 'better-half'. In fact there is so little to compensate in Mr. Burbidge, to whom we shall proceed bye and bye, for his positive demerits, that he may easily be dispensed with. The volume, then, would well represent the two phases of Tennyson, grave and sportive, the inner and outer world. If Mr. Clough is a mountain stream, 'A' is a sparkling fountain. 'A' is more likely to be popular. He gives the head less work—the eye is not so introverted— the enigma of life is not so sternly grappled with. . . .

. . . On the whole, reverting [after discussing Burbidge], as we gladly do to Mr. Clough and 'A', we think we may congratulate the present age in England on its poetry. As fragments, their poems are all the better specimens of what might be done. It is the foot of Hercules. Depth of thought and feeling, finding its characteristic exponent in a more emphatic and logical, if less strictly grammatical, order of words, than in the last century, in fewer redundancies, and less of that vagueness of expression which is, in part, the unlucky incident of our language being so composite, and thus so rich in quasi-synonyms,[1] (and a similar improvement may be noted in prose, for instance, in some of the least extreme imitators of Mr. Carlyle's diction), this is the brightest side of our present poetry. In these respects Mr. Clough and 'A' seem well fitted to give voice to the blind motions of the age. If they elevate and purify that to which they lend utterance, they will worthily have fulfilled a poet's mission.

[1] e.g.: Let *Observation*, with extended view,
   Survey mankind from China to Peru.

   Johnson's Juvenal Imitated [The critic's note.]

18. Unsigned review of *Ambarvalia* in the *Literary Gazette*

21 April 1849, lxv, 292–3

The *Literary Gazette* had already given *The Bothie* a hostile reception, complaining in its notice of 18 August 1849, of its 'affectations, absurd terms, and ridiculous versifying' (see No. 9).

Arcades Ambo[1] and a queer couple. Clough goes it through sixty-four pages, and Burbidge finishes off the volume. To do our best office for the former, we quote some lines which may compare with the poetry of the period of gentlemen who wrote with ease two centuries agone.

[Quotes 'Away, haunt thou not me' and 'My wind is turned to bitter north' entire.]

Who would expect from one that could write such passable verse as this, such trash as the annexed, entitled *Natura Naturans*?

> Beside me,—in the car,—she sat,
> She spake[2] not, no, nor looked to me:
> From her to me, from me to her,
> What passed so subtly stealthily?
> As rose to rose that by it blows
> Its interchanged aroma flings;
> Or wake to sound of one sweet note
> The virtues of disparted strings.
>
> Beside me, nought but this!—but this,
> That influent as within me dwelt
> Her life, mine too within her breast,
> Her brain, *her every limb she felt:*
> We sat: while o'er and in us, more
> And more, a power unknown prevailed,

[1] 'Both Arcadians' (Virgil, *Eclogues* VII, 4).
[2] For spoke. [Critic's note.]

85

Inhaling, and inhaled,—and still
'Twas one, inhaling or inhaled.

The scene is a second-class carriage on the railroad, where this unconscious inhaling takes place, and the poor girl, as if mesmerized,
feels her every limb,—

As unsuspecting mere a maid
As, fresh in maidhood's bloomiest bloom,
In casual second-class did e'er
By casual youth her seat assume.

This casual youth informs us that '*her life was in him then*', and that
they 'fused in one', or something of that mysterious sort, and the
circumjacent world began to partake of this wondrous influence,
most alliteratively:—

Flashed flickering forth fantastic flies
Big bees their burly bodies swung,
Rooks roused with civic din the elms,
And lark its wild reveillez rung;

In Libyan dell the light gazelle,
The leopard lithe in Indian glade,
And dolphin, brightening tropic seas,
In us were living, leapt and played.

Their shells did slow crustacea build,
Their gilded skins did snakes renew,
While mightier spines for loftier kind
Their types in amplest limbs outgrew;
Yea, close comprest in human breast.

And then there is some nonsense about our first parents in Eden.

When, naked both, its garden paths
They walked unconscious, unashamed.

And the Cloughage concludes and the Burbidge-age begins, in a style
no less remarkable, as the following will prove to the meanest
capacities:—

Lilie, a Myth

Within this bosom she was born,
I say not if 'twas day or night
I say not if 'twas eve or morn
When Lilie saw the light.

A vision that for seventeen years
Had floated in men's eyes was she;
A bright machine of smiles and tears,
No more—till she knew me.

Into my arms that vision crept,
And nothing knew she there should find!
And I breathed on her as she slept,
And she became a Mind.

Some of the rest of this rhapsody is so expressed as to be indecent, and so we only transcribe fragments.

I was a coarse and vulgar man,
I vile and vulgar things had done;
And I, as Nature's instincts ran,
Was wont to let them run.

And yet to such a man as I
Did Lilie her pure fancy fling;
And loved me—as a butterfly
May love a flower of Spring.

[Pretty Flower!]

She sought my breast, she nestled there,
For nought knew she that should forbid.

One stanza of a picture of Sicily in 1846, ridiculous as it is, induces a wish that the producers there were now as profitably employed,—

Goodman Tobacco-farmer spreads out his store to dry;
Row and row the green leaves in a seemly order lie;
The open shore invites him, row and row he spreads them there,
Binding neatly into bundles, as they answer to the air.
Today's are fat and scentless, today's are green with dew;
Yesterday's are shrunk and brown, but the scent is creeping through.

From the absurd to the pathetic is but a step: over leaf to 'An Anniversary'.

Two years ago, this day, he died;
In silence to the grave he stole.

As if a corpse walked itself off and buried itself with maimed rites! We think the brother bards are worthy of being bound in the one same volume.

19. John Conington(?), from a review, 'Recent Poetry, and Recent Verse', in *Fraser's Magazine*

May 1849, xxxix, 580–5

Conington (1825–69) was Professor of Latin at Oxford (1854–69); he published verse translations of Horace, the *Aeneid* and half the *Iliad*. For the convincing ascription of this article to Conington see *A. H. C. Descr. Cat.* 66.

Most of the quotations from Burbidge have been retained here for their comparative interest.

The next book on our list is one far superior in poetic power to any of the works we have noticed, except the *Strayed Reveller*, and far superior to that volume in faith and earnestness of purpose. Its name, *Ambarvalia*, perhaps, is a mistake; for it leads us to expect something of a pastoral, or rather a purely Bucolic nature. On the contrary, the short lyrics and fragments of blank verse of which it consists are almost entirely of a subjective and meditative cast, principally religious and philosophic. Especially in Mr. Clough's half of the book there is often an obscurity of thought, and a careless roughness of form, which more time spent in polishing, and more exertion given to throwing his thoughts into a concrete and truly imaginative form, might easily have remedied. We must complain, too, of the fragmentary state of the whole book. It is true every scrap is worthy reading and remembering. The authors have a right to say, 'Whatever we have not done, we have, at least, given you a worthy thought embodied in a worthy form, to help your comprehension and recollection.' But still we must ask, Why these mere scraps—very often without titles? Why were they not kept to be inserted as parts of some continuous whole? Why, as we said before, should an artist begin publishing his sketches before he has painted us one perfect picture? He fritters away his own talents by the habit of throwing into verse unconnected his passing thoughts, unless he have some one higher object in view which will hereafter unite them all. The only case in which such a method is allowable is when each little poem is in itself a defined and perfect organic whole, such as almost all Mr. Tennyson's earlier short poems were; for it is but fair that an artist should try his power upon small pictures before he advances to vast and complicated ones. But let them be wholes, and not desultory *disjecta membra poetæ*; and let the poet be sure that the sooner he tries to compose a large work the better for him, even though he fail. The habits of method, and of continuous thought and purpose; the insight into the laws of art, above all of the *più nel uno*—the unity in multiplicity, which was, according to the old Italian painters, the ground law of all composition; in short, the self-discipline, moral and intellectual, which he will gain by labouring for months or years at one great work, will go further to make a poet and a man of him, than thousands of 'fugitive pieces'—fugitive in every sense of the word. We were deeply struck with this truth in reading, the other day, the poetical works of the late Mr. Motherwell, in which a quantity of talent, which if united and inspired by one great object might have produced an immortal poem, seems to us to have been utterly thrown away by dribblets upon innumerable subjects, which taken separately were of little interest, while they might have shone brilliantly, each in its place, as parts of a great whole. The moral in the old fable of the bundle of sticks, that division is weakness, holds as true in art as it does in politics and in war. We speak, of course, of those only who have the great faculty of concentration,—of arranging and wielding large masses of thought in obedience to a single idea. Those who have not, must either aim at perfect finish in short poems, which, we believe, is almost necessary to their naturalness and effectiveness,—in fact, to their being poetry at all, or else—which, perhaps, is the wiser plan—they must give up poetry, and turning essayists, philosophers, politicians, or whatsoever else their hand findeth to do, do that with all their might, and not trouble themselves at all with writing verses, if they cannot write first-rate ones. We do not mean to recommend such a course to Mr. Clough, for he has shewn the public, in his poem of *The Bothie*, that he is capable of better things than fragments; though in that too, as here, we miss both the dramatic faculty of projecting himself out of himself into the characters whom he describes, and also that rhythmic inspiration, that instinctive melodiousness, which throws all the thoughts of the lyric poet into the form of a song,—that faculty which is the secret of the great effect which Moore has been able to produce with thoughts and images generally of the shallowest and most commonplace kind. But we do think, on the shewing of his own poems, that Mr. Clough is meant to be something higher than a third-rate versifier,—that he is meant to be an earnest thinker and prose writer upon some of the deepest questions of our day; and though we would not advise him to give up verse, yet we would counsel him, while he has so much matter to express, not to lose time over the manner of it, as he seems to have done, for instance, in the following beautiful fragment,—beautiful and wise, but which, unless it was intended to be inserted in a longer poem, might, with the exception of the last three lines, have been written in prose without sacrificing a particle of its imagery:—

[Quotes 'Roused by importunate knocks I rose' ('Blank Misgivings . . . ,' VII).]

We would not complain thus, were there not some things among Mr. Clough's poems which make us believe that he can finish, and that he can cast his into a truly song-like form; for instance, the first piece in the book, which struck us much, not only for its noble moral, but also for the genuine and appropriate melody of its soft and melancholy rhythm:—

[Quotes entire 'The human spirits saw I on a day'.]

We must speak with diffidence in criticising the poems of two young men, who seem, from this little book, far more able to sit in judgment on us than we are on them; but we think that Mr. Burbidge gives more promise than Mr. Clough does of taking a high place among the lyrists of the day. In both there is a full consciousness, that to affect the present generation they must sing about the present; but in Mr. Burbidge there is more natural melodiousness, more polish, more objectivity, if not of thought, still of expression. Yet in him, too, we miss that Tyrtæan fire and passion, that lilt and roll, by which the true people's poet can stir the hearts of men. He is too calm as yet for an Orpheus; 'the brutes' may listen, but it will require much more energy on his part to make them 'dance.' But his sonnets are very beautiful; this one, for instance:—

To the revered Memory of Thomas Arnold, D.D.

Yes, noble Arnold, thou didst well to die!
Needed but this, that the dark earth should hide
The seed, to have the harvest far and wide.
Long (with a voice that echoed in the sky)

> Didst thou pour forth thy fervent prophecy:
> Vain seer!—for thou amongst us didst abide;—
> This world was then thy country;—at our side
> Thou spak'st scarce heard. But now thou art on high
> Among the immortal and invisible quire.
> And straight like thunder (silent till the fire
> Which caused it dies), thy soul's majestic voice
> Is rolling o'er the wonder-smitten land;
> And Truth that sate in drought, dares to rejoice,
> Marking that all admire, some understand.

And this one, again, in a different key, which, with several others of both gentlemen's *Devotional Poems*, seem to be the harbingers of a healthier and deeper school of religious poetry than any we have seen of late. True, it, like many more of their thoughts, is melancholy; but it is not the morbid Werterism of men discontented with God, His universe, and history, which is the track of His footsteps through time, as was the melancholy of the *Lyra Apostolica*, but of righteous discontent with the evil within them and without them, which is at discord with God and with His purposes in this day; and it is, therefore, that for one verse complaining of others we have fifty complaining of themselves. We hope to see many more such devotional poems as this book contains, and only beg Mr. Burbidge, in his next work, not again to seem to yield to one of the Manichæan lies of the age, which he nobly contradicts throughout the poems themselves. We mean not to countenance the fancied separation between Sacred and Profane, by putting his devotional poems apart from the rest, and under a separate title.

> The evil birds which I have fed so long,
>   In the foul mansion of my sinful soul,
> Now with their pinions, horrible and strong,
>   They battle with me for their usual dole.
> Hungrily barking, a discordant song,
>   They hang upon the outlets of my mind,
> Or on the roof sit patiently and long,
>   Heavy as autumn clouds, the loathsome kind.
> Lord, give me air and light! I pant for breath!
>   And Thy sweet residence, once warm and bright,
>   Is close, confined, and small, and full of night;
> It is clay-cold and damp—it smells of death!
> Yet Thou art there!—And where Thou deignest to be,
> My blessed Lord! is good enough for me.

Another feature, which excuses the sadness of some of these poems, is the healthy, cheerful, and truly godly eye which they have for Nature, for Love, and all human relations. We can allow those who delight simply and innocently in the beauties of God's universe as He created it, to lament as much as they will over the sad deflexions from it which man's sin has caused. We will listen respectfully to the sighs of a man who can write in the same breath such a poem as the following:—

New-old Philosophy

Un vrai Philosophe est homme, fait gloire de l'être.—MARMONTEL

Let Love be Love, my best philosophers!
  As Motion is the regent Law of life,
Even so 'tis Passion only which confers
  The power of Love. All contest is not strife.
It is not peace, but death, where nothing stirs.

*   *   *

So is Love's genuine calm, by Passion's strife
  Kept rich and full, else falling soon away,

Or (keeping semblance) sad in lack of life,
  As that cold impress fair the adulterous clay
Took on the bounteous heart of Diomed's Wife.[1]

Beneath the tents which sacred Love invests,
  Blush not, true man, the rosy wreath to take;
Nor, while within thine arms the dear one rests,
  With overstooping kisses to awake
The little Love asleep between her breasts.

The true philosopher is he whose eye
  Reads truly Nature, God's appointed plan—
He who obeys her rule instinctively,
  Or wittingly, or not, the genuine man.
Wisdom is to obey her, knowing why!

[The reviewer concludes by quoting the lengthy 'Goodman Tobacco-Farmer', which he considers 'one of the best political ballads . . . for a long time'; finally, he recommends *Ambarvalia* 'to all who read poetry, not for passing amusement, but as food for earnest meditation'.]

1 In the museum at Naples, is shewn the mould of a woman's bosom in indurated ashes—supposed to be that of the wife of Diomed, the possessor of the villa called by his name, at the gate of Pompeii. [Burbidge's note.]

20. Unsigned review, 'Clough's Poems', the *Rambler*

July 1849, iv, 201–5

Mr. Clough's poems, which it is our intention principally to notice . . . belong to that description of poetry which to ourselves is more interesting than any other. It is an everyday observation, that in all persons, more or less, but more especially in all persons of lively and keen sensibilities, there is an inward life, in which they far more truly *live*, than in the external and visible one. The customs of society, the necessities of every-day duties, the hopelessness of meeting with sympathy, these and other causes conspire in giving a certain external sameness to all educated men. The devout religionist, the man of the world, and the debauchee, may unite for political or other purposes, or may meet together, if they so please, and sustain conversation on no very unequal terms. Nay, even in his domestic circle, where the Englishman especially loves to unbend, his deepest thoughts, those which are most of all the centre round which his whole life turns, are often still secrets; he cannot disclose them even if he would. But if he have the divine gift and publish poetry,—poetry, we mean, of that particular kind which is here in question,—then we begin to see his real self, stripped of disguises and conventionalities; then we learn what are those cherished and deeply enshrined objects, on which his heart and his imagination rest and are supported.

It is impossible that poetry of this nature shall be written at all, without thus unveiling the innermost thoughts. Many a man, indeed, will write a cut and dry *imitation* of this style, and unveil nothing except the profound unreality and sophistication of his own mind; but it requires no very deep or discerning criticism to discover such pitiful imposture, and estimate it at its proper value. We are speaking of *genuine* poetry, belonging to (what may be called) the autobiographical kind: and we say that it is of especial interest, because it discloses in a way peculiar to itself the inward belief and principles of a man; it shews us what he really feels as his *summum bonum*; it makes clear what is that standard whereby he measures himself and the world around him. In one such poet you will see, as the prevailing principle, a yearning for human sympathy; in another a thirst for keen and ecstatic enjoyments of a lower and more sensual kind; in a third, the burning ardour for intellectual attainments, for clearer knowledge as to our position in this life and our prospects in another; in a fourth, the longing for power and influence over the minds of others stands confessed; in a fifth, the benevolent love of his fellow-men; in a sixth, these several desires mixed in various proportions; and so on *ad infinitum*. And, in like manner, the devout Catholic, if *he* write such poetry, will expend himself in musings on the wonderful grace of God, which has followed after him for so many years of careless wandering, and has found him at last; or on the treasures of love stored in the Sacred Heart of his Saviour; or on the glories of the Queen of his affections; or on the bitter root of sin ever springing up within the soul; or on the happy prospect of future rest both from sin and suffering; or again, in lamentations on the miserable appearance presented by the sinful world, and hopes and prayers that souls may be gathered in to Christ.

All impartial persons, we are confident, will at once admit that Mr. Clough's poetry is of the real genuine kind described above, and in no way of the artificial or sophisticated sort. On the other hand, his general principle and view of things differs essentially from any one of those we have enumerated. It differs no less from those ordinarily called worldly than from the Catholic; it differs no less from the Catholic than from those ordinarily called worldly. We think, then, it may interest our readers if we endeavour to set before them this his general view of things, and as nearly as possible in his own words. We shall make no attempt to appreciate and describe his poetical excellences, though we are inclined to place them in a very high rank; but merely to draw out what may be called the *doctrine* of these poems. Such an effort may make not an uninteresting chapter in the history of the contemporary English religious mind in general, and in particular of one school which appears at present to have considerable influence, the school founded by the late Dr. Arnold; for Mr. Clough, as is well known, was one of Dr. Arnold's ablest and most cherished pupils. It may be added, that Mr. Clough has been for some years a Fellow of Oriel College; that during his residence at Oxford he has published one or two pamphlets of a practical tendency (one on the importance and the best method of diminishing undergraduate expenditure, another on the duty of subscribing largely for the relief of Irish distress), which are most highly spoken of; that he has ceased from residence (we believe) without taking orders; and is now the Principal of an Unitarian establishment in connexion with University College, London—a position, however, we imagine, which does not necessarily imply that he has himself adopted Unitarian opinions.

We cannot make an in every way fairer beginning of our extracts, than the first poem in the volume; of its great beauty we suppose there can be no second opinion.

[Quotes entire 'The human spirits saw I on a day'.]

This principle, viz. of doing our duty for duty's sake, may almost be called the key-note of the whole series, and has evidently complete possession of the author's mind. It is not necessary to say how far higher and nobler a principle this is than any merely worldly or merely interested standard of action; and yet, as held by Mr. Clough at least, it does not contain all that might be desired. Of course, one who has unhappily not been educated in any creed in which he can have *faith*, must begin by taking his conscience for his one authority; but ought he to expect that he shall end there? He knows that there are various voices in the world purporting to be immediate revelations from God; is he justified in *taking for granted* that none of them are really so? This is one element which we greatly desiderate in Mr. Clough:—a strong sense of the *à priori* probability that among these alleged revelations some one is true, and of the fearful irreverence towards God which is implied in passing over their claims without examination;—an anxious desire thence resulting to discover if possible that one truth;—and a pious purpose to submit his mind to it when found. He seems quite contented, as the passages we have put into italics[1] especially shew, to remain in darkness all his life.

Mr. Clough, however, is very far from implying by the term 'duty' merely that particular code of morality which one happens to have been taught; for he has written a spirited poem ['Duty, that's to say complying'] against so miserable a notion, and in favour of giving full heed to 'the questing and the guessing of the soul's own soul within.' That the conscience can by degrees clear itself more and more of error, and find for itself more and more of moral truth, he admits; that there may possibly be a divine fabric of both moral and supernatural truth, requiring the implicit submission of intellect and will, and that, if there be such, it probably admits of being recognised—this he does not so much *deny*, as ignore the very question.

[1] ll. 33, 44, 46, 51.

But, returning to this principle of the authority of conscience, is not this beautiful?

[Quotes from 'Why should I say I see the things I see not', ll. 29–end: 'Are there not, then, two musics' to 'mid multitudes alone'.]

[Quotes from 'Look you, my simple friend', ll. 21–34: 'And can it be' to 'though in anger'—italicizing the last four lines.]

Nor can we bring ourselves to omit the following (though it bears less directly on matters of controversy), as being about the most beautiful specimen of blank verse we have happened to see in any modern writer:

[Quotes entire 'Light words they were, and lightly, falsely said'.]

We wish we had room to quote part of a very interesting series called by the author somewhat unintelligibly 'Blank Misgivings of a Creature Moving About in a World Not Yet Realized', which present in fact the utterance, in various shapes, of the most touching repentance and self-abasement for past faults and unrealities: but it is difficult to make a selection. . . .

There are two poems in which the author expresses an earnest conviction, that minds which honestly act under a sense of duty are really holding the same course, even when they appear to differ most widely. There is a sense in which, and qualifications under which, this is true; but in our humble judgment, there is a more obvious and more ordinary sense in which it is most false. The first of these poems occurs at p. 9;[1] the second is of such great poetical merit, that we shall quote it.

[Quotes entire 'Qua Cursum Ventus'.]

The most singular poem of the whole, theologically speaking, is ['When Israel came out of Egypt']. In this he is speaking of the *atheistical* tendency of speculation at the present day, the tendency to represent that

> Earth goes by chemic forces; Heaven's
> A Mécanique Celeste,
> And heart and mind of human kind
> A watch-work like the rest;

and compares this state of speculation to the cloud of darkness on Mount Sinai, while Moses was within, communing with God. He bids

---

[1] 'Sic Itur'.

us to be quite confident that some Moses will come from behind the cloud in due time, if we will only be content to wait, and will 'bring some worthy thing for waiting souls to see; some sacred word that he hath heard.' In the mean time the great evil he fears is, lest humble souls, seeing the evil tendency of this free speculation, should fall back on some one of the old forms of religion; forms which he respectfully parallels to the *Golden Calf* worshipped by the Israelites during Moses' absence. As yet, up to the nineteenth century, we know nothing of real religion: existing creeds are but golden calves, and all true reasoning seems to lead towards atheism: only let us have patience, however, he says, and something better will at last come. It quite baffles comprehension how a thinker, in many respects so humble and so profound as Mr. Clough, can be blind to the strange, the absolutely incredible audacity, of such a mode of thinking. What does *he* know of all existing creeds, what pains has he taken to acquaint himself with their claims and their nature, what amount of confidence does he claim for his own judgment, that he thus quietly and self-complacently sneers at them as golden calves? What hope can there be of his arriving at religious truth, while such is his demeanour?

But the most painful criticism we have to make is yet to come. We have always had deep misgivings as to the ultimate result of the principles held by Dr. Arnold and the Protestant world generally in regard to marriage; of the blasphemies they utter against the beauty and the merit of virginity; of the allegations they make as to what they are pleased to call the unnaturalness of Catholic morality. These principles of theirs, even as they hold them, in regard to the sacredness of *nature*, are indeed hateful and anti-Christian enough; but we have always feared, that when heartily embraced and fairly carried out to consequences by ardent and consistent thinkers, they would assume a shape from which such men as Dr. Arnold would recoil in dismay. It is with deep regret that we cite these poems in corroboration of this misgiving. In the mere matter of language, and as judged only by the conventionalities of society, there are passages bordering most closely (to say the least) on the indelicate: but as to the matter itself, we will only say, that thoughts and feelings, to which, were a good Catholic so unhappy as to give consent, he would be off at once to his confessor in anguish of soul, are here recorded as mere phenomena, with no hint of regret or shame. We allude especially to the poem called 'Natura naturans;' but the following poem also is not free from blame on the same score.[1]

[1] 'Farewell, my Highland Lassie!'

And this fact is the more significant, from the company in which Mr. Clough's poems appear; for as to Mr. Burbidge's,—it will be enough to say, that the latter gentleman uses the phrase, 'the *sacred* fire of youth', openly and undisguisedly, to express the feeling of sensual passion in a married man.

And now our readers have some general idea of the ethical tone of Mr. Clough's poems. To examine into this ethical tone, to endeavour, *e.g.* to decide how far on the whole it is hopeful or the reverse in regard to his chance of ultimately reaching to the truth; or how much is praiseworthy and how much reprehensible;—this would lead us to far too great a length, even if the task were in the compass of our ability. On their *poetical* merit, again, it is needless to speak; for the quotations we have given will enable our readers to judge for themselves. So much only we may say, that, to judge from our own experience, these poems possess one characteristic of high excellence, viz. that they grow greatly on the mind by repeated perusal, and that a first reading does them no sort of justice.

21. From an unsigned review, 'Recent Poetry', *Prospective Review*

1850, vi, 134–6

The extract given below consists of that part of the review devoted to Clough, the general remarks on the differing qualities of Burbidge together with one sample of the reviewer's taste for the latter poet.

The same serious spirit, the same sense of mystery, the same vivid consciousness of the Unseen in which we live and move—which characterises the poetry of Mr. Kingsley and Mr. Trench—appear in the little volume called *Ambarvalia*. Mr. Clough's poems are generally more remarkable for spiritual than for poetical thought: his language is often stiff, and his ideas obscure and involved, which makes it difficult to arrive at his meaning. He is too fond of alliteration, e.g. these phrases occur—'mortal moral strife,' 'sure assured,' 'seem to see,' 'dare not dare,' 'wills thy will,' 'priceless prize,' 'dreamier dreams,' 'bloomiest bloom,' 'primal prime,'—and are certainly awkward and unpoetical. The first poem we like much: it expresses well that mystery in which the mind gets entangled, in endeavouring to solve the difficulties which press upon the thoughtful.[1] 'Qui laborat orat' contains a true and noble thought, and reveals (as do all this writer's lines) a lowly yet manly and aspiring soul. He has more concentration of thought and expression than Mr. Trench, more metaphysical subtlety, but less of the poetical temperament. There are some fine verses under the title 'When Israel came out of Egypt'. The most poetical piece of all we think is the 'Silver Wedding' celebrated in Germany when a couple have been married five-and-twenty years;—there is true poetical and deep human feeling in it, doing justice to our highest nature: it is too long to quote here. 'Qua cursum ventus,' lines suggested by a common experience of life, is forcible and earnest as well as beautiful; it is the only specimen we have space for in this short notice of Mr. Clough's miscellaneous effusions, where, it must be candidly allowed, that a want of taste is sometimes discernible:—

[Quotes 'Qua Cursum Ventus'.]

We should say that Mr. Burbidge (to repeat an expression already frequently used for want of a better) had a more decidedly poetical temperament than Mr. Clough: his lines throughout flow more easily, and there is more fancy and imagination, and less metaphysical thought in his poems. We like his opening lines upon Florence, and others further on in the volume, suggested also in that city, when walking in the Boboli gardens. The following lines entitled 'Portraiture' we think must be admired:—

> With pain her gloomy eyes did she uplift,
> That woman old; with many a tempest torn,
> Of sins and sorrows spent ere we were born,
> Her sallow brow appeared, o'er which a drift
> Of massive snow-white hair lay dead and still,
> Or flew across, by fits, without her will.
>
> There stood before her the enquiring child:
> On the frail lids of his uncentred eyes

[1] 'The human spirits saw I on a day'.

Lay no weight heavier than a light surprise;
His tresses soft, like silver undefiled,
Hung on his sunbright face, or in a (floating) wreath
Clouding his lips, moved mildly with his breath.

A rock long-bearded with cold weeds marine,
In whose wet womb the ocean-creatures sleep,
Should it uplift its scalp above the deep,
Were likest to that hellish Woman seen;
But he a Lily stood, caressed by eve,
And which the morning mists are loth to leave.

22. An unsigned review, 'Clough's Poems', the *Saturday Review*

30 November 1861, pp. 564–5

The author of these poems [*The Bothie* and *Ambarvalia*] has lately died, leaving a very high reputation in a very narrow circle. His was the old case of a boy who outshines and surpasses other boys—of a young man whose life seems full of promise—and then of a grown man in whom the promise seems to fade away, and who, if he does anything to reveal his powers to the outer world, does far less than his friends hoped for. Sometimes a disappointment of this sort is due to there being nothing really in the character or mind of the man that has any permanent value; and then no career can be much less interesting. But sometimes, as in the case of Mr. Clough, the failure is due to the particular type of the mind—to an excess of feeling and scrupulousness and intellectual activity, and a deficiency in clearness of thought, in the gift of expression, and in physical spirits. In 1849, Mr. Clough published a small volume of poems, which were, in some measure, a record of the struggles and trials through which he had passed. His friends found a few striking passages in them, an enormous preponderance of obscure and confused meditations, and a very unequal power of versification. The world at last never read them at all; but within the circle to which Mr. Clough was known in England and America, these poems made no difference in the general impression he produced on those who came in intimate contact with his high thoughts, his proud and shy bearing, and his intense love of truth. Now that he is gone, the general public is not likely to care much for his poems, even if the only poetical work he produced of real interest— his *Long Vacation Pastoral*—which has long been out of print, were again issued. But when a man has a high position in a small knot of friends, it is always interesting to know why he has it. It is not by accident that men win the confidence and admiration of their friends; and as Mr. Clough's friends included many persons of eminence both here and on the other side of the Atlantic, it cannot be quite in vain to ask what are the qualities of heart and head that give a man high standing in such a circle, even when it is acknowledged that he has done nothing appreciable by strangers to justify the estimation in which he is held. It so happens, also, that Mr. Clough's career is bound up in a very marked way with the recent history of Oxford. What he felt and did and thought is very illustrative of all that was going on in his University during his early manhood; and as the future historian of English thought cannot possibly omit to notice the general features of an intellectual movement so conspicuous in its time as that which has been going on at Oxford during the last thirty years, every biography and every notice of men who have been participators in, or have been conspicuously affected by this movement, has a sort of adventitious value.

It is impossible to give in a few words the general character of such a movement, lasting, in different phases, through many years, and passing through the channels of many men in several important respects wholly dissimilar to each other. It is too intimately mixed up with the present to wear to us the clear, sharp outlines by which often, beyond the clearness and sharpness of truth itself, we define the past. Theology has also played a great part in Oxford during the last quarter of a century, and we do not intend to discuss theology. But there are one or two features of this movement to which it is quite safe to advert, and about which there can be no doubt. Anyone who is acquainted with the recent history of the University must have observed that the temper of men's minds there has been such as to give great weight to personal character and personal influence. There has been something in the opinions and feelings of men generally that has led them to throw themselves unreservedly, and with an almost unreasoning warmth of tenderness and fulness, on the support and comfort which a few eminent thinkers or actors have known how to afford. Of course, these leaders and their contemporaries have been very different in gifts and acquirements, and have come intellectually to very different conclusions. But still, there are some points in which they exhibit a very striking resemblance. They have all been men capable of feeling keenly intellectual doubts. They have been prone to weigh everything, to see difficulties, to reject explanations, to like subtleties that had any sort of affinity to their mental constitution. On the other hand, the general tendency of their influence has been to inspire, not doubt, but convictions—to force upon the minds of all those whom they have largely affected a strong sense of the existence of something which is beyond the reach of doubt, which alone gives value to investigation, as without it human inquiry would degenerate into the whirling of a wheel forever spinning round, but never grinding corn. They always clung, as their last and surest hope, to the notion of duty. To keep on doing right—not to speculate only, but to act, not to think only, but to live—was not so much a part of their teaching as a doctrine woven into their being. Lastly, they all exhibited what is so attractive, and is the only source of attraction that cannot be outgrown—that tenderness and sweetness which has its roots in a constant sense of the mysterious, the sacred, and the sublime. Had the Oxford movement been one of mere theological inquiry, or of the reconstruction of English philosophy, or of the remodelling of the higher course of English education, it need not have given room for men of such a stamp as this to exercise more influence than able and good men must always exercise in every generation. But when a movement is at once intellectual and moral, when the centres of men's being are disturbed, when glimpses into new worlds of feeling and thought are constantly being opened, and closed, and reopened, then men who think, and dare to say what they think—who cleave to the truth so far as they can grasp it, but who offer the type of the duty which balances and steadies, and of the tenderness and sense of heavenly things which beautifies existence—wield a power which is altogether extraordinary. They overwhelm, they captivate, they satisfy those who are confused, dissatisfied, and hesitating. At any rate, there can be no doubt that uprightness and love are good, even if we cannot unravel ourselves the problems of our life, or see that those whom we follow have a clue that will guide them through the whole labyrinth.

A very few names would comprise all those who have had this personal influence in its highest completeness. But there are always persons at such a time who shade off the interval between those endowed with the gifts and qualities that place them in the first rank and those who merely follow. There are men whose thinking is original, whose inquiry is honest, who are firm in duty, and full of tenderness, but who have not that gift of poetical outpouring, not that readiness of sympathy, that aptness for expression, which mark the leading men of such an epoch. These less prominent, but scarcely less noble and beautiful characters are, however, often viewed with exceptional regard by the few whom the accidents of daily life throw across their path, and these few spread the fame of their friend. This was the position that Mr. Clough occupied at Oxford. He had all the mental and moral qualities which gain respect in such a period as that we have been describing, but he possessed them in such a way as to make him very little known. Any one who turns to the volume of poems which Mr. Clough published in 1849 will see dimly reflected through those puzzling compositions the keen sense of difficulties, the nice regard for the minutiae of truth, the manly love of duty, and the delight in all objects of human love, and in the beauties of nature, which have gone to make up the Oxford ideal of recent years. We are even overpowered with his questioning of himself, with his diffidence as to his own feelings and opinions having any truth in them, with the puzzles which society and active life present to his nervous and agitated mind. On the other hand, these poems are sometimes pervaded with a very different atmosphere. They are full of the calm and purity of a love of duty which is offered as the only escape from the vexations and embarrassments of human existence. They contain also many passages in which the impressions of a young man happy in slight lovemaking and unhappy in serious lovemaking are revealed. They are rich in the overpourings of a heart brimful of affection to old friends and cherished companions. They are interspersed with very pretty and neatly turned descriptions of the scenery that has most struck the author's fancy. So much even strangers must see in these poems, and they may derive a certain pleasure from what they read in spite of the crabbed language in which the thoughts are often expressed, and of the obscurity of the thoughts themselves. But to old friends and those who had seen in the man all that is very imperfectly set out in his printed words, these musings and confessions had an interest which was only to be measured by the feelings with which they regarded the author.

Whether poetical genius of any order could throw into the shape of intelligible and attractive versification the thoughts that Mr. Clough tried to express may be doubtful. Those, perhaps, who admire Shakespeare's sonnets will think it could be done; but most certainly Mr. Clough's poetical genius was not equal to the task. Sometimes, however, creative power and facility of expression, which otherwise seem wanting in a writer, are all at once revealed by the chance of a very happy subject. It was so with Mr. Clough. There was one subject which might easily be made full of poetry, and which Mr. Clough, of all men, from personal experience and the tone of his mind, was fitted to handle. In a lucky hour he set himself to write a poetical story describing the life and adventures of an Oxford reading party in a Long Vacation. Perhaps the English public would not much care for this poem, although the first edition was soon sold out, and the poem is much admired in America. It is full of the harmless slang in vogue at Oxford; it abounds in allusions to the books and authors appointed for study at Oxford; and it is written in a very peculiar metre—in a kind of prosaic, halting, indistinct hexameter, in which no one but a classical scholar could see any metre at all, and which would at every third line oblige a classical scholar to read again and again the words before him, in order to discover how they were meant to run. These attributes do not tend to make a poem popular in England, and it is a very good thing that they do not. But still, this Pastoral, to those who can make up their minds to enjoy it, is a most delightful poem. It is in exact keeping with its subject. It is full of fun, of jokes bad and good, of discussions, of adventure, of lovemaking, of deep feeling. It embodies all that is ordinary and extraordinary in the lives of a happy group of young men, in beautiful scenery, with perfect liberty allowed them, and yet with fixed tasks which they set themselves to do. It is Oxford undergraduate life seen at its best, not on stilts, nor pedantic, nor averse to solemn thought, but still full of boyish jollity and an eager delight in bodily exercise. As very few of our readers will have seen it, we may explain that this Pastoral narrates the adventures of a party of five or six undergraduates who go to read in Scotland with a tutor, 'a grave man nick-named Adam.' A Highland gathering and a ball dispose the less studious to go off on a three weeks' wandering, during which Philip, the hero, falls in love successively with a peasant girl, or 'lovely potato-uprooter,' as she is called, with a Lady Maria, and with the heroine Elspie, who is perfection, and lives in a bothie. There is thus introduced a sufficient variety of female charms; and as even the tutor gracefully talks upon the characters of women, and as the whole drift of the book is to show the qualities most desirable in women, there is no want of romance and lovemaking to carry the tender-hearted reader on. No Oxford men will forget the impression it made on them when they first read it. It offered them at once a glorification of their youthful happiness, and a serious though often playful examination of the deeper feelings of young men. Perhaps those who have never seen the book may like to have a specimen of it. We cannot select the best passages, for they are too intimately connected with the thread of the story to be intelligible when standing by themselves. But every here and there there is a passage which can be detached, and, perhaps, the following is as good as any. It contains a description of the basin in a mountain stream in which the happy party took every day their morning bathe. Even those who have never bathed in a mountain stream, and have never attempted to scan spondaic hexameters, will recognise a power of graphic description and a hearty love of nature in the following lines:—

[Quotes *The Bothie*, III. 34–62: 'But in the interval!' to 'they shrieked and shouted'.]

23. Arnold's last tribute

1861

Last Words on Translating Homer (1861), reprinted in *The Complete Prose Works of Matthew Arnold*, R. H. Super (ed.), Vol. I, 156.

The passage given below forms the closing paragraphs of 'Last Words on Translating Homer', a lecture which Arnold delivered at Oxford on 30 November 1861, shortly after receiving news of Clough's death.

The successful translator of Homer will have (or he cannot succeed) that true sense for his subject, and that disinterested love of it, which are, both of them, so rare in literature, and so precious; he will not be led off by any false scents; he will have an eye for the real matter, and, where he thinks he may find any indication of this, no hint will be too slight for him, no shade will be too fine, no imperfections will turn him aside,—he will go before his adviser's thought, and help it out with his own. This is the sort of student that a critic of Homer should always have in his thoughts; but students of this sort are indeed rare.

And how, then, can I help being reminded what a student of this sort we have just lost in Mr. Clough, whose name I have already mentioned in these lectures? He, too, was busy with Homer; but it is not on that account that I now speak of him. Nor do I speak of him in order to call attention to his qualities and powers in general, admirable as these were. I mention him because, in so eminent a degree, he possessed these two invaluable literary qualities,—a true sense for his object of study, and a single-hearted care for it. He had both; but he had the second even more eminently than the first. He greatly developed the first through means of the second. In the study of art, poetry, or philosophy, he had the most undivided and disinterested love for his object in itself, the greatest aversion to mixing up with it anything accidental or personal. His interest was in literature itself; and it was this which gave so rare a stamp to his character, which kept him so free from all taint of littleness. In the saturnalia of ignoble personal passions, of which the struggle for literary success, in old and crowded communities, offers so sad a spectacle, he never mingled. He had not yet traduced his friends, nor flattered his enemies, nor disparaged what he admired, nor praised what he despised. Those who knew him well had the conviction that, even with time, these literary arts would never be his. His poem, of which I spoke before, has some admirable Homeric qualities;—out-of-doors freshness, life, naturalness, buoyant rapidity. Some of the expressions in that poem,—'Dangerous Corrievreckan . . . Where roads are unknown to Loch Nevish,' [*The Bothie*, IX. 79, and IV. 12]—come back now to my ear with the true Homeric ring. But that in him of which I think oftenest is the Homeric simplicity of his literary life.

POEMS BY ARTHUR HUGH CLOUGH
(1862)

(*including* Amours de Voyage, *first published,* Atlantic Monthly, 1858)

---

24. Francis Turner Palgrave's 'Memoir' to *The Poems by Arthur Hugh Clough*

(1862; 1863)

Palgrave (1824–97) was a poet and critic, a close friend of Tennyson and editor of the *Golden Treasury*; he was Professor of Poetry at Oxford, 1885–95. The 'Memoir' is the final revised version of an article printed in *Fraser's Magazine*, LXV, April 1862, 527–36.

Arthur Hugh Clough, born at Liverpool, 1st January 1819, was educated at Rugby. His career there has been sketched by a distinguished schoolfellow, from whose interesting notice the following lines are extracted. Arthur Stanley thus writes:

Of all the scholars at Rugby School, in the time when Arnold's influence was at its height, there was none who so completely represented the place in all its phases as Clough. He had come there as a very young boy, and gradually worked his way from form to form till he reached the top of the school. He did not, like some of the more distinguished of his contemporaries, hold aloof from the common world of schoolboy life, but mingled freely in the games and sports of his schoolfellows. He received also into an unusually susceptible and eager mind the whole force of that electric shock which Arnold communicated to all his better pupils. Over the career of none of his pupils did Arnold watch with a livelier interest or a more sanguine hope. By none, during those last years of school life, or first years of college life, was that interest more actively reciprocated in the tribute of enthusiastic affection than by Clough.

He came up to Oxford, and carried away the Balliol scholarship with a renown beyond that of any of his predecessors. I remember, even to this day, the reverberation of the profound sensation occasioned in the Commonroom of that College, already famous, when his youthful English essay was read aloud to the assembled Fellows. From Balliol he was elected (1842) to a Fellow-ship at Oriel—a distinction still at that time retaining something of its original splendour, and rectifying the sometimes ill-adjusted balance (as had happened in Clough's case) of the honours of the University.[1]

Clough's residence at Oxford was cast at a time when one of the theological tempests, which during the last hundred years have so often arisen there, was raging at its fiercest. It was a controversy from which few could hold aloof—least of all, a mind lively, susceptible, and speculative. And for a while the movement of that day attracted him, by holding out the ideal of a more devoted and unselfish life, and a higher sense of duty, than the common. But he learned early to distrust a theory not resting on honest acceptance of our human nature, and was soon named as one of the foremost who battled for just freedom of opinion and speech, for liberation from what he esteemed archaeological formulas, for more conscientious fulfilment of obligation towards the students—for a wider course of studies, lastly, than those who had grown up under the older system were willing to contemplate. Hence all who longed for that more compre-hensive university, of which they have since seen the beginning, looked on Clough as amongst their leaders; and his influence was always towards whatever should incline others to a liberal view of the ques-tions of the day, of the claims of the feeble, and the feelings of the poor;—verging gradually to what, in a phrase which now seems itself an echo from the past, were considered 'democratic tendencies'. Plainer living and higher thinking were the texts on which he gave us many a humorous and admirable lesson. In all his dealings, the most casual observer would have felt, here was a man who loved truth and justice, not coldly and afar off, as most, but with passion and intensely; and against what he judged wrong and meanness in high places, he fought with an unselfish courage and a spirit which did good to all honest hearts.

One instance is too characteristic of the man to be passed over. He always held in horror the selfish deductions which (he thought) were often made from some doctrines of Political Economy:—and when the Irish famine took place, he advocated the relief fund which was set up in Oxford in a very plain-spoken and vigorous pamphlet, urging

1 Obituary notice, the *Daily News*, 9 January 1862.

the immediate suppression of certain academical luxurious habits, and, above all, requiring from us sympathy with the distressed as an imperious duty.

It would, however, be no true picture of Clough in his youth, that presented him mainly as a 'practical man'; indeed a certain unaptness or want of shrewd rapidity (as shown in his honours' examination), a sensitive fairness and chivalrous openness of dealing, marked him rather as the poet who walked the world's way as matter of duty, living a life, meanwhile, hidden with higher and holier things, with the friends and books he loved so fondly, with deep solitary thought, with Nature in her wildness and her majesty. Cast on days of change and development, his strong moral impulses threw him into the sphere of warfare; yet he was no 'born reformer'; was diffident of his own conclusions; had no clean-cut decisive system, nay, thought experience proved the narrowness of such; and was beyond those fetters of 'logical consistency' which played so great a part in the controversies of the time. Many fragments of his verse show that whilst roused to a spirit of resolute self-reliance by what went on around him, he felt how much the war of conscience and conviction must be carried on within, until some clearer light should break upon the enquirer.

> O let me love my love unto myself alone,
> And know my knowledge to the world unknown;
> No witness to the vision call,
> Beholding unbeheld of all;
> And worship thee, with thee withdrawn apart,
> Whoe'er, whate'er thou art,
> Within the closest veil of mine own inmost heart.
>
> [*Dipsychus*, IV, 82–8, *Poems* (1951)]

Or, again, we find the voice of sound worldly wisdom expressing itself in the Siren strains which are not confined to the invitations of pleasure:

> Better it were, thou sayest, to consent;
> Feast while we may, and live ere life be spent;
> Close up clear eyes, and call the unstable sure,
> The unlovely lovely, and the filthy pure.
>
> [*Dipsychus*, IV, 89–92, *Poems* (1951)

Here, too, 'there is much to be said on both sides'; but one can foretell the poet's answer.

To these years belongs, also, the series of poems published in 1849 (and now reprinted with omissions marked by the author), under the title *Ambarvalia*. This contains several pieces of which it has been justly said, 'that they will hold their place beside those of Tennyson and Browning':[1]—to friends looking at the little volume, however, as an exhibition of Clough's own mind, we trace him characteristically in a certain caprice or over-fantasy of taste, in a subtle and far-fetched mode of reasoning which returns to plain conclusions through almost para-doxical premises, in a singular toleration and largeness towards views opposed to his own; it may be added, in an honesty of mind which confesses itself not only perplexed with the 'riddle of the universe', but indignant at the complacent explanations which those who proclaim it insoluble are too apt, he thought, to enforce upon the diffident.

But whilst this conflict went on within, towards friends what might be called the imaginative side of his nature was dominant. The sun-shine and animated smiles which, many will remember, he brought with him into college society, came, not from ordinary and slighter causes, but from a heart to which affection was at once a delight and a necessity, and a mind 'haunted like a passion' by the loveliness of poetry or of scenery. During several summer vacations he had searched out the glens and heights, lakes and moors, of Wales, and Westmore-land, and Scotland, with that minute and reverent care, in absence of which travelling is idle, and with that love for the very soil and configuration of his country which almost always implies high-heartedness. And it was noticed that when speaking of spots of any special beauty or impressiveness—Grasmere, or Pont-y-Wern by Snowdon, or the lochs and valleys of the Western Highlands—his eyes brightened as at the thought of something personally dear, and his voice softened at names and remembrances which carried with them so much of poetry. And to this youthful enthusiasm for Nature he united that other enthusiasm for energetic walks and venturesome wanderings, bathing, swimming, and out-of-doors existence in gen-eral, which may, perhaps, be claimed as an impulse peculiarly English.

All this, with much else, Clough summed up in his first published poem, brought out in the autumn of 1848, as if his farewell to his university. The *Bothie of Tober-Na-Vuolich* (as, for euphony's sake, he finally wished the Gaelic name to stand) is a true Long Vacation pastoral, in style and thought intensely Oxonian; yet with this, which so much amused us at the time, are other and deeper features not less characteristic of the writer. Such are the profound and vital interest in the ancient master-works of prose and poetry, which an Oxford

[1] From 'Arthur Hugh Clough . . . In Memoriam', *Spectator* xxxiv, 23 November 1861, p. 1285.

man at least cannot recognize elsewhere in such reality; the profound sympathy with those who live by the labours we too slightingly call mechanical, and with minds which owe more to Nature than to society or study; the delight in friendship and in solitude; the love of wild wandering, and the intense—not appreciation of, say rather 'acceptance in', the natural landscape, in which Arthur Clough, more than any man known to the writer, seemed to have inherited a double portion of the spirit of William Wordsworth. A sense of fresh, healthy manliness; a scorn of base and selfish motives; a frank admiration for common life; a love of earth, not 'only for its earthly sake', but for the divine and the eternal interfused in it—such, and other such, are the impressions left. These noble qualities are rare in any literature; they have a charm so great that, like Beauty before the Areopagus, they almost disarm the judgment. Viewed critically, Clough's work is wanting in art; the language and the thought are often unequal and incomplete; the poetical fusion into a harmonious whole, imperfect. Here, and in his other writings, one feels a doubt whether in verse he chose the right vehicle, the truly natural mode of utterance. It is poetry, however, which truly belongs to a very uncommon class. Even where the last touches have been given, the matter almost everywhere much outruns the workmanship: it should be judged by the thoughts awakened, rather than by the mode of expressing them.

Such writing, it might be imagined, from its merits equally with its faults, addresses itself to no numerous audience; yet the *Bothie* was quickly known and valued; and as a true man, from whom much might be hoped, the author was henceforth spoken of, not only in the sphere of friendship and of Oxford, but in many places where the life around them, from different circumstances, rendered men sensitive to his tone of thought:—in Northern England especially, in America, and in those wide regions over seas to which Englishmen have carried endurance of toil, and energy of intellect.

This poem has been already alluded to as the author's farewell to Oxford. Having held a tutorship in his college now for several years, and joined in all efforts onward, a sense that he had done his work in Oxford, that he was a little too alien in speculative and in practical thought from the tone of the University, to be of further use, or to find a fit abode there; that he might honourably seek a more unshackled career without, led Clough to withdraw, in 1848, from Oriel. There was much in the spirit of that day with which he could not reconcile himself:

To finger idly some old Gordian knot,
Unskill'd to sunder, and too weak to cleave,
And with much toil attain to half-believe,

['Come back, come back . . .']

as he once expressed it, could not be his portion. Chivalrously generous
in allowing liberty of opinion in others, he might now seek at least a
fuller freedom for himself. Other half-external causes, it has been
stated, co-operated in this; but more influential with so conscientious
and brave a man, was the conviction of antagonism to the form of
thought which Oxford exacted, or appeared to exact from her children.
That world was not his friend, he fancied, nor that world's law. Yet
this divergence was not such as ever estranged him in heart from that
noble corporation which, more than any other of modern times, is
apt to retain a life-long hold on the affections and the honour of its
members; nor was it, again, such as, after his withdrawal, could be laid
at rest within the bounds of some different system. This was no logical
tangle, no scepticism in the common sense, no sudden imagined discovery, caprice of vanity, fanciful reverie, far less pride of heart or of
intellect. Rather, if frank submission to the inexplicable mysteries of
creation, if a reverence which feared expression, a faith in the eternal
truth and justice, be the attributes of a religious mind, Clough possessed
it with a reality uncommon in the followers of any religion. But the
consciousness of the strange things of life, verbally recognized by most
of us, and then explained by some phrase, or put by as unpractical,
was to him the 'heavy and weary weight' which men like Wordsworth or Pascal felt it. The *'voyant trop pour nier, et trop peu pour
s'assurer'*[1] of the greatest of French thinkers, as truly expressed Clough's
conviction; and, convinced thus, it was with mingled perplexity and
wrath that he listened to the popular solutions which he heard so
confidently, often so threateningly vaunted—to the profane pretence
of knowledge (as he thought it)—disguised under the name of Provi-
dential schemes, or displayed in dogmatic formulas. Far other was the
pure and lowly confession of man's incapacity to search out God,
with which at this time he spoke in a few of his most characteristic
and deeply-felt poems, which will be found in this collection. What
pathetic tenderness, what manly courage, is concentrated in the lines
referred to—how deep, practical, and modest a faith—how devout a
submission! Those who knew Clough know how truly he has here

[1] 'Seeing too much to deny and too little to trust': source in Pascal untraced.

rendered, not only the conviction, but the practice of a life of high and unwearied industry—a life in which the thought of self, except as regarded the fulfilment of duty, had no share; not will they feel the phrase too serious, if it be added, that he who 'lived in the spirit of this creed' was surely already not far from the kingdom of Heaven.

The pages he then wrote contain the record of Clough's essential life during this second, or transitional, portion of that brief career, and have hence been dwelt on with greater minuteness. He meanwhile was spending the spring and summer of 1849 in Italy: drawn thither in part by the charm of that country to so sympathetic a student of the ancient literature; in part by the attraction which any effort to gain national liberty exercises over all noble natures. Such efforts, or what seemed such, notably at this period engaged much of Clough's best thoughts and warmest sympathies. Thus in 1848 he wrote thus, in his half-humorous, half-pathetic strain, from Paris:

I do little else in the way of lionizing than wander about the Tuileries' chestnuts, and about bridges and streets, *'Pour savourer la république'*. I contemplate with infinite thankfulness the blue blouse garnished with red of the Garde Mobile, and emit a perpetual incense of devout rejoicing for the purified state of the Tuileries'. But a few days later comes the reverse of the picture—'Ichabod, Ichabod, the glory has departed.' Liberty, Equality, Fraternity, driven back by shopkeeping bayonet, hides her red cap in dingiest St. Antoine. Wellto-do-ism shakes her Egyptian scourge, to the tune of 'ye are idle, ye are idle'; —the tale of bricks will be doubled, and the Moses and Aaron of Socialism can at the best only pray for plagues: which perhaps will come, paving-stones for *vivats*, and *émeutes* in all their quarters.

Meantime the glory and the freshness of the dream is departed. The very Garde Mobile has changed its blouse for a bourgeoisie-prætorian uniform with distinctive green hired-soldier epaulets.

The voice of Clubs is silent. Inquisitors only and stone walls of Vincennes list the words of Barbes. *Antirappel* Courtais no longer hushes the drum, which, as he said, *'fâche le peuple'*. Wherefore, bring forth, ye millionaires, the three-months-hidden carriages; rub clean, ye new nobles, the dusty emblazonries; ride forth again, ye cavalier-escorted amazons, to your Bois de Boulogne. The world begins once more to move on its axis, and draw on its kid gloves. The golden age of the Republic displays itself now, you see, as a very vulgar parcel-gilt era.

It is needless to add that a similar discouragement awaited Clough in Rome. Unable or unwilling to believe what at least bore the name Republic could really lead the crusade on behalf of despotism, he lingered on till the investment of Rome by a French army rendered departure impossible. Many details of that memorable siege he recorded in letters sufficiently refuting the calumnies which England at that time was not ashamed to borrow from the natural enemies of freedom. He witnessed self-restraint under privation and provocation, the firm, proud submission to overwhelming force, and a conquest where all of honour was with the defeated,—the high national qualities, in a word, with which Italy has made Europe familiar. 'Whether the Roman Republic will stand, I don't know', he wrote during the struggle, 'but it has, under Mazzini's inspiration, shown a wonderful energy and a glorious generosity'. Readers will find many of Clough's impressions and feelings of that period recorded in the *Amours de Voyage* and other shorter pieces. Then from the temporary triumph of shame and super-stition, he turned to the Power which 'never did betray the heart that loved her', and through the Italian Lakes and Switzerland wandered homewards to resume more active duties.

From a poem now written at Venice, may be taken a traveller's wish that he might

> In one unbroken passage borne
> To closing night from opening morn,
> Uplift at whiles slow eyes to mark
> Some palace front, some passing bark;
> Thro' windows catch the varying shore,
> And hear the soft turns of the oar.
> How light we move, how softly! ah,
> Were life but as the Gondola!
>
> [Cf. *Poems* (1951), *Dipsychus*, IV, 27–34.]

Though not altogether accomplished, something of this easy tenor of the happy life was in store for the writer during the twelve years of useful and energetic labour, which the 'blind Fury' Fate of the poet had measured out for him. At first indeed he found in the Wardenship of University Hall, London, an employment not altogether congenial to his disposition: yet even here, in the comparative solitude of the new abode, the discovery that withdrawal from Oxford had no ways shaken the affection of those he trusted, cheered the hours which, to a disposition so tenderly sensitive as Clough's, were apt to catch a gloom from the sight of unfamiliar walls and faces. This was, perhaps, the most lonely part of his life: and in the streets of London many strange passages of what he called the *philosophia metropolitana* presented themselves, and have found their way into verses of a peculiar pathos and sarcasm.

But such depressing humours came and went, whilst in the increased respect of those he most valued, whether alien from his tone of thought or not, he received now part of the reward with which truth recompenses self-sacrifice. Soon, too, when resident for a few months in America, whither in 1852 he went to try his fortunes, he found amongst the most distinguished men of Boston and its neighbourhood a renewal of the deep interest which he had aroused in his earlier companions. 'He had nothing of insular narrowness', one of them writes, 'none of the prejudices which too often interfere with the capacity of English travellers or residents among us, to sympathise with and justly understand habits of life and thought so different from those to which they have been accustomed'. The friendships then formed were the main result—a sufficient result, Clough held it—of the trial: England drew him towards her before he could find a footing in the west, with the one irresistible word—homewards. Yet the resolution to return was not taken without some reluctance to quit the new world.

I like America all the better [he wrote in 1853] for the comparison with England on my return. Certainly I think you were more right than I was willing to admit, about the position of the poorer classes here. Such is my first reimpression. However it will wear off soon enough, I daresay.

There are deeper waters of ancient knowledge and experience about one here, and one is saved from the temptation of flying off into space; but I think you have, beyond all question, the happiest country going.

An appointment, however, in the education department of the Privy Council-office decided him to return to England.

> —The universal instinct of repose,
> The longing for confirm'd tranquillity,
> Inward and outward; humble, yet sublime;
> The life where hope and memory are as one:[1]

—What life was ever wholly true to this great ideal? Yet in its most essential features, at peace with himself and with circumstances, happy in his home and the blessing of his children, Clough may be held to have fulfilled it.

A career such as this had been naturally watched by his friends with a certain anxiety, heightened by the sight of a character at once so sensitive and so self-sacrificing, and by the warmth of affection which it excited. Henceforward, however, until failing health raised them,

---

[1] Wordsworth, *The Excursion*, III, 397-400.

there was no cause for anxious thoughts. It was evident, indeed, that rest or leisure were not in his prospect; that not less than in his earlier days, Clough would be still, in its most emphatic and highest sense, a working man. His official employment was varied, but hardly diminished, by the Secretaryship to the Commission of Report on Military Education, which in 1856, carried him again to France, and finally to Vienna. Meantime he gradually completed the long revision of Dryden's *Translation of Plutarch*, begun in America; comparing that inaccurate though spirited text throughout with the original, and retouching it with a skill and taste in which his careful study of Chaucer and our early literature gave him a special mastery. These tasks were more than enough, as it proved, for a constitution never robust; and when, with his usual energetic sympathy for all that touched the welfare of the poor or the wretched, he further undertook much anxious work to assist his wife's cousin, Florence Nightingale, in her own arduous labours, Clough's health gave way, and travelling was prescribed.

His first journey, to Greece and Constantinople, was of great interest to so good a scholar; and he summed up the chief features on his return in a few lines placed in one of the *Tales* [i.e. *Mari Magno*], of which the most complete are printed within this volume.

[Quotes *Mari Magno*, 'The Lawyer's First Tale', IV, 57–8 ('Aware it might be first and last' to 'I did it eagerly and fast') followed by 38–55 ('Counted the towns' to 'the blind to sight'). This tale was not printed by Palgrave.]

Finding his health not thoroughly restored, after a short visit to England he returned southwards for the winter. By one of the Italian lakes he was struck by malaria fever, and with difficulty completed the journey to Florence, where it carried him off on 13th November 1861. He lies in the little cypress-crowded cemetery beyond the walls of the Fair City, on the side towards Fiesole.

This truly was a life of much performance, yet of more promise Clough did the work of a man within his two and forty years; yet we must feel now the bitterness and irony of that fate which seemed to secure him outward prosperity, but never left him a brief interval in which, as one who best knew him said, 'to be himself', and to realize for his own advantage, if not for ours, powers rarely given in such curiously subtle combination. Perhaps his speculative activity was beyond his powers of co-ordination, the discursive element of thought too dominant, the fear of partial conclusions over-scrupulous. But from what he might have been it is best to turn to what he was. It appears to the writer an idle demand, though now a demand often made, that a man should publish to the world the results of his thought or study:—to live a lofty life, within the limits of this existence,—to carry out for himself a perfect scheme, so far as human weakness may allow, is a far higher thing, as unhappily a far rarer: and in this aspect, those who knew him will confess it is no phrase of partial affection to say that Clough ranked with the best of his contemporaries. The reader will find many charming stanzas, some excellent, amongst those belonging to the later period of his life. Yet in the larger sense, it might be truly said, that he rather lived than wrote his poem. It must not be imagined that, with the more prosperous circumstances above noticed, he became false to his convictions, or, as some do, put away from himself as unpractical the thought of those deeper problems which had perplexed his earlier years, not less by the sense of their darkness than of their close and unavoidable pressure on our daily life; that he now recoiled from them in fear, or forgot them in felicity. No one could be more conscience-pure from that self-deceiving concession to ease and cowardice by which honest doubt and insoluble difficulty are so often stifled. But with a modest reserve, the frequent companion of frank simplicity,—with a sense, it may be, of the increased perplexities which darken wider horizons,—he kept mainly to himself the results of his riper speculative experience; satisfied to express them henceforth only by a larger charity towards opponents, and an even more fervent earnestness on his own part to make truth and justice and generosity his sole guides for action. As said above, Clough lived his poem. Few, it has been observed, have looked on Nature more entirely in the spirit which his favourite Wordsworth expressed in the immortal lines on Tintern: fewer, perhaps, in this age have more completely worked out his ideal, 'plain living and high thinking'. Let it not be said that Clough's gifts were inadequately realized, when he has eft us this example.

It is a second, nay, to Fancy a more final farewell, thus to review the memories of lost affection. We would willingly, in his friend's pathetic phrase,

> Treasuring the look we cannot find,
> The words that are not heard again—[1]

[1] Tennyson, *In Memoriam A.H.H.*, XVIII ('. . . the look *it* cannot find').

willingly linger yet a little more over the now visionary remembrance
of outward form and manner; yet the youthful blitheness and boyishness of heart with which he welcomed the sight of those he cared for,
contrasted with the signs of age before its time in his scant and silvery
hair: the gait, almost halting at times, which seemed hardly consistent
with so much physical resolve and energy; the perplexed yet encour-
aging smile that met the speaker, if chance talk touched on matters
of speculative or moral interest; the frown and furrows of the massive
forehead at any tale of baseness or injustice; the sunny glance or healthy
homely laughter at any word of natural kindness, or brilliancy, or
innocent humour.

There were days, indeed—months, perhaps—of darkness from more
quarters than most men are accessible to: yet this was on the whole a
happy life, though in a sense remote from the world's happiness. Here
was little prosperity in common parlance; years of struggle and toil,
fightings within and without, the *otia dia*[1] of the poet within view
only to be snatched away; no fame or recognition of abilities much
beyond what he saw crown others with celebrity. But his mind was
free from the 'last infirmity': he lived in the inner light of a pure
conscience, the healthfulness of duty fulfilled, the glorious liberty of
absolute utter unworldliness. And even in the midnight of meditative
troubles, the ever-youthful hope of the 'royal heart of innocence' was
never wanting. Nor were other elements of human happiness absent
within his home and without it—society and solitude by turns, Nature
and poetry glorious throughout life as on the first day, friendships
equal, open, and enduring—reverence, even from many who knew
him but slightly, for one so signalized and authenticated as a true Man
by the broad seal of Nobleness. This must be reckoned the first, as it
is the rarest, feature in human character. But in him it was equally
balanced by another, which in such degree is hardly less rare, Tenderness. Clough might be said not so much to trust his friends, as to trust

---

[1] From the passage in *De Rerum Natura*, V. 1384-7, where Lucretius describes how
men came to learn the soothing power of music:

> inde minutatim dulcis didicere querellas,
> tibia quas fundit digitis pulsata canentum,
> avia per nemora ac silvas saltusque reperta,
> per loca pastorum deserta atque otia dia.

'—then little by little they learnt the sweet lament, which the pipe pours forth, stopped
by the players' fingers, the pipe invented amid the pathless woods and forests and glades,
among the desolate haunts of the shepherds, and the lovely places of their rest' (tr.
Cyril Bailey, Oxford: Clarendon ed., 1947).

himself to them. Friendship in his eyes, as in the ancient days he felt with so deeply, was a high and sacred thing, a duty and a virtue in itself, and he guarded it with scrupulous sensitiveness. It was natural that one so gifted should be looked up to with unusual warmth and honour. Many will remember how much Clough's opinion on acts or thoughts, on literature or on nature—remote from ordinary judgments or humorously paradoxical as it might be—was tacitly referred to; how often the difficulties and doubts of the tangled passages of life were laid before him for counsel. A resolution was not always ready, but they never failed to find that which is better than most men's decisive clearness—a judgment noble, tender, courageous, conscientiousness: if not always practical advice, no little measure, at least, of that wisdom which is from above.

25. *Amours de Voyage:* an exchange of letters between Clough and J. C. Shairp

November 1849 (*Corr. I*, 275–8)

John Campbell Shairp (1819–85) was a fellow student of Clough's at Balliol. Clough's Philip in *The Bothie* may be modelled upon him to some extent. He was a critic and minor poet, his only remembered poem now, perhaps, being 'Balliol Scholars', in which he celebrates his friends and contemporaries Clough, Arnold and John Duke Coleridge. He became Professor of Poetry at Oxford in 1877. This exchange of letters arose, nine years before the poem's publication, because Shairp was one of the friends amongst whom Clough passed round the poem in MS. soon after its completion.

(i) From Shairp's letter to Clough [5?12? November 1849]
The latter half as being more downright pleases me more than the former. But taken as a whole—bating some few pages—it does not give me much pleasure. The state of the soul of which it is a projection I do not like. It strikes me as the most Werterish (not that I ever read Werter) of all you have yet done. There is no hope, nor strength, nor belief in these;—everything crumbles to dust beneath a ceaseless self-introspection and criticism which is throughout the one only inspiration. The gaiety of manner where no gaiety is, becomes flippancy. In the Bothie, though I was not its warmest admirer, there was strength and something positive in the men's characters and the Highland Hills—but here this fresh element is wanting and blasé disgust at men and things rampant. The *Ambarvalia*, if Werterish, was honest serious Werterism—but this is Beppoish or Don Juanish (if I remember them right). The Hexameters still do not go down with me. They give me a sense of Travestie—which is their place I think. The snatches of longs and shorts are very nice, but they would not do to be more than snatches. One page or two of the Hexameters rise into music— that 'Falling Falling still to the ancient Lyrical cadence' and that about

the statues on Monte Cavallo. But I need not go on to enumerate minor things which I liked. No, I would cast it behind me and the spirit from which it emanates and to higher, more healthful hopeful things purely aspire. I won't flatter; but you were not made, my dear Clough, to make sport before the Philistines in this way, but for something else. . . . Why this superabundance of oaths and other sweary words? They weaken the lines, are in bad taste and not good for yourself, if I may say so. On the whole I regard *Les Amours* as your nature ridding itself of long-gathered bile. . . . Don't publish it—or if it must be published—not in a book—but in some periodical. For if you live, you will leave this mood of mind behind I hope, and then books which are its echo might be a clog about your neck. . . . Should it strike you that my estimation of the amours comes from my 'rosewaterish sentimental' nature—that though I may go that way nature has not meant you nor do you intend to go that but another road—should this occur to you, I may add that I doubt much whether *Les Amours* will arride the public as much as either of your two former works.

It is hard to speak out and yet to seem friendly, but forgive any seeming bluntness or hardness of speech.

(ii) Clough's reply to (i) [November 1849]
. . . You are a very gentle beast and of a good conscience and roar me like any sucking dove—*Parturiunt montes*[1]—You are not half trenchant enough. You don't at all sting, I assure you. Yet your criticism is not exactly what I wanted. What I want assurance of is in the way of execution rather than conception. If I were only half as sure of the bearableness of the former as I am of the propriety of the latter, I would publish at once. Gott und Teufel, my friend, you don't suppose all that comes from myself!—I assure you it is extremely *not* so.

You're a funny creature, my dear old fellow—If one don't sing you a ballant, or read you a philosophical sermonette, if one don't talk about the gowans or faith—you're not pleased. However I believe that the execution of this is so poor that it makes the conception a fair subject of disgust. . . .

(iii) Shairp to Clough [November 1849]
Your friend Goethe says in Eckerman—'Yes—Such things one has to suffer from friends—How few men are capable of understanding the

---

[1] *Parturient montes, nascetur ridiculus mus:* 'Mountains will be in labour, a single laughable mouse will be born' (Horace, *Ars Poetica*, 139).

proper law of a production! Instead of taking its ground, and seeing what it should be, they praise or blame according as it harmonises with their own condition.' I confess I have always done so and *pace* Goethe intend to continue to do so. That is if I do not like the 'law of any production' I cannot like the carrying out of that law, however faithfully this may [be] done. Making reserve of some passages which I should willingly preserve, I do not like the conception. There is nothing hearty and heart-whole in it—no strength except in its raillery at all men and things and in its keen, ceaseless self-introspection. I do not like the point of view nor atmosphere from which it looks out on the world. It does not seem true or at least very partially so: and certainly is not refreshing. Every feeling of love for M. Trevellyn as it rises is cut to shreds by this; if carried out it would cut the whole world up into shreds and oneself to the bargain. I *can* like other things besides a Ballad and a Sermonette but one has supped one's fill of negations and now would prefer a draught of something stronger.

As to the execution I am not a good judge because the Hexameter does not take me, but has always a feeling of parody. But even for Hexameters many of them are slovenly. Not that I dislike your roughness, but then it should be more rock-like ruggedness not so slip-slop— not so many Well's and other monosyllables, and not so many *oaths* above all.

The execution is wanting too in dramatic power, scenes and scenery. The analysis *is too absorbing*. . . .

(iv) Clough to Shairp [November 1849]
You cannot possibly be too severe and truculent about the execution— and I agree quite as to the correctness (which is the only question) of what you say.—Except that I am not sure that Scenes and Scenery, after which you always go awhoring, would exactly improve the matter.

But do you not, in the conception, find any final Strength of Mind in the unfortunate fool of a hero? I have no intention whatever of sticking up for him, but certainly I didn't mean him to go off in mere prostration and defeat. Does the last part seem utterly sceptical to your sweet faithful soul?—

. . . I probably shan't publish for fear of a row with my Sadduccees.[1]

[1] i.e. The Management Committee of University Hall, of which Clough was Principal at the time.

26. Emerson to Clough

1858

From a letter dated 17 May 1858 (*Corr. II*, 548).

I cannot forgive you for the baulking end or no end of the *Amours de Voyage.* . . . . I read the first *livraison* of your poem with joy, and said, Behold that is what cannot be written here. Tis the sincerity of British culture. Here is a man tremulous all over with sensibility, and he holds a fine pen that delicately finds the right word,—gift that brings with it all other gifts. We watched from month to month our beloved star. The hexameters frightened some citizens. But all the good readers I know gave this poem every advantage over all the rest. And when we began to build securely on the triumph of our poet over all gainsayers, suddenly his wing flags, or his whim appears, and he plunges to a conclusion, like the ending of the Chancery suit in *Bleak House*, or like the denouement of Tennyson's *Princess*. How can you waste such power on a broken dream? Why lead us up to the tower to tumble us down? There is a statute of Parnassus, that the author shall keep faith with the reader; but you choose to trifle with him. It is true a few persons compassionately tell me, that the piece is all right, and that they like this veracity of much preparation to no result. But I hold tis bad enough in life, and inadmissible in poetry. And I think you owe us a retribution of music, and to a musical argument. As I wish now to give due emphasis to my objection, I shall say nothing of all the merits that shine in the poem.[1]

[1] Writing in June 1858 to C. E. Norton Clough reported Emerson's reprimand 'for the termination of the *Amours de Voyage*' and went on: 'he may be right and I wrong and all my defence can only be that I always meant it to be so and began it with the full intention of its ending so—but very likely I was wrong all the same. . . .' (*Corr. II*, 551).

27. Charles Eliot Norton, from 'Arthur Hugh Clough', *Atlantic Monthly*

April 1862, ix, 462–9

Charles Eliot Norton (1827–1908), founding editor of the *North American Review* and the *Nation* and critic, taught fine arts at Harvard; like Clough, he won a reputation as an unflinching freethinker in religious matters.

Most of the biographical part of this article (which is more eulogistic than Palgrave's), has been omitted: it consists mainly of liberal quotation from 'Arthur Hugh Clough—in Memoriam' (*Spectator* xxxiv, 23 November 1861), an anonymous article which Norton attributes in his later 'Memoir' prefixed to *The Poems of Arthur Hugh Clough* (Boston, 1862) to Thomas Hughes; Norton also quotes freely from Clough's letters to him, which he describes as 'reflections of himself, full of thought, fancy, and pleasant humour, as well as of affectionateness and true feeling' (for the Clough-Norton correspondence see Mulhauser). Norton's 'Memoir' is itself virtually a reprint of this article, from which critically relevant extracts are given below.

To win such love as Arthur Hugh Clough won in life, to leave so dear a memory as he has left, is a happiness that falls to few men. In America, as in England, his death is mourned by friends whose affection is better than fame, and who in losing him have met with an irreparable loss. Outside the circle of his friends his reputation had no large extent; but though his writings are but little known by the great public of readers, they are prized by all those of thoughtful and poetic temper to whose hands they have come, as among the most precious and original productions of the time. To those who knew him personally his poems had a special worth and charm, as the sincere expression of a character of the purest stamp, of rare truthfulness and simplicity, not less tender than strong, and of a genius thoroughly individual in

125

its form, and full of the promise of a large career. He was by Nature endowed with subtile and profound powers of thought, with feeling at once delicate and intense, with lively and generous sympathies, and with conscientiousness so acute as to pervade and control his whole intellectual disposition. Loving, seeking, and holding fast to the truth, he despised all falseness and affectation. With his serious and earnest thinking was the play of a genial humour and the brightness of poetic fancy. Liberal in sentiment, absolutely free from dogmatism and pride of intellect, of a questioning temper, but of reverent spirit, faithful in the performance not only of the larger duties, but also of the lesser charities and the familiar courtesies of life, he has left a memory of singular consistency, purity, and dignity. He lived for conscience, not for show, and few men carry through life so white a soul.

. . . Clough was at Oxford in 1847,—the year of the terrible Irish famine, and with others of the most earnest men at the University he took part in an association which had for its object 'Retrenchment for the sake of the Irish.' Such a society was little likely to be popular with the comfortable dignitaries or the luxurious youth of the University. Many objections, frivolous or serious as the case might be, were raised against so subversive a notion as that of the self-sacrifice of the rich for the sake of the poor. Disregarding all personal considerations, Clough printed a pamphlet entitled, *A Consideration of Objections against the Retrenchment Association*, in which he met the careless or selfish arguments of those who set themselves against the efforts of the society. It was a characteristic performance. His heart was deeply stirred by the harsh contrast between the miseries of the Irish poor and the wasteful extravagance of living prevalent at Oxford. He wrote with vehement indignation against the selfish pleas of the indifferent and the thoughtless possessors of wealth, wasters of the goods given them as a trust for others. His words were chiefly addressed to the young men at the University,—and they were not without effect. Such views of the rights and duties of property as he put forward, of the claims of labor, and of the responsibilities of the aristocracy, had not been often heard at Oxford. He was called a Socialist and a Radical, but it mattered little to him by what name he was known to those whose consciences were not touched by his appeal. 'Will you say,' he writes toward the end of this pamphlet, 'this is all rhetoric and declamation? There is, I dare say, something too much in that kind. What with criticizing style and correcting exercises, we college tutors perhaps may be likely, in the heat of composition, to lose sight of realities, and pass into the limbo of the factitious,—especially when the thing must be done at odd times, in any case, and, if at all, quickly. But if I have been obliged to write hurriedly, believe me, I have obliged myself to think not hastily. And believe me, too, though I have desired to succeed in putting vividly and forcibly that which vividly and forcibly I felt and saw, still the graces and splendors of composition were thoughts far less present to my mind than Irish poor men's miseries, English poor men's hardships, and your unthinking indifference. Shocking enough the first and the second, almost more shocking the third.'

It was about this time that the most widely known of his works, *The Bothie of Toper-na-Fuosich, a Long-Vacation Pastoral*, was written. It was published in 1848, and though it at once secured a circle of warm admirers, and the edition was very soon exhausted, it 'is assuredly deserving of a far higher popularity than it has ever attained.' The poem was reprinted in America, at Cambridge, in 1849, and it may be safely asserted that its merit was more deeply felt and more generously acknowledged by American than by English readers. The fact that its essential form and local coloring were purely and genuinely English, and thus gratified the curiosity felt in this country concerning the social habits and ways of life in the mother-land, while on the other hand its spirit was in sympathy with the most liberal and progressive thought of the age, may sufficiently account for its popularity here. But the lovers of poetry found delight in it, apart from these character-istics,—in its fresh descriptions of Nature, its healthy manliness of tone, its scholarly construction, its lively humor, its large thought quickened and deepened by the penetrating imagination of the poet.

'Any one who has read it will acknowledge that a tutorship at Oriel was not the place for the author. The intense love of freedom, the deep and hearty sympathy with the foremost thought of the time, the humorous dealing with old formulas and conventionalisms grown meaningless, which breathe in every line of the *Bothie*, show this clearly enough. He would tell in after-life, with much enjoyment, how the dons of the University, who, hearing that he had something in the press, and knowing that his theological views were not wholly sound, were looking for a publication on the Articles, were astounded by the appearance of that fresh and frolicsome poem. Oxford (at least the Oriel common room) and he were becoming more estranged daily. How keenly he felt the estrangement, not from Oxford, but from old friends, about this time can be read only in his own words.' It is in such poems as the 'Qua Cursum Ventus,' or the sonnet beginning, 'Well, well,—Heaven bless you all from day to day!' that it is to be read. These, with a few other fugitive pieces, were printed, in company with verses by a friend, as one part of a small volume entitled *Ambarvalia*, which never attained any general circulation, although containing some poems which will take their place among the best of English poetry of this generation.

[Quotes 'Qua Cursum Ventus'.]

'In 1848–49 the revolutionary crisis came on Europe, and Clough's sympathies drew him with great earnestness into the struggles which were going on. He was in Paris directly after the barricades, and in Rome during the siege, where he gained the friendship of Saffi and other leading Italian patriots.' A part of his experiences and his thoughts while at Rome are interwoven with the story in his *Amours de Voyage*, a poem which exhibits in extraordinary measure the subtlety and delicacy of his powers, and the fulness of his sympathy with the intellectual conditions of the time. It was first published in the *Atlantic Monthly* for 1858, and was at once established in the admiration of readers capable of appreciating its rare and refined excellence. The spirit of the poem is thoroughly characteristic of its author, and the speculative, analytic turn of his mind is represented in many passages of the letters of the imaginary hero. Had he been writing in his own name, he could not have uttered his inmost conviction more distinctly, or have given the clue to his intellectual life more openly than in the following verses:—

> I will look straight out, see things, not try to evade them:
> Fact shall be Fact for me; and the Truth the Truth as ever,
> Flexible, changeable, vague, and multiform and doubtful.

Or, again,—

> Ah, the key of our life, that passes all words, opens all locks,
> Is not *I will*, but *I must*. I must,—I must,—and I do it.

And still again,—

> But for the steady fore-sense of a freer and larger existence,
> Think you that man could consent to be circumscribed here into action?
> But for assurance within of a limitless ocean divine, o'er
> Whose great tranquil depths unconscious the wind-tost surface

Breaks into ripples of trouble that come and change and endure not,—
But that in this, of a truth, we have our being, and know it,
Think you we men could submit to live and move as we do here?

... In November, 1852, he arrived in Boston. He at once established himself at Cambridge, proposing to give instruction to young men preparing for college, or to take on in more advanced studies those who had completed the collegiate course. He speedily won the friendship of those whose friendship was best worth having in Boston and its neighborhood. His thorough scholarship, the result of the best English training, and his intrinsic qualities caused his society to be sought and prized by the most cultivated and thoughtful men. He had nothing of insular narrowness, and none of the hereditary prejudices which too often interfere with the capacity of English travellers or residents among us to sympathize with and justly understand habits of life and of thought so different from those to which they have been accustomed. His liberal sentiments and his independence of thought harmonized with the new social conditions in which he found himself, and with the essential spirit of American life. The intellectual freedom and animation of this country were congenial to his disposition. From the beginning he took a large share in the interests of his new friends. He contributed several remarkable articles to the pages of the *North American Review* and of *Putnam's Magazine*, and he undertook a work which was to occupy his scanty leisure for several years, the revision of the so-called Dryden's *Translation of Plutarch's Lives*. Although the work was undertaken simply as a revision, it turned out to involve little less labor than a complete new translation, and it was so accomplished that henceforth it must remain the standard version of this most popular of the ancient authors. ...

28. Unsigned review, 'Clough's Poems' in the *Saturday Review*

26 July 1862, 109–10

Mr. Clough's poems have been collected into a volume, and the outer world has now a fair opportunity of judging a man whose friends have spoken of him so highly. A memoir by Mr. Palgrave precedes this collection, and tells the simple story of Mr. Clough's life. It is impossible that a career so absolutely unmarked by outer events should have much interest, and the only feature of attraction which the biography of a man of thought and retirement can offer—that of a selection from his correspondence—is not present here. Mr. Palgrave has nothing to do except to record that Mr. Clough was a very promising boy at Rugby—that he was successively fellow and tutor at Oriel—that he resigned his tutorship in 1848, and went to Italy, where he was present at the siege of Rome—that he was for a short time head of an institution in connexion with the University of London— that he took a voyage to America—that he returned, obtained a situation in the Privy Council Office, married, and worked on until his health gave way, and he set out on the tour which was brought to an end by his death in Italy last year. This simple outline is filled up with a sketch of Mr. Clough's character, and some observations on his poetical powers and productions. To write this sort of memoir of a man just dead, and known only in a very limited circle, is by no means an easy task. If the writer is warm in his praise, the outside world thinks he is amusing himself by magnifying an obscure friend into post-humous fame. If he is guarded, the few people who really care about the book, and who watch with a generous jealousy over the memory of one long loved and lately lost, exclaim that the biographer has been unjust to the dead. On the whole, Mr. Palgrave may be said to have done well what he had to do. He points forcibly and truly the main traits of Mr. Clough's character—his scrupulous justice and honour, his tolerance and largeness of mind, his constant endeavour to 'live plainly and think highly.' He also sums up very fairly the chief characteristics of Mr. Clough's poetry—the love of nature it shows, the power with which it expresses the fluctuations of mental conflict, and the liveliness and humour by which it is relieved. The only objection we have to make is to the style. Mr. Palgrave seems to have much less command over his pen than might be expected in a man so well read in English literature and so fond of the best authors. He is always at the mercy of any masters of bad style who tempt him to stray. It jars upon the taste of ordinary readers, and upon the recollections of those acquainted with Mr. Clough's simplicity and good sense, to read that 'he inherited a double portion of the spirit of William Wordsworth,' and that he was 'authenticated as a true Man by the broad seal of nobleness.' The gentle satire that runs through life could scarcely have been brought home more curiously to Mr. Clough than it would have been could he have dreamt that one day it would be said of him that something or other 'authenticated him as a true Man.'

It is quite right that when a man stamps himself upon the minds of his acquaintances as extraordinary in gifts or character, and when those acquaintances have reason to think themselves capable of forming a true judgment, they should, after his death, honour his memory and justify themselves by explaining what he seemed to be to them, and how superior the man himself was to his writings. Poems such as those which Mr. Clough has left behind him necessarily reveal much of their author's character, and it helps strangers to understand them if they have a key to that character in the friendly reminiscences of a biographer. But, after all, published poems must be finally taken for what they are worth in themselves, and not for what they may be worth in connexion with certain elements of a dead man's character, or certain powers residing in him, but only partially developed. If these poems are to be considered as having permanent value, they must be criticized apart from the history of their author. The only question that will occupy the outside world is whether they have substantial, intrinsic merits great enough to repay the trouble of reading them. It seems to us that they have, in spite of the many drawbacks to which they are obviously subject. The greatest of these is obscurity. It is very hard to see what the short poems are about before they are over. We finish them before we can find out the sense of the first stanza. They are also monotonous, as they express very few emotions of the mind, and have only very slight connexion with the external world; and lastly, they only appeal to a limited class, and embody sorrows and aspirations with which persons of only a special kind of education, and of a special temperament, can really sympathize. On the other hand, they express one or two things so well, and those things are in themselves so great, that poetry so successful in its own walk must be held to have an indisputable value.

There is nothing more difficult to convey in words than the exact meaning of the doubts of a philosophical mind of the present day. Perhaps the doubts of all doubters are substantially the same, and the Book of Job has as much philosophy in it as this world is likely ever to come to. But every generation has its own way of putting things; and we might suppose ourselves capable of stating without much trouble what are the chief doubts and conflicts in which we are engaged; but to state them shortly, and to speak of any individual as thinking in a particular way about them, is almost sure to give an opening for ridicule. It is not so much the thought as the vividness with which the thought is held and expressed, and its whole bearing upon the life and other thoughts of the thinker, that attract us. Mr. Clough was extremely impatient of all subterfuges, he was scrupulously anxious not to be led away by half thoughts, he was sincerely desirous not to deceive himself. He shunned anything like half-belief. At the bottom of all reflection, however, he found the image of a wise and just God. This fear of half-belief—this searching out of God, as a being disclosed to him in the recesses of his own heart, but not lightly to be clothed with attributes and credited with schemes and plans of creation—Mr. Clough expressed as well as he could in verse. That which he had to say is perhaps as old as the human race, and is certainly as old as religious philosophy. His verses are full of power, and of happy, unexpected terms; but are obscure, inharmonious, and incomplete. A man cannot be said to have necessarily done much who has put such thoughts into such verses. He may not have done much, but he also may have done much. All depends on the sense of reality which the thinking produces on us, and on the feelings the verse awakens. If we put the substance of the Book of Job into the form of a logical proposition, it does not seem as if we had got hold of much more than a truism. But there are men to whom the truisms of religious philosophy are living realities, and whose life is spent in dwelling on thoughts which ordinary men dismiss after a moment's hasty reflection. That one writer is superficial and another profound on such points, is a fact only to be learnt by experiment. When we read them we feel the difference, but unless we read them we cannot see where the difference lies. We cannot describe what it is that makes the verses of Mr. Clough seem to us to embody, better, perhaps, than those of any other writer of our generation, these ancient doubts and truths in their modern shape; but as we read what he has written, we become conscious of his superiority.

Mr. Clough has also expressed, with far more than ordinary truth and feeling, the emotions which a man of tender heart and full of the sadness of philosophy experiences when he throws himself upon his fellows and basks in the grateful sunshine of friendship. The best, or at least the most intelligible and harmonious of all his short poems, describes the satisfaction with which he welcomes the belief that all honest men, however they are separated in thought and aim, are carried to the same port at last. He compares them to two ships lying side by side at night, and then carried far apart by dawn of day, although they fancied the same breeze was bearing them on. Mr. Clough also saw much of the humour of innocent society, and his *Bothie* is infinitely the best picture ever given of University life. He alone of the many who have undertaken to describe Oxford has done justice to the subject, and has pictured young men as they really exist— full of nonsense, and pedantry, and animal spirits, interested in all manner of discussions, moral and intellectual, working, rowing, bathing, walking and talking, and smoking for ever. This was the form of external life with which Mr. Clough was acquainted, and he managed to describe it as no one else has ever done. That he has done this, and that he has contrived to invest his description with a glow of poetry, and to glorify the life he yet faithfully represents, is quite enough to show that he was not merely a meditative man of reflection, delighting for ever to weave into verse those questionings which vex the meditative mind. It was unfortunate for his permanent reputation that he had little in his life to force the representation of the outer world and of society on him, and that his distrust of his own poetical powers led him to substitute for poetical effort that absorption in the slavery of exhausting labour which killed him before his time, and at last seemed to him the only worthy end of life, and the only proper result of philosophy.

This volume contains two new pieces of considerable length. One is called *Amours de Voyage*, and embodies what its author was thinking and observing and studying, during his stay at Rome in 1849. It is in the form of letters, supposed to be written by an English traveller to his friend, and by an English young lady to her friend. The pair gradually fall in love, although the gentleman is very long in deciding whether he feels more than the passing tenderness which results from being thrown in the way of a sympathizing and pretty girl. His doubts on this point fill up a large portion of the poem, and he has scarcely ascertained that his feelings are serious when the young lady's family leave Rome, and he has to set off in chase of them. He visits them at Florence, at Milan, and at Como; and the story ends as a story never ended before, in the lover giving his mistress up in sheer weariness and despair, because he cannot find her direction. Of course, the interest of such a story cannot be in the story itself. It lies in the humorous sketches of English society abroad, in the playfulnesses of the young lady in her unbosomings, and in the description of the people, the city, and neighbourhood of Rome. It is not nearly equal to the *Bothie*, but it has many of the same excellences. There are fine passages in it, and many subtle trains of thought, and some spirited satirical sketches. Perhaps the first account of the Trevellyns—the family out of whom, by the aid of juxtaposition, he selects his Mary—is as amusing as any:—

[Quotes *Amours de Voyage*, I. 115–34: 'which of three Misses Trevellyn' to 'nor God's, God knoweth!'.]

The doubts of the lover are, however, a little wearisome. He is always in a state of flux and reflux of thought. He cannot make up his mind whether he likes the girl, or whether he would take the trouble to save her life if she was in danger, or whether he ought to save her if he did not wish; or whether he might lawfully fight for the Roman Republic, or whether he would wish to fight if he might. It is, perhaps, not unnatural that a man substantially good, affectionate, and grave, should have all these thoughts pass through his mind, if he accustomed himself to the intricacies of casuistical self-inspection. But there is no very good reason why he should put his feelings and opinions into English hexameters. The other new poem, or rather collection of poems, is called *Mari Magno*, and consists of stories or recollections supposed to be narrated by a group of passengers on their passage to America. These tales are very unfinished, and are not very interesting. In one, however, called the 'Clergyman's Tale', there are some lines that show deep and noble feeling, and a strong sense of the sinfulness of sin. There is also a short poem inserted in the early portion of the book, and now first published, which may fairly be quoted as a proof, that although Mr. Clough was distracted by the difficulties which the wars of foreigners suggest to a philosophical stranger, he yet had moments when he could strongly feel all the nobleness and romance attached to the then falling cause of Italy:—

[Concludes by quoting 'Peschiera'.]

29. [Henry Fothergill Chorley], review of *Poems* in the *Athenaeum*

26 July 1862, 107–9

Chorley (1808–72) was a music and literary critic with the *Athenaeum*, 1833–66, an unsuccessful novelist and dramatist and a close friend and admirer of Browning.

The writer of the biographical notice prefixed to this volume makes little of his hero. Mr. Clough, born a Liverpool man, was, we are reminded, 'first favourite' among the remarkable company of youths trained and moulded by the good, genial Arnold at Rugby, and was there considered as a youth of no ordinary promise. Subsequently he won the hearts of all who came near him when a tutor at Oxford, as he had done when a Rugby school-boy, by his manliness, his genius, and his resolution to *be* and to *do* everything which is right and hon-ourable. But he was vexed by vain longings, which his biographer shall describe in his own language:—

[Quotes the passage 'Having held a tutorship in his college' to 'or Pascal felt it' from Palgrave's 'Memoir': see pp. 112–13 above.]

On leaving Oxford, Mr. Clough travelled and wrote letters home from Paris, in the Carlyle dialect, concerning 'well-to-do-ism', 'vulgar parcel-gilt era,' and such matters. He was in Rome during the period when the Eternal City was in the hands of the Mazzini Triumvirate,—sympathized keenly with the daring and disappointment of the Re-publicans,—and came home 'from the temporary triumph of shame and superstition,' depressed at heart, to undertake the Wardenship of University Hall, London. This did not suit him. He then tried America, which answered no better, and returned to an appointment as Secretary to the 'Commission of Report on Military Education.' His frame seems to have been worn out, possibly by the heart within eating itself away, ere he made this last attempt at reconciling position with propensities; and he died, aged forty-two, in 1861.

It is evident that this man, described as a man of many gifts and many virtues, did not 'pant upon the thorns of life,'—that he had no struggle from without to disquiet him. His memorialist it is true, says that he—

did the work of a man with his two-and-forty years; yet we must feel now the bitterness and irony of that fate which seemed to secure him outward prosperity, but never left him a brief interval in which, as one who best knew him said, 'to be himself,' and to realize for his own advantage, if not for ours, powers rarely given in such curiously subtle combination. Perhaps his speculative activity was beyond his powers of co-ordination, the discursive element of thought too dominant, the fear of partial conclusions over-scrupulous.

We must add another high-flown paragraph:—

[Quotes from Palgrave, 'It appears to the writer an idle demand' to 'sole guides for action': see p. 118 above.]

What does the above mean? An appeal to sympathy for struggles from within?—an apology for the discontent of an unsettled mind?— an explanation why promises so golden failed to be fulfilled? 'Living a poem' is a phrase which has deep and authoritative sound; but the phrase rings hollow, if the sense to be conveyed thereby is the excuse for, not the admission of, discontent and failure. It will appear to others besides ourselves, that Mr. Clough had no definite idea of the form in which he should *do* and *be* 'his poem.' There was a time when young gentlemen were 'sad as night for very wantonness': at present we are wandering through an age of straggling thought and comfortless aspiration, great as is our reputed gain in health of tone. During such a period the sensitive and the mediocre, and those lacking that inbred, abiding sense of duty and dignity which makes a man munificent and gentle amid success, patient without bitterness under hope deferred, stand a fair chance of being placed on pedestals too high for their real stature. It is no very sublime thing to doubt; with some minds it is an instinct. It is no very tragical thing to own that effort has been wasted—that the bread cast into the waters has been lost in the whirl-

pool. If the above hints and explanations be perverse in misrepresenta-
tion, as bearing on the life of an amiable man who never, we are
assured, found his right place—perhaps because he never came to an
agreement with himself,—the fault lies in part with the ambiguity
and incomplete reasoning of his biographer.

The incompleteness of Mr. Clough's life—the motto of which we
are invited to believe was 'plain living and high thinking'—is reflected
in his poems. The serious ones, we fancy, are a reprint of those in
Ambarvalia—a collection published by him in 1849, conjointly with
Mr. Burbage [*sic*]. In these 'the high thinking' has neither found clear
utterance nor poetical diction. The author has no objection, when
other inspiration fails, to help himself out with slang. Here and there,
it is true, are gracious fancies and smooth versification; but it may be
asserted, that volumes by the dozen of as much or more promise are
put forth every year without exciting the slightest wonder or hope.
As we go on with the book, we get deeper and deeper into the slough
of affectation. *The Bothie of Tober-na-Vuolich, a Long-Vacation Pastoral*,
is a long poem in which hexameters and the *Whistlecraft*[1] style are
attempted, with no great felicity. What manner of waistcoats the
Oxford men wore when dressing for a Highland dinner—how they
bathed in a morning, (Mr. Clough seems to have thought a bath
something so heroic and extraordinary, that he could never return
sufficiently often to cold water,) are told somewhat in this vein:—

[Quotes *The Bothie*, I, 25–44; 'Somewhat more splendid' to 'leaving
his ample Olympian chamber'.]

Not so many years ago the bread-and-butter simplicity of Voss's
'Louise'[2] used to be a favourite laughing-stock with our wits and
critics. They must henceforth be silent when they encounter a tale
made up of familiarities like these—not laid aside with a man's '*hob-
badiboyhood*' (the word is Mr. Clough's), seriously put in among the
claims for the man who was unsuccessful, yet 'lived his poem.'

The book, indeed, is full of coxcombry. '*Amours de Voyage*' is a
tale, told also in lame hexameters, devoted to the republican days of
Rome,—in which, among high thoughts, patriotic sentiments and
love-breathings, are interspersed passages outdoing the most prosaic

[1] Whistlecraft: the pseudonym under which John Hookham Frere published his mock-
heroic 'King Arthur and his Round-Table' (1817–18).
[2] *Louise* (1784; 1795) by Johann Heinrich Voss (1751–1826); this idyll was the prototype of Goethe's *Herman and Dorothea*.

passages which flaw 'Aurora Leigh,' or are to be found in *Lucille*[1] and 'The Angel in the House'. Take merely some ten lines from a lady's letter. Hundreds of the same quality could be cited:—

> Mary allows she was wrong about Mr. Claude *being selfish*;
> He was *most* useful and kind on the terrible thirtieth of April.
> Do not write here any more; we are starting directly for Florence:
> We should be off tomorrow, if only Papa could get horses;
> All have been seized everywhere for the use of this dreadful Mazzini.
> P.S.
> Mary has seen thus far.—I am really so angry, Louisa,—
> Quite out of patience, my dearest! What can the man be intending?
> I am quite tired; and Mary, who might bring him to in a moment,
> Lets him go on as he likes, and neither will help nor dismiss him.

Again:—

> Mr. Claude, you must know, is behaving a little bit better;
> He and Papa are great friends; but he really is too *shilly shally*,—
> So unlike George! Yet I hope that the matter is going on fairly.
> I shall, however, get George, before he goes, to say something.
> Dearest Louise, how delightful to bring young people together!

Not being among the initiated, we take leave to characterize the above as poor stuff—doubly impertinent as put forth by one purported to be sincere in his life—which should imply sincerity in art. Any man whose song is of manly sports and wholesome ambitions, who is sick of conventionalisms, should find better use for his powers than committing to paper the boarding-school nonsense which passes in reams through the post-office every day.

Gymnastic enterprises and namby-pamby sentimentalities make a strange mixture. Howsoever the compound be extolled as representing that union of 'plain living and high thinking', which serves for watchword and catch-word to many of our rising men,—your 'muscular' poet, with his thews and sinews, and his '*matutine*' bath, and his delight in marrying a Highland *lassie*—who digs potatoes, alternately with his keen appreciation of the epistolary prattle and tattle of Sarah Maria to Elizabeth Jane about papa and flirtations and *beaux*—may, after all, be intrinsically as much of a 'sham' as was *Jemmy Jessamy*[2] with his muff and his sedan, or *Damon*,[3] who dropped *bouts rimés* into Lady

---

[1] *Lucille* (1860), by Owen Meredith (pseud. Edward Robert Lytton Bulwer-Lytton, 1831–91).

[2] *The History of Jemmy and Jenny Jessamy*, 3 vols., 1753, by Eliza Haywood.

[3] *The Genuine Distresses of Damon and Celia*, 2 vols., 1771, by William Renwick.

Miller's Bath-Easton vase, or *Rugantino*,[1] who *out*-Corsaired the Corsair.

30. David Masson in *Macmillan's Magazine*

August 1862, vi, 318–31

Masson (1822–1907) edited *Macmillan's Magazine* from its inception in 1859 to 1867. He was a Professor at University College, London (succeeding Clough), and later at Edinburgh. He was the author, in a *North British Review* article entitled 'Theories of Poetry and a New Poet' (1853), of the view Arnold attacks in his 1853 Preface, that 'a true allegory of the state of one's mind . . . is perhaps the highest thing that one can attempt in the way of fictitious art' (which includes, for Masson, poetry).

A man of very shy demeanour, of largish build about the head and shoulders, with a bland and rather indolent look, and a noticeable want of alertness in his movements—such, to a stranger meeting him casually, appeared that Arthur Hugh Clough, of whom, till his death the other day at the age of forty-two, all those who knew him intimately were wont to speak in terms of such unusually high regard. Many persons to whom the name of Clough was only beginning to be adequately known when a premature death removed him will now take up with interest the beautiful little volume in which his Poems are first collected, and in which they are introduced by a brief Memoir from the pen of his friend, Mr. F. T. Palgrave.

A collected volume of Poems may either be read with a view to enjoying and appreciating them individually on their own account, without much reference to their connexion with the mind that produced them; or it may be read throughout with a special attention to that connexion, and with a desire to detect, underneath each, that

---

[1] Reference untraced.

mood or moment of the author's mind of which it was a product, and so, in the whole series, taken chronologically, to see the representation of a completed intellectual life. Whether the one mode of reading or the other shall be pursued depends greatly on the nature of the Poems. It were a morbid excess of the biographical spirit that, in reading the collected metrical romances, ballads and songs of Scott, should always be groping through the heroic stir of the action, and the descriptions of natural scenery, for more and more definite conceptions of Scott's own personality. No one can think that much would be made by the process. Yet, notwithstanding what such an instance may suggest, it may be asserted that, in all cases in which we have the collected remains of a poet before us after he is dead, there is a certain necessity, as well as propriety, in viewing them as the representative relics of a human spirit, thus and thus fashioned and circumstanced while it lived, and so in thinking back, page after page, as we read, to the vanished hand that wrote and the heart that the writing expressed. If there has been a deepening and improvement of our style of current literary criticism since the days when Jeffrey was the chief master of that older style which consisted in the application to book after book of what may be called 'the alternate beauty-and-blemish principle,' it has been owing chiefly to an increased habit of trying to discern, even through each successive work of a living poet, the peculiar cast of his philosophy, the nature of the real thoughts that are occupying or besetting him. Poets may complain of this, and may have ground for complaint in the mistakes made about them from the direct interpretation of what they conceive and express only vicariously. But there is soundness in the method, however it may be misused. At all events, when the remains of a poet are put forth collectively after his decease, there is, in the fact, a kind of solicitation to the reader not only to accept and enjoy each piece or poem separately for what it is worth, but also so to read as to figure to himself deliberately and distinctly this one more physiognomy, to be added to the portrait-gallery of the dead whom he is bound to remember.

In the present case there is no need to argue this matter farther. These poems of Clough are, indeed, interesting in themselves. They have such merits of thought and expression that, were the volume torn up, and the anonymous leaves scattered here and there, in Australia or Western America, or wherever else afar off the English language is spreading, there would be some, doubtless, whom the fragments would arrest, and who would con them and repeat them as fine things by some unknown author. And yet to us, receiving the volume as it is now published, it becomes plain, after the first glance at the nature of its contents, that we should not half understand it, unless we kept before us, in reading it, the image of the author, Arthur Hugh Clough—nay, unless we remembered that he was born in 1819, was known in his boyhood as Arnold's favourite pupil at Rugby, went thence to Oxford and became one of the brightest hopes of the place, but in 1848 gave up his connexion with Oxford, and thereafter, till his death in 1861, led a life more at large.

In a vague way there are two periods of Clough's life represented in the poems—which periods are also discriminated in Mr. Palgrave's Memoir. The first is the period, beginning with Clough's twenty-first and ending in his twenty-ninth year, during which he was still an Oxford scholar; the second is the period, extending from his twenty-ninth year to his death, during which he had no official connexion with the University, but was living, as we have said, 'more at large.'

If we were to say that, during the first or earlier period, Clough is presented to us as one of those who, in the language of that time at Oxford, would have been described, and would, in the language of many, still be described, as Sceptics, Rationalists, or Radicals, we should be probably hitting the right nail roughly on the head. Considering, however, how unpleasantly exact are the common associations with these names, we should then certainly be doing him an injustice, except with those who can surround a definite designation with the due penumbra. It is better, therefore, to quote Mr. Palgrave's more general words respecting the Oxford period of his friend's life.

[Quotes Palgrave's 'Memoir', 'Clough's residence at Oxford' to 'willing to contemplate': see p. 109 above.]

So far the information given by Mr. Palgrave might amount simply to this, that Clough, after a moment of attraction towards Puseyism, swung decidedly the other way—becoming, in general and academic politics, a noted liberal, and in theology one of that band of free and then struggling young thinkers to the influence of some of whom, carrying their tendencies into the Church, and developing them within its bounds, may be traced the present *Essays and Reviews* outburst.[1] But that this is hardly enough, Mr. Palgrave seems to indicate by subsequent expressions.

---

[1] *Essays and Reviews* (1860), by Benjamin Jowett and others.

[Quotes Palgrave, 'It would be no true picture' to 'and her majesty': see p. 110 above.]

In other words, Clough at Oxford was mainly a meditative spirit, trying to the very core the beliefs in the midst of which he found himself, and coming to peculiar speculative conclusions. The nature of these conclusions is also indicated.

[Quotes Palgrave, 'the consciousness of the strange things of life' to 'displayed in dogmatic formulas': see p. 113 above.]

The meaning of all which, expressed in the rough and ready language of the religious newspapers, certainly is that Clough had come to be a 'sceptic' in his relations to the established theology. But, as Mr. Palgrave feels, there is a coarseness, apt to be very unjust in the case of such a mind as Clough's, in this rough and ready mode of designation, practised by those who are so fond of sorting their fellow-creatures accurately beforehand into the two divisions of the sheep and the goats, and who, it is pretty certain, will find themselves mistaken, in not a few instances on both sides, when the partition comes to be made by the true authority. Hence Mr. Palgrave prefers general language in describing the sum of his friend's speculative conclusions, even on their negative side. Hence, too, he adds a caveat, of positive purport, intended to prevent people from supposing that, when they have learnt that Clough was a truant from the established theology, they have merely to call up certain flagrant contemporary instances of similar truancy, in order to understand his mood and his company.

[Quotes Palgrave on Clough's 'divergence from the beliefs and forms of Oxford' not being 'such as ever estranged him' to 'followers of any religion': see p. 113 above for revised version.]

This is also true. Clough, in parting from the existing theology, made no attempt to turn again and rend it. His was no combative or aggressive scepticism. On the contrary, he remained singularly tolerant and courteous in his relations to those whom he had himself quitted. Nor, on quitting them, did he walk across to any of the refuges already marked out and palisaded on the other side of the great plain of opinion. He did not range himself with the Unitarians; he did not behave as if it occurred to him that one extraordinary Frenchman might really have effected in our day the final generalization of all things for ever and ever, and so betake himself either to the earlier or the later Comtism; above all, there was no sign of a tendency in his case to that far-off part of the plain, strewn with skeletons and dead dogs, where waves the senna-coloured banner of Atheistic Secularism. He walked forth, if anything, a pure natural Theist, or perhaps this with such additions, such constitutional sympathies with the good in what he was leaving, that, had there been any prospect of that Church of the Future so often talked of, but the requisite broadness of which as yet defies our art of ecclesiastical architecture, he might not have walked forth at all. He walked forth, at all events, really himself— Arthur Hugh Clough.

Now there is record of all this in the poems, and especially in the shorter pieces at the beginning of the volume. These poems bring Clough distinctly before us as the scholarly young Oxonian of high promise and sociable habits, genial and respected, more than most in his college, and in the whole venerable city of colleges, but liking much to be alone with himself, and, when thus alone, meditating, meditating. For example—

[Quotes 'Blank Misgivings of a Creature Moving About in Worlds not realised', VII.]

But the tenor of his meditations, whether in the secrecy of his own rooms, or at the college lectures, or abroad in his daily walks, is also recorded. For a time the mood is that of pure doubt—of ascertained severance of his intellect from surrounding beliefs, of consequent uncertainty how he ought to conduct himself, and of longing for more light. Thus—

[Quotes 'In a Lecture Room', and 'Away, haunt thou not me.]

Many more passages might be quoted, indicating, under various modes of expression, the constant settling of his mind in the same course of thought, together with the anxiety which thence resulted as to his own proper conduct in the circumstances in which he found himself—an anxiety which gradually ripened into a conviction that he could pursue the ecclesiastical career to which a prolonged connexion with Oxford naturally pointed, only by reconciling himself—

> To finger idly some old Gordian knot,
> Unskill'd to sunder, and too weak to cleave,
> And with much toil attain to half-believe.

The following passage, written perhaps before this conviction was so clear as it ultimately became, is worth noting for the peculiar strain of prayer that runs through it.

[Quotes 'Blank Misgivings . . .', IX, ll. 62–77: 'So be it: yet, O Good and Great', to 'earthly swine'.]

The notion which pervades these lines is one which recurs again and again in Clough's verses, and on which, as being the standard recipe always offered to persons in his mental condition, he had evidently ruminated a great deal.

'Do the law and thou shalt know the doctrine,' is the profound aphorism of Scripture itself—an aphorism the attenuated form of which, in modern religious casuistry, is that, if the doubter will only persevere in the routine of plain and minute duties lying before him, and will abstain as far as he can, during this regimen, from the questionings that have been perplexing him, he will find light unawares breaking in upon him, and will come out of the tunnel at last. Now this notion, we say, is one which Clough ruminated with peculiar persistency. For a time he had evidently considerable hopes from it. It may have been noted, and it is certainly worth noting, how many of the most daring sceptics in matters of theology have been strict and even fanatical in their conformity to the established ethics—refraining almost with horror from themselves applying the spirit of investigation to what has come down rooted in the common convictions of men in this department, and discouraging all disintegration of the common morality by others, notwithstanding that it might be supposed, from their own point of view, that the two sets of common beliefs, the theological and the ethical, do intertwine at the roots, and that, at all events, there might be the chance of error and of premature conclusion, as well in the theory of earthly duty and of social arrangements as in that of man's metaphysical relations. In Clough it is evident that there was this apparent inconsistency, and that, even when he doubted in theology most, he was firm and orthodox in his creed as to what is moral, noble and manly. Hence as respected the essentials of duty, as respected fidelity to the common sense of right and wrong in all greater things, he *was* prepared to accept the recipe offered to doubters, and to trust in it. Thus—

> The Summum Pulchrum rests in heaven above;
> Do thou, as best thou may'st, thy duty do:
> Amid the things allowed thee live and love;
> Some day thou shalt it view.

But, in the actual circumstances of his case, and in the form in which the maxim was urged upon him and on others, as an easy common-place of modern religious casuistry, his feelings towards it were different. Duty! yes; the great law of the heart and of all noble tradition; the 'whatsoever things are just, whatsoever things are honourable, whatsoever things are lovely and of good report'—it is not about this that there is the difficulty! In this sense, who would not be contented to do his duty in hopes of the dawning of the doctrine? But action in the vast region of contingent morality; the choice, among a hundred ways of activity, of that which is fittest and in which one may do one's duty best; and then, moreover, the question of the actual morality or immorality of those very so-called 'duties', a quiet perseverance in which is prescribed as the proper regimen—the little compliances and hypocrisies, the small concealments and strains of conscience, the eating of the meats offered to idols! Looking at the matter from this point of view, Clough finds by no means such comfort in the usual recipe for the doubter as he had acknowledged in the broader aphorism and the broader interpretation. He becomes impatient of it. It was not, indeed, till a somewhat later period, and after he had pondered the maxim on various sides in freer circumstances, that he put into words, in one of his poems, the following striking and subtle verdict upon it:

> *Action will furnish belief;* but will that belief be the true one?
> This is the point, you know. However, it doesn't much matter.
> What one wants, I suppose, is to predetermine the action,
> So as to make it entail, not a chance belief, but the true one.

There is something far more bitter in the following poem, written at the time when he was first turning the maxim round and round, and hearing from others and pronouncing to himself the word 'Duty' without having the benefit of a suitable working definition of it.

[Quotes entire poem beginning 'Duty—That's to say, complying With whate'er's expected here'.]

We do not know that in any of the poems Clough reaches a greater depth of sceptical sarcasm than this; but there are some later ones in which he indulges in a kind of playful irony, under which something of the same spirit is concealed.

As even in these pieces, where the sentiment is mocking or satirical, one can discern the writer's natural theistic faith inspiring the expression and giving it pungency, so the pieces which are truly most characteristic of Clough are those in which this positive or really religious faith avows itself more strongly and directly, and the strange truth is hinted, that it is jealousy for the purity of this faith, and nothing else, that is the actuating principle in what others would call his scepticism. Here, surely, is a prayer, the general solemnity of which so overtones the discords from common belief which the expert ear may nevertheless detect in it, that, if read in the diary of an old saint, it would seem not out of keeping:

[Quotes 'Qui Laborat, Orat'.]

On the whole, there is, perhaps, nothing in the volume so characteristic of Clough,—exhibiting so exactly the blending of the positive and the negative in his conclusions—as the following, dated 1845:—

[Quotes 'The New Sinai' (originally entitled 'When Israel Came out of Egypt') ll. 1–104: 'Lo, here is God' to 'wait it out, O Man!']

In the poems of subsequent date to this, passages may be found in which, sometimes the positive side of this speech, sometimes the negative part, may seem urged in greater proportion; but never through them all, as far as we have been able to see, is there any real recantation of the sum of the speech, or any advance beyond it. In other words, we have here, as in the tantamount parts of contemporary poems, that conclusion, or that generalization in matters of speculative theology, from which Clough never budged. He had found here— one may not call it, perhaps, his resting-place, but the platform on which it was to be his life to walk and wait. It was as if the last words we have quoted of the poem were addressed to himself, and he obeyed them punctually. And here is a peculiarity in Clough's intellectual career, as compared with the career suppositiously assigned to men of his class in most Art and Culture novels. The supposition is, that a man in his mental condition cannot rest in it—that, as by a law of the human constitution, he must go either backward or forward, in search of other ground, of a more definite footing. The supposition is that a man in this mental condition must walk incessantly to and fro as a maniac, till at length his paroxysm will be ungovernable, and he will overleap walls, so as to be caught and bound. Such is the almost invariable representation in the Art and Culture novels that treat of the phenomenon of modern scepticism; and there are instances in abundance in real history which seem to verify it. It may be questioned, however, whether, in the case of men who have once worked themselves exactly or nearly into Clough's speculative state, the representation is correct; and certainly in Clough's own case it does not hold true. On the contrary, a kind of resigned and humble satisfaction with that speculative state as the truest attainable, a kind of jealous watchfulness lest he should be lured or driven out of it, a kind of resolution never to go backward or forward from it, and to regard all promises of more definite certainty inducing him to do either as temptations of evil—this is what we see in Clough. As we have said, the very actuating principle of that which seemed and might be called his scepticism was his zeal for the purity of that which he conceived to be true religion. True religion with him consisted, it would seem, in the firm, resolute, unswerving conviction of the inscrutability of the Supreme. With the purity of this conviction, he seems to have thought, was bound up no one could tell what potency of varied intellectual and moral consequence for the human spirit. There were temptations from within and without to abandon it, and to clutch at systems and certainties; but, as all these proceeded on the assumption of the scrutability of that which had been declared to be inscrutable, it was man's never-ending duty to beware of them as nothing else than inclinations or baits to idolatry and Baalism. It is astonishing how explicitly this strange notion, perceptible in the pieces already quoted, is avowed in passages in the later poems; and the passages which do avow it are peculiarly noteworthy as revealing Clough's speculations in their essence. Here is one:—

> O Thou, in that mysterious shrine
> Enthroned, as we must say, divine!
> I will not frame one thought of what
> Thou mayest either be or not.
> I will not prate of 'thus' and 'so',
> And be profane with 'yes' and 'no',
> Enough that in our soul and heart
> Thou, whatsoe'er Thou may'st be, art.

The same contentedness 'not to know' is expressed and recommended more at large in one entire poem:—

[Quotes 'The Questioning Spirit'.]

Again, in the following passage in one of the long poems of the volume, where, if we suppose himself the speaker (as we must) he actually turns the tables upon those who insist upon the necessity of theological certainty, and bids Certainty avaunt as Humanity's evil genius:—

[Quotes *Amours de Voyage*, Canto V, ll. 95–112 'What with trusting myself' to 'while I can, will repel thee'.]

If we have dwelt so long among the poems illustrating the nature of Clough's speculative philosophy, it is because here a critic may hope to be of use in elucidating what is not quite patent; whereas, with respect to the rest of the volume, he can do little more than make extracts, or note what every reader will note for himself. But the proportions of things must not be mistaken. Necessary as it is to assign importance to Clough's speculative tendencies and conclusions, not only because they are the key to his life, but also because they really pervade his poetry in a latent manner, it must not be forgotten that Clough did not spend all his time in such 'thinking about thinking', but pretty soon packed his speculations up, as every poet is bound to do, into the form of a working and producing mind. Even in his Oxford time he was not always pondering 'the problem of the Universe'; he was reading, joining in sprightly talk, indulging in sweet bachelor fancies, taking splendid long walks, and enjoying vacation excursions. Mr. Palgrave tells us how 'during several summer vacations he had searched out the glens and heights, lakes and moors of Wales and Westmoreland and Scotland;' how such was his passion for natural beauty that, in describing any spot that had impressed him, his eyes would brighten and his voice soften at the remembrance; moreover, that 'to his enthusiasm for nature he united that other enthusiasm for energetic walks and venturesome wanderings, bathing, swimming, and out-of-doors existence in general which may perhaps be claimed as an impulse peculiarly English.' Accordingly, even among his earlier short poems there are some which testify to this range of his tastes and activities, and which are records of general feelings and impressions, or even small exercises of imagination on selected topics, rather than personal confessions or meditations.

It is, however, chiefly the poems written after his separation from Oxford—making about two-thirds of the contents of the present volume—that are of this general kind. The passing from the 'subjective' to the 'objective' (if we may venture once more on these ill-liked but not yet superseded phrases) in the style and aim of his poetry is, indeed, that which chiefly marks the epoch of his separation from Oxford. It was as if, considering the nature of the speculations which had so long been occupying him, and which it was now becoming desirable that he should have done with in that form, and should pack up into a faculty for working and producing, he saw that he could not complete the packing-up, or even honestly pack up at all, unless he transferred himself from Oxford, where there *are* local rules of contraband, to that more general world where everybody may go about with his packages and no one has a right to stop or examine them.

His farewell to Oxford, as Mr. Palgrave says, was his *Bothie of Tober-na-Vuolich*, published in the autumn of 1848. Here certainly was as healthy a burst as Goethe himself could have desired to see, out of the 'subjective' into the 'objective'. Who does not know *The Bothie*—in its form, a new feat in our literature, inasmuch as it really settled in the only true way, namely, by a capital example, the question, still argued, whether hexameter verse will do in English; in its matter, such a hearty and delightful story of the adventures of a reading party of young Oxonians, who have gone, with their tutor, to the Highlands for the long vacation, and, in particular, of the marriage theories of one of them, Philip Hewson, ending in his love for the demure Highland maiden Elspie, whom he at last marries and takes with him to New Zealand? Or, if there are any of our readers who do *not* yet know *The Bothie*, they are to be envied the pleasure which remains for them of a first acquaintance with it. It is as good as a month in the Highlands for oneself to read of those glorious young fellows there.

> How they had been to Iona, to Staffa, to Skye, to Culloden,
> Seen Loch Awe, Loch Tay, Loch Fyne, Loch Ness, Loch Arkaig,
> Been up Ben Nevis, Ben More, Ben Cruachan, Ben Muick-dhui;
> How they had walked, and eaten, and drunken, and slept in kitchens,
> Slept upon floors of kitchens, and tasted the real Glen-livat,
> Walked up perpendicular hills, and also down them,
> Hither and thither had been, and this and that had witnessed,
> Left not a thing to be done, and had not a copper remaining.

Evidently Clough threw into this poem a great deal of rich humorous substance that had been accumulating in him during his Oxford days—reminiscences of his own Highland excursions, literary impressions, and thoughts upon all things and sundry. One knows not whether to admire most the delight in open-air scenery and sports, and the power of describing them which the poem exhibits, or the power which it also exhibits of the brief and graphic hitting-off of physiognomy, costume, modes of thinking and character. And then the humour all through, the happy phrases, the surprises in the turns and variations of the hexameters, and the breaks of powerful feeling, high imagination, and the fine sense through the humorous medium. It would be too much to say that Clough had any special or pervading meaning of which he intended the poem as a whole to be the vehicle; but, so far as we may fix on anything of the kind, it is to be found doubtless in Hewson's Radical theories on the subject of women and their education. These theories are urged by Hewson himself in vehement protests against modern fine-ladyism, and enthusiastic pictures of what women might be if they would abandon boudoir, toilette, carriage, drawing-room and ball-room, and become once more natural and healthy beings, doing needful household work, or even milking the kine in the field, like Rachel, and watering cattle.

[Quotes *The Bothie*, II, ll. 34–67: 'Never I properly felt' to 'a prize carnation without it'.]

The rest of the Oxonians laugh at Philip's exaggerations, and chaff him; but one of them, Hobbes, the dreamy and corpulent, comes to his rescue, and, catching at an analogy that has been started in the course of talk, between architecture and feminine beauty, takes Philip's part, if only from the momentary fascination of this analogy. There shall be a Pugin of women, Hobbes declares; and Philip shall be the man.

[Quotes *The Bothie*, II, ll. 144–53; 'Philip shall write us a book' to 'Modern-Florid, modern-fine-lady?']

But all this chaffing and theorizing ends, as regards Philip, in his love for Elspie, in which what is good in his theories is carried out with no great shock to the conventionalities. In the love-making of Philip and Elspie there are some really noble passages.

The poem entitled *Amours de Voyage*, written in 1849, or about a year after *The Bothie*, is in the same English hexameter verse, with little interspersed specimens of English elegiacs in alternate hexameters and pentameters. There was, indeed, a natural affinity of Clough's scholarly genius for these classic forms of metre. But, on the other hand, while thus obeying an instinctive fondness for the disused forms of the classic metres, he seems to have had as decided an instinctive conviction that the *matter* in which a poet should deal should be contemporary circumstance, the things and men of his own day. The *Amours de Voyage*, at all events, is a thoroughly contemporary poem. The little Epilogue in elegiacs, appended to it, tells what is its general tenor, and when and where it was written.

So go forth to the world, to the good report and the evil!
  Go, little book! thy tale, is it not evil and good?
Go, and if strangers revile, pass quietly by without answer.
Go, and if curious friends ask of thy rearing and age,
  Say, 'I am flitting about many years from brain unto brain of
  Feeble and restless youths born to inglorious days:
But', so finish the word, 'I was writ in a Roman chamber,
  When from Janiculan heights thundered the cannon of France.'

In other words, the poem was written in Rome during the Mazzinian defence of that city and of the Roman Republic against the
French in 1849, and it is the expression of a number of miscellaneous
thoughts and feelings, such as may be supposed to have been flitting
about in the minds of restless youths in those days, through the medium
of the story of one such English youth, Claude, making the tour of
Italy, and at Rome casually thrown into the society of an English
family, and, against his will, falling in love with one of the girls. The
story, stragglingly told in the form of letters from Claude himself, or
from one or other of the girls, has no proper *dénouement*; and the
interest and the power of the poem lies in the passages of general
thought and feeling (one or two of which we have already quoted by
anticipation) and in the historical notes and allusions which it contains.
Here is Claude's first impression of Rome.

Rome disappoints me much; I hardly as yet understand, but
Rubbishy seems the word that most exactly would suit it.
All the foolish destructions, and all the sillier savings,
All the incongruous things of past incompatible ages,
Seem to be treasured up here to make fools of present and future.
Would to Heaven the old Goths had made a cleaner sweep of it!
Would to Heaven some new ones would come and destroy these churches!
However, one can live in Rome as also in London.
Rome is better than London, because it is other than London.

Again, going more into particulars with respect to Rome as the
seat of the Papacy—

[Quotes *Amours de Voyage*, Canto I, ll. 87–114: 'Luther, they say,
was unwise' to 'and thy clear stars, Galileo!'.]

But the most remarkable thing about the poem is the testimony
borne all through it to the nobleness of that Mazzinian defence of
Rome, and to the fine behaviour of the people in those last days of their
brief Republic.

Their brief Republic! Yes, though we are now apt to forget the fact, there *was*, in 1849, an independent Republic in the Roman States, instituted by the all but unanimous vote of the Roman people in their own legal parliament assembled, and maintained for a time without doing harm to anybody,—except perhaps the impalpable harm done to the genteel feelings of diplomatists, and fine personages like my Lord Normanby, disgusted that a new thing calling itself a Republic should dare to exist on an earth honoured by their temporary residence in it— till France sent her cannon to blow it to atoms, and Great Britain, sneaking in the wake of France in that blessed transaction, assured France privately through that identical Lord Normanby, then her Britannic Majesty's ambassador at Paris, that the suppression of the Republic, and 'the restoration of the Pope under an improved form of government' was an enterprise in which Britain wished France well, and her success in which would delight the British Protestant soul. Oh, we are a generous and a far-seeing nation! We are wise always at the right moment; we never make mistakes. What man among us, what newspaper, but now holds the doctrine of the necessary unity of Italy, exults in that doctrine, treats it as an axiom in European politics? And yet, methinks, as I write, I could count back, by not a great many months, to the time when, with ninety-nine out of every hundred even of our liberal public men, and with all our newspapers, or nearly all, this unity of Italy, now an axiom which it would be a shame to question, was a blackguard chimera, a mad dream of a few Italian idiots, Mazzini in their midst. Give me a pair of scissors and access to files of our leading newspapers, and I could fill sheets of letter-press with rather astonishing proofs to that effect, in the shape of extracts from the speeches and the articles of men who have now conveniently forgotten their own words, and flaunt in a rhetoric magnificently opposite. Oh, but we are a wise and generous people! We can change our views, accept blackguard chimeras, and still, to prove our consistency, go on reviling their authors and preachers, and calling them fools and blackguards, as we did before!

It is refreshing, we say, in the midst of all this, to turn back to what a man like Clough felt and said at the time and in the place. As an independent and cultured Englishman travelling in Italy, he was not a partisan. Italian politics were no particular concern of his. Possibly, he was rather bored with them, and with all that tumult of democracy, the worth of which he had doubtless estimated in the course of his historical readings. And so with his Claude in the poem. He represents him as rather a *blâsé* intellectual youth, cold and critical, wanting only to see the marbles and antiquities of Rome, and somewhat put about by the fact that the time of his visit chanced to be that of a patriotic tumult. But, being on the edge of such a tumult, he can look on and see; and what he sees with his own eyes he can report honestly, without caring whether it is what people at a distance want to have reported or not. Well, gradually, in the midst of the fighting Romans—of those Romans whom, with all the rest of the world, he had supposed to have no fighting stuff in them, and whom he is glad to see really having the pluck after all—in the midst of these Romans, manning their walls against the French, replying with cannon to the French cannon, and meeting the French at their gates, he begins himself to be stirred with the battle-spirit. Shall he get a horse and join them? No, it is no business of his; but, hang it! he almost wishes it were! For, if there is a wrong and a right in the world, they are thoroughly in the right in what they are doing; they are behaving splendidly, poor fellows; it does his heart good to hear that in this and that sally they have drubbed the Frenchmen. Let them write in the newspapers at home what they like about Rome being in a state of terrorism, in the hands of a few foreigners, Socialists, and Red-Republicans, who are actually selling the Roman works of art to the Yankees! It is not true; don't believe a word of it! He has himself, indeed, seen one priest, who was said to be trying to escape to the Neapolitans, murdered in the streets by the furious people. At least, he saw a great crowd, a scuffle in one part of it, hands raised, blows falling, and then, after a while, a man's legs in an unusual position. This he did see; it was a pity; but what of it?—you can't have a city in siege, and holy men sneaking out to the enemy, without such things happening! And how well the government behaves, condemning and discouraging all acts of the sort, so that the docile people are raised even above their instinct of vengeance, and, one or two such acts done and repented of, are really a marvel of good order!

> Ah, 'tis an excellent race,—and even in old degradation,
> Under a rule that enforces to flattery, lying, and cheating,
> E'en under Pope and Priest, a nice and natural people.
> Oh, could they but be allowed this chance of redemption!—but clearly
> This is not likely to be. Meantime, notwithstanding all journals,
> Honour for once to the tongue and the pen of the eloquent writer!
> Honour to speech! and all honour to thee, thou noble Mazzini!

Clough's writings during the rest of his life were not so numerous as might have been expected. . . . A labour of this portion of his life was his revision, published some time ago, of the old English translation of Plutarch; but with this exception, so far at least as there is indication in the present volume, his writings, not already named, consist only of a few short occasional pieces of verse, appended in the volume to the similar short pieces of earlier dates, and of a little metrical sketch and tales, composed but a month or two before his death, and printed at the end of the volume under the title of *Mari Magno*. Some of the short pieces have a peculiar wit and sprightliness, with a certain flavour of Burns and of Béranger perceptible in two or three of them. The Tales entitled *Mari Magno*—supposed to be stories told on board a steam-ship by one or two passengers to America—are in the plain, hard manner of Crabbe, with even a repetition, hardly to have been expected in Clough, of Crabbe's fault of distorting, sheerly for the rhyme's sake, the natural prose order of the words. In their kind, however, they are good; and they are interesting as being different from anything else of Clough's. The last of the three, called 'The Clergyman's Tale,' is particularly powerful in its execution and in its ethical purpose.

31. G. H. Lewes on *Poems* (1862) in *Cornhill Magazine*

September 1862, vi, 398–400

Lewes (1817–78), best known for his relationship with George Eliot and as the author of *The Life and Works of Goethe*, was also one of the most versatile critics of his time, his range including the drama, history, philosophy and numerous scientific subjects.

Certain books have an indirect interest, personal or historical, which renders them more attractive than many that are intrinsically better. The *Poems of Arthur Clough*, for example, claim but a very modest place as poems, but they are attractive as the writings of a man of sweet, sincere, sensitive nature, and of high culture. A poet he was not; neither by the grace of God, nor by the acquired cunning of ambitious culture, could he become a singer; and it is mere rhetorical evasion in his friendly biographer, to say that 'Clough *lived* his poem instead of writing it.' Yet the feeling which prompted this evasion suggests the source of interest we feel in this volume; it is the intense conviction, produced in friends, of some supreme excellence which Clough *might* have achieved, *ought* to have achieved, but somehow *did not*. In a word, he was one of the prospectuses which never become works: one of that class whose unwritten poems, undemonstrated discoveries, or untested powers, are confidently announced as certain to carry everything before them, when they appear. Only they never do appear. Sometimes attempts are made; they fail, and the failure is 'explained,' the attempts being repudiated as any real indication of the man's genuine powers. 'Under happier circumstances,' we are assured . . . as if the very seal and sign of genius were not precisely the regal superiority to circumstances, making them aids and ministers to success, instead of becoming their captive and slave!

We hear on many sides the freest scorn of all the imperfect workers who have at least done something; who have achieved some success, though not by faultless works; and this scorn is often uttered by men who announce an unknown paragon *about* to achieve great things. It is also curious to remark how very rarely the unknown man, who suddenly leaps into fame by a splendid deed, or by a noble work, was much believed in by his friends. The man of genius, even after he has proved his power, usually disappoints spectators. 'He looks so very different from what I should have expected.' His figure is unimposing; his head is so far from ideal; his trousers are decidedly ill-cut; and though perhaps there is no demonstrable relation between the cut of trousers and the intellectual power, somehow or other men cannot help feeling disappointed. And if this is the case *after* success, how much more so will it be before the genius has proved itself? . . . Had Arthur Clough never written a line, we could have better understood the expectations of his friends. But he has written enough to furnish a tolerably decisive estimate of his quality. As a man, he was doubtless loveable and loved; as a writer, he can claim but a very modest place. He was thoughtful and cultivated, and all thoughtful, cultivated minds will recognize this in his poems. They will also recognize a sincere and sensitive nature, shrinking from the rough and ready acquiescences of conventional beliefs, and withdrawing from the conflicts of life, conscious of being unfitted for them. But as to poetry, there is little or none. The nearest approach to poetry is perhaps in the following:—

[Quotes 'Qua Cursum Ventus'.]

We shall have misled the reader if he have understood us to say that this volume is only interesting as an example of the actual work achieved by a man who greatly impressed his friends. It is interesting, though less so, for its own sake. The verses are not good, but they are far from commonplace. They express real thoughts and real feelings, and in the *Bothie of Tober-na-Vuolich* there is considerable promise; for, in spite of its being exclusively a bit of Oxford-student life, in spite of its intentional imitations of Homer and Goethe, and its classical allusions, there is enough humour and fancy, and enough originality, to make it popular in a wider circle, and suggest that the writer, in ripening years, might have produced a remarkable work in prose. His later writings, however, are inferior to it.

32. Unsigned review, 'Arthur Hugh Clough' in *Church and State Review*

1 October 1862, i, 240–1

One of the most significant and the worst conceits of the time is its conceit of poetry. The rhapsodies of scepticism, unbelieving thoughts, blasphemous words—the thoughts dark and hopeless, the words obscure and twisted into all manner of unnatural and pedantic shapes—the very metres employed showing a restless craving after something new, and in their happiest use falling harsh and rugged on the English ear: this is some account of a good deal of what goes by the name of poetry in England now.

There is a great deal of this sort of stuff in the 'poems' of Arthur Hugh Clough. Now the intellectual life of many of us has its period of doubt. There comes a time when the world seems a painful enigma—a labyrinth devoid of clue. In the mind of Arthur Clough this state was unhappily permanent: and there seems little reason to suppose that, had he lived longer, he would have escaped from it. Not only was he perplexed by 'the riddle of the universe,' but by questions of practical life. His motto to the *Amour de Voyage*,—'*Il doutait de tout, même de l'amour,*'—furnishes the key to his nature. He was a poetical casuist. *Amours de Voyage*, the longest of his recent poems, relates in prolix hexameters how a loiterer in Italy met an English girl there, fancied himself in love with her, but was by no means sure of it; and finally, losing sight of her by the accidents of travel, gave her up with perfect calmness. Thus writes Claude, the hero, to his friend Eustace:—

After all, do I know that I really cared about her?

*   *   *

Do nothing more, good Eustace, I pray you. It only will vex me.
Take no measures. Indeed, should we meet, I could not be certain;
All might be changed, you know. Or perhaps there was nothing to be changed.

Really Miss Mary Trevellyn might think herself fortunate in escaping from so very indecisive a lover. Although *Amours de Voyage* contains some fine passages, the subject is quite unworthy of poetic treatment; and we soon weary of reading the letters of a gentleman whose chief characteristics are unbelief and weakness of will. To quote Mr. Tennyson's noble lines:—

> He seems as one whose footsteps halt,
> Toiling in immeasurable sand.[1]

Clough's Pyrrhonism was inalienable from his temperament; and, as his hero doubted of the love between man and woman, so the poet doubted of that greater love on which the universe depends. In most of his minor poems this theme is dominant. Take *The Questioning Spirit*:—

[Quotes ll. 12–25: 'Dost thou not know' to 'I will do my duty, said the last'.]

This final line may be taken as an embodiment of Clough's creed. Having framed and fixed for himself the lowest conception of duty' he never went farther. He never escaped from this 'true ignorance., He always 'did his duty' well, and seems to have enjoyed life in his way, and made many friends; but he had nothing in the way of belief save that—

> We are such stuff
> As dreams are made on, and our little life
> Is rounded with a sleep.

Some of his lyrics, written at sea, have by their vague suggestiveness an attraction for morbid and unhealthy tempers.

> Where lies the land to which the ship would go?
> Far, far ahead, is all her seamen know.
> And where the land she travels from? Away,
> Far, far behind, is all that they can say.

Here the mystery of ocean is made to indicate that mystery of the universe which always perplexed the poet, haunting his most serene moments. The same feeling runs through another melancholy and musical lyric, whence we quote one stanza:—

> Come home, come home! And where a home hath he
> Whose ship is driving o'er the driving sea?
> Through clouds that mutter, and o'er waves that roar,
> Say, shall we find, or shall we not, a shore
> That is, as is not ship or ocean foam,
> Indeed our home?

[1] 'Will', ll. 15–16.

Clough's scepticism ran through all his actions, and he may fairly be said to have mistaken his vocation. By nature he was a poet, as *The Bothie of Toper-na-Fuosich* suffices to prove; but he surrendered himself to dull forms of labour, and his last literary work was a careful revision of Dryden's *Plutarch*. Comparing his later poems with the immortal *Bothie*, we find with regret that the life of the man was withering away in him. That poem, simple as Wordsworth, idyllic as Theocritus or Goethe, full of the joyous spirit of young Oxford men, fresh with the cool breezes of the Highland hills in autumn, is unique in English literature. It is not too much to say that in mere originality it transcends all the writings of Mrs. Browning, and Mr. Tennyson. There is an almost Homeric freedom in it. Its hero, Philip Hewson, is to some extent a reflection of the author. Chartist and poet, with paradoxical notions about the duties of women, and with a tendency to fancy himself in love with every pretty face he encounters, he is only saved from a life of indecision and flirtation by meeting a young lady with somewhat stronger will than his own. Elspie, a Highland lassie, supplies the element wanting in Philip's character. The story is delightfully told. Although we do not agree with Mr. Palgrave that Clough inherited a double portion of Wordsworth's spirit, we admit that he was *almost* as true and hearty a lover of nature as the greater poet.

Clough's humour and subtlety are not inferior to his picturesqueness: the love-scenes between Elspie and Philip are very subtle and beautiful. When she compares herself to one side of the arch of a bridge, building itself up slowly and toilfully to meet another from the other bank—till 'a great invisible hand' drops the keystone, and produces 'a queer happy sense of completeness'—the idea is so good that we do not pause to inquire whether Highland lassies often have such notions when they are sweethearting. The same may be said of her comparison of Philip to the sea, and herself to a 'quiet stream of inland water,' forced to mingle with the tyrannous tide. If the daughters of Highland blacksmiths talk in this poetico-metaphysical style, wooing must be no joke in the braes of Lochabar.

The fastidiousness which naturally grew upon a man of Clough's peculiar character led him to make many unnecessary alterations in the *Bothie*. He changed its title because 'Toper-na-Fuosich' has some ludicrous meaning. He eliminated some of the slang, which gives so truthful an air to the poem. It is a great mistake for a man at forty to think he can improve a poem written before he was thirty. He may make it more elegant and accurate, but every touch will decrease its freshness and vigour. In Clough's case this was particularly true, for the buoyancy of his youth departed too soon, leaving only a sentimental melancholy.

Clough's politics were as indefinite as his theology, but with a touch of republicanism in them. He thought the United States 'the happiest country going,' not having lived to see the tragical end of its greatness. Writing the *Amours de Voyage* at Rome, in 1848, he exclaims—

Honour to speech, and all honour to thee, thou noble Mazzini!

This is not the place to discuss the amount of honour due to Mazzini; but it may be observed that English journalists are in much confusion of thought in regard to the relations of Mazzini, Garibaldi, Victor Emmanuel, and Louis Napoleon. At the commencement of any of Garibaldi's wild enterprises our liberal journals gravely remonstrate with him for attempting to unsettle the Italian people. When he succeeds they write him down a hero who always embraces a just cause, and is always triumphant. When he fails they are in much distress to know what is to be done with him.

Clough was very fond of the hexameter, and has written many that are as good as such lines can be in English; but he was too careless in the use of the metre to do much towards its naturalisation. His last poem is entitled *Mari Magno*, and consists of a series of tales supposed to be told on shipboard. They are very much in Crabbe's manner; one of them, 'The Clergyman's Tale', is very beautiful, and shows that the poet's conscience was still tender. Beautiful also is an interlude— 'Currente calamo'—whence we quote the opening lines:—

[Quotes 1–20: 'Quick, painter, quick' to 'full of Southern grace'.]

His biographer tells us that he was 'signalized and authenticated as a true Man by the broad seal of Nobleness.' This is, we suppose, what is called 'fine writing.' What it may mean we do not profess to know; and, having belief in Revelation, it is, perhaps, not possible that we should. We are afraid that it is the scepticism of Mr. Clough rather than his 'poetry' which has been his chief recommendation to some of his principal admirers.

There is an English line worth all the hexameters of Mr. Clough's 'poetry,'—

No very great wit, he believed in a GOD.

33. Walter Bagehot, 'Mr. Clough's Poems' in *National Review*

October 1862, xiii, 310–26

Bagehot (1826–77) was a barrister, an economist and a copious writer on literary and social questions. From 1860 till his death he was editor of the *Economist*; his book, *The English Constitution* is a standard work.

No one can be more rigid than we are in our rules as to the publication of remains and memoirs. It is very natural that the friends of a cultivated man who seemed about to do something, but who died before he did it, should desire to publish to the world the grounds of their faith, and the little symptoms of his immature excellence. But though they act very naturally, they act very unwisely. In the present state of the world there are too many half-excellent people: there is a superfluity of persons who have all the knowledge, all the culture, all the requisite taste,—all the tools, in short, of achievement, but who are deficient in the latent impulse and secret vigour which alone can turn such instruments to account. They have all the outward and visible signs of future success; they want the invisible spirit, which can only be demonstrated by trial and victory. Nothing, therefore, is more tedious or more worthless than the posthumous delineation of the possible successes of one who did not succeed. The dreadful remains of nice young persons which abound among us prove almost nothing as to the future fate of those persons if they had survived. We can only tell that any one is a man of genius by his having produced some work of genius. Young men must practise themselves in youthful essays; and to some of their friends these may seem works not only of fair promise, but of achieved excellence. The cold world of critics and readers will not, however, think so; that world well understands the distinction between promise and performance, and sees that these laudable *juvenilia* differ from good books as much as legitimate bills of exchange differ from actual cash.

If we did not believe that Mr. Clough's poems, or at least several of them, had real merit, not as promissory germs, but as completed performances, it would not seem to us to be within our province to notice them. Nor if Mr. Clough were now living among us, would he wish us to do so. The marked peculiarity, and, so to say, the *flavour* of his mind, was a sort of truthful scepticism, which made him anxious never to overstate his own assurance of anything; disinclined him to overrate the doings of his friends; and absolutely compelled him to underrate his own past writings, as well as his capability for future literary success. He could not have borne to have his poems reviewed with 'nice remarks' and sentimental epithets of insincere praise. He was equal to his precept:

> Where are the great, whom thou wouldst wish to praise thee?
> Where are the pure, whom thou wouldst choose to love thee?
> Where are the brave, to stand supreme above thee,
> Whose high commands would cheer, whose chiding raise thee?
> Seek, seeker, in thyself; submit to find
> In the stones bread, and life in the blank mind.
>
> [*Dipsychus*, IV, 122–7, *Poems* (1951)]

To offer petty praise and posthumous compliments to a stoic of this temper is like buying sugar-plums for St. Simon Stylites. We venture to write an article on Mr. Clough, because we believe that his poems depict an intellect in a state which is always natural 'to such a being as man in such a world as the present,' which is peculiarly natural to us just now; and because we believe that many of these poems are very remarkable for true vigour and artistic excellence, although they certainly have several defects and shortcomings, which would have been lessened, if not removed, if their author had lived longer and had written more.

In a certain sense there are two great opinions about everything. There are so about the universe itself. The world as we know it is this. There is a vast, visible, indisputable sphere, of which we never lose the consciousness, of which no one seriously denies the existence, about the most important part of which most people agree tolerably and fairly. On the other hand, there is the invisible world, about which men are not agreed at all, which all but the faintest minority admit to exist somehow and somewhere, but as to the nature of locality of which there is no efficient popular demonstration; there is no such compulsory argument as will *force* the unwilling conviction of any one disposed to denial. As our minds rise, as our knowledge enlarges, as our wisdom grows, as our instincts deepen, our conviction of this invisible world is daily strengthened, and our estimate of its nature is continually improved. But—and this is the most striking peculiarity of the whole subject—the more we improve, the higher we rise, the nobler we conceive the unseen world which is in us and about us, in which we live and move, the more unlike that world becomes to the world which we *do* see. The divinities of Olympus were in a very plain and intelligible sense part and parcel of this earth; they were better specimens than could be found below, but they belonged to extant species; they were better editions of visible existences; they were like the heroines whom young men imagine after the young ladies of their vicinity—they were better and handsomer, but they were of the same sort; they had never been seen, but they might have been seen any day. So too of the God with whom the Patriarch wrestled: he might have been wrestled with even if he was not; he was that sort of person. If we contrast with these the God of whom Christ speaks—the God who has not been seen at any time, whom no man hath seen or can see, who is infinite in nature, whose ways are past finding out, the transition is palpable. We have passed from gods— from an invisible world which is similar to, which is a *natural appendix* to, the world in which we live,—and we have come to believe in an invisible world, which is altogether unlike that which we see, which is certainly not opposed to our experience, but is altogether beyond and unlike our experience; which belongs to another set of things altogether; which is, as we speak, transcendental. The 'possible' of early barbarism is like the reality of early barbarism; the 'may be', the 'great perhaps', of late civilisation, is most unlike the earth, whether barbaric or civilised.

Two opinions as to the universe naturally result from this fundamental contrast. There are plenty of minds like that of Voltaire, who have simply no sense or perception of the invisible world whatever, who have no ear for religion, who are in the technical sense unconverted, whom no conceivable process could convert without altering what to bystanders and ordinary observers is their identity. They are, as a rule, acute, sensible, discerning, and humane; but the first observation which the most ordinary person would make as to them is, that they are 'limited'; they understand palpable existence; they elaborate it, and beautify and improve it; but an admiring bystander who can do none of these things, who can beautify nothing, who, if he tried, would only make what is ugly uglier, is conscious of a latent superiority which he can hardly help connecting with his apparent inferiority. We cannot write Voltaire's sentences; we cannot make things as clear as he made them; but we do not much care for our deficiency. Perhaps we think 'things ought not to be so plain as all that.' There is a hidden, secret, unknown side to this universe, which these picturesque painters of the visible, these many-handed manipulators of the palpable, are not aware of, which would spoil their dexterity if it were displayed to them. Sleep-walkers can tread safely on the very edge of any precipice; but those who see, cannot. On the other hand, there are those whose minds have not only been converted, but in some sense *inverted*. They are so occupied with the invisible world as to be absorbed in it entirely; they have no true conception of that which stands plainly before them; they never look coolly at it, and are cross with those who do; they are wrapt up in their own faith as to an unseen existence; they rush upon mankind with, 'Ah, there it is! there it is!— don't you see it?' and so incur the ridicule of an age.

The best of us try to avoid both fates. We strive, more or less, to 'make the best of both worlds.' We know that the invisible world cannot be duly discerned, or perfectly appreciated. We know that we see as in a glass darkly; but still we look on the glass. We frame to ourselves some image which we know to be incomplete, which probably is in part untrue, which we try to improve day by day, of which we do not deny the defects,—but which nevertheless is our 'all' which we hope, when the accounts are taken, may be found not utterly *unlike* the unknown reality. This is, as it seems, the best religion for finite beings, living, if we may say so, on the very edge of two dissimilar worlds, on the very line on which the infinite, unfathomable sea surges up, and just where the queer little bay of this world ends. We count the pebbles on the shore, and image to ourselves as best we may the secrets of the great deep.

There are, however, some minds (and of these Mr. Clough's was one) which will not accept what appears to be an intellectual destiny. They struggle against the limitations of mortality, and will not condescend to use the natural and needful aids of human thought. They will not *make their image*. They struggle after an 'actual abstract.' They feel, and they rightly feel, that every image, every translation, every mode of conception by which the human mind tries to place before itself the Divine mind, is imperfect, halting, changing. They feel, from their own experience, that there is no one such mode of representation which will suit their own minds at all times, and they smile with bitterness at the notion that they could contrive an image which will suit all other minds. They could not become fanatics or missionaries, or even common preachers, without forfeiting their natural dignity, and foregoing their very essence. To cry in the streets, to uplift their voice in Israel, to be 'pained with hot thoughts,' to be 'preachers of a dream,' would reverse their whole cast of mind. It would metamorphose them into something which omits every striking trait for which they were remarked, and which contains every trait for which they were not remarked. On the other hand, it would be quite as opposite to their whole nature to become followers of Voltaire. No one knows more certainly and feels more surely that there is an invisible world, than those very persons who decline to make an image or representation of it, who shrink with a nervous horror from every such attempt when it is made by any others. All this inevitably leads to what common practical people term a 'curious' sort of mind. You do not know how to describe these 'universal negatives,' as they seem to be. They will not fall into place in the ordinary intellectual world any how. If you offer them any known religion, they 'won't have that;' if you offer them no religion, they will not have that either; if you ask them to accept a new and as yet unrecognised religion, they altogether refuse to do so. They seem not only to believe in an 'unknown God,' but in a God whom no man can ever know. Mr. Clough has expressed, in a sort of lyric, what may be called their essential religion.

[Quotes 'ὕμνος ἄυμνος' ('A hymn, yet not a hymn'), 1–24: 'O Thou whose image' to 'whatso'er Thou mayst be, art'.]

It was exceedingly natural that Mr. Clough should incline to some such creed as this, with his character and in his circumstances. He had by nature, probably, an exceedingly real mind, in the good sense of that expression and the bad sense. The actual visible world as it was, and he saw it, exercised over him a compulsory influence. The hills among which he had wandered, the cities he had visited, the friends whom he knew,—these were his world. Many minds of the poetic sort easily melt down these palpable facts into some impalpable ether of their own. To such a mind as Shelley's the 'solid earth' is an immaterial fact; it is not even a cumbersome difficulty—it is a preposterous imposture. Whatever may exist, all that *clay* does not exist; it would be too absurd to think so. Common persons can make nothing of this dreaminess; and Mr. Clough, though superficial observers set him down as a dreamer, could not make much either. To him, as to the mass of men, the vulgar outward world was a primitive fact. 'Taxes *is* true,' as the miser said. Reconcile what you have to say with green peas, for green peas are certain; such was Mr. Clough's idea. He could not dissolve the world into credible ideas and then believe those ideas, as many poets have done. He could not catch up a creed, as ordinary men do. He had a *straining*, inquisitive, critical mind; he scrutinised every idea before he took it in; he did not allow the moral forces of life to act as they should; he was not content to gain a belief 'by going on living.' He said,

> Action *will furnish belief:* but will that belief be the true one?
> This is the point, you know.
>
> [*Amours*, V, 20–1]

He felt the coarse facts of the plain world so thoroughly, that he could not readily take in anything which did not seem in accordance with them and like them. And what common idea of the invisible world seems in the least in accordance with them or like them?

A journal-writer, in one of his poems, has expressed this:

[Quotes *Amours de Voyage*, V, 86–103: 'Comfort has come to me here' to 'thou subtle, fanatical tempter!'.]

Mr. Clough's fate in life had been such as to exaggerate this naturally peculiar tempter. He was a pupil of Arnold's; one of his best, most susceptible, and favourite pupils. Some years since there was much doubt and interest as to the effect of Arnold's teaching. His sudden death, so to say, cut his life in the middle, and opened a tempting discussion as to the effect of his teaching when those taught by him should have become men and not boys. The interest which his own character then awakened, and must always awaken, stimulated the discussion, and there was much doubt about it. But now we need doubt no longer. The Rugby 'men' are *real* men, and the world can pronounce its judgment. Perhaps that part of the world which cares for such things has pronounced it. Dr. Arnold was almost indisputably an admirable master for a common English boy,—the small, apple-eating animal whom we know. He worked, he pounded, if the phrase be used, into the boy a belief, or at any rate a floating, confused conception, that there are great subjects, that there are strange problems, that knowledge has an indefinite value, that life is a serious and solemn thing. The influence of Arnold's teaching upon the majority of his pupils was probably very vague, but very good. To impress on the ordinary Englishman a general notion of the importance of what is intellectual and the reality of what is supernatural, is the greatest benefit which can be conferred upon him. The common English mind is too coarse, sluggish, and worldly to take such lessons too much to heart. It is improved by them in many ways, and is not harmed by them at all. But there are a few minds which are very likely to think too much of such things. A susceptible, serious, intellectual boy may be injured by the incessant inculcation of the awfulness of life and the magnitude of great problems. It is not desirable to take this world too much *au sérieux*; most persons will not; and the one in a thousand who will, should not—Mr. Clough was one of those who will. He was one of Arnold's favourite pupils, because he gave heed so much to Arnold's teaching; and exactly because he gave heed to it was it bad for him. He required quite another sort of teaching: to be told to take things easily; not to try to be wise overmuch; to be 'something beside critical;' to go on living quietly and obviously, and see what truth would come to him. Mr. Clough had to his latest years what may be noticed in others of Arnold's disciples,—a fatigued way of looking at great subjects. It seemed as if he had been put into them before his time, had seen through them, heard all which could be said about them, had been bored by them, and had come to want something else.

A still worse consequence was, that the faith, the doctrinal teaching which Arnold impressed on the youths about him was one personal to Arnold himself, which arose out of the peculiarities of his own character, which can only be explained by them. As soon as an inquisitive mind was thrown into a new intellectual atmosphere, and was obliged to naturalise itself in it, to consider the creed it had learned with reference to the facts which it encountered and met, much of that creed must fade away. There were inevitable difficulties in it, which only the personal peculiarities of Arnold prevented his perceiving, and which everyone else must soon perceive. The new intellectual atmosphere into which Mr. Clough was thrown was peculiarly likely to have this disenchanting effect. It was the Oxford of Father Newman; an Oxford utterly different from Oxford as it is, or from the same place as it had been twenty years before. A complete estimate of that remarkable thinker cannot be given here; it would be no easy task even now, many years after his influence has declined, nor is it necessary for the present purpose. Two points are quite certain of Father

Newman, and they are the only two which are at present material. He was undeniably a consummate master of the difficulties in the creeds of other men. With a profoundly religious organisation which was hard to satisfy, with an imagination which could not help setting before itself simply and exactly what different creeds would come to and mean in life, with an analysing and most subtle intellect which was sure to detect the weak point in an argument if a weak point there was, with a manner at once grave and fascinating,—he was a nearly perfect religious disputant, whatever may be his deficiencies as a religious teacher. The most accomplished theologian of another faith would have looked anxiously to the joints of his harness before entering the lists with an adversary so prompt and keen. To suppose that a youth fresh from Arnold's teaching, with a hasty faith in a scheme of thought radically inconsistent, should be able to endure such an encounter was absurd. Arnold flattered himself that he was a principal opponent of Mr. Newman; but he was rather a principal fellow-labourer. There was but one quality in a common English boy which would have enabled him to resist such a reasoner as Mr. Newman. We have a heavy apathy on exciting topics, which enables us to leave dilemmas unsolved, to forget difficulties, to go about our pleasure or our business, and to leave the reasoner to pursue his logic: 'any how he is very *long*'—*that* we comprehend. But it was exactly this happy apathy, this commonplace indifference, that Arnold prided himself on removing. He objected strenuously to Mr. Newman's creed, but he prepared anxiously the very soil in which that creed was sure to grow. A multitude of such minds as Mr. Clough's, from being Arnoldites, became Newmanites. A second quality in Mr. Newman is at least equally clear. He was much better skilled in finding out the difficulties of other men's creed than in discovering and starting a distinct basis for his own. In most of his characteristic works he does not even attempt it. His argument is essentially an argument *ad hominem*; an argument addressed to the present creed of the person with whom he is reasoning. He says: 'Give up what you hold already, or accept what I now say; for that which you already hold involves it.' Even in books where he is especially called on to deal with matters of a first principle, the result is unsatisfactory. We have heard it said that he has in later life accounted for the argumentative vehemence of his book *against* the Church of Rome by saying: 'I did it as a duty; I *put* myself into a state of mind to write that book.' And this is just the impression which his arguments give. His elementary principles seem *made*, not born.

Very likely he would admit the fact, and yet defend his practice. He would say:

Such a being as man is, in such a world as this is, *must* do so; he must make a venture for his religion; he may see a greater probability that the doctrine of the Church is true than that it is false; he may see before he believes in her that she has greater evidence than any other creed; but he must do the rest for himself. *By means of his will* he must put himself into a new state of mind; he must cast in his lot with the Church here and hereafter; *then* his belief will gradually strengthen; he will in time become sure of what she says.

He undoubtedly in the time of his power persuaded many young men to try some such process as this. The weaker, the more credulous and the more fervent, were able to persevere; those who had not distinct perceptions of real truth, who were dreamy and fanciful by nature, persevered without difficulty. But Mr. Clough could not do so; he felt it was 'something factitious.' He began to speak of the 'ruinous force of the will,' and 'our terrible notions of duty.' He ceased to be a Newmanite.

Thus Mr. Clough's career and life were exactly those most likely to develop and foster a morbid peculiarity of his intellect. He had, as we have explained, by nature an unusual difficulty in forming a creed as to the unseen world; he could not get the visible world out of his head; his strong grasp of plain facts and obvious matters was a difficulty to him; too easily one great teacher inculcated a remarkable creed; then another great teacher took it away; then this second teacher made him believe for a time some of his own artificial faith; then it would not do. He fell back on that vague, impalpable, unembodied religion which we have attempted to describe.

He has himself given in a poem [*Amours de Voyages:*] now first published,[1] a very remarkable description of this curious state of mind. He has prefixed to it the characteristic motto, '*Il doutait de tout, même de l'amour.*' It is the delineation of a certain love-passage in the life of a hesitating young gentleman, who was in Rome at the time of the revolution of 1848; who could not make up his mind about the revolution, who could not make up his mind whether he liked Rome, who could not make up his mind whether he liked the young lady, who let her go away without him, who went in pursuit of her, and could not make out which way to look for her, who, in fine, has some sort of

---

[1] i.e. in England: Bagehot was evidently ignorant of its publication in the *Atlantic Monthly* in 1858.

religion, but cannot himself tell what it is. The poem was not published in the author's lifetime,[1] and there are some lines which we are persuaded he would have further polished, and some parts which he would have improved, if he had seen them in print. It is written in conversational hexameters, in a tone of semi-satire and half-belief. Part of the commencement is a good example of them:

[Quotes *Amours*, I, 13–50: 'Rome disappoints me much' to 'the Tourist may answer'.]

As he goes on, he likes Rome rather better, but hazards the following imprecation on the Jesuits:

[Quotes *Amours*, I, 101–14: 'Luther, they say, was unwise' to 'and thy clear stars, Galileo!'.]

The plot of the poem is very simple, and certainly is not very exciting. The moving force, as in most novels of verse or prose, is the love of the hero for the heroine; but this love assuredly is not of a very impetuous and overpowering character. The interest of this story is precisely that it is not overpowering. The over-intellectual hero, over-anxious to be composed, will not submit himself to his love; over-fearful of what is voluntary and factitious, he will not make an effort and cast in his lot with it. He states his view of the subject better than we can state it:

[Quotes *Amours*, II, 252–83: 'I am in love, meantime' to 'And love be its own inspiration?'.]

It appears, however, that even this hesitating hero would have come to the point at last. In a book, at least, the hero has nothing else to do. The inevitable restrictions of a pretty story hem him in; to wind up the plot, he must either propose or die, and usually he prefers proposing. Mr. Claude, for such is the name of Mr. Clough's hero, is evidently on his road towards the inevitable alternative, when his fate intercepts him by the help of a person who meant nothing less. There is a sister of the heroine, who is herself engaged to a rather quick person, and who cannot make out anyone's conducting himself differently from her George Vernon. She writes:

> Mr. Claude, you must know, is behaving a little bit better;
> He and Papa are great friends; but he really is too *shilly-shally*,—
> So unlike George! Yet I hope that the matter is going on fairly.

[1] See footnote on previous page.

> I shall, however, get George, before he goes, to say something.
> Dearest Louise, how delightful to bring young people together!

As the heroine says, 'dear Georgina' wishes for nothing so much as to show her adroitness. George Vernon does interfere, and Mr. Claude may describe for himself the change it makes in his fate:

[Quotes *Amours*, III, 214–39: 'Tiber is beautiful too' to 'to reinstate Pope and Tourist', and 268–92: 'Yes, on Montorio's height' to 'this time it shall not be a failure'.]

But, of course, he does not reach Florence till the heroine and her family are gone; and he hunts after them through North Italy, not very skilfully, and then he returns to Rome; and he reflects, certainly not in a very dignified or heroic manner:

[Quotes *Amours*, V, 141–80: 'I cannot stay at Florence' to 'if you love me, forbear interfering'.]

And the heroine, like a sensible, quiet girl, sums up:

> You have heard nothing; of course, I know you can have heard nothing.
> Ah, well, more than once I have broken my purpose, and sometimes,
> Only too often, have looked for the little lake-steamer to bring him.
> But it is only fancy,—I do not really expect it.
> Oh, and you see I know so exactly how he would take it:
> Finding the chances prevail against meeting again, he would banish
> Forthwith every thought of the poor little possible hope, which
> I myself could not help, perhaps, thinking only too much of;
> He would resign himself, and go. I see it exactly.
> So I also submit, although in a different manner.
> Can you not really come? We go very shortly to England.

And there let us hope she found a more satisfactory lover and husband.

The same defect which prevented Mr. Claude from obtaining his bride will prevent this poem from obtaining universal popularity. The public like stories which come to something; Mr. Arnold teaches that a great poem must be founded on a great action, and this one is founded on a long inaction. But Art has many mansions. Many poets, whose cast of thought unfits them for very diffused popularity, have yet a concentrated popularity which suits them, and which lasts. Henry Taylor has wisely said 'that a poet does not deserve the name who would not rather be read a thousand times by one man, than a single time by a thousand.' This repeated perusal, this testing by continual repetition and close contact, is the very test of intellectual poetry;

unless such poetry can identify itself with our nature, and dissolve itself into our constant thought, it is nothing, or less than nothing; it is an ineffectual attempt to confer a rare pleasure; it teazes by reminding us of that pleasure, and tires by the effort which it demands from us. But if a poem really possess this capacity of intellectual absorption—if it really is in matter of fact accepted, apprehended, delighted in, and retained by a large number of cultivated and thoughtful minds,—its non-recognition by what is called the public is no more against it than its non-recognition by the coal-heavers. The half-educated and busy crowd, whom we call the public, have no more right to impose their limitations on highly educated and meditative thinkers, than the uneducated and yet more numerous crowd have to impose their still narrower limitations on the half-educated. The coal-heaver will not read any books whatever; the mass of men will not read an intellectual poem: it can hardly ever be otherwise. But timid thinkers must not dread to have a secret and rare faith. Little deep poetry is very popular, and *no* severe art. Such poetry as Mr. Clough's, especially, can never be so; its subjects would forbid it, even if its treatment were perfect: but it may have a better fate; it may have a tenacious hold on the solitary, the meditative, and the calm. It is this which Mr. Clough would have wished; he did not desire to be liked by 'inferior people'—at least he would have distrusted any poem of his own which they did like.

The artistic skill of these poems, especially of the poem from which we have extracted so much, and of a long-vacation pastoral published in the Highlands, is often excellent, and occasionally fails when you least expect it. There was an odd peculiarity in Mr. Clough's mind; you never could tell whether it was that he would not show himself to the best advantage, or whether he *could* not; it is certain that he very often did not, whether in life or in books. His intellect moved with a great difficulty, and it had a larger inertia than any other which we have ever known. Probably there was an awkwardness born with him, and his shyness and pride prevented him from curing that awkwardness as most men would have done. He felt he might fail, and he knew that he hated to fail. He neglected, therefore, many of the thousand petty trials which fashion and form the accomplished man of the world. Accordingly, when at last he wanted to do something, or was obliged to attempt something, he had occasionally a singular difficulty. He could not get his matter out of him.

In poetry he had a further difficulty, arising from perhaps an over-

cultivated taste. He was so good a disciple of Wordsworth, he hated
so thoroughly the common sing-song metres of Moore and Byron,
that he was apt to try to write what will seem to many persons to
have scarcely a metre at all. It is quite true that the metre of intellectual
poetry should not be so pretty as that of songs, or so plain and impressive as that of vigorous passion. The rhythm should pervade it and
animate it, but should not protrude itself upon the surface, or intrude
itself upon the attention. It should be a latent charm, though a real
one. Yet though this doctrine is true, it is nevertheless, a dangerous
doctrine. Most writers need the strict fetters of familiar metre; as soon
as they are emancipated from this, they fancy that *any* words of theirs
are metrical. If a man will read any expressive and favourite words of
his own often enough, he will come to believe that they are rhythmical;
probably they have a rhythm as he reads them; but no notation of
pauses and accents could tell the reader how to read them in that manner; and when read in any other mode they may be prose itself. Some
of Mr. Clough's early poems, which are placed at the beginning of this
volume, are perhaps examples of more or less of this natural self-
delusion. Their writer could read them as verse, but that was scarcely
his business; and the common reader fails.

Of one metre, however, the hexameter, we believe the most accomplished judges, and also common readers, agree that Mr. Clough
possessed a very peculiar mastery. Perhaps he first showed in English
its *flexibility*. Whether any consummate poem of great length and
sustained dignity can be written in this metre, and in our language, we
do not know. Until a great poet has written his poem, there are commonly no lack of plausible arguments that seem to prove he cannot
write it; but Mr. Clough has certainly shown that in the hands of a
skilful and animated artist it is capable of adapting itself to varied
descriptions of life and manners, to noble sentiments, and to changing
thoughts. It is perhaps the most flexible of English metres. Better than
any others it changes from grave to gay without desecrating what should
be solemn, or disenchanting that which should be graceful. And Mr.
Clough was the first to prove this, by writing a noble poem, in which
it was done.

In one principal respect Mr. Clough's two poems in hexameters,
and especially the Roman one, from which we made so many extracts, are very excellent. Somehow or other he makes you understand what the people of whom he is writing precisely were. You may
object to the means, but you cannot deny the result. By fate he was

thrown into a vortex of theological and metaphysical speculation, but his genius was better suited to be the spectator of a more active and moving scene. The play of mind upon mind; the contrasted view which contrasted minds take of great subjects; the odd irony of life which so often thrusts into conspicuous places exactly what no one would expect to find in those places,—these were his subjects. Under happy circumstances he might have produced on such themes something which the mass of readers would have greatly liked; as it is, he has produced a little which meditative readers will much value, and which they will long remember.

Of Mr. Clough's character it would be out of place to say anything, except in so far as it elucidates his poems. The sort of conversation for which he was most remarkable rises again in the *Amours de Voyage*, and gives them to those who knew him in life a very peculiar charm. It would not be exact to call its best lines a pleasant cynicism; for cynicism has a bad name, and the ill-nature and other offensive qualities which have given it that name were utterly out of Mr. Clough's way. Though without much fame, he had no envy. But he had a strong realism. He saw what it is considered cynical to see—the absurdities of many persons, the pomposities of many creeds, the splendid zeal with which missionaries rush on to teach what they do not know, the wonderful earnestness with which most incomplete solutions of the universe are thrust upon us as complete and satisfying. '*Le fond de la Providence*,' says the French novelist, '*c'est l'ironie*.'[1] Mr. Clough would not have said that; but he knew what it meant, and what was the portion of truth contained in it. Undeniably this *is* an *odd* world, whether it should have been so or no; and all our speculations upon it should begin with some admission of its strangeness and singularity. The habit of dwelling on such thoughts as these will not of itself make a man happy, and make unhappy one who is inclined to be so. Mr. Clough in his time felt more than most men the weight of the unintelligible world; but such thoughts make an instructive man. Several survivors may think they owe much to Mr. Clough's quiet question, 'Ah, then you think—?' Many pretending creeds, and many wonderful demonstrations, passed away before that calm inquiry. He had a habit of putting your own doctrine concisely before you, so that you might see what it came to, and that you did not like it. Even now that he is gone, some may feel that recollection of his society a check on unreal

---

[1] Bagehot slightly misquotes Balzac, *Eugénie Grandet* (1833): 'L'ironie est le fond du caractère de la Providence'—'Irony is the essence of Providence (or Fate)'.

theories and half-mastered thoughts. Let us part from him in his own words:

[Quotes entire 'Some future day when what is now is not'.]

34. W. Y. Sellar, from a review in *North British Review*

November 1862, xxxvii, 323–43

William Yonge Sellar (1825–90), classical scholar and Fellow at Oriel, was a friend of both Clough and Arnold. Arnold refers to his first reaction to *The Bothie* in the letter given as No. 1.

It is now nearly a year since the author of this volume of poems died at Florence, in the forty-second year of his age. Much regret for his untimely loss, and admiration of his genius and character, were expressed at the time of his death by friends who had been intimate with him at Rugby, at Oxford, and in later life, and who had other means of estimating his power of mind and purity of character than were accessible to those who only knew him by his writings. To few men, with equal justice, could the pathetic words of the old Roman poet be applied—

Multis ille bonis flebilis occidit.[1]

There were some, also, who did not know him personally, but had long known him as the author of a few remarkable poems, which seemed to them never to have been adequately appreciated. They will gladly welcome this republication of the best of the old poems, with the addition of others equally powerful, and equally characteristic of their author. But the knowledge of these poems is no longer confined

---

[1] 'Many a good man may weep for his death' (Horace, *Odes*, I, xxiv, 9).

to the old friends of the author, or to a small circle of admirers. The notices, both favourable and unfavourable, which this new volume has already attracted, must be satisfactory to all who believe that the more the author is examined, the more certain will be the ultimate recognition of his worth. An interest in these poems has been awakened among the readers and critics of our higher literature; who will, uninfluenced by any personal regard for the man, finally decide whether or not this small volume deserves to be ranked among the real and precious additions to the original thought and feeling of our time.

The volume consists of a number of short poems, chiefly expressive of personal feeling and experience; and of three longer poems, viz., *The Bothie of Tober-na-vuolich*, the *Amours de Voyage*, and a collection of tales, under the title *Mari Magno*. About one-half of the shorter poems and *The Bothie*, have already appeared. They have all been revised by the author, and those only have been republished which his mature judgment approved. Although some good thoughts and powerful lines have been lost in this process, yet the book, as a whole, has gained by the omissions. The ruggedness and obscurity of expression, and the caprices of taste which met the reader of the *Ambarvalia*, on first attempting to penetrate their meaning, were displayed most prominently in the poems that have been rejected. The chief alteration in *The Bothie* consists in its change of name. We have noticed also a few omissions and verbal changes, which leave the substance of the poem undisturbed, while they soften some of its grotesquer features. Readers to whom these poems have long been known, will acknowledge, with gratitude to the publisher, an immense improvement in the external form in which they now appear. The uncouth shape in which *The Bothie* was first sent into the world, was a real drawback to its success, and to the pleasure of reading it. Mr Macmillan has satisfactorily shown, that whatever may be the other objections to the admission of hexameters into English literature, the length of the lines is not incompatible with elegance and convenience in the volume which contains them.

The poems are accompanied by a short memoir of the author, from the pen of his friend, Mr Palgrave, the accomplished editor of the *Golden Treasury*. Although the life of a scholar and a thinker is not usually so rich in the materials of biography as that of a man of action or social prominence, yet some disappointment will be felt that there is scarcely any other record of the thoughts and feelings of so interesting a man than what is contained in these poems. Their evidence attests the powerful and profound impression made upon his mind by the great religious and political movements which have agitated the minds of this generation, and of which we are every day seeing new phases and results, in action and speculation, at home or abroad. A few letters, or other personal memorials, would have enabled a reader, interested in the author, to enter more easily into the spirit of his writings. But with the exception of two or three slight extracts, recording some impressions of Paris and Rome in 1848 and 1849, and of a visit to America in 1852, Mr Palgrave does not appear to have found any memorials of the kind suited to his purpose. In the absence of such personal memorials, his short memoir will help the reader to understand the circumstances and the state of feeling under which most of the poems were written, and to form for themselves some true image of the author. He has said just enough to prepare our minds for the kind of thought, sentiment, inward and outward experience, of which these poems are the result. He has performed his part with the warm feelings of personal affection; but also in the spirit of a critic, too honest, and too well acquainted with the highest literature of every age, to over-estimate the genius of his friend. Many traits of character are brought before us with singular fidelity, and with much grace and beauty of expression. Thus, for example, the following sentence vividly represents to us Mr Clough's exceeding love of nature:—

And it was noticed that, when speaking of spots of any special beauty or impressiveness—Grasmere, or Pont-y-wern, by Snowdon, or the lochs and valleys of the western Highlands—his eyes brightened as at the thought of something personally dear, and his voice softened at names and remembrances which carried with them so much of poetry.

The memoir is written throughout in the serious, reflective, and elevated tone of a man who feels deeply the seriousness and elevation of his subject. The language in which it is written, if seemingly highly pitched, is carefully chosen, and never vague nor irrelevant. It is the language of a man applying to human life the standard of our highest feelings and impulses; but the author of these poems appears to have been one of the very rare men to whom such a standard can be applied without exciting the suspicion of partial or enthusiastic exaggeration.

[A brief summary follows of the main events of Clough's life, quoting Palgrave.]

Mr Clough might have been recognised as a greater poet if he had not all his life been so hard-working a man. The conditions under which the germs of creative art and poetic accomplishment may be matured, are indeed manifold and inscrutable. In some cases, poetry seems to be poured out of wells of happiness beyond the common lot: others, we know, 'are cradled into poetry by wrong.' There have been poets who were associated with the foremost men of their age, and who lived prominently before the eyes of the world; others, again, who have kept themselves free from all the cares of life, and lived more in communion with nature than with their fellow-men. A poet may reach the perfection of his powers by living in London or Edinburgh, by the lakes of England or in the Highlands of Scotland—anywhere almost, at home or abroad. But while so facile in many things, in one respect 'the Muses' are hard task-mistresses. They will scarcely admit divided service. The constant pressure of alien cares and duties lies heavily on the imagination, and deadens the creative energies. Possibly, more freedom and leisure might not have made Mr Clough a happier or more useful man. His sense of the duty and necessity of taking his own share, and more than his own share, of practical work, may have been a safer guide for him to follow than the impulses of his poetic and speculative faculty. But freedom and leisure would have given him a better chance of becoming a great poet. And we notice, in looking at the dates affixed to the different poems, that the time of his most active production was the time of his unsettlement between leaving Oxford and undertaking his duties in the Education Office. A few of the poems were written in the earlier years of his Oxford life, and betray the deep under-current of the theological agitation of the period; and his faculty appears to have awakened again into activity, although under the disadvantage of feebler bodily health, in the leisure obtained by illness during the last years of his life.

Although every poet or thinker must be finally estimated, not by our idea of what he might have been, but by what he proved himself to be, it is well to bear these facts in mind as an explanation of the inequality subsisting between the thought or substance of many of these poems, and their artistic execution. Evidently the author was not a man to whom the expression of his thought came readily. He learned slowly to 'beat his music out.' Facility is either the happy and exceptional gift of the rarest genius, or the snare of mediocrity. The first he did not inherit; his conscientious thoroughness of mind would have saved him from the last. To have attained to perfect accomplishment in the highest and most enduring of the arts, would have demanded, in his as in most cases, the unimpeded energies and the undivided cares of the best years of a lifetime.

Mr Palgrave, while fully appreciating the elements of poetry in the genius of his friend, expresses a doubt 'whether in verse he chose the right vehicle, the truly natural mode of utterance.' These poems are obviously more remarkable as the expression of genuine thought and feeling, than as finished works of art or of creative power. Yet *The Bothie* shows that the author possessed the last faculty in a considerable measure; and many of his later poems show a great advance in facility and graceful execution. For a poet of this age, he has singularly little of that picturesque fancy, which turns the whole universe into imagery as pretty, as varied, and as transient as the changing forms and colours of a kaleidoscope; and critics, who regard what they call 'wordpainting' as the chief end and evidence of the poetic faculty, need not be expected to rank his claims very highly. His mode of writing is the furthest removed from what has been called 'the invertebrate type' of literature. He was perfectly honest and true to himself in every line that he wrote, and appears to have been totally uninfluenced by the mere ambition of literary success. His book is the sincere and real expression of the various phases through which his mind passed, and of the great emotions and affections which filled his heart. It is the record of much high feeling and 'high thinking' on the most substantial interests of human life. The substance of his poetry was formed out of a character, of rare depth and purity, a strong and tender conscience, generous and romantic enthusiasm, warm and stedfast affections;—

> High nature, amorous of the good,
> But touched with no ascetic gloom;
> And passion pure in snowy bloom
> Through all the years of April blood.[1]

His thought was the pure product of his own mind, exercised upon the subjects on which he felt most deeply. There is a kind of desperate sincerity and intensity of feeling in his readiness to sacrifice everything for the attainment of a certainty of conviction which, even till the last, was denied to him. This impulse was the ruling passion of his life, the chief stimulus to intellectual effort, the chief source of all the 'noble pain' which he endured. He was, his friends say, shy and reserved in his outward bearing; but the real temper of his mind seems to have been a fervent, almost an unguarded, enthusiasm. He seems

---

[1] Tennyson, *In Memoriam A. H. H.* (1850), CIX.

sometimes ready to follow any truth of human nature into all its practical consequences; but he regards also each question long, anxiously, and from many points of view; and thus the prevailing attitude of his mind was doubt, for a time deepening into despondency, and even a sadder bitterness of feeling, but at the last settled into a calmer and happier state of patient expectancy.

Mr Clough was well known at Oxford to be an excellent scholar; and it is to his careful revision that we owe our only trustworthy translation of Plutarch's *Lives*. These poems prove, further, that he had a very living sympathy with the great writers of antiquity,—a gift which does not always accompany even an exclusive devotion to classical studies. Readers of the poems will often come upon modes of thought and expression, which recall old familiar tones in Homer and Plato, in Virgil, Horace, and Lucretius; and they will remark how, in the darkest time of his despondency, a new life and inspiration seem to come to him from the art and ruined grandeur of antiquity. But, although the two longest of the poems contained in this volume are written in the metres of ancient poetry, the substance and the form of all of them are intensely modern. His mind had been fed, not on ancient literature only, but also on the original thinkers and imaginative writers, who have most powerfully moved their contemporaries in England, France, and Germany. But, deep under all his rich and manifold culture, there were more powerful impulses than any which come from ancient or modern books. What moved him to write was his personal interest in great questions, which, although they appear to some to lie apart from our practical life, yet are among the things which impart to that practical life all its substance and dignity. These questions or subjects are, in their essence, neither ancient nor modern; but they are most vitally realized when they force themselves into prominence in the experience of our own times.

We might classify the subjects out of which these poems were formed in some such way as this: I. The results of moral and religious experience; II. The doubts and the certainties of friendship and love; III. The cause, or what seemed to him the cause, of popular rights and freedom throughout the world; and IV. The power and the beauty of nature. These were to the author the most real sources of the pleasure and of the pain of existence. They are the subjects on which most of the shorter poems, which are chiefly the direct expression of personal feeling and conviction, are founded; and they are thoroughly inwoven with the serious, the humorous, and the satiric representation of life in

The Bothie and the *Amours de Voyage*. In the earliest poems, written when the author was about one-and-twenty years of age, the thought is perhaps as mature, the feeling as intense, as in the latest. The improvement perceptible in the later poems, consists in a wider knowledge of men, in more happy ease and musical sweetness of expression, in greater power of escaping out of his inner thought, and shaping the natural incidents of life into poetry. The earliest poems bear the date of 1840. In them we had the author closely questioning his own inner life,

> As ever in his great Taskmaster's eye,[1]

with an anxious conscientiousness, very different from the untruthful and immodest airs of literary egotism. Though his mind was then directed inwards, yet his genius does not prey upon itself—does not question or assert its own existence. But he questions anxiously his spiritual life and his affections, to see whether they are conformable to the pure ideal to which his own heart and conscience bore witness. We quote the following poem, not by any means as one of the most perfect in form and expression, but as representative of the earliest moral and religious impressions recorded in this volume:—

[Quotes the poem beginning 'I have seen higher holier things than these' ('Blank Misgivings', X).]

But, with advancing years and riper experience, greater and more arduous questions confronted him. The thoughts which now troubled him were not so much concerning his own inward state, as concerning the ultimate grounds of belief for himself and all men. Three of the most remarkable poems in the earlier part of the volume,—viz., 'Qui laborat orat,' 'The New Sinai,' and 'The Questioning Spirit,'— represent the state of a soul 'perplexed in the extreme,' yet hopefully and devoutly believing in God and duty. Of all the earlier poems, 'The New Sinai' is the most impressive; but it must be read as a whole, and it is too long to quote in full. 'The Questioning Spirit' is also one of the most beautiful of the early poems, both in thought and expression; but it is one of the very few that appear to us to recall something of a Tennysonian echo. The conclusions of all of these poems, although dashed with uncertainty, are yet bright and hopeful in comparison with the bitter pain and deep despondency of 'Bethesda,'

---

[1] Milton, 'On his having arrived at the Age of Twenty-Three'.

the sequel to 'The Questioning Spirit.' In the earlier poem, the human spirits have been represented as giving their various answers,—

Some querulously high, some softly, sadly low,—

to the spirit that questions them as to their lives, until the true answer is elicited,—

I know not, I will do my duty, said the last.

But in the sequel, even this trust has failed. The conclusion of the second poem, which we quote, reveals perhaps the deepest stage of that despondency, which the author was for a time destined to undergo. The expression of that despondency is, however, relieved by gleams of imaginative power, which recall the simple majesty of the old masters of painting. The human spirits are here represented, waiting for their release from their weariness and doubt, under the symbolical figure of 'the maimed and halt, diseased and impotent,' waiting at the pool of Bethesda:

[Quotes 'Bethesda', 17–41: 'And I beheld that' to 'I saw not, neither know'.]

The later poems, although they do not tell of a faith absolutely restored, yet evince a more hopeful and patient mood. There is a tone of plaintive sadness in the following stanzas, which is far less depressing than the deeper tones of the 'Bethesda,' and the more bitter outburst of feeling in the *Amours de Voyage*:—

'Old things need not be therefore true,'
O brother men, nor yet the new;
Ah! still awhile the old thought retain,
And yet consider it again!

The souls of now two thousand years
Have laid up here their toils and fears,
And all the earnings of their pain,—
Ah, yet consider it again.

* * *

Alas, the great world goes its way,
And takes its truth from day to day;
They do not quit, nor can retain,
Far less, consider it again.

After all his wanderings in the mazes of anxious thought, he returns at last to rest on the old and simple trust, thus expressed in another poem:—

[Quotes 'What we, when face to face we see', 21–32: 'Ah yet, when all is thought and said' to 'together, here'.]

The reader will indeed find in these poems much 'honest doubt' expressed with a deep sense of pain, but a still deeper sense of the guilt of stifling

> All the questing and the guessing
> Of the soul's own soul within.

But we will find also the strength that arises from faithfulness to the sense of truth and duty; and, in some of the poems, the higher strength which comes from the perception of a divine presence in the soul, 'unnamed, though not unowned.'

> Nor times shall lack, when, while the work it plies,
>   Unsummoned powers the blinding film shall part,
> And, scarce by happy tears made dim, the eyes
>   In recognition start.
>
> But, as thou willest, give or e'en forbear
>   The beatific supersensual sight,
> So, with Thy blessing blest, that humbler prayer
>   Approach Thee morn and night.

It would have been impossible to give any account of the substance of these poems, and of the author's deepest thoughts and most anxious feelings, without approaching ground which should be touched with as much reserve as possible in mere literary criticism or discussion. On that subject we shall say no more than this, that it appears impossible for any candid mind to confound the doubts expressed in these poems with the commonplace scepticism of an irreligious nature. Doubt seems to have clouded the author's mind in proportion almost as he felt most deeply on any subject. Next to religious truth and duty, he seems to have prized the affections of love and friendship. Even on these subjects his thoughts are for a time dashed with doubt; but they grow clearer and clearer with the growing experience of life, and rise in the later poems into absolute confidence and serenity. None of the poems has been more generally and deservedly admired than the 'Qua cursum ventus,' representing the accidental estrangement of friends, arising out of the change of thoughts and sympathies accompanying their separate growths. But the pains and pleasures of love fill a still larger space in this volume than the more tranquil phases of friendship. The depth, purity, and ennobling influence of passion, are here represented with the ideal colouring of romance, and also in the real light of human experience. But the peculiarity, although we cannot say the poetical merit, of his treatment of the subject, is, that he shows here also something of the same analytic tendency, the same kind of doubt, scruple, and hesitation, with which he encounters the metaphysical perplexities of our being. In his earlier poems he discusses in a kind of abstract way, but with a real discernment of fact and intuitive knowledge of human nature, the doubts and difficulties of the heart in making 'the one irrevocable choice;' and the same phases of feeling meet us again in *The Bothie*, the *Amours de Voyage*, and the 'Lawyers' Tale.' In a poem written in 1841, he contrasts 'love' with 'duty,' and then utters his warning against any sacrifice whatever of the highest affections:—

[Quotes 'Thought may well be ever ranging', 8–21: 'Hearts, 'tis quite another thing' to 'had never gone!'.]

This aspect of the passion of love was ever present to the author's mind, and gave the prevailing colour to all the narrative poems in the volume. It is his sense of the depth, and strength, and mystery of love, which makes him consider the subject so curiously, seeing the dangers of delusion and of hasty impulse; the difficulty of discerning between 'the good' and 'the attractive,' and the infinite consequences depending on the decision. Thus it is that Philip, in *The Bothie*, passes through two other passionate phases before his final choice is made. It is this same 'wayward modern mood' which causes the *Amours de Voyage* to end in the most lame and impotent conclusion which perhaps has ever yet been given to a tale of love. It is the same frailty of 'something introspective overmuch' characterizing the hero of the 'Lawyer's Tale,' which makes him very nearly miss altogether the happiness that awaited him. A curious instance of the same introspective tendency may be seen in a beautiful Idyllic song, written with much of the natural feeling and musical cadence of Theocritus, in which a peasant girl of the Alps or Pyrenees pours out the simple fears and pains of her heart as she is driving her cattle home from the mountain:—

> Ah dear, and where is he, a year agone,
> Who stepped beside, and cheered us on and on?

My sweetheart wanders far away from me,
In foreign land or on a foreign sea.
Home, Rose, and home, Provence and La Palie.

It is quite natural to find her, in her lonely walk through the gloom of that wet and stormy evening, thinking with some doubt of her lover's constancy:—

For weary is work, and weary day by day
To have your comfort miles on miles away.

But it does strike us as something of a false note, a touch of over-refinement, to find her thus questioning the permanence of her own feeling:—

Or may it be, that I shall find my mate,
And he, returning, see himself too late?
For work we must, and what we see, we see,
And God, He knows, and what must be, must be,
When sweethearts wander far away from me.
Home, Rose, and home, Provence and La Palie.

We confess that we never can like 'Elspie,' the heroine of *The Bothie*, so well as we should wish; chiefly, we think, because she has thought so much and so wisely about her own feelings, and has, 'in her ignorant Highlands,' worked out her theory of love as completely as a strong-minded woman familiar with all the aids and appliances of modern fiction.

These poems contain also many signs of the strong political sympathy with which the author watched the struggles of 1848 and 1849. The hero of *The Bothie* is full of the 'democratic fervour' of that time; and the *Amours de Voyage* was

Writ in a Roman chamber,
When from Janiculan heights thundered the cannon of France.

The ardent and generous tones of some of the shorter poems in this volume,—as, for instance, that called 'Peschiera,'—remind us of a similar sympathy with Italian freedom, expressed at a time when that cause had not so many advocates in England, in the fine 'political poems' of the late Henry Lushington. As perhaps the best specimen, among his shorter poems, of the poetical expression of Mr Clough's political feeling, we quote the following lines, addressed, as it seems, to those who despaired of the cause of liberal opinions and institutions after the successful reaction of 1849:—

[Quotes 'Say not, the struggle nought availeth'.]

The presage of these lines we have seen partially fulfilled, and all men now know that the struggle was not then over, and that 'the labour and the wounds' have not been in vain.

In our review of these shorter poems, we have limited ourselves to the purpose of illustrating the most striking modes of sentiment and opinion characteristic of the author. We have desired rather to give readers unfamiliar with his manner a key to his meaning, than to extract the poems most remarkable in point of expression and artistic grace. But, if our space allowed, we might quote several exquisite pieces,—such, for instance, as the poem at page 76:—

> O stream descending to the sea,
> Thy mossy banks between;

and the one immediately following:—

> Put forth thy leaf, thou lofty plane,
> East wind and frost are safely gone;—

the beauty and musical flow of which entitle them to be ranked in any collection of the best poetry which this age has produced. There is in the later poems a great advance in poetical style, from the grave severity and frequent obscurity which were the characteristics of many of the poems that first appeared in the *Ambarvalia*. It is unreasonable to demand, in poetry of this kind, that immediate perspicuity which is an essential excellence in a narrative or a simple lyrical poem. The finest reflective poetry in the language,—viz., the sonnets of Shakspeare, and the *In Memoriam*,—are very far from being immediately intelligible, even to the most competent readers. Still it is the case that, as a writer becomes more familiar with, and more completely master of, his thought and feeling on any subject, it becomes more natural to him to express himself, whether in prose or poetry, by means of simple and familiar language. And we look upon it as a great improvement in these later poems, that whatever difficulty they present, does not arise from intricacy or abruptness of language, but consists in the subtlety and novelty of the thought and sentiment. This difficulty, arising more from the state of the reader's than the writer's mind, attaches to all original reflective poetry, and is nowhere more sensibly felt than in the lyrical and dramatic poetry of the Greeks,—the greatest masters of simplicity and clearness of expression. Fortunately, the class of readers who are likely to be interested in these poems will not, if they have any reason to think their trouble will be repaid, be deterred from examining a book which demands some thought and some capacity of serious feeling on their own part. Other objections might perhaps be urged against some of these poems with more justice than the charge of obscurity. There are still, we think, in this volume a few examples of the misapplied power and the capricious taste which were much more visible in the earlier edition of the *Ambarvalia*. The author is more uncertain in his satire and humour (although he has much of these qualities that is genuine and excellent) than in his serious efforts. We could gladly have spared such poems as 'The Latest Decalogue', the satire of which is not nearly so effective as that of the earlier poem,

> Duty, that's to say, complying
> With whate'er's expected here;

or that beginning—

> How in Heaven's name did Columbus get over?

or those mystical elegiacs—

> Trunks the forest yielded, etc.

And we should have liked to see them replaced by some stanzas, at least, from the 'Silver Wedding' or the '*Ἐπὶ Λάτμῳ*,' which appeared in the former edition. The only poems in the volume that seem decidedly common-place are those entitled 'The Song of Lamech' and 'Jacob.' The faculty, so remarkably manifested by our two greatest living poets, of giving life, substance, and personality to the modes of thought and feeling of other ages, does not seem to have been conspicuous among Mr Clough's poetical gifts. His art is almost confined to the reproduction of what he had felt, seen, and sympathized with in actual life.

If Mr Clough had written only the poems with which we have hitherto been occupied, and which fill less than one-third of the volume, their intrinsic worth would have entitled him to be ranked among the few poets of his generation. But many readers will be more attracted by the longer poems, which are tales and descriptions of modern life;—the first, a half-humorous, half-romantic pastoral;—the second, a kind of novelette in metre, partly serious, partly satirical;—the last, unfortunately left unfinished, being a collection of simple tales, illustrating various phases of love and affection in ordinary life. These poems are more exceptional in point of artistic design and execution, but they evince much more varied power than the shorter pieces. *The Bothie of Tober-na-vuolich* is the most lively and natural description of a phase of real modern life which we know of in English verse. The work, although grotesque and unequal, has yet many of the rarest qualities of poetry. It is in many places humorous, picturesque, eloquent; it is throughout rich in thought, sense, passion, dramatic representation of character, outward description of nature. The author's thoughts and doubts on human life are here not presented to us as the refined ore of his meditation, but are poured out in overflowing floods of language from the activity of a speculative mind first meeting the new experience of life, and coming into active contact with the hearts and minds of others. And the conception and execution of the whole poem are so vivid, that every reader must feel as if he had known all the characters represented, and been present with them in all the scenes and actions that are there described.

Yet, with all these merits, which it would not be easy to exaggerate, the poem is so exceptional in form and subject, that it is easier to estimate and enjoy it by itself, than to attempt to fix its relative place in comparison with other poems. The subject, in the first place, is too slight to entitle the work to be regarded as a great poem. The story of an Oxford reading-party in the Highlands of Scotland, one of the members of which falls three times in love in the course of six weeks, and finally marries Elspie, daughter of David M'Kay, blacksmith, and tenant of a bothie in Lochaber, could not, consistently with our ordinary associations, be treated in 'the grand style.' Yet, while many writers have tried to interest the public in undergraduate life,—some painting it in facetious, some in satirical, and some in soberer colours,—nowhere else do we find that life presented with such truth and attractiveness, and with so much of the romance and humour that brighten and enliven existence. It would be difficult to imagine a more agreeable picture of the health and strength, the friendliness and natural enjoyment of youth, than what is here presented. There is a pleasant air of nature and simplicity, in union with grace and accomplishment, in the various delineations of character. The men represented can feel passion or poetic emotion, without becoming silly or sentimental; they can express humour and fun without the premature and second-hand cynicism in which ignorance of the world tries to disguise itself; they have the most keen and 'sensuous' delight in their open-air life of bathing and mountaineering, without attaching undue importance to their muscular energy; and they enjoy their reading and the fresh exercise of their thought without exhibiting any tinge of youthful priggishness or pedantry. This kind of life must be delightful to live, and is very pleasant to read about; but it is not the stuff out of which great poems have been produced in any age of literature.

The form of the poem is a still greater drawback to its artistic claims than the subject. In the first place, it requires the very finest touch to give consistent grace to a delineation which is professedly partly serious, partly humorous; and to the merit of graceful design this poem makes no pretension. It is, in every way, a new, a bold, and somewhat grotesque experiment. The hexameter verse, in which it is written, has still to fight its way into the recognized metres of English poetry. Mr Clough, we think, uses that metre far more happily than any other English poet by whom it has been employed. But the question of its adaptation to serious and elevated poetry, must still, we think, be considered *sub judice*. Hitherto, when continuously employed, it has generally tended to a lifeless monotony of cadence. In Mr Clough's hands it appears an admirable vehicle for the occasional expression of vivid or impetuous emotion; and it has all the virtues of rapid and direct force, which are claimed for it by Mr Arnold.[1] But the elevated passages in *The Bothie*, and the *Amours de Voyage*, seem to produce their powerful metrical effect, by rising out of the lower undulations of a kind of rapid and rhythmical prose. It is owing to the inequality and irregularity of the metre, that it is so admirably adapted to the subjects treated in the two poems. If we could receive Mr Newman's premises in his controversy with Mr Arnold, and accept the *Iliad* as a quaint, grotesque, and unequal poem, we might admit Mr Arnold's practical conclusion, and consider the experiment of *The Bothie* almost decisive in favour of translating Homer in English hexameters. But as we agree with nearly every word of the admirable criticism in which Mr Arnold establishes his premises, we are compelled to suspend our assent to his conclusion, till we see a poem in which the occasional metrical excellence of *The Bothie* is continuously and equally sustained.

We might, from this poem, illustrate all the peculiar characteristics

---

[1] *Lectures on translating Homer.*

of the author. His philosophy of life, of love, and of society, of which we only gather the results in the shorter poems, is here worked out and exemplified. But we shall confine ourselves to quoting a few passages, in which he exhibits his love of nature, and his power of representing her outward aspect, and interpreting the deeper meaning which she conveys to our minds. Mr Arnold has drawn attention to flashes of the spirit of Homer, in such expressions as '*by dangerous Corryvreckan,*' '*where roads are unknown to Loch Nevish,*'[1] and the like. Many more of these might be added. No modern English poet is so truly Homeric,— not through conscious imitation so much as the gift of a kindred spirit,—in seizing immediately the real aspects and simple effects of nature, which may be perceived and felt every day by the peasant as well as by the poet, but which are often lost from the excitement, the routine, and even the cultivation of modern life. Mr Clough has much, too, of the spirit of that other ancient poet, who, next to Homer, had the most vivid perception of the outward world; and who also has proclaimed, with more power than any other, the majesty of nature's laws, and has penetrated more deeply into that secret and all-pervading life:—

> Cæli subter labentia signa
> Quæ mare navigerum, quæ terras frugiferentis
> Concelebras.[2]

Many, however, of the readers of this *Review* will find a nearer source of interest in the scenery of the poem. No writer in prose or verse has shown so true a feeling of the beauty of Scotland, since Wordsworth gave a perfect voice to the music and the pastoral loveliness of Yarrow. We feel, as we read, that a sympathetic mind is bringing us nearer than we ever were before to the grandeur and the force of nature, as they are displayed in the rivers and woods of our inland Highlands, and over the immense range of the mountains, seas, and islands of the west.

We quote a few short passages, the descriptive truth and power of which we think our readers will acknowledge, whether they like or dislike the metre in which they are written:—

[1] *Last Words on Homer.*
[2] 'who beneath the gliding stars of heaven fillest with thy presence the sea that carries the ships and the land that bears the crops': Lucretius, *De Rerum Natura*, I, 2–4 (tr. C. Bailey, Oxford: Clarendon ed., 1947); Lucretius is invoking 'Alma Venus'—'Venus the life-giver'.

There is it, there, or in lofty Lochaber, where, silent upheaving,
Heaving from ocean to sky, and under snow winds of September,
Visibly whitening at morn to darken by noon in the shining,
Rise on their mighty foundations the brethren huge of Ben-Nevis?
There, or westward away, where roads are unknown to Loch Nevish,
And the great peaks look abroad over Skye to the westernmost islands?
There is it? there? or there? we shall find our wandering hero?
Here, in Badenoch? here, in Lochaber anon, in Lochiel, in
Knoydart, Moydart, Morrer, Ardgower, and Ardnamurchan,
Here I see him, and here: I see him; anon I lose him!
Even as cloud passing subtly unseen from mountain to mountain,
Leaving the crest of Ben-More to be palpable next on Ben-Vohrlich,
Or like the hawk of the hill which ranges and soars in its hunting,
Seen and unseen by turns, now here, now in ether eludent.

What if autumnal shower came frequent and chill from the westward,
What if on browner sward, with yellow leaves besprinkled,
Gemming the crispy blade, the delicate gossamer gemming,
Frequent and thick lay at morning the chilly beads of hoar-frost.

Duly there they bathed and daily, the twain or the trio,
Where in the morning was custom, where over a ledge of granite
Into a granite basin the amber torrent descended;
Beautiful, very, to gaze in ere plunging; beautiful also,
Perfect as picture, as vision entrancing that comes to the sightless,
Through the great granite jambs the stream, the glen, and the mountain;
Beautiful, seen by snatches in intervals of dressing,
Morn after morn, unsought for, recurring; themselves, too, seeming
Not as spectators, accepted into it, immingled, as truly
Part of it as are the kine in the field lying there by the birches.

It was on Saturday eve, in the gorgeous bright October,
Then when brackens are changed, and heather blooms are faded,
And amid russet of heather and fern green trees are bonnie;
Alders are green, and oaks; the rowan scarlet and yellow;
One great glory of broad gold pieces appears the aspen,
And the jewels of gold that were hung in the hair of the birch-tree,
Pendulous, here and there, her coronet, necklace, and ear-rings
Cover her now, o'er and o'er; she is weary, and scatters them from her
There, upon Saturday eve, in the gorgeous bright October,
Under the alders knitting, gave Elspie her troth to Philip.

As at return of tide the total weight of ocean,
Drawn by moon and sun from Labrador and Greenland,

Sets in amain, in the open space betwixt Mull and Scarba,
Heaving, swelling, spreading, the might of the mighty Atlantic;
Then into cranny and slit of the rocky, cavernous bottom
Settles down, and with dimples huge the smooth sea-surface
Eddies, coils, and whirls; by dangerous Corryvreckan:
So in my soul of souls, through its cells and secret recesses,
Comes back, swelling and spreading, the old democratic fervour.

Our admiration of the *Amours de Voyage* must be expressed in much
more qualified terms. It is written in a spirit the very reverse of the
healthy tone and sunny cheerfulness of *The Bothie*. Into the one poem
the author seems to have thrown all the sanguine buoyancy; into the
other, all the weary, hopeless feelings of his life. Each poem produces
the impression of absolute sincerity, and is marked by its own peculiar
power. But the sincerity of the *Amours de Voyage* is the painful sincerity of a man scrupulously anxious not to think too well of himself
or too hopefully of life. The power displayed is often the power of
insight into the under-side of human nature—into the doubts, weakness, and self-deception which underlie that aspect of things on which
it is most pleasant, and perhaps most profitable, to dwell. There is
often a jar produced on the feeling of the reader by some bitter or weary
expression of despondency or self-distrust, after some transient outburst of the old enthusiasm. The prevailing feeling of the poem is too
real for satire. It is rather like the 'misery that makes sport to mock
itself.' We do not for one moment suppose that Mr Clough has
represented himself in this poem, any more than in any of the characters in *The Bothie*; but he has expressed, in the person of Claude, much
of the unsettlement and despondency which are uttered more directly
in other poems of the same date. He has expressed, especially in that
character, the sense of the vanity of thinking and of knowledge apt to
come over a mind which has passed from youth into manhood in a
kind of hot-house air of contemplative studies, without having been
braced by the free air and natural life of the outer world. It is the old
character of the man, weak in purpose and in conduct, but endowed
with the subtle perception, the broad speculative power, the delicate
and sensitive feelings of genius,—all of which finer qualities render
their possessor more unfit for happiness and usefulness. A very modern
Hamlet is seen playing a weak and common-place part in the very
common-place drama of modern English society in Rome. Mr Clough
may have passed through some transient phases of feeling and inward
experience, which gave him insight into such a character; but the

evidence of his other writings, and the respect of his friends, prove that his own manly nature was in no way identified with this subtle but unfortunate creation of his mind.

But there are other sources of interest in the poem besides that derived from the love story. There is here more subtle observation, both of outward and inward fact, than, perhaps, in any other of the author's writings; and a few passages (as, for instance, the letters II. and IV. of Canto III.), in which speculative ideas are expressed and embodied in an imaginative form, rise into high and impassioned poetry. The poem is interesting further, as recording some impressions formed during the memorable siege of Rome in 1849. We recognize here, in the expression of his political sympathies, the same questioning spirit of doubts, especially doubt and distrust of himself, which were found to be characteristic of the author in other matters. Yet, if there was some distrust, there was no divided sympathy in his mind. His heart went entirely with the popular cause, and with the brave defenders of Rome and Venice; and no shadow of doubt qualifies his scorn for the superstition and misgovernment against which the Roman people rebelled, and his indignation against the base policy which restored and supports the papal administration.

To some readers, the most agreeable passages in the poem will be those, of which the one subjoined is an example, which record the impressions formed on his mind by the art and poetry of the past. The following lines afford as good a specimen of the elegance of which the English hexameter is capable as any which we can select:—

[Quotes *Amours de Voyage*, Canto III, 214–28: 'Tiber is beautiful, too,' to 'the valley and villa of Horace'.]

We have no space left to speak of the last poems, the tales included under the title *Mari Magno*. They were written only a short time before the author's death, and were never revised by him. They are evidently left incomplete; but we think that he had here struck on one of his happiest veins. The poems, while bearing the marks of haste and unfinished execution, are written with great ease and simplicity. They have all the old moral strength and beauty of the author's mind, no longer clouded by any morbid misgivings. The most powerful of the tales is the one called 'The Clergyman's Tale;' but we prefer quoting the denouement of 'The Lawyer's Tale,' which presents a charming picture of secure and natural happiness. The reader will see that these poems are written in the good old English metre of Chaucer and of

Dryden, to which we wonder that our poets do not oftener return, leaving the Tennysonian blank verse to its own perfect master and inventor. Mr Clough uses the metre, as is best suited for narrative poetry, in a style which recalls the freedom of Dryden and the homeliness of Crabbe; not the rhetorical point and concentrated energy of Pope, nor the equable elegance of Goldsmith:—

[Quotes *Mari Magno*, 'The Lawyer's Tale', 226–51: 'Wandering about, with little here to do', to 'in each other's arms'.]

It is useless now to speculate as to what Mr Clough might have done, had longer life been granted to him; or had circumstances allowed him more freedom and leisure; or had not the weight of anxious thought pressed too heavily upon his early years. There were in him, undoubtedly, the materials of a much greater poet than he actually became. But with this volume in our hands, we will not think of applying to him the melancholy words of 'unfulfilled promise.' Whether these poems are destined to obtain a wide and permanent popularity, the actual result only can show. We do not expect nor desire for them that sudden and enthusiastic favour, which is often repaid by subsequent neglect and injustice. Their original merit and permanent value appear to us to consist in the truth and worth of that moral power which lay behind the poetical and speculative capacity of the author. They will be most admired by those who value the artistic accomplishment less than the thought, or power, or character revealed through poetry. They demand, indeed, a 'fit audience,' who can think and feel seriously, largely, and with toleration; but that audience need not be a limited one. And we are confident that those who are once impressed by these poems, will find this impression confirmed and enlarged by time. They will value them, not as a source of amusement for their idler hours, but as a solid treasure of thought and experience,—an aid, in many ways, to their better aspirations.

35. From 'Arthur Hugh Clough', an unsigned review of *The Poems of Arthur Hugh Clough* (Boston, 1862), the *Boston Review*

March 1863, iii, 132–8

The Boston edition of *The Poems of Arthur Hugh Clough* was prefixed with a memoir by Charles Eliot Norton; for details of the very slight differences in contents from the English edition see *A.H.C. Descr. Cat.* p. 34. For Norton on Clough see No. 27.

The thoughts of a rare, choice spirit lie entombed in these pages. Clough was one of those men who leave a marked impression upon the circle in which they move. He had the magnetism of personal influence. He could charm by word, by cheer, by the indefinable air of intellectual superiority, those among whom he familiarly lived. To these his poems, the truthful revelations of the man, have more than ordinary attraction. Memory gives each of them a special meaning. To us who never knew him, until this little volume came to hand, they have a charm, as they reveal a singularly honest and earnest nature. And more, they are instructive, as showing the intellectual spirit of the times. It was given to Clough, as to Sterling and to Blanco White to pass through the region of modern doubt. Each of these men came to nearly the same conclusion; each threw aside hereditary opinions; each pushed out into great vagueness of speculation; each, after a long flight, like a bird spent of its strength, fluttered to the ground; each is now learning for himself those secrets which to mortal eyes are not revealed.

Hence Clough, aside from his merely literary character, is a representative man in religious thought. He would not be called a religious thinker. In this respect, he only claims our notice as one who rejected, at much personal loss, his ancestral faith, and tried to solve the problems of our spiritual nature. His minor poems are mainly occupied with suggestions upon these. They touch upon doubt, necessity, duty, fidelity to truth; they show fully the longing for peace and hope; but they set forth only that contentment which arises from baffled purpose. They exhibit a negation of warm religious belief; they are sad from a want of Christian faith. The man is 'representative' because he tried the pathway of religious doubt, with intellectual gifts and scholarly endowments which ought to insure success, if it were possible. Because he did not succeed, he is worthy of notice in these pages. He had a stronger mind than Sterling; he had a stronger grasp of truth than Blanco White; but his splendid powers were of no avail in the solitary march for peace and rest, away from Christ. We honor the noble honesty of Clough, but we regret the misuse of his religious nature. It is too common that the whole influence of a unversity education is to undermine one's faith in Christianity. The spirit of doubt is not confined to the young men of Oxford and Cambridge. It is in our own universities. It is a strong undercurrent at Harvard and Yale, at Amherst and Brown and Williams. The young men who are first in intellectual power, are weakest in their belief in religious truth. Clough is the very type and leader of these. He is honest, as they are; he tries to explore the whole realm of religious thought, as they do; he frankly gives up the church, as they do; he fritters away fine powers of thought, as they do; and the golden season of manhood is spent in doubt, when under a more genial sky, it would have been spent in service to Christ. Our finest minds engage, as the work of life, in occupations which are far below them, perhaps chiefly because they have no settled religious faith. Yet where is the remedy? It seems to be a necessity for these men to prove their belief. But they are readiest to do it, when they have least fitness for it. And besides, the intellectual leaven of this age is at work in nearly every ingenuous mind. It was the spirit of Arnold which gave the impulse to Clough's mind; and then the Tractarian movement only helped to spur it on when he came to Oxford. His eminence there made him perhaps a sort of leader among radical young men. And it is not strange that, when the Oxford honors were all in his hands, and life looked bright before him, he should feel compelled to resign his Fellowship and bid *Alma Mater* adieu. And he does this in the following sonnet, which is also a good sample of his shorter poems:

[Quotes 'Well, well—Heaven bless you all from day to day' ('Blank Misgivings', III).]

But he never returned to the Oxford cloisters. His mind was too radical for that. The pupil of Arnold had gone beyond him. And so has the spirit which Arnold aroused gone beyond the bounds which he would have assigned to it. Its legitimate fruit is the *Essays and Reviews*, which has made an epoch in theological literature.

Now the real value of all this writing and thinking is slight; it is negative; it would not be worth writing about, did not these men win the ear of those whose minds are yet unformed. Here is precisely their evil influence. Men, like Arnold, and Carlyle, and Sterling, and White, and Clough, and Jowett, are the very ones who have intellectual raciness and zest for the young men in our colleges. Their spirit is noble, earnest, winning. But however honest they may be with themselves, their principles are unsound. He who follows them will soon feel his Christian beliefs giving away. The men themselves feel their religious unsoundness. Here are some passages from Clough's *Amours de Voyage* which reveal his religious condition. 'Had he been writing in his own name,' says Mr. Norton, in his charming memoir, 'he could not have uttered his inmost conviction more distinctly, or have given the clue to his interior life more openly, than in the following verses':

> I will look straight out, see things, not try to evade them:
> Fact shall be Fact for me; and the Truth the Truth, as ever,
> Flexible, changeable, vague, and multiform and doubtful.

> Ah, the key of our life that passes all wards, opens all locks,
> Is not *I will*, but, *I must*, I must—I must—and I do it.

> But for the steady fore-sense of a freer and larger existence,
> Think you that man could consent to be circumscribed here into action?
> But for assurance within of a limitless ocean divine, o'er
> Whose great tranquil depths unconscious the wind-tost surface
> Breaks into ripples of trouble that come and change and endure not,—
> But that in this, of a truth, we have our being and know it,
> Think you we men could submit to live and move as we do here?

This man persists in relying upon those very things in human belief that are most involved in doubt. He has doubted so long that he sees every truth double, and is uncertain which side to accept. He finally comes to the sceptic's jumping-off place—not the '*I will*, but *I must.*' Clough's poems are often disfigured, many of them made obscure by the spirit of restless mental questioning. They may give many thoughts peculiar to our time exceedingly well; but most of them seem as if written by a man whose heart is ill at ease. There is a tone of sadness, at times almost pathetic. This is true more especially of the minor poems. There is little of genuine poetry in the misgivings of mental doubt. It is unfortunate for his reputation that these were ever printed; and yet they are valuable for insights into his intellectual character. To apply his own words used for another purpose:

> Our native frailty haunted him—a touch
> Of something introspective overmuch.

He analyzed his emotions, his thoughts, too keenly. His doubt became his disease, precisely as with Sterling and Blanco White.

Yet all his poems are not of this *doubtful* character. *The Bothie of Tober-na-Vuolich* is full of frolicsome and hearty playfulness. One would never guess, from reading it, that at the time it was published, the author's opinions were too radical for Oxford. It is a Long-Vacation Pastoral, an Idyll of the Highlands. Its peculiarity is the freshness of its scenes, its fidelity to nature, and the quaint Homeric simplicity of its language and structure. The hexameter verse is here successfully employed. We have come even to enjoy the measure as Clough uses it in his two longest poems. He truly says: 'It is not an easy thing to make readable English hexameters at all; not an easy thing even in the freedom of original composition, but a very hard one indeed, amid the restrictions of faithful translation.' Yet he has overcome the difficulty; very often his verses have 'the true Homeric ring.' In these lines there is even music in the flow:

> Tiber is beautiful, too, and the orchard slopes and the Anio
> Falling, falling yet, to the ancient lyrical cadence;
> Tiber and Anio's tide; and cool from Lucretilis ever,
> With the Digentian stream, and with the Bandusian fountain
> Folded in Sabine recesses, the valley and villa of Horace.

And again in these lines from the *Tober-na-Vuolich*:

> There, in the bright October, the gorgeous bright October,
> When the brackens are changed, and heather blooms are faded,
> And amid russet of heather and fern green trees are bonnie,
> Alders are green, and oaks, the rowan scarlet and yellow,
> Heavy the aspen, and heavy with jewels of gold the birch-tree,
> There, when shearing had ended, and barley-stooks were garnered,
> David gave Philip to wife his daughter, his darling Elspie;
> Elspie the quiet, the brave, was wedded to Philip the poet.

There is nothing unhealthy in all this. *The Bothie* is made out of the experiences of Oxford students while rusticating in the Highlands. In its way, it is perfect; it is interesting because it gives pictures of the Highlands; it is full of student life; it is also more a work of art than his other poems, which seem to be rather the unstudied utterance of his mind; but it is too scholarly, in spite of its peculiar beauty, ever to win many readers; those, however, who can understand it always will prize it highly.

It happened to Clough, as to many other recent English writers, to be more truly recognized in America than in England. We are in more sympathy with such earnest, searching minds, than the mass of Englishmen. . . .

[An outline of the main events of Clough's life has been omitted.]

He has left behind him, so his friends claim, no adequate memorial of his powers. He revised, and almost retranslated, Plutarch; he wrote for the *North American* and for *Putnam's Monthly*; but he was never an easy writer. His style is jerky and fitful, yet his choice of words is often inimitable. His poetry is his chief legacy to literature. His *Mari Magno, or, Tales on Board*, is on the plan of the *Canterbury Tales*, but has not the finish of *The Bothie*, or of the shorter poems. The conception, however, is good, and could he have wrought it out carefully, we think this would have proved a very happy success. The spirit of these sketches is more quiet and subdued than in the earlier poems, and even the measure into which he runs the verse indicates a more balanced and reposeful mental state. There are signs in his later writings that faith was gaining ground upon his unbelieving habit of mind. He had a rare gift for describing natural scenery. He could have excelled, too, had he written poems like 'The Song of Lamech' or 'Jacob.' To our mind these, if less piquant, are more complete than perhaps any of his other works. But he had a humorous vein. The 'Spectator ab Extra' is full of genuine humor; so also is the poem beginning—

How, in Heaven's name, did Columbus get over?

There are few poems more finished in every respect than Clough's 'Highland Lassie,' quoting which we must bid adieu to the little volume which is to keep his memory green:

[Quotes 'ὁ θεὸς μετὰ σοῦ' ('God be with you!').]

LETTERS AND REMAINS OF ARTHUR HUGH CLOUGH

('*For private circulation only*')
1865

---

36. William Allingham, from 'Arthur Hugh Clough, 1819–1861', *Fraser's Magazine*

October 1866, lxxiv, 525–35

Allingham (1824–89), an Irishman, was a poet and editor of *Fraser's Magazine*, 1874–9.

Most of the biographical part of this survey of Clough's life and work, about two-thirds of the whole, has been omitted.

The name of Arthur Hugh Clough is held in regard by many readers of books in England and America, and in affection by his personal friends. He was an Englishman of our own day with its novelties and problems, intellectual, cultivated, thoroughly honest and singleminded, and possessing moreover a marked degree of originality, which after all is the truly interesting thing. Originality or 'genius,' that which is born with a man, and peculiarly distinguishes him from all others, is what we seek in every one; this *is* the man. But, though every human creature has a genius, it is in most cases so small, and so overlaid in a few years with all kinds of extraneous matter and rubbish, as to be scarcely discoverable, at all events not worth much pains to discover.

Clough's mind, naturally of a grave reflective turn, was occupied in early life with the studies of a public school and college career, and a good deal at the same time with moral and theological questions; English ecclesiasticism had a large share in his training; later, he took interest in politics, though not in parties; the picturesque in nature attracted him much, and he delighted in rambles afoot; first and last he had a constant literary impulse, which expressed itself mainly in poetic forms, in part perhaps because his habitually reserved mind had thus the advantage of a thicker veil when venturing into public view. Reserved and reticent, cautious almost to a fault in forming opinions, everything Clough said, did, and wrote was genuine—was from himself, and imbued with his truthful, generous, and manly nature.

From a volume of *Letters and Remains* printed 'for private circulation only,' we gather, by permission, some traits of his life, assisted by our own personal acquaintance with the man. The book in question has a high and rare simplicity of presentment, and as far as it goes is one of the honestest pieces of biography. . . .

The first specimens we have of Clough's poetry are dated about this time (1839), and have a decidedly Wordsworthian tone. First and last, Wordsworth was for him the chief among modern poets. He had also much liking for Crabbe, and but little for the rich aerial colourists, such as Keats and Shelley, being always uneasy when he felt his legs taken off the ground.[1] He required a tangible intellectual basis, and was rather suspicious of sentiment and imagination. Of the old English poets, he seemed clearly to prefer Chaucer. . . .

In the autumn [of 1848] he was at home with his mother and sister at Liverpool, and during this time he wrote his poem of the *Bothie*. It made at first little impression on the public, but select readers in England, and more in America, found in these hexameters (metrically irregular as they are, and not seldom prosaic) a well-spring of original and healthy thoughts upon modern manners, combined with a delightful freshness and picturesqueness in description. Of an Oxford reading-party in the Highlands, one young man falls in love with a beautiful and fine-minded girl, a farmer's daughter; they marry and emigrate to New Zealand. Such the story.

> There he hewed, and dug; subdued the earth and his spirit;
> There he built him a home; there Elspie bare him his children,
> David and Bella; perhaps ere this too an Elspie or Adam;
> There hath he farmstead and land, and fields of corn and flax-fields
> And the Antipodes too have a Bothie of Tober-na-vuolich.

---

[1] Allingham confided to his diary a severe comment on Clough's want of the mystical Wordsworthian response to Nature: though Clough did love it, in his descriptions 'Something of the land-surveyor . . . mingles with the poet' (*A Diary*, ed. H. Allingham and D. Radford (1907), 143).

As to the metre, 'it was a reading' (he says) 'of *Evangeline* aloud . . . which, coming after a re-perusal of the *Iliad*, occasioned this outbreak of hexameters.' . . .

Many of the views of life and of art are found in his letters from Rome, which were afterwards worked into his second long hexameter poem, entitled *Amours de Voyage*, first published in America. Like the *Bothie*, incondite in metrical form, and frequently ultra-prosaic, the *Amours de Voyage* also is filled with fine and valuable observations made at first-hand, expressed usually with great precision and point, and often with singular beauty. *Ambarvalia*, a volume of short poems, half by Clough ('the casualties of at least ten years') and half by his old school friend Mr. Burbidge, appeared shortly after the *Bothie*. In 1850, during a visit to Venice, Clough began a longish poem, somewhat of the *Faust* kind, called *Dipsychus*, which 'shows the mark of Venice in all its framework and its local colouring.' This was Clough's method. His mind full of the scenery and impressions of some notable locality—the Scotch Highlands, or Rome, or Venice—he made therefrom a mould, as it were, and poured into it the reflections, guesses, theories, and beliefs that were occupying him, or had occupied him. There is much of the sarcastic in the Venice poem, put chiefly into the mouth of a 'Spirit,' who is, in fact, our old friend Mephistopheles, and who drives the well-intending but puzzled Dipsychus to exclaim—

> . . . if indeed it be in vain
> To expect to find in this more modern time
> That which the old-world styled, in old-world phrase,
> Walking with God! It seems His newer will
> We should not think at all of Him, but turn,
> And of the world that He has given us make
> What best we can.

These latter lines are quoted by Clough in a subsequent letter in the following connection:—'It was odd that I was myself in a most Romanising frame of mind yesterday, which I very rarely am. I was attracted by the spirituality of it. But what has hitherto always come before me as the truth, is rather that

> It seems His newer will,' &c. . . .

. . . Clough's poems (excepting those which appear in the volume of *Letters and Remains*), fill a close-printed volume of over 300 pages, and consist of two long poems in hexameters—the *Bothie*, and *Amours de Voyage*; a set of five stories in rhyme grouped under the general title of *Mari Magno*; and some threescore minor effusions. Of all the larger compositions, and several of the smaller, the main subject matter is the same, namely, Love, as seen from one point of view, though with various circumstances, by an educated young Englishman of the present day,—neither 'platonic' love by any means, nor on the other hand sensual or lawless, but love as a desire and search for what is truest and best in matrimonial union. This love, as our poet represents it, this hoping and longing for hymeneal happiness, is self-questioning, self-tormenting, fearing shams, fearing self-deception, fearing to lose what is solid through over-refinement, a substance for a shadow; fearing still more to sell its birthright for a mess of pottage. The hero of the *Bothie*, an Oxford man, yet a radical, is troubled chiefly, both in his general views, and particularly in his character of aspirant to matrimony, by his thoughts as to the condition, duties, and mutual relations of the upper and the lower classes.

The *Amours de Voyage* (first published in America) was all but unknown in England during the author's lifetime, and is still much less widely known than the *Bothie*. This poem (to which one of the mottoes is '*Il doutait de tout, même de l'amour.*' *French Novel.*) recounts the slight adventures of one Claude, a young Englishman of our time, one of the—

> Feeble and restless youths born to inglorious days.

Sick of London, he makes a tour to Italy and Switzerland. He is disappointed or dissatisfied, or at best unsatisfied, with almost everything and every one he sees,—not ignobly, but with the discontent of a subtle, inquiring, and aspiring soul, which is least of all contented with *itself*. At Rome he meets three Miss Trevellyns, and likes them, especially Mary, not forgetting, however, to remind himself—

> Well, I know there are thousands as pretty and hundreds as pleasant,
> Girls by the dozen as good, and girls in abundance with polish
> Higher and manners more perfect than Susan or Mary Trevellyn.
> Well, I know, after all, it is merely juxtaposition,—
> Juxtaposition, in short; and what is juxtaposition?

Claude's attitude throughout is that of a questioner. He is, perhaps, the best type yet given us in literature of the scepticism of modern England. He is high-minded, pure, benevolent, intellectual; but he questions of religion, of morals, of love, of men and women, of history and art, and above all of himself. He is not an ingenious quibbler, he has no touch of affectation; to question and doubt, to consider and reconsider, is as natural to him as thinking or breathing. Of Rome he asks—

> Is it illusion? or does there a spirit from perfecter ages,
> Here, even yet, amidst loss, change and corruption, abide? &c.

When the French besiege the city, he thinks—

> Am I prepared to lay down my life for the British female?
> Really, who knows, &c.

He writes to his friend Eustace—

> I am in love you say; I do not think so exactly.

As Georgiana Trevellyn remarks, 'he really is too shilly-shally.' Does he care very much for Mary Trevellyn? Does she care very much for him? He cannot decide, and in his indecision allows her and her party to travel northwards without him. Then he pursues, but, by a series of misadventures, fails to find them, and gives up the pursuit, saying by and by—

> After all, do I know that I really cared so about her?
> Do whatever I will, I cannot call up her image;

> After all, perhaps there was something factitious about it;
> I have had pain, it is true: I have wept, and so have the actors.

Meanwhile Mary Trevellyn, who has been anxiously looking for Claude, submits on her part, 'although in a different manner,' to the closing of their acquaintance. In a letter of Clough's of June 1858, he says:

> I have had, mirabile dictu, a letter from Emerson, who reprimanded me strongly for the termination of the *Amours de Voyage*, in which he may be right, and I may be wrong; and all my defence can only be, that I always meant it to be so, and begun it with the full intention of its ending so; but very likely I was wrong all the same.

Love, and Self-questioning, singly or in combination, form the staple of the minor poems, whereof the following may be named as very characteristic:—'Duty,' 'When panting sighs the bosom fill,' 'O tell me, friends,' 'The questioning Spirit,' 'O thou whose image.' Several short pieces printed in the volume of poems reappear embodied in the long composition, which remains a fragment, given in the volume of *Letters and Remains* and entitled *Dipsychus*, that is, the two-

souled or two-minded, a man who cannot come to an agreement
with himself, 'This way and that dividing the swift mind.' Some of
the pieces in question assume a different meaning as part of the long
composition. For example, the lines given in *Poems*, page 61, 'Submit,
submit!' and which there seem to belong to the poet's own way of
thinking, are in *Dipsychus* put into the mouth of the devil; though,
again, as the author says in his Epilogue, 'perhaps he wasn't a devil at
all. That's the beauty of the poem; nobody can say!' There is a kind of
bitter humour, a sarcastic philosophy, of which we find traces in
Clough's other poems, appearing in larger measure in this *Dipsychus*,
as in the lines ' "There is no God" the wicked saith;' or 'How pleasant
it is to have money,' &c.; or these:—

> This world is very odd we see,
> We do not comprehend it;
> But in one fact we all agree,
> God won't, and we can't mend it.

> Being common sense, it can't be sin,
> To take it as I find it;
> The pleasure to take pleasure in;
> The pain, try not to mind it.

On one side of his mind, at least, Clough had a good deal of sympathy with the way of looking at life which we find in such poets as
Horace, Goethe, Byron, Béranger.

Dipsychus is tormented by 'twisted thinkings,' he fears action, and
also fears lest he may drone and dream away his life:

> Is it a law for me
> That opportunity shall breed distrust,
> Not passing till that pass?

The Spirit taunts him:—

> Heartily you will not take to anything;
> Whatever happen, don't I see you still,
> Living no life at all? . . .
> Will you go on thus
> Until death end you? if indeed it does.
> For what it does, none knows. Yet as for you,
> You'll hardly have the courage to die outright;
> You'll somehow halve ev'n it. Methinks I see you,
> Through everlasting limbos of void time,

Twirling and twiddling ineffectively,
And indeterminately swaying for ever.

Clough's last work comprises five love-stories under the general title of *Mari Magno, or Tales on Board*, being supposed to be told by certain passengers in a steamer during the voyage from England to Boston U.S. They are all very modern and matter-of-fact both in style and substance, and include many characteristic and interesting remarks on life.

Clough's poetry is in every part full of matter and meaning; of mere beauty and melody for their own sakes there is but little. Picturesque he often is, but (to compare one art with another) it is in the style of Clarkson Stanfield, never in that of Turner or of David Cox. He was comparatively inattentive to the subtle effects of language and metre, caring much for conveying his thought strongly and clearly, and but little for giving delight by the way.[1] Indeed, he generally felt metre as a hindrance, and was very impatient of the bonds of rhyme. Yet, in writing in verse, he doubtless felt also that he had more scope for originality: there was less risk of seeming odd in manner, or of 'committing himself' in matter. This criticism, however, is partly opinion, partly surmise; the main fact is that he *has* expressed himself effectively, has spoken to the world out of the thought and experience of a man, and a 'man of genius', *unus e multis*, a true word which remains. From the higher mind of cultivated, all-questioning, but still conservative England, in this our puzzled generation, we do not know of any utterance in literature so characteristic as the poems of Arthur Hugh Clough, 'some-time fellow of Oriel College, Oxford.' Freely he thinks and speaks; yet always as an Englishman. His sympathies are general, but his tastes and standards are still national. . . .

1 Allingham again puts this more strongly in his diary; in an entry dated 1 October 1866, which was evidently connected with the writing of this article: there he writes plainly of finding Clough's poetry 'often too truthful to be good as art' (*A Diary*, 143).

37. W. H. Smith, from 'Dipsychus and the Letters of A. H. Clough', Macmillan's Magazine

December 1866, xv, 89–102

William Henry Smith (1808–72) was a philosopher, author of two philosophical dialogues, the evolutionist novel 'Thorndale' (1857) and 'Gravenhurst' (1857) and a minor poet.

. . . Clough, when alive, if spoken of as a poet, was quoted as the author of the *Bothie of Tober-na-vuolich*; henceforth, he will be known as the author of *Dipsychus*, and of some lyrics of unsurpassable beauty, where deep reflection meets with a pathetic and musical utterance.

We hardly know to which first to turn—the *Letters*, or this poem of *Dipsychus*, so much light does each throw upon the other, and both on the man whom we still seem to have but lately lost from amongst us. For our own part, it is long since we have taken up a book that has so riveted our attention, or so stirred our thoughts, as these *Letters and Remains*. Any one wishing to study our age, in a phase of it at once most noble and most sad, could not do better than peruse this volume. He must, however, bring to it a candid and intelligent spirit, and perhaps some sad experience of his own, or he will not read the lesson aright.

There is but one pen that could do full justice to Arthur Clough—the same that gave us the living portraiture of Sterling. Both of these men had the happiness of being friends of Carlyle. Both may be said to have been his disciples, if such men are the disciples of any one; both, at least, were followers of the gospel of labour—of work performed for its own good results, come what may to the worker. Both were distinguished by the personal influence they exercised over their contemporaries, an influence by no means to be measured by their literary reputation; an influence of the man and the character, not of the writer or public teacher; an influence, in short, which is but another name for the love they called forth. Both were men of rare energy, lovers of truth, bold in their search for it, yet feeling ever as they moved the weight of a grave responsibility. Not theirs the audacity that is but another name for recklessness,—the audacity that, in throwing off personal fear, throws off all fear whatever; they had the courage of the brave man who, when he has ceased to fear for himself, fears for others, and the great cause he has espoused. Both were men who had great faiths and great doubts—faiths and doubts of being alike unsettled, perhaps, to the very end; for of both it may be said that they left the world before their opinions appear to have been fully matured. Wine of a certain vintage takes a long time, it seems, to ripen. Sterling had the more enthusiastic temperament; yet, as the poet, Clough proved himself indisputably superior. Sterling, strange to say, with all his fire and his rare oratorical power, when he wrote poetry, glided down into a tamer mood, and a lower intellectual level, than of right belonged to him; he partly deserted himself, imitated some model—Wordsworth or another—or, let us say, thought as the artist, dropping the philosopher. Clough, on the contrary, threw the whole man into his verse—we speak of his highest efforts—and poured forth subtle thoughts which could not help being poetry because they were steeped in feeling.

In one respect, the Letters before us would fail to give an adequate impression of Clough. They were written chiefly from abroad, when he was touring, in holiday time in short, or (as in the last journey) in a period of leisure forced on him by illness. They might lead a hasty reader to conclude that the writer of them led a very nomadic life, restless, changeful, in which the pleasant dissipation of the tourist had a large share. But, in fact, these periods of idleness were but a very scanty portion of a life which was given up, day by day, and hour by hour, to work which was often felt most monotonous and tasteless. He, the poet and the thinker, slaved at the public mill of tutorship, or, in later years, was sedulous over the necessary but subordinate labours of a government office; in both cases it was the work which was put before him to be done—it was an honest work, and he scrupulously performed it, leaving for himself little time to bestow on the labours of his predilection. The great peculiarity of his character was precisely this, that the desire for fame or wealth—or, as we now delight to call it, a social position—was not requisite to his industry. We presume that he would have preferred the higher work to the lower, but he looked at the industry itself, and its results. The only thing absolutely essential to him was the approval of his own conscience. This man, so free in speculation, who had sounded all the perilous depths of human thought who had cast off dogmas as the serpent casts his skin, and with as little idea of returning to them again, was a very slave to the sentiment of duty. The thing that was right—the doing of this stood to him in the place of ambition; and it had sometimes to stand in the place of doctrine too. Faith in the right—this never forsook him; nor in that Being whom, when the reason refuses to clothe in any mythological or objective form, it still finds—even in itself! This is expressed in a poem which commences with these lines:—

> O Thou, whose image in the shrine
> Of human spirits dwells divine:
> Which from that precinct once conveyed,
> To be to outer day displayed,
> Doth vanish, part, etc.

He showed as little eagerness for literary reputation as for any other social distinction. The best he had written he allowed to lie in his desk. It was not till after he had left the scene that the world at large knew that there had been a poet amongst them. Then there was much clapping of hands. Could he who had passed in behind the veil have returned, at our summons, to receive our plaudits, we feel persuaded that, for such a purpose, he would not have relifted the fallen curtain . . .

We must now pass from the 'Memoir' and *Letters* to the posthumous poem of *Dipsychus* (the Two-Souled), which is here printed in as complete a form as was possible.[1] Fragment as it is, we think it deserves no meaner title than that of our 'English *Faust*.' Of the many writers who have been influenced by the great German, no one has so happily succeeded in combining the grave and solemn with the light and ironical. It has been often remarked that we have no good translation of *Faust*, because, in the first place, the translator of *Faust* should be himself a poet; and, in the next, this poet must be alike capable of the profound and the lively, the pensive and the satirical. Now this requisite combination we have here in *Dipsychus*. But we must not let it be understood for a moment that, because we allude to the influence of Goethe, the poem itself is one of an imitative character. If the fact that the materials are drawn entirely from the writer's own experience constitute originality, this is pre-eminently an original poem. It is the expression of the man himself, of various thoughts that,

[1] In the remainder of this article the reader is referred for the sources of quotations to the current printed version of *Dipsychus* in *Poems* (1951).

at different times, have come unbidden into his mind. And here let us at once make an observation which it is well to bear in mind in reading and appreciating this poem. It deals with great subjects, and these are treated from opposite points of view. But the subtleties, or the audacities of thought we meet with, are never cold inventions or elaborate ingenuities. We have no paradoxes designedly contrived to startle or amuse. The subtlety or audacity of thought is always a genuine product of the thinker. There is a charming levity of manner in parts, but no great subject is really *played with*. Taken as a whole, it is the gravest of all colloquies a man could hold with himself.

The idea of a dialogue of a mind with itself, a debate between the higher and the lower self, is by no means new. Tennyson has something of the kind in his 'Two Voices'; and in that pleasant little volume, *Voyage autour de ma Chambre*,[1] the author gives to his more material self the title of *l'autre*, and *l'autre* expresses his view of things very piquantly at times. Clough has converted *l'autre* into his Mephistopheles, a spirit that follows Dipsychus like his shadow, and whispers in his ear what could be called his worldly thoughts. The design, we think, is happy. If the Evil Spirit or Tempter of our day can be nothing but a personification of a certain mode of feeling and thinking, the most accurate way of representing him would be as a personification of the very thoughts and desires of the man who is tempted. Each one of us has his own Mephistopheles.

But it is not certain that Clough intended to limit his poem to a dialogue of the soul with its other self. It is probable that he would have introduced other characters. Indeed, in the second part, of which a brief sketch was made, we catch sight of a certain Delilah, who would, no doubt, have been brought forward in a more prominent manner had the work been completed. It was growing up gradually in the mind of the author (just as did its greatest predecessor *Faust*), and the artist himself could not perhaps have told us what shape it would finally assume. One thing is evident, that the 'Easter Day' which precedes it, and is printed as if it were a separate poem, must be looked on as a part of *Dipsychus*. The dialogue commences with a reference to it. It acts as a prologue. There is another 'Easter Day' at the conclusion—as hopeful as the first is desponding—which takes the place of epilogue. It is true there is also a prose prologue and epilogue very cleverly written. How the author would finally have adjusted the materials he has left behind, it is not easy to guess. Per-

[1] By Xavier de Maistre, 1794.

haps he would have determined on omitting these two slight conversations in prose.

Dipsychus is in Naples, which, if not the most vicious town in Europe, is certainly the town where vice looks most odious by its glaring juxtaposition with a degraded form of Christianity. Everywhere monks and Madonnas, lies and rascality. 'If Christianity has come to this,'—so muses the solitary man—'where is the Christ who undertook the regeneration of the world? Yes, He lived; yes, He taught and suffered; but does He live *now*? Does He, from the heavens, rule and save the world?' And he bursts forth in the passionate exclamation, 'Christ has *not* risen!'

[Quotes 'Easter Day', ll. 1–8: 'Through the great sinful streets' to 'Christ is not risen!' and 48–63: 'As circulates in some great city crowd' to 'Christ is not risen!'.]

The whole poem is written with great vigour, and also with great pathos. 'It has,' as the poet himself somewhere observes, 'a strong Strauss smell about it;' but this, we presume, could not be avoided. Scene the First transports us to Venice. Dipsychus is sitting in the piazza apart from the crowd, with the attendant Spirit beside him.

[Quotes *Dipsychus*, Scene 1, 43–68: 'The whole great square' to 'How he likes doing it!—ha, ha!' and 78–9: 'While these do what? Ah, heaven, too true, at Venice Christ is not risen either'.]

Scene Second is in the public garden. Scene Third in the hotel, but much the same dialogue is pursued in both.

> *Di:*   Oh, great God!
> Why, why in wisdom and in grace's name,
> And in the name of saints and saintly thoughts,
> Of mothers and of sisters, and chaste wives,
> And angel woman-faces we have seen,
> And angel woman-spirits we have guessed,
> And innocent sweet children and pure love,
> Why did I ever one brief moment's space
> But parley with this filthy Belial?
>   ... Was it fear
> Of being behind the world, which is the wicked?
> *Sp:*   Come, then,
> And with my aid go into good society.
> Life little loves, 'tis true, this peevish piety;

E'en they with whom it thinks to be securest—
Your most religious, delicatest, purest—
Discern and show, as pious people can,
This feeling that you are not quite a man.
Still the thing has its place, and with sagacity
Much might be done by one of your capacity.
A virtuous attachment, formed judiciously,
Would come, one sees, uncommonly propitiously;
Turn you but your affections the right way,
And what mayn't happen, none of us can say;
For, in despite of devils and of mothers,
Your good young men make catches, too, like others.
Di: To herd with people that one owns no care for;
Friend it with strangers that one sees but once;
To drain the heart with endless complaisance.

To waste the priceless moments of the *man*
In regulating *manner.* Whether these things
Be right, I do not know; I only know 'tis
To lose one's youth too early. Oh, not yet,
Not yet I make the sacrifice.
Sp: *Du tout!*
To give up nature's just what would not do.
By all means keep your sweet ingenuous graces,
And use them at the proper times and places,
For work, for play, for business, talk, and love.
I own as wisdom truly from above,
That scripture of the serpent and the dove.[1]

We perceive that this worldly temptation to lay himself out for
what is called a good marriage will not succeed with our solitary
thinker. There is, indeed, but one alternative for such a man: either
he must love outright, and start to his feet, and energetically pursue
his phantom; or some woman, not the purest of her sex, must seek
him out, break down the barriers of his shyness and reserve, and carry
him off, a slave for a season. It is this last branch of the alternative that
describes (as we have related it in the second part) the fate of our
Dipsychus.

Scene the Fourth is in the Piazza again. Our much meditative man
has been insulted by some German officer, and the question is, Shall
he fight or not? Of course the worldly Spirit urges an immediate

[1] For the passages corresponding to these lines see *Poems* (1951), *Dipsychus,* Scenes IIA
and III.

challenge, taunts him with cowardice, and even argues the case on moral grounds, for ought not all offenders be punished for the benefit of society at large? Dipsychus answers in a noble strain:

> *Di:* It falls from off me like the rain.
> . . . I seem in spirit to see
> How he and I at some great day shall meet
> Before some awful judgment-seat of truth;
> And I could deem that I behold him there
> Come praying for the pardon I give now,
> Did I not think these matters too, too small
> For any record on the leaves of Time.
> O Thou great Watcher of this noisy world,
> What are they in Thy sight? or what in his
> Who finds some end of action in his life?
>
> *Sp:* Certainly. Take our lives,
> Sweet friends, and please respect our wives;
> Joy to the Croat! Some fine day
> He'll see the error of his way,
> No doubt, and will repent and pray.
> At any rate he'll open his eyes,
> If not before, at the Last Assize.
> Not, if I rightly understood you,
> That even then you'd punish, would you?[1]

Dipsychus, however, is immovable. To draw his sword in a great cause, that he thinks would be 'the flower and top of life,'

> But things so merely personal to myself
> Of all earth's things do least affect myself.

In Scene Fifth, on the Lido, two aspects of one momentous thought —the supposition that there is NO Divine Governor of the world— are put before us. In this case Dipsychus himself gives utterance to the two opposite views: 1, the awe and terror and sense of anarchy that follows the denial, and 2, the sense of freedom and perfect self-will which the same denial would procure for mankind. His thoughts take the shape of a dream. The reckless libertine denial is ushered in by the *tinkling*, the awe-struck denial by the solemn *tolling*, of a bell. It is a contrivance which reminds us of some of the pieces of Edgar Poe; we cannot say that we altogether like it, and we may observe, in passing, that Clough appears to us to have rather an excessive fondness

---

1 For the passages corresponding to these lines see *Poems* (1951), *Dipsychus*, Scene VI.

for a *refrain*, or the repetition of some verse or line. Such repetition is very effective, only it must not grow into a mannerism.

When Dipsychus has told his dream the Spirit takes up the theme, and here is introduced one of the most perfect little pieces that ever were written. Heine himself has done nothing more terse, or more *spirituel*.

[Quotes *Dipsychus*, Scene V, ll. 154–61, 166–85; '"There is no God!"' to '*something very like Him*'.]

Then follows a cluster of beautiful little poems. The Spirit revels in his wit, and Dipsychus himself assumes a gayer vein. It is he who breaks forth in these lines:—

> Afloat, we move. Delicious! Ah
> What else is like the gondola?
> This level floor of liquid glass
> Begins beneath us swift to pass.
> It goes as though it went alone
> By some impulsion of its own;
> How light it moves, how softly! Ah,
> Were all things like the gondola! &c. &c.
>
> [Scene IV, 3–10]

Yet the next minute he cannot but bethink him of the boatman at work out there in the hot sun to procure him this delicious movement of the gondola.

[Quotes Scene IV, ll. 43–60: 'Our gaieties, our luxuries' to 'we shall pay' and 114–17, 'This world is very odd', etc.]

Then the Spirit chants these jovial lines, which will meet with an echo far and wide, and which are distinguished by the refrain:—

> How pleasant it is to have money, heigh ho!
> How pleasant it is to have money!

These and some others have been already printed separately in the first volume—more is the pity; for we are persuaded that if *Dipsychus* had been given to the world, in all its freshness, in the form it has here, there is not a critic in the three kingdoms who would not have been loud in its praise. It is difficult to compare it with the more imaginative poetry of Tennyson or Browning, but there is a third name among our still living poets which may suggest an apt comparison. Those who are fond of arranging or classing their favourite poems according to their degree of merit would perhaps bracket together *Philip van Artevelde* and *Dipsychus*. The masterpiece of Taylor[1] has all the advantage of completeness, and it has far greater variety of character; the fragment of Clough, on the other hand, deals with a subtler range of thought, and with speculative moods which awaken the deeper sympathies of the age. Both writers are distinguished by pure and forcible English; both desire first of all to be understood, and, for this end, take care that they understand themselves. We, for our own part, are not given to make this sort of catalogue of our favourite writers—we should never be quite satisfied with the order in which we had arranged them; but we venture on this parallel in order to show unmistakably the high estimation we have of *Dipsychus*.

It has, as the author left it behind him, very little plot or dramatic structure of any kind, yet we have still to mention what may be said to be the knot of the poem, the urgent problem that Dipsychus has to solve with himself. The soul wants action as well as thought, and where is noble action to be found? Shall a man sit idle till a grand purpose unfolds itself? Do grand purposes come to idle men? or does idleness fit us for them when they do come? Yet again, if a man, for commonplace ends, gives himself to a laborious routine, will not this commit him irrevocably to the mean and ignoble? He and the Spirit together pass in review the several professions, as of arms, the Church, and the law, and of course with little result. Yet there must be activity of some kind. No great opportunities come to men who sit idle upon the ground:

> High deeds
> Haunt not the fringy edges of the fight,
> But the pell-mell, of men. O what and if
> E'en now by lingering here I let them slip,
> Like an unpractised spyer through a glass,
> Still pointing to the blank, too high?

But he has no sooner uttered this sentiment than the opposite fear of debasing the mind by sordid habits returns upon him—

> O and to blast that Innocence, which though
> Here it may seem a dull unopening bud,
> May yet bloom freely in celestial clime!

---

[1] Sir Henry Taylor (1800–86): his psychological drama *Philip van Artevelde* was acclaimed upon publication in 1834, but failed on the stage in 1847. The preface to the play is now best remembered as representing the 'classical' Victorian reaction against Romanticism.

Ay! but this innocence—will idleness secure it any better than ordinary selfish action?

> Life loves no lookers-on at his great game,

>   . . . The dashing stream
> Stays not to pick his steps among the rocks,
> Or let his water-breaks be chronicled;
> And though the hunter looks before he leaps,
> 'Tis instinct rather than a shaped-out thought
> That lifts him his bold way. Then instinct, hail;
> And farewell hesitation. If I stay,
> I am not innocent; nor if I go—
> E'en should I fall—beyond redemption lost.

But irresolute, deliberating men may talk of surrendering themselves up to their instincts; they cannot do it; they have passed, by deliberation itself, out of the sphere of instinct. An awakened instinct, or passion, may seize on them; they cannot deliberately choose for it. What Dipsychus wants is action that shall be—

> In its kind, personal, in its motive not.

What refined Socialism is to give us this? and would it not be action of a very mechanical kind, however pure its motive?

>   For indeed
> The earth moves slowly, if it move at all,
> And by the general, not the single force
> Of the linked members of the vast machine
> In all its crowded rooms of industry
> No individual soul has loftier leave
> Than fiddling with a piston or a valve.

The Spirit interposes. We must, after all, submit to do as the rest are doing.

> *Sp:* To move on angels' wings were sweet;
> But who would therefore scorn his feet?
> It cannot walk up to the sky;
> It therefore will lie down and die.
> Rich meats it can't obtain at call;
> It therefore will not eat at all,
> Poor babe, and yet a babe of wit!
> But common sense—not much of it—

Or 'twould submit,
Submit, submit!

We have quoted already with unusual length: we must hurry up what remains to be said. From the Second Part, of which but very little seems to have been written, we learn that Dipsychus found the requisite impulse for action in a love not of the most virtuous order. But, having received the requisite impulse, he has toiled and risen in the profession of the law till he has attained the dignity of Lord Chief Justice. The close is somewhat enigmatical. The reader perhaps will be better pleased to excogitate his own interpretation than to receive one from us.

The whole terminates with a second 'Easter Day,' the burden of which is that Christ *has* risen! As joy and grief intermingle in life, and yet, on the whole, joy conquers grief, so belief and unbelief will mingle, but finally faith is conqueror.

For all that breathes beneath the heaven's high cope,
Joy with grief mixes, with despondence hope.

It does not fall to us to pass in review the poems of the previous volume, and we are glad that such a task has not devolved on us. We should, indeed, on one ground be quite incapacitated for it. A large portion of these poems is written in English hexameters, and, do all we can, we (that is, of course, the present individual writer) are unable to reconcile ourselves to this verse, if verse it is to be called. If we force ourselves to read a poem in this metre we should not be able to enjoy, or do justice to such substantial merits as it might really possess; the constant irritation of the (to us) detestable cadence would unfit us for any enjoyment at all. Of course there are many who do like English hexameters, or they would not be written, and we are prepared to be told that we have neither ear nor taste, nor a scholar's predilection. So let it be. But the fact remains; as we are unable to enjoy, so we should be unable fairly to criticise, a poem in this metre. But we were delighted with many of the pieces addressed to the non-scholastic ear. Let us be allowed to close the present notice, which has unavoidably led us into grave and intricate topics, with a quotation from a pleasant idyll:—

[Quotes 'On Grass, on Gravel, in the Sun', ll. 1–12: 'On grass, on gravel' to 'compare with this?' and ll. 37–48: 'The high-titled cares' to 'compare with this?'.]

THE POEMS AND PROSE REMAINS

1869

NOTE ON THE CONTENTS

With the partial exception of H. S. Milford's *Poems of Clough*
(1910), this was the most complete edition of Clough's work to
have been published before the standard edition which appeared
in 1951. It was re-issued in 1871 with Mrs Clough's 'Memoir'
abridged, and subsequently in 1874, 1877, 1878, 1879, 1880 and
1882. All these printings were called by the publishers, Macmillan,
the 'Third Edition'—Palgrave's *Poems* of 1862 being the First and
his revised version of 1863 the Second. A Fourth Edition, identical
with the Third, appeared in 1883 and was reprinted in 1885.

Mrs Clough's edition contains many important poems previously unpublished (for full details see *A.H.C. Descr. Cat.* 35–8).
Her 54-page 'Memoir' is considerably longer than Palgrave's,
filled out by lengthy reminiscences contributed by several of
Clough's friends and acquaintances, but it contains no noteworthy
critical comment; neither is its tone of extenuation better calculated than Palgrave's to win Clough fresh readers. Palgrave's
briefer and better phrased 'Memoir' has therefore been preferred
for inclusion here as the earliest and probably most influential
representative of the well-intentioned apologias Clough's reputation had to contend with.

In her Preface Mrs Clough pays tribute to 'the valuable assis-
tance which she has received in making these selections and in
arranging these volumes from Mr J. A. Symonds, to whose taste
and judgment any measure of success that may have been achieved
is chiefly due'. This, no doubt, being the case, the essay by Symonds that follows here, though it antedates the publication of
The Poems and Prose Remains by a few months, may be regarded
as, in effect, the true editor's Introduction.

38. John Addington Symonds, from 'Arthur Hugh Clough', article in the *Fortnightly Review*

1 December 1868, xxiv, 589–617

Symonds (1840–93) was a prolific minor poet, classical scholar, author of the *History of the Italian Renaissance* and of studies of Dante and Whitman.

He had written an earlier long essay on Clough which had been intended to supplement Palgrave's 'Memoir', but after its appearance in *Cornhill Magazine* in October 1866 he wrote to Mrs Clough regretting any misconceptions he might have fostered through ignorance of Clough's life. He thinks Allingham's article in *Fraser's* (see No. 36) must have been better informed than his. Accordingly, he begins this article with an uncontroversial résumé of the life and a careful discussion of Clough's religious standpoint. He had also, by this time, become Mrs Clough's friend and was helping her to prepare the *Poems and Prose Remains* of 1869 (we first learn of this joint venture in his letter to her of 4 May 1868, *The Letters of John Addington Symonds*, I, 804, ed. Schueller and Peters). Since he refers in another letter of 1 January 1869, to 'Jowett's approval of the general plan' of the collection, it seems reasonable to regard the article printed here as relevant to the more complete *Poems and Prose Remains* which are the subject of this section, though they did not appear until later in 1869.

It is also interesting to note that in the first letter to Mrs Clough to which I have referred Symonds felt able to assure her that 'there are several at Cambridge and Oxford' of his generation 'who look on Mr Clough's poems as the expression of their deepest convictions and seek in him a mirror of themselves, deriving strength and support from his example' (*The Letters of J.A.S.*, I, 670).

It is not our purpose to dwell upon the biography of Mr. Clough, which has lately been much discussed in various contemporary publications, but rather to examine his works, and to show in what their real and vital excellence consists. Yet in order to understand these works, and to explain away some misconceptions which have arisen as to the alleged 'wasted genius,' 'baffled intellect,' 'unfulfilled purpose,' and 'disappointed life' of Mr. Clough, which many of his recent critics bitterly deplore, we may preface our review of his poems by a short notice of this biography.

[There follows a brief summary of Clough's life.]

Such is the briefest outline of Clough's life. Its chief value is to bring out the essential point that the *Bothie*, *Amours de Voyage*, *Dipsychus*, and *Mari Magno*—the four principal monuments of his poetical genius—were all of them composed in the course of two short periods of holiday and relaxation: the first three during the quiet time which intervened between the first and second period we have marked, after he had broken with Oxford and when he had not yet engaged in other work; the last, immediately before his death and during his last journey. The poems themselves bear traces of the scenes and times that gave them birth. The *Bothie* is a record of Highland reading parties; *Amours de Voyage* is full of Roman associations; *Dipsychus* carries us to Venice; *Mari Magno* combines the influences of a voyage across the Atlantic with several touches caught from Pyrenean, Swiss, and Greek scenery. In so true a sense were Clough's poems the product of his life, and so clearly were the powers of his genius limited, not by their own feebleness or by the wasting action of a morbid intellect, but by the lack of time and opportunity for fuller and more studied compositions. Indeed, we believe that none but those who judge Clough's life and writings by the lowest standard will maintain that his work was insufficient. On the contrary, if we regard the quality rather than the quantity of literary production, our feeling will be surprise at the mere amount of his poetry, especially if we reflect upon the nature of the topics which he handled, the conscientious scrupulosity of his nature, both as a poet and as a man, and the various distractions of his life. Clough had nothing of the self-conscious artist or of the ordinary *littérateur* about him. His poems are not flashes on the surface, occasional pieces, or set compositions upon given themes; but the very pith and marrow of a deeply-thinking, deeply-feeling soul—the most heartfelt utterances of one who sought to speak out what was in him in the fewest and the simplest words. His horror of artificial language was often carried to excess. His hatred of affectation betrayed him into baldness. But one thing we may be sure to find in him—sincerity and sense.

Those, again, who can divest themselves of social and religious prejudices, and who are strong enough to breathe the fine rare atmosphere of thought in which he moved, will acknowledge that it was not he who was irreligious, but that this reproach might rather be cast on those of us who blind our eyes, and palter with our conscience, and endeavour to impose our intellectual forms and fancies upon God. Clough happened to live during a period of transition in the history of human thought, when it was impossible for a thinking man to avoid problems by their very nature irresoluble in one lifetime. Loving truth for its own sake, he laid himself open with singular purity and candour of mind to all the onward moving forces in the world around him. He did not try to make things other than he found them. He refused to tamper with his conscience for the sake of repose in the Romish, or of distinction in the English Church; nor yet was he inclined to buy freedom at the price of irreligion. Some natures are capable of these courses. Truth is not all-important to them: they acquiesce in traditional methods of holiness, and in the respectabilities of time-hallowed creeds. But Clough was by no means one of this sort. Manfully and boldly he admitted all the difficulties that occurred to his mind, faced them, scrutinised them, and maintained in spite of them an invincible confidence in the moral supremacy of good, and in the relation of his own soul to God. He had the strength to cast off much that was dear and honoured in his earliest beliefs, and to fling himself upon a sea of anxious questioning.

Determined to be free and independent, he resigned the valuable post he held as tutor and fellow of Oriel. And in all these things he triumphed: for no one gained a purer or keener insight into the *essence*, as distinguished from the *forms*, of religion and morality; no one grasped abstract truths more firmly; no one possessed a fuller humanity, or higher faculties of helping and sympathising with his fellow-men. It was the reality of his religion, its perfect simplicity, its comprehensiveness and spirituality, which made it unintelligible to men of duller intellects and less sensitively scrupulous consciences. They required something more definite than he could give them; something more rough and ready, more fitted for immediate use. They did not care if part of the truth were sacrificed so long as they had solid dogmas to repose upon, and comfortable hopes to cling to. But Clough dreaded everything like 'adding up too soon' and incomplete conclusions. The insight which most men are impatient to exercise at the outset of life, he hoped might possibly be granted to him at its end, or, if not then, in after stages of existence.

The chief value of Clough's religious poetry appears to consist in this—that he sympathised at a very early period with the movement that is unquestionably going on towards the simplification and purification of belief, and that he gave an artistic expression to the thoughts of earnest seekers and questioners in the field of faith. In doing so he did not innovate, or ruthlessly destroy, or sentimentally bewail the past. He simply tried to reduce belief to its original and spiritual purity —to lead men back to the God that is within them, witnessed by their consciences and by the history of the human race. The primal religious instincts of mankind are apt in the course of centuries to gather round them metaphysical husks, which are partly protective of the germs within, and partly restrictive of their true vitality. Times arrive at which these outward shells are felt to have become too hard and narrow. They must then be broken through in order to free the kernels that lie within them. The most clear-sighted men at such periods try to discriminate between what is essential and what is unimportant in religion; but the majority cling always to the human and material rubbish with which it is clogged, as if it were the very living and life-giving divine truth. We might use Plato's simile, and compare the present condition of the Christian faith, as contrasted with the teaching of its great Founder, to the Glaucus of the deep, who rises overgrown with weeds and shells from the ocean, where he has been hidden. To pull away these weeds, and to restore the god-like form to its own likeness, is the desire of all thoughtful men whose minds have been directed to religious questions, and who have not bound themselves to support the existing order of things, or undertaken for their own interests to solidify the prejudices of the mass. Christ himself, by his answers to the questions of the Jews, taught us the principle of returning to simplicity in religious beliefs. He also, by his example, justified us in assuming that the Gospel is not stationary, but progressive; that we may come to know more of God than we knew centuries ago; and that the human race, by extending its intelligence, extends its spiritual insight. It is from this point of view that Clough approaches topics of religious belief and Biblical inquiry.

My own feeling [he says] certainly does not go along with Coleridge, in attributing any special virtue to the facts of the Gospel history. They have happened, and have produced what we know, have transformed the civilisation of Greece and Rome and the barbarism of Gaul and Germany into Christendom. But 1 cannot feel sure that a man may not have all that is important in Christianity, even if he does not so much as know that Jesus of Nazareth existed. And I do not think that doubts respecting the facts related in the Gospels need give us much trouble. Believing that in one way or other the thing is of God, we shall in the end perhaps know in what way, and how far it was so. Trust in God's justice and love, and belief in his commands as written in our conscience, stand unshaken, though Matthew, Mark, Luke, and John, or even St. Paul, were to fall.[1]

Again he says, with the same confidence in spiritual truth which is the essence of belief in God:—

It is far nobler to teach people to do what is good, because it is good simply, than for the sake of any future reward. It is, I dare say, difficult to keep up an equal religious feeling at present, but it is not impossible, and is necessary. Besides, if *we* die and come to nothing, it does not therefore follow that life and goodness will cease to be in earth and heaven.[2]

This thought is further expressed in a fragment of verse:—

> It fortifies my soul to know
> That, though I perish, Truth is so:
> That, howsoe'er I stray and range,
> Whate'er I do, Thou dost not change.
> I steadier step when I recall
> That, if I slip, Thou dost not fall.

The power and dignity of this repose on what is great and good, this total unselfishness and confidence in the Unseen, belong to the highest sphere of religious faith. But it is not the religion of the emotions so much as of the intellect; and therefore it cannot be widely understood and accepted. When the hearer is bidden to discard his hopes of personal reward, and to embrace some exalted conception of the divine character more remote than that of old Anthropomorphism—when he is informed that neither at Jerusalem nor on this mountain must he worship, and that his God is in reality a Spirit—he begins to murmur that there is nothing left for him to live by, no solid and substantial ground to stand upon, no sufficient inducements to virtuous action. And the preacher of so abstract and refined a faith is stigmatised as sceptical, if no worse name be given him. Thus

[1] Clough to his sister, May 1847 (printed in *PPR I*, 110–11).
[2] Clough to his sister, December 1848 (*ibid.* 135).

Spinoza, who by the most intelligent men of this century has been represented as a God-absorbed, if not a 'God-intoxicated' man, was called an Atheist for professing a theology, the essence of which might be summed up in the one proposition, that he loved God too much to want love back from Him again. And to ordinary minds he *was* Atheistical; for in their sense of the word God he had no God. He had refined and abstracted the idea until it vanished from the sphere of their intelligence.

One great quality of Clough's mind in regard to religion was its wholly undogmatic character. He regarded all problems with impartiality and calmness. One of his MSS. consists of a series of arguments in which he discusses the great question of belief.[1] Nothing could better illustrate his perfect openness of mind than this process of reasoning. It begins by stating the impossibility that scholars should not perceive 'the entire uncertainty of history in general, and of the origin of Christianity in particular.' In this position he coincides with all the fairest and profoundest thinkers of the century. Niebuhr, Grote, Sir Cornewall Lewis, Strauss, Baur, Renan, have all in their own departments shown the doubtfulness of early history, and have endeavoured with more or less success to sift the truth from a mass of error. The historian of Christianity has greater difficulties to contend with than the historians of Rome or Greece; for he has no corroborative evidence of what is narrated in the sacred books, and all his endeavours to bring the truth to light meet with furious antagonism from minds wedded to the old system. But, continues Clough, it is equally impossible for a man who has lived and acted among men not to perceive the value of what is called Christianity. The more he is convinced of this, the less inclined will he be 'to base it on those foundations which, as a scholar, he feels to be unstable. MSS. are doubtful, records may be unauthentic, criticism is feeble, historical facts must be left uncertain.' This then is the antithesis with which we have to deal: on the one hand, the history of the origin of Christianity involves the greatest amount of uncertainty; on the other hand, Christianity, as a real and vital principle, is indispensable to the world. Meanwhile, our own personal experience is small and limited; our own powers are narrow, and not to be relied on. 'A sane and humble-minded man' (concludes Clough), who is disinclined to adopt the watchword of a party or to set up new views, has no alternative 'but to throw himself

---

[1] This MSS. was to be printed in *PPR I*, under the heading 'Notes on the Religious Tradition' (reprinted *SPW*).

upon the great Religious Tradition.' One step is gained; but here another difficulty presents itself to the thinker.

I see not [he continues] how any upright and strict dealer with himself, how any man, *not merely a slave to spiritual appetites, affections, and wants*—any man of intellectual as well as moral honesty (and without the former the latter is but a vain thing) can dare to affirm that the narrative of the four Gospels is an essential integral part of that tradition.

The words which we have italicised are peculiarly characteristic of Mr. Clough. He was sensitively, almost Quixotically, afraid of accepting even a respectable and harmless creed for the sake of merely being comfortable. He saw that in an age of doubt it was a sort of self-indulgence to cling to the old formulas of faith, and that, in one sense, honest questioning was less sceptical than conscious acquiescence. Pursuing this vein of reflection, he condemns the weakness of ignoring scientific or historic doubts 'for the sake of the moral guidance and spiritual comfort' implied in submissive belief, or of 'taking refuge in Romish infallibility.' At the same time, he is eager to deny that there is anything great or noble or very needful in showing up the inconsistencies of the New Testament: 'it is no new gospel to tell us that the old one is of doubtful authenticity.' But cannot a simple-minded man steer between the opposite dangers of bragging Scepticism and Iconoclasm on the one hand, and, on the other, of self-indulgent mysticism? 'I believe that I may, without any such perversion of my reason, without any such mortal sin against my own soul, which is identical with reason, and against the Supreme Giver of that soul and reason, still abide by the real Religious Tradition.' But 'where,' he asks, 'since neither in rationalism nor in Rome is our refuge, where then shall we seek for the Religious Tradition?' The answer to this question is the answer which all good men and all sincere thinkers are becoming more and more ready to accept; it is the answer made by the Church in earlier days; the answer still implied in an old picture which represents Aristotle and Plato among the Apostles of Pentecost: —'Everywhere. But above all,' he adds, 'in our own work, in life, in action, in submission so far as action goes, in service, in experience, in patience, and in confidence.' Then follows a very significant sentence which reveals to us the seriousness of Clough's mind upon this subject, his sense of its deep mystery, his persuasion that all a man's life is too little in the search for God. 'I would scarcely have any man dare to say that he has found it till that moment when death removes his power of telling it.' The answer, however, requires to be expanded. We must look for the Religious Tradition everywhere, and not expect to find it in Protestantism only, or in the Roman Church, or in Unitarianism. Take the good from each and all. 'Whether Christ died for us upon the cross I cannot tell; yet I am prepared to find some spiritual truth in the doctrine of the Atonement. Purgatory is not in the Bible; I do not therefore think it incredible.' Again, we must seek it among clergymen, religious people, 'among all who have really tried to order their lives by a high standard.' Johnson, Hume, and Butler, each in his own way, contributes something to the total. Search the Scriptures, but also search the Laws of Menou and the Vedas, the Persian sacred books and Hafiz, Confucius, the Koran, Greek and Roman literature. Homer, Socrates, Plato, Lucretius, Virgil, Tacitus, can tell us something. This comprehensiveness and liberality of soul correspond with the true spirit of Christianity, of Christianity which is universal and divine because it is truly human; of Christianity which speaks alike to Jew and Greek, barbarian, Scythian, bond and free, which needs no better evidence than that which is afforded by its parallels in India, China, Persia, Greece—the soul of man in every clime and age. Nor will this comprehensive creed render us less appreciative of Christianity itself. We may travel far and wide, yet not become disqualified for returning 'to what assuredly, *primâ facie*, does appear to be—not indeed the religion of the majority of mankind—but the religion of the best, so far as we can judge in past history, and (despite of professed infidelity) of the most enlightened in our own time.' To cease to be Christians, to separate ourselves from the peculiar form of Christianity adopted by our forefathers, would be unnatural, if not impossible; for special religions seem to be adapted to special races. Yet we may remember that there are many more Buddhists than Christians in the world, and not imagine that on us alone God's sun has shone. Finally,

it is much more the apparent dispensation of things that we should gradually widen than that we should narrow and individualise our creeds. Why are we daily coming more and more into communication with each other, if it be not that we learn each other's knowledge, and combine all into one? I feel more inclined to put faith in the current of the river of things than because it runs one way to think I must therefore pull hard against it to go the other.

But it is time to pass from these reflections on the nature of Religion to the poems in which Clough has embodied the fervent spirit of his creed. '*Qui laborat, orat*'—is the title of a few stanzas in which the poet questions whether it be not profane to give even the most abstract form to God, and concludes that work is the truest expression of earnest prayer. A similar train of thought is carried out in loftier language in another called 'The New Sinai.' After tracing the gradual development of the monotheistic idea, and adverting to the cloud and darkness which in modern times have, through the influence of science on the one hand and superstition on the other, seemed to gather round the throne of God, he eloquently and emphatically expresses his content to trust and wait for the hour of God's own revelation. This is the essence of his religion—to believe in the Unseen, and bravely to embrace a faith without sight, instead of forging an image, and falling down to worship it. A third poem, of a strictly devout character, even more solemn in expression, more full of weighty and condensed thought, develops the same idea: its first stanza may be quoted as an index to the whole:—

> O Thou, whose image in the shrine
> Of human spirits dwells divine;
> Which from that precinct once conveyed
> To be to outer day displayed,
> Doth vanish, part, and leave behind
> Mere blank and void of empty mind,
> Which wilful fancy seeks in vain
> With casual shapes to fill again.

It is very difficult for those who did not know Clough personally to gather from such notices as we can give, how deep and fervent— how absolute and unshaken—were his religious convictions. But the witnesses of his life are unanimous in assuring us that the principles expressed in the poems we have quoted were the fixed and unvarying rules of his own conduct, the supporting and strengthening springs of his action in the world. Contrasted with these devotional poems are some of a more analytical character, which, however, tend to the same conclusion, that God, falsely figured by the world to itself in various fanciful or obsolete shapes, or else denied with insolence and scorn, is yet supreme and spiritual, felt by those who have preserved an honest and untainted soul, and dreaded with blind terror even by those who pretend to disbelieve in him. Of these, two songs in *Dipsychus*, 'I dreamed a dream,' and its companion, 'There is no God the wicked saith' (published in the volume of collected poems), may be cited as specimens. An ironical tone runs through them, and is strangely blended with bitterness, gravity, and a kind of tender regret. They ought not to be separated; for nothing is more true of Clough's mind than that it worked by thesis and antithesis, not reaching a clear synthesis, but pushing its convictions, as it were, to the verge of a conclusion. The poems, for instance, which begin, 'Old things need not be therefore true,' 'What we, when face to face we see,' and 'Say not, the struggle nought availeth,' are in their tone almost timid and retrogressive when compared with 'Easter Day;' and yet we feel that none of them contain the *dernier mot*. Clough could take the world's or the devil's point of view with wonderful force and vigour. This is clear throughout *Dipsychus*; but it also appears in a published poem, entitled, 'The Latest Decalogue.' To imagine that when he did so he was expressing his *own* view would be to mistake the artist's nature altogether. Yet some people are so dull as to do this. They are shocked at any one venturing to state a base or wicked opinion, even though his object be to call attention to the contrary, and, by revealing ugliness, to lead the eye in silence to the contemplation of beauty.

In Clough's works there are many stumbling-blocks for such readers —none greater than 'Easter Day,' a poem about which it is hard to speak, whether we regard its depth of meaning or its high literary excellence. Of the general scope of this poem it is impossible to give a better account than that which is prefixed to it in the volume of *Letters and Remains*. There it is styled

a semi-dramatic expression of the contrast he (Clough) felt between the complete practical irreligion and wickedness of the life he saw going on, and the outward forms and ceremonies of religion displaying themselves at every turn. How can we believe, it seems to say, that 'Christ is risen' in such a world as this? How, if it was so, could such sin and such misery continue until now? Yet if we must give up this faith, what sadness and what bitterness of disappointment remain for all believers who thus lose all that is most dear to them! And he abandons himself to this feeling of grief and hopelessness, only still vaguely clinging to the belief that in earth itself there may be, if nowhere else, a new refuge and a new answer to this sad riddle. The mood of mind which he depicts in such terrible colours is not to be regarded as his own habitual belief. The poem is in no sense a statement of facts or opinions, but a strong expression of feeling—above all, the feeling of the greatness of the evil which is in the world.[1]

More, however, remains to be said. For though 'Easter Day' 'is not to be regarded as his own habitual belief,' we cannot but consider it to

[1] This note by Mrs Clough illustrates her anxiety that her husband's more sceptical poems should not mar his posthumous reputation (see above, p. 10).

be the expression of a mind steeped in the disintegrating solvents of nineteenth-century criticism. The author has clearly absorbed everything that German commentators have to say upon the subject of the resurrection—nay, more, has, at least one time of his life, most keenly felt the cogency of their destructive arguments, and in a mood of bitterness provoked by human degradation has given the form of fiery language to the shapeless and uncertain doubts which crowd the minds of a beliefless generation. 'Easter Day' is unique in the history of literature. It is a poem fully worthy of that name, in which a train of close and difficult reasoning is expressed in concise words—such words as might have been used by a commentator on the Gospels, yet so subtly manipulated by the poet, with such a rhythm, such compactness, such vitality of emotion, as to attain the dignity of art by mere simplicity and power.

For the sake of those who may not have this poem in their hands, we subjoin some extracts. But it must be remembered that quotation in this case is akin to mutilation, and that the poem itself is liable to be misunderstood in its incomplete form:

[Quotes 'Easter Day', ll. 1–8, 27–35, 64–112, 126–36.]

It must not be thought that religious problems are the only ones which occupied the mind of Mr. Clough. On the contrary, whatever is important in the life of man attracted his eager thought, and received from him the same minute and scrupulous consideration. His large humanity was one of his most prominent qualities; nor was there anything of real or of serious significance, however painful, in the world from which he shrank. Two principal topics beside that of religion seem to have been always present to his mind. One of these was the question of love, the other of action, or of work in life. We shall now proceed to consider his poetical treatment of both of these points, which, together with religion, form the most important subjects that a poet can approach.

Passing from Clough's religious poems to those in which he has dealt in detail with the problems of human life and love, we may make the preliminary remark that here, as in his more abstract compositions, he is manly and clairvoyant—unflinching—affecting nothing, and avoiding nothing which he sees to be true and weighty in the facts presented to his notice. Though minutely analytical—as, for instance, in *Dipsychus* and some parts of *Amours de Voyage*—he is never morbidly so. We feel his personality as we do that of all true

and sincere poets; and perhaps these poems are a better record of that
personality than any memoirs which could possibly be written. But
there is nothing self-conscious or unhealthily introspective in this
revelation of himself. What strikes us in these poems of the second
class is their perfect sincerity and truth to life. They are like pictures
painted from natural objects in the fair light of day—no Fuseli or
Blake translations from a world of spirits and of murky gloom. Nor
is this impression altered where the remote and uncommon nature of
his subject obliges him to have recourse to psychological anatomy.
We find no 'supreme moments,' no passionate and fiery experiences
in which life is lost as in a furnace glow, either in his philosophy or his
art. He yields, indeed, its full part to passion, but a far larger part to
law—the law of conscience and humanity. The pathos that he stirs is
of no maudlin or sentimental kind, but is purely natural and sincere—
gushing, as in the last story of *Mari Magno*, from the flinty rock of fact
and dire necessity. In this respect he is a kind of better Crabbe; more
full of natural tenderness and fine distinctions, if less sternly powerful
and less deeply tragic.

But if Clough has nothing in common with poets of the De Musset
type, he is equally far removed from the trivial domesticities of the
Angel in the House.[1] Clough was not, indeed, a misogynist or indifferent to marriage. On the contrary, a great number of his poems
prove that the problems of married love and life were among those
which most deeply occupied his mind. But he did not shut his eyes
and dream that the Englishman's paradise of a clean hearth and a
kind wife is the only object of existence, or, that if it were, it would
be easy to obtain entrance into it. The patient insight, refusing to
be deceived by any illusion, however sweet, in its unwavering courage,
which we have traced in his treatment of religion, appears no less
in his treatment of love. He is able to see men and women as they
are, very imperfect in their affections, often too weak even to love
without an *arrière pensée*, letting priceless opportunity slip by, and
killing the flower of one part of their nature by the drought and dryness of the other part.

In attempting to illustrate these general remarks by an analysis of
Clough's poems, we might begin with a notice of the tales called
Mari Magno, the last of his works, and therefore in some ways the
ripest product of his mind. But these tales are already *in extenso* before
the public, and are so likely to be the most popular portion of his works,

[1] Coventry Patmore, *The Angel in the House* (1854–6).

that we may perhaps content ourselves with reference to them. The first two are very speculative. Their moral seems to be that love is fellow-service, and that the *à peu près* of human relations must be accepted cheerfully. To follow the absolute, and to expect to realise an idea, is vain. Let life school us to love as men, with the whole force, indeed, of our natures, but with no fantastic yearnings after impossibilities. If we fail to learn these lessons, and refuse the natural good of human life, we shall be disciplined with disappointment. The thought of these two poems is so subtle—so delicately shadowed forth and illuminated with cross lights—that in order to present a faithful picture of them, it would be necessary to transcribe the tales themselves. The rest are more simple. They have less of speculation and more of incident and human pathos. Indeed, the story called 'Christian,' or the Lawyer's Second Tale, is one of the most dramatic poems of its kind in the English language. When we remember that this story was actually completed during Clough's last hours, while paralysis was rapidly invading the very stronghold of life, it forms the most convincing proof of the genuine and irresistible force of his poetic genius.

Amours de Voyage is, perhaps, the most highly finished, various, and artistically complete of all his works. It consists of a series of letters supposed to be written from Rome by an Englishman called Claude, and two sisters of a family of Trevellyns whose acquaintance he made there. It was composed by Clough at Rome in 1848, during the short life of Mazzini's Republic and the French siege. The chief incidents of this stirring time are so wrought into the narrative part of the poem as to contrast in a striking manner with the Hamlet-like indecision of the hero's character. '*Il doutait de tout, même de l'amour*' is one of the mottoes on the title-page; and the last two couplets of the 'Envoy' well describe the peculiar contrast which runs through the whole work:—

> Say, 'I am flitting about many years from brain unto brain of
> Feeble and restless youths born to inglorious days;
> But,' so finish the word, 'I was writ in a Roman chamber,
> When from Janiculan heights thundered the cannon of France.'

Amours de Voyage has three distinct subjects: the criticism of Rome from a traveller's point of view, involving many religious and æsthetical reflections; politics and the events of the siege; and the love-story of an over-refined and irresolute spirit. The two former topics are gradually merged in the last. Indeed, they serve chiefly to enliven the poem, and to illustrate the character of the sceptical hero and his ladylike innamorata. Clough has managed with great delicacy to introduce the theme of love, at first quite incidentally, into Claude's letters, and to let it grow by degrees until it swallows up the others, and forms the whole subject of the poem. But it must not be imagined that the love-story is the only important part of *Amours de Voyage*. On the contrary, there is a singular richness in the woof and texture of this poem, a variety which we miss in compositions like *Werter* or *Maud*. The descriptions of character are humorous and racy. Very delicate satire, for instance, adds an interest to Miss Georgina's letters; and the whole Trevellyn family is hit off with dramatic nicety. Claude himself appears before us as a many-sided man, and we get a good notion of his personality long before his love drama begins.

Claude is a young English gentleman, well born and well connected, but naturally shy and rather satirical. His education has rendered him fastidious; and he is by temperament inclined to dream and meditate and question rather than to act. We soon find that he has the trick of introspection, and of nineteenth-century yearning after the impossible. It is curious that in his delineation of this state of mind Clough should remind us of Alfred de Musset—his antipodes in moral tone and mental calibre. Yet it is so. Both poets describe the *maladie du siècle*— the nondescript cachexy, in which aspiration mingles with disenchantment, satire and scepticism with a childlike desire for the tranquillity of reverence and belief—in which self-analysis has been pushed to the verge of monomania, and all springs of action are clogged and impeded by the cobwebs of speculation. But while De Musset presents us with a French picture of this condition, very feeble, sickly, and disagreeable, Clough is true to the national vigour of the English character. We cannot mistake the irony with which he treats Claude, or fall into the error of identifying him with the poet.

Claude's first letters are devoted to the impressions produced on his mind by Rome. 'Rubbishy' is the best word he can find to express the Eternal City: indeed, it resembles its own Monte Testaceo, a 'mass of broken and castaway wine-pots.' In the midst of such grumblings a hint is dropped of a family called Trevellyn, who, a letter further on, are thus cleverly described:—

Middle-class people these, bankers very likely, not wholly
Pure of the taint of the shop; will at table-d'hôte and restaurant
Have their shilling's worth, their penny's pennyworth even:

Neither man's aristocracy this, nor God's, God knoweth!
Yet they are fairly descended, they give you to know, well connected;
Doubtless somewhere, in some neighbourhood have, and are careful
    to keep some
Threadbare genteel relations, who in their turn are enchanted
Grandly among country-people to introduce at assemblies
To the unpennied cadets our cousins with excellent fortunes.
Neither man's aristocracy this, nor God's, God knoweth!

Meantime Claude begins to make way with these Trevellyns. He owns it is pleasant to be with them. His aristocratic refinement and fastidious tastes are even shocked at finding that he delights in 'pleasing inferior people.' But, after all, it is only a matter of accident and travelling sociability, of—

       Juxtaposition, in short; and what is juxtaposition?

This supplies him with much food for very Cloughian contemplation. Meantime, a few scraps from the Miss Trevellyns to their friends introduce us to these young ladies, and let us know that Mary thinks Mr. Claude 'a superior man,' but 'terribly selfish;' and so the first canto ends. The second opens with Italian politics. Claude sympathises with the patriots more than he chooses to admit, or than his habits of disdainful self-analysis permit him to be aware of. Once or twice he flashes into real enthusiasm; but he never gives himself a free rein. In the midst of details about the siege, and of wonderings whether he would be prepared in the event of danger 'to lay down his life for the British female,' he exclaims: 'I am in love, meantime, you think?' and after, for the space of ten lines, articulating the charms of Mary's feminine good taste and sense, decides that he 'is not exactly.' Then follows letter after letter about love. Claude is clearly getting into the thick of it—summoning to his aid all his heavy casuistical battalions and squadrons of light sophistry. The real misery of a state of mind like Claude's is, that it produces a confusion in the moral instincts: the higher, as well as the lower parts of the nature, become objects of dread and suspicion. Claude fears sophistication in every virtue, and is nervously alarmed by his own impulses. It may easily be conceived that he puzzles the Trevellyns not a little. Georgina thinks Mr. Claude 'really is too shilly-shally,' and induces her own *fiancé* to sound him with regard to his intentions as to her sister Mary. The third canto opens with a series of similar reflections, for Claude is now in the very centre of indifference, having cast off the No, and not yet reached the Yes of loving.

Then he takes up a question which he had suggested at an earlier period. 'What is Juxtaposition?' We travel in a railway-train, and, to pass the time, talk with the girl we find next us. This is a true allegory of most marriages. Yet we prate at the same time about 'eternal ties and marriages made in heaven.' But if we *really* believed in this pretence—if the bridegroom *really* thought he was linked for ever to the bride—if he did not foresee the release of burial while he signed the bond of matrimony—how do you think he would then accept his situation? Claude's friend seems to hint that Juxtaposition may be great, but that Affinity is greater. 'Ah!' says Claude, 'there are many affinities of different degrees and forces:—

> But none, let me tell you,
> Save by the law of the land and the ruinous force of the will, ah,
> None, I fear me, at last quite sure to be final and perfect.

Yet, he sighs, it is pleasant to be deluded, and the love-makings of the earth are very beautiful:—

> Could we eliminate only
> This vile hungering impulse, this demon within us of craving,
> Life were beatitude, living a perfect divine satisfaction.

But soon another word, more abrupt than Affinity, more cogent than Juxtaposition, breaks the serene sphere of his dubitations like a bombshell. It is Obligation. His intentions are asked. Mary, indeed, has herself never held him bound in any way; and this is one of her charms in his eyes. Every morning he may meet her afresh, and find no old debts to pay. But just as Claude is on the eve of starting for Florence with the Trevellyns and their Vernon friends, one of the latter hints that he ought to declare himself one way or the other. Thereupon Claude breaks loose, and excuses himself from the party:—

> How could I go? Great heavens! to conduct a permitted flirtation
> Under those vulgar eyes, the observed of such observers.

This brings us to the fourth canto, when Claude, having let his opportunity slip, and missed, as he expresses it, the tide in his love affairs, feels an irresistible desire to be again, at any cost, with Mary Trevellyn. He leaves Rome; but they have left Florence,—for Milan, it appears. Then follows a weary chase after them, through Bellagio, over the Splügen, the Stelvio; back again to Como, Florence, Pisa, and Rome. Every place is searched; every friend applied to. But by a natural accident of travelling, when once missed, they cannot be

caught up again. The whole of this fifth canto is occupied with hurry-
ings to and fro, blank researches, and vain self-reproaches. There is
something piteous and pathetic in its feverishness. Mary Trevellyn,
in the meantime, is at Lucerne, waiting, not without anxiety, for
Claude, and ready, it is clear, to make him happy. Indeed, we feel that
it is very stupid on the part of Claude to give her up after so short a
pursuit. He is meant, however, to be a poor creature, distracted by his
own waywardness of speculation, and confused in his impulses.
Amours de Voyage concludes with a series of those dubitations, halts,
and turning-points of thought, in which Clough delighted as an
artist, and which serve, with admirable irony and humour, to pourtray
the feebleness of Claude.

We have entered so fully into the analysis of this poem that there is
little need for comment. Yet we cannot refrain from calling attention
to its subtle discussion of a subject which to most men is so simple.
Clough shows us in the character of Claude the effect of a speculative
intellect acting upon the instincts and affections. We can scarcely
wonder that Clough is not more generally read and admired, because
the problems with which he is occupied are rare and remote. There
are but few characters like Claude in the world. Indeed, it might be
wondered, whether it is worth while commemorating those perplexed and sceptical conditions of the consciousness in verse. Ought a
poet not rather to lead the world, and to show the ultimate truth, than
to represent the waverings of a discontented spirit ill at ease? Clough's
vindication, however, lies in this: first, that it is the poet's function to
hold up a mirror to his age, as well as to lead it; and secondly, that we
still admire Hamlet and Faust. Claude belongs to the same race as these
princes of metaphysical perplexity. However exceptional, his scepticism is natural to himself, and to the temper of his century. In painting
him, Clough reproduced the experience which he obtained from
commerce with the world, and drew a picture of his times.

Omitting all notice of the *Bothie*, the best known of Clough's works,
we may now proceed to discuss *Dipsychus*, a dramatic composition
which has not yet been given to the public. This fact, besides the
intrinsic importance of the poem, which contains in the most condensed form, all Clough's speculations about life and action, must be
our excuse for the length of the extracts we propose to make, and for
the minuteness of our analysis. Hitherto we have seen him occupied
with the problems of Religion and Love. Having shown us the cor-
rosive action of the human intellect in both of these fields he comes

forward to display the further operation of this sceptical *aqua fortis* upon the philosophy of Life itself in Dipsychus. The hero of this poem is not, like Hamlet, indisposed to fulfil a single and difficult duty; or, like Faust, exhausted with the world of thought; or, like Claude, unnerved for decision and unable to obey his instincts. His difficulties are deeper, and more general. He passes in review the whole casuistry of Life, and Duty, and Action, involving religion, love, and morality, in his speculation. The theme of the poem is therefore, in some sense, the metaphysic or supreme abstraction of Human Doubt.

It was written at a period of the poet's life when he was thinking and feeling deeply about the choice of work. Oxford had been given up. University Hall in London had not proved very satisfactory. Clough felt the need of action without confidence in any special sort of action. Subtle analysis and high aspirations seemed to unfit him for the coarser work of the world. Mere pleasure or the luxury of living or domestic felicity could not satisfy the whole of such a nature. He asked himself, What is to be done? What is the value of any work that a man can do? How shall we preserve the soul's virginity upon the crowded highways of the world? Is it worth while to sacrifice beautiful illusions for doubtful truths of fact? Is it right to exchange the poet's golden sunset skies for the world's palpable coin—itself the root of all evil as well as of all comfort?

These meditations are cast in the mould of a dialogue between a man's soul and a spirit. But the title *Dipsychus* seems to intimate that the spirit is but a mode of the soul which externalises itself. Or, to speak more clearly, this spirit is not the true man, but it is that second self which usage with the world and the unnumbered centuries of human tradition have imposed upon the soul. Clough calls him Mephistopheles and Belial. He is made to name himself Cosmarchon or Cosmocrator:—

> This worldly fiend that follows you about,
> This compound of convention and impiety,
> This mongrel of uncleanness and propriety.

He is in truth the spirit of this world, the spirit of fact and reality, as opposed to aspirations and ideals, the spirit of those conditions under which men have to labour in their commerce with the world; the spirit of those lower necessities which environ action. Reflection, it was long ago said by the philosophers, belongs to God and to godlike men. But action is proper to mankind and to the mass of human beings. By cleaving to action we renounce our heavenly birthright of contemplation. Yet if we confine ourselves to reflection and aspiration, we separate ourselves from the life of men. No one has yet solved the problem of acting without contracting some stain of earth.

The form of Dipsychus and the character of the Spirit remind us of Faust, and prove that Clough was to a certain extent influenced by Goethe's great work. But the problems agitated by Clough are of a more subtle and spiritual nature than those which Goethe raised. They are worked out with less attention to artistic finish and dramatic effect than the speculations which underly the play of *Faust*. In their narrow compass they strike many students as being more forcible in thought and more full of feeling than the meditative scenes of Goethe's drama. Clough was content to be wholly undramatic and monotonous. Instead of presenting us with numerous highly-coloured pictures, he dissected a portion of the troubled brain of one man with marvellous skill and delicacy. Thus the two works are essentially different in their scope and aim; and the resemblance between them is superficial. Besides, the Spirit in *Dipsychus* has not much in common with the Mephistopheles of Goethe. We find in *Dipsychus* no tempter beyond the casuist that everyone carries in his bosom; no contract but that which everyone makes when he leaves the Thebaid of his contemplation for the service and the pay of the great world; no greater duality of existence than that which every self-conscious man of the century contains within his own nature. The dialogues of Dipsychus and the Spirit are the communings of a heart given to self-examination. Their strife is a modern version of the old battle carried on between the spirit and the flesh, or rather between St. Paul's Pneumatic and Psychic, spiritual and natural, man. But the strife is even, and no Zeus holds the balance. The combatants are twins, inseparable in this life. The one that is the stronger, though confessedly the viler, rules the other, because he conformed to the existing conditions under which the individual is forced to live and act. The fate of the forlorn, indignant, and defrauded soul is hidden from us at the end. Dipsychus seeks to act as a man, and not to keep aloof from human passions and the pains of life: but in doing so he falls, and is entangled in the snares of the world. It is hard to say how Clough intended his drama to conclude. The second part of *Dipsychus*, as we have it, is incomplete. But so far as one can judge from this fragment, one is surprised at the common-place and rather vulgar *dénouement* which the poet seems to have designed. It contrasts so strangely with the elevated and subtle tone of the first part, and forms so distinct a bathos or anti-climax, that we are disposed to abandon any attempt at its interpretation, believing that in its present mutilated state it cannot be fairly criticised, and to confine our attention to the first part. This part consists of a series of short scenes, which fall naturally into two chief groups. In the first of these groups Dipsychus and the Spirit discuss several questions of theology and social ethics, setting forth in broad and well-defined contrast the double point of view which may be taken by a scrupulous and an easy conscience; the discord between the spirit of the Gospel and the spirit of the world; and the divergence between a craving after spiritual things and an acquiescence in the order of carnal and conventional routine. The second group is devoted exclusively to the casuistry of action.

Dipsychus opens at Venice, with a reminiscence of 'Easter Day.' Though the scene is changed, and months have passed, the old refrain of 'Christ is not risen,' keeps running in the poet's head. The Resurrection, in any real and modern sense of the word, is just as inconceivable at Venice as at Naples. The spirit of Christianity is just as absent from the Rialto as from the Toledo. While Dipsychus is repeating the opening lines of 'Easter Day,' the Spirit intervenes and begins to criticise it:—

> Dear, how odd!
> He'll tell us next there is no God.
> I thought 'twas in the Bible plain,
> On the third day He rose again.

The Spirit accepts all that the world has agreed to believe—all the ὁμολογούμενα[1] and stereotyped conventions of his Church and State. Theology and metaphysics, indeed, are not his trade. But he recommends general religious observances as a matter of prudential policy, and occupies a pew on Sundays in obedience to the third commandment of his own amended Decalogue:—

> Oh,
> You'll go to church, of course, you know;
> Or, at the least, will take a pew
> To send your wives and servants to.
> Trust me, I make a point of that;
> No infidelity,—that's flat.

On the present occasion at Venice, however, he prefers to enjoy the sun, and watch the humours of the crowd on the Piazza. Dipsychus

[1] 'dogmas'.

238

converses with him, sullenly enough, and they carry on their dialogue through a visit to the Public Gardens, where the higher musings of the man are constantly broken with ever so slight a revelation of the spirit's carnal nature. Dipsychus is disgusted, and exclaims:—

> O moon and stars, forgive! and thou, clear heaven,
> Look pureness back into me. Oh, great God!
> Why, why, in wisdom and in grace's name,
> And in the name of saints and saintly thoughts,
> Of mothers, and of sisters, and chaste wives,
> And angel woman-faces we have seen,
> And angel woman-spirits we have guessed,
> And innocent sweet children, and pure love,
> Why did I ever one brief moment's space
> But parley with this filthy Belial?
> ... Was it the fear
> Of being behind the world, which is the wicked?[1]

But when he has regained his hotel, the Spirit begins once more to reason with him on the duties of society, and the necessities of acquiescence in the ways of the world. Social conventions are discussed; Dipsychus fretting against formal lies and diplomacy of manners and outward show, the Spirit proving how wise it is to leaven our sincerity with tact, our purity with *savoir faire*, the dove with the serpent, piety with polish. His final argument on all these points is that,—

> What we all love is good touched up with evil:
> Religion's self must have a spice of devil.

Or again:—

> Life little loves, 'tis true, this peevish piety;
> E'en they with whom it thinks to be securest—
> Your most religious, delicatest, purest—
> Discern and show, as pious people can,
> Their feeling that you are not quite a man.

The same argument is reasoned on a different thesis, after Dipsychus has been insulted by a Croat, and the Spirit is urging him to seek satisfaction. Here, as before, Dipsychus wants to adhere to the pure precepts of the Gospel. The Spirit shows how unfit they are for actual

---

[1] Cf. *Poems* (1951), where these lines appear, not, as in the 1869 volume, at the end of Scene II, but opening Scene IIA, the whole of which Mrs Clough omitted. She also omitted after line 9 in this quotation the line, 'To this insidious lewdness lend chaste ears' and Clough's 'Or' in the next line was altered to 'But'.

life, and sums up with a crushing satire on his comrade's peaceful mood.

In the next scene we are on our way to the Lido, and the question, 'Is there no God?' is being reasoned by the two spirits—Dipsychus taking the mournful and regretful side, expressing the sadness of a soul that longs to believe in a God and hears it knelled that there is none, while the Spirit makes the best of things, and shows that we can get on very well without one. The little song, 'There is no God, the wicked saith,' occurs in this scene. In the Second Act—if we may use this word to express the group of unconnected scenes which follow— we are brought to consider the great problem of the choice of work. Here we may admire that subtlety of modern thought, which seeks no longer with the ancient philosophers a Criterion of Happiness or Knowledge, or with the theologians a Criterion of Faith, but which, having, as it were, abandoned happiness, knowledge, and faith, as hopeless and irresoluble questions, to their fate, is no less puzzled to discover the Criterion of Life itself—of Action—of a man's place in the world of men. This part opens with a further discussion of the thoughts suggested by 'Easter Day,' in which the Spirit takes occasion to develop his religious opinions, and thus impresses their practical result upon Dipsychus:—

> Take larger views (and quit your Germans)
> From the Analogy and Sermons;
> I fancied, you must doubtless know,—
> Butler had proved, an age ago,
> That in religious, as profane things,
> 'Twas useless trying to explain things;
> Men's business-wits, the only sane things,
> These and compliance are the main things.
> God, Revelation, and the rest of it,
> Bad at the best, we make the best of it.
> Like a good subject and wise man,
> Believe whatever things you can.
> Take your religion as 'twas found you,
> And say no more of it, confound you![1]

Then, while afloat in his gondola, Dipsychus begins to wish that all life were after this wise:—

> How light we move, how softly! Ah,
> Were life but as the gondola!

[1] Cf. *Poems* (1951), Scene VII.

So live, nor need to call to mind
Our slaving brother here behind!

The contemplative indisposition for action in Dipsychus is mocked
and baffled by the perplexing and tormenting riddles which the in-
equalities of the world offer to his mind. Life might be beautiful,
and enjoyable, and easy, he thinks, were it not for a craving within
us after the unseen, and could we divest ourselves of all sympathy for
our toiling, suffering fellow-creatures. In this mood, riches and luxurious
pleasures seem to him 'mere insolence and wantonness.' But the Spirit,
as may be imagined, shares none of these difficulties. He sings. 'How
pleasant it is to have money, heigho!' and sums up his Welt-philosophie
in two common-place stanzas:—

> The world is very old, we see,
>   We do not comprehend it;
> But in one fact we all agree,
>   God won't, and we can't mend it.

> Being common sense, it can't be sin,
>   To take it as I find it;
> The pleasure to take pleasure in;
>   The pain, try not to mind it.

To these verses Dipsychus replies with the exquisite lines, 'O let
me love my love unto myself, alone' . . .

In the next scene Dipsychus resolves to commune more seriously
with the Spirit, and to question him. The design is scarcely formed
before the Spirit is at his elbow, and Dipsychus, after some hesitation,
asks:—

> Should I form, a thing to be supposed,
> A wish to bargain for your merchandise,
> Say what were your demands?—what were your terms?—
> What should I do? What should I cease to do?
> What incense on what altars must I burn?
> And what abandon? What unlearn or learn?
> Religion goes, I take it.

By no means, replies the Spirit. We have here no blood-signed contract, no tragic price of soul's damnation for the pomps and pleasures
of the flesh. All you have to do is to follow the world's ways—take
orders, if you like, but keep within the serviceable limits of routine

religion, and do not indulge in vague emotions. If that does not suit
you, choose the law. Marry, too, by all means; and—

> Trust one who knows you,
> You'll make an admirable Sposo.

This is the result of the incantation. Dipsychus, with his high-flown
aspirations and shy sensitiveness, is cast upon a sea of doubt. He seeks
action, and has to choose between two common-place professions. The
Spirit of the world tempts him with no magnificent pleasures, with
no promises of power. Sneering at him, he offers in exchange for his
soul's virginity the merest humdrum of diurnal life in a marriage
without illusions and a business without enthusiasms. Dipsychus is
fairly staggered:—

> I had hoped
> Midst weakness, indolence, frivolity,
> Irresolution, still had hoped; and this
> Seems sacrificing hope.

Would it not be better, he asks, to wait—to let inferior opportunities
slip by, and to seize the supreme chance of heroic action when it
comes? But what if, when it comes, we should prove incapable of
seizing it or using it by want of action? Is it not safer to engage in the
great battle as a common soldier, and work up to the captaincy?—

> High deeds
> Haunt not the fringy edges of the fight,
> But the pell-mell of men.

Yet again there is danger in this course. We may reasonably fear—

> In the deft trick
> Of prentice handling to forget great art,
> To base mechanical adroitness yield
> The Inspiration and the Hope a Slave!

Ah, but suppose I relinquish action altogether? Even that is unsafe:—

> Contamination taints the idler first.

I will away with hesitation, at last he cries, and obey my instinct—
if only, alas! I had an instinct!—

> No, no:
> The life of instinct has, it seems, gone by,
> And will not be forced back. And to live now,

> I must sluice out myself into canals,
> And lose all force in ducts. The modern Hotspur
> Shrills not his trumpet of 'To Horse, to Horse!'
> But consults columns in a Railway Guide.

But even thus to act, humbly and by routine, might be sufficient for
the yearnings of the soul, if only we could believe that the work done
were worth doing, and that we were integral and indispensable parts
of the life of the great world:—

> If indeed it work,
> And is not a mere treadmill! which it may be,
> Who can confirm it is not? We ask action,
> And dream of arms and conflict; and string up
> All self-devotion's muscles; and are set
> To fold up papers. To what end?—we know not.
> Other folks do so; it is always done;
> And it perhaps is right.

After all, if really bidden to bathe in this common-place Jordan of
unapparent efficacy, let us bathe. 'I submit.' As an echo to this word
the Spirit is heard from within singing:—

> Submit, submit!
> 'Tis common sense and human wit
> Can claim no higher name than it.

Still, though on the verge of action, Dipsychus wavers. Is he now,
so swiftly and irrevocably, 'to lose in action, passion, talk, the soul?'
To abandon, for the uncertain good of work in the world, those
moments of illumination which have come upon him hitherto at
intervals, and seemed to solve the riddle?—

> O happy hours!
> O compensation ample for long days
> Of what impatient tongues call wretchedness!
> . . . No, no!
> I am contented, and will not complain.
> To the old paths, my soul! Oh, be it so!
> I bear the work-day burden of dull life
> Above these footsore flags of a weary world,
> Heaven knows how long it has not been; at once,
> Lo! I am in the Spirit on the Lord's day
> With John in Patmos. Is it not enough,
> One day in seven? and if this should go,

If this pure solace should desert my mind,
What were all else? I dare not risk this loss.
To the old paths, my soul!

Overhearing this soliloquy, the Spirit gibes:—

Oh, yes.
To moon about religion; to inhume
Your ripened age in solitary walks,
For self-discussion; to debate in letters
Vext points with earnest friends; past other men
To cherish natural instincts, yet to fear them
And less than any use them . . .
. . . to pervert
Ancient real facts to modern unreal dreams,
And build up baseless fabrics of romance
And heroism upon heroic sand;
To burn forsooth, for action, yet despise
Its merest accidence and alphabet.

Once in a fortnight say, by lucky chance,
Of happier-tempered coffee, gain (great Heaven!)
A pious rapture.[1]

We regret that our space admits of only these broken extracts from a speech which is full of the most searching satire on a scholar's solitary life—of irony terrible in its remorseless truth—of worldly wisdom crushing down in proud superiority of strength the dreamy aspirations of a timid soul. Dipsychus, stung and quickened by a sense of his own impotence and by the ruthless logic of the carping voice, cries with a return of discontented determination:—

Must it be, then? So quick upon my thought
To follow the fulfilment and the deed?
I counted not on this. I counted ever
To hold and turn it over in my hands
Much longer.

Yet he cannot now escape the law which his own speculations have imposed on him. It is in vain that the thirst for action leaves him for a moment, and he cries:—

What need for action yet? I am happy now;
I feel no lack. What cause is there for haste?
Am I not happy? Is not that enough?

[1] See *Poems* (1951), Scene X.

bidding the Spirit depart. The Spirit will not go, but turns upon him with a new menace:—

> What! you know not that I too can be serious,
> Can speak big words, and use the tone imperious,
> Can speak, not honiedly, of love and beauty,
> But sternly of a something much like Duty.

The casuistry of action becomes very serious when the voice of the world imposes upon the soul one of its own laws, and goads it on by an appeal to its own higher impulses. Dipsychus is daunted and shaken:—

[Quotes Scene XI, 73–86: 'It must be, then' to 'welcome, welcome, welcome!'.]

In the midst of this mental anguish and moral conflict, the Spirit of the world sneers at him. What are you dreading to give up? What is the work you have set yourself? Is it literature—novels, reviews, poems, perhaps a little philosophising—vague scepticism, dilettante dreamings about life? Or else you'll try teaching and tutoring of youth, not so as to absorb your whole time, but always keeping leisure for your meditations and illuminations:—

> Heartily you will not take to anything;
> Whatever happen, don't I see you still
> Living no life at all? Even as now
> An o'ergrown baby, sucking at the dugs
> Of instinct, dry long since. Come, come! you are old enough
> For spoon-meat surely.
>   Will you go on thus
> Until death end you? If indeed it does:
> For what it does, none knows. Yet as for you,
> You'll hardly have the courage to die outright;
> You'll somehow halve even it. Methinks I see you.
> Through everlasting limbos of void time,
> Twirling and twiddling ineffectively,
> And indeterminately swaying for ever.[1]

In this way, with continual sarcasms and much home truth, seasoned with a reiteration of the philosophy of submission, the Spirit drives Dipsychus on to engage in the world's work. Having bowed and given up the contest, Dipsychus still abjures his counsellor:—

[1] Cf. *Poems* (1951), Scene XI, 170–88.

Not for thy service, thou imperious fiend,
Not to do thy work or the like of thine;
Not to please thee, O base and fallen spirit!
But one Most High, Most True, whom, without Thee,
It seems I cannot.

He still sets the law of life and the law of the Gospel at variance:

Do we owe fathers nothing—mothers nought?
Is filial duty folly? Yet He says,
'He that loves father, mother, more than Me;'
Yea, and 'the man his parents shall desert,'
The ordinance says, 'and cleave unto his wife.'
O man, behold thy wife! the hard, naked world;
Adam, accept thy Eve!

With many protestations, and reservations, and antinomian arguments, Dipsychus at length accepts the yoke of the prince of this world, not without having his eyes open to what he is about, but seeing no other course. And the Spirit says:—

O, goodness! won't you find it pleasant
To own the positive and present;
To see yourself like people round,
And feel your feet upon the ground!

After this long analysis of Dipsychus, we have only to call attention to the skill with which Clough has sustained his two characters. In the course of their protracted dialogue, they never change, except in so far as an alteration of will and purpose is wrought in the weaker spirit by the stronger and more persistent tempter. The force of unscrupulous and narrow power, firmly planted upon the solid facts of common life, is displayed with wonderful vigour by the poet, in his Mephistopheles, who, at the same time, has never failed to make the most of the humours and satirical side of his character. There is nothing tragic in this Mephistopheles, just as there is nothing tragic (melodramatically speaking) in the final concession of Dipsychus. But beneath the ironical sneers of the one, and the helpless struggles of the other, lurks the deep and subtle tragedy of human life and action—of free souls caged, and lofty aspirations curbed—a vulgar and diurnal tragedy over which no tears are shed in theatres, but which, we might imagine, stirs the sorrow of the angels day by day as they look down upon our world.

This same most piteous chord is touched even more deeply and with a keener sense of hopelessness in the poem called 'The Questioning Spirit'—one of the most perfect among Clough's earlier compositions, written, perhaps, at the darkest and most troubled period of his life, on the theme of what may be described as the Criterion of Duty. As another appendix or gloss upon the philosophy of Dipsychus, we may mention the lines beginning, 'Duty—that's to say complying,' the concentrated verjuice of the satire of which is very characteristic of one of Clough's moods. An answer or antidote to these more gloomy views of common life is found in the elegiac lines beginning, 'Hope evermore and believe, O man!' which contain this cheerful stoicism:—

> Not for the gain of the gold; for the getting, the hoarding, the having;
> But for the joy of the deed; but for the Duty to do.

It remains to consider Clough's artistic qualities more in detail than we have hitherto done. But neither is it easy to do this, nor have we left ourselves much space for doing it in. In the course of our notice, however, we have been at pains to select passages for quotation which might illustrate his style, as well as supply the matter necessary for explaining his subject. There is a certain dryness, hardness, and severity —a want of colour, tone, and richness—in most of what Clough has written. In daily life he was a man of few words, and difficult utterance; nor does he seem ever to have gained real facility of poetical expression. His last poems, the *Mari Magno Tales*, have indeed more fluency; but here the *copia verborum* tends to a somewhat prosaic prolixity, instead of adding warmth and splendour to his style. Those readers who have accustomed their ears to the sublime harmonies of Milton, or to the exquisite lyrical music of Shelley, or to the more artificially melodious rhythms of Mr. Swinburne, or to Tennyson's elegant and complex cadences, will complain that Clough is harsh and unadorned. He rough-hews indeed (as it has been said) like a Cyclops; but he cannot finish like a Canova. Occasionally he attains to perfect style and form *per saltum*, by a sudden flash of native energy and fire. He pours forth torrid thought and feeling like a lava jet into the adamantine mould of stately and severe expression. 'Easter Day' is a specimen of this success. The poem owes nothing to its rhythm, or its rhymes, or the beauty of its imagery, or the music of its language. It is plain and natural, and without allurements of any sort. But the emotion is so intense, and so thoroughly expressed—the thought is so vigorous and vital in every line—that the grandest poetry is wrought out of the commonest materials, apparently without effort, and by the mere intensity of the poet's will. 'Easter Day' is a bronze poem. It is the most perfect illustration in English literature of the artistic canons which Wordsworth preached, and upon which his own practice brought contempt. 'Qui laborat orat' and many more of the minor religious poems are likewise cast of red-hot feeling, in a stern and simple mould.

But, such being the style by which alone Clough attains to excellence, it follows that when he is not perfectly simple and clear he has no excuse: when he is prolix he becomes prosy. There is no gorgeousness of language, pomp of sound, or playfulness of fancy to cover the faults of ill-constructed or feebly-designed poems, and to yield ample matter for quotation when the subject fails to interest.

Passing to matters of mere detail, we may observe that Clough apparently rhymed with some difficulty, and that he was too fond of a jingling refrain carried through a poem of many stanzas, as in the lyrics of *Dipsychus*. It was only when he felt with intensity, and when the expression of his feeling welled up spontaneously within his heart and overflowed, that his poems were perfect; and then we imagine that few writers had the power of more exactly and touchingly saying what they wished.

Connected, apparently, with this inadequacy of utterance in any of the more complex and rhymed forms of verse, was his predilection for hexameters. The English hexameter has always been confessed to be a somewhat rough and jolting metre, when compared with heroic or blank verse or the Spenserian stanza. Yet it served Clough's purpose. In those loose, yet rhythmical lines he was able to express with the exact fidelity required by his artistic conscience all essential realities of fact, all delicate shades of feeling—to turn from sentiment to satire, from the incidents of travel to æsthetical or religious meditations, from landscape pictures to philosophy or argument or analysis. A good judge of poetry has lately pronounced it as his opinion that Clough never intended his hexameters for metre, but for cadenced prose. But it is impossible that Clough could have meant these hexameters for an essay in prose, since they are utterly unlike any sort or kind of prose writing, and are extremely suggestive, to say the least, of Horace's epistles and of Goethe. No artist of taste would make experiments in one species of writing by importing into it the peculiar rhythm of another species. If a man chooses to cast his thought into the world-old form of the hexameter, he is not asking us to compare him with the *Religio Medici*, the *Areopagitica*, the *Opium Eater*, and *Modern*

Painters, but with the *Iliad*, the *De Rerum Naturâ*, *Hermann and Dorothea*, and *Evangeline*. Judged by these latter standards, Mr. Clough takes a high place for the subtlety, variety, and racy flavour of originality which he has imparted to this ancient vehicle of thought. His hexameters are *sui generis*, unlike those of any other writer in any language, and better, we venture to assert, in spite of Mr. Arnold, than those of any other English author. If he sets prosody at defiance, and makes such dactyls as 'pace slowly,' he yet produces periods of majestic and sonorous music like those which might be quoted from the earlier parts of *Amours de Voyage*. But, leaving these questions of style and form, we may pass to other poetical qualities of Mr. Clough. In his painting from nature, and in his descriptions of character, we trace the marvellous sincerity and accuracy of his mind. The *Bothie* is full of the most delightful pictures of highland scenery, the fidelity of which can only be tested by a minute comparison of Clough's words with the actual places they refer to. *Amours de Voyage*, in the same way, yields many most highly finished and exquisitely faithful pictures of Rome. Everything Clough wrote he drew from personal experience as far as the locality and *mise en scène* are concerned. And this accounts for the strict truthfulness to nature which we find in his chief poems.

As for his power of analysing and sustaining character, for his irony and humour, and pathos, we have already said and quoted enough to show that he possesses these higher faculties of genius in no small degree. What is particularly important in the present age of literature, he is powerful without being ostentatious, passionate and intense without extravagance, profound without obscurity, perfectly simple in form and solid in matter. He is a poet who will bear being frequently read; and who, each time we read him, astonishes us with some fresh beauty, or some new reach of thought.

39. R. H. Hutton, 'Arthur Hugh Clough', from *Essays Theological and literary*

London, 1871, II, 368–91

This is a revised and expanded version of a review in the *Spectator*, xlii, 11 September 1869, pp. 1073–5. Like the review, the essay incorporates the substance of Hutton's earlier notice of the *Bothie*, in the *Spectator*, xxxv, 25 January 1862, pp. 104–5.

Richard Holt Hutton (1826–97) was a mathematician, theologian and man of letters. He succeeded Clough as Principal of University Hall, London, and was joint editor of the *Spectator*, 1861–97.

These two volumes, as they now stand, contain as adequate a picture of the singular but large, simple and tender nature of the Oxford poet as is attainable, and it is one which no-one can study without much profit, and perhaps also some loss; without feeling the high exaltation of true poetry and the keen pleasure caused by the subtlety of true scholarship, at every turn; nor also without feeling now and again those 'blank misgivings of a creature moving about in worlds not realized,' which are scattered so liberally among those buoyant ardours, disappointed longings, and moods of speculative suspense, and which characterize these singular letters of reticent tenderness and rough self-satire.

Everyone who knew Clough even slightly received the strongest impression of the unusual breadth and massiveness of his mind. Singularly simple and genial, he was unfortunately cast upon a self-questioning age, which led him to worry himself with constantly testing the veracity of his own emotions. He has delineated in four lines the impression which his habitual reluctance to converse on the deeper themes of life made upon those of his friends who were attracted by his frank simplicity. In one of his shorter poems he writes:

> I said my heart is all too soft;
> He who would climb and soar aloft

> Must needs keep ever at his soul
> The tonic of a wholesome pride.

This expresses the man in a very remarkable manner. He had a kind
of proud simplicity about him, singularly attractive, and often singularly disappointing to those who longed to know him well. He had a
fear, which many would think morbid, of leaning much on the appro-
bation of the world; and there is one characteristic passage in his
poems, in which he intimates that men who lean on the good opinion
of others might even be benefited by a *crime* which would rob them
of that evil stimulant:

> Why, so is good no longer good, but crime
> Our truest, best advantage, since it lifts us
> Out of the stifling gas of men's opinion
> Into the vital atmosphere of Truth,
> Where He again is visible, tho' in anger.

So eager was his craving for reality and perfect sincerity, so morbid
his dislike even for the unreal conventional forms of life, that a mind
quite unique in simplicity and truthfulness represents itself in his poems
as

> Seeking in vain, in all my store,
> One feeling based on truth.

Indeed, he wanted to reach some guarantee for simplicity deeper than
simplicity itself. I remember his principal criticism on America, after
returning from his residence in Massachusetts, was that the New
Englanders were much simpler than the English, and that this was
the great charm of New England society. His own habits were of the
same kind—sometimes almost austere in their simplicity. Luxury he
disliked, and sometimes his friends thought him even ascetic.

This almost morbid craving for a firm base on the absolute realities
of life was very wearing in a mind so self-conscious as Clough's, and
tended to paralyse the expression of a certainly great genius. As a rule,
his lyrical poems fall short of complete success in delineating the mood
which they are really meant to delineate, owing to this chronic state
of introspective criticism on himself in which he is too apt to write,
and which, characteristic as it is, necessarily diminishes the linearity
and directness of the feeling expressed, refracting it, as it were, through
media of variable density. As he himself—no doubt in this stanza

delineating himself—says of one of his heroes in 'The Clergyman's first tale':

> With all his eager motions still there went
> A self-correcting and ascetic bent,
> That from the obvious good still led astray,
> And set him travelling on the longest way.

And in the same poem there are descriptive touches which very skil-fully portray the nature of those dispersive influences, as I may call them, in his character, which, while they may injure his lyrical, add a great wealth of criticism to his speculative and disquisitional poems:

> Beside the wishing-gate which they so name,
> 'Mid northern hills to me this fancy came,
> A wish I formed, my wish I thus expressed:
> *Would I could wish my wishes all to rest,*
> *And know to wish the wish that were the best!*
> O for some winnowing wind, to the empty air
> This chaff of easy sympathies to bear
> Far off, and leave me of myself aware!

That is clearly self-portraiture, and it describes an element in Clough's nature which, no doubt, contributed greatly to diminish the number of his few but exquisite lyrical poems, and sometimes to confine even those to the delineation of feelings of a certain vagueness of drift. Yet there was, besides this most subtle and almost over-perfect intellectual culture in Clough, much also of a boyish, half-formed nature in him, even to the last, which, when fully roused, contributed a great deal of the animation, and, when least roused, contributed not a little of the embarrassed, shy, half-articulate tone to some of the most critical passages of his finest poems. He describes this side of boyish feeling admirably in one of his *Mari Magno* tales:

[Quotes 'The Lawyer's First Tale', II, ll. 141–53: 'How ill our boy-hood' to 'and unexplained'.]

And even in his latest and most finished poems you see the working of this half-developed element of Clough's massive and rich but to some extent inert imagination; and you see, too, how powerfully it operated to discontent him with his own productions, to make him underrate vastly their real worth. Rapidly as his genius ripened at an age when, with most men, the first flush of it would have passed over, there was something of conscious inertia, not unlike immaturity in it to the last, which gives a tone of proud hesitation, a slowness of hand, to the literary style of his finest poems. He calls himself, in his *Long Vacation Pastoral*, 'the grave man, nicknamed Adam,' and there is really something of primeval earth, of its unready vigour and crude laboriousness, about his literary nature. Even when he succeeds best, the reader seems to see him 'wipe his honourable brows bedewed with toil.' And he is impatient with himself for not succeeding better, and despises his own work.

The *Long Vacation Pastoral* belongs to a class of poems that is scarcely naturalized in England—the class of which Goethe's *Hermann and Dorothea* is perhaps the most perfect specimen, though in vigour and breadth of imagination Clough's pastoral is certainly not inferior. Goethe's influence over the school of poetry of which Matthew Arnold and Clough have been the most considerable English disciples, is very powerfully marked. There is the same longing after the old Homeric simplicity—less successful perhaps in a cultivated Englishman than in the more childlike German—the same love of homely naturalness of manner, of the wholesome flavour of earth, an even deeper desire to tame or exorcize all romance that is alien to common sense, and the same intellectual disposition to give common sense the casting vote, wherever there seems to be a conflict between it and the thirst of their own natures for something deeper. Moreover, in Clough's poem there is the same underlying theme which haunted Goethe so constantly— the wish to analyse the true secret of womanly fascination, and finally, the key-note of the *Hermann and Dorothea*, that the highest charms of woman consist in a certain union between homely usefulness and classical beauty, in the graceful cutting of bread-and-butter, like Werther's Charlotte, or graceful 'potato-uprooting', like Philip's heroine in Clough's pastoral. As one of his 'reading' party expresses it:

> All Cathedrals are Christian, all Christians are Cathedrals,
> Such is the Catholic doctrine; 'tis ours with a slight variation;
> Every Woman is, or ought to be, a Cathedral,
> Built on the ancient plan, A Cathedral pure and perfect,
> Built by that only law, that Use be suggester of Beauty,
> Nothing concealed that is done, but all things done to adornment,
> Meanest utilities seized as occasions to grace and embellish.

But if the school of art and predominant thought which marks Goethe's *Hermann and Dorothea* and Clough's poem are the same—if they both alike seek and find their ideal of women in 'the freshness of the early world,' in some well-born or well-taught maiden,

Milking the kine in the field, like Rachel, watering cattle,
Rachel, when at the well the predestined beheld and kissed her,
Or, with pail upon head, like Dora beloved of Alexis,
Comely, with well-poised pail over neck arching soft to the shoulders,
Comely in gracefullest act, one arm uplifted to stay it,
Home from the river or pump moving stately and calm to the laundry;

yet all the imaginative form and framework of Clough's poem are entirely his own—entirely original, and marked strongly with the stamp of its Oxford origin.

The almost Homeric vigour with which all the characteristics of the reading party are dashed off, the genial humour with which their personal peculiarities are coloured in, the buoyant life of the discussions which arise among them, the strength with which the Highland scenery is conceived and rendered in a few brilliant touches, the tenderness and simplicity with which now and then the deeper pathos of life is allowed to be seen in glimpses through the intellectual play of the poem, are all Clough's own. He is far more terse, far less prolix than the great German poet in his style of painting homely nature. There is more of that relaxed fibre which makes scoffers say that Goethe is a little spooney on his Charlotte's bread-and-butter, and his Dorothea's proficiency as a waggoner. Clough's poem is masculine throughout, though the sentiment is perhaps not entirely healthy, and the humour, therefore, is of a kind of which Goethe had little trace. Here, for example, is Airlie, the high dresser of the party:

Airlie descended the last, effulgent as god of Olympus;
Blue, perceptibly blue, was the coat that had white silk facings,
Waistcoat blue, coral-buttoned, the white-tie finely adjusted,
Coral moreover the studs on a shirt as of crochet of women:
When the four-wheel for ten minutes already had stood at the gateway,
He, like a god, came leaving his ample Olympian chamber.

And here is a Highland dance, in which Airlie again figures, described with all the humour and force of a modern Homer:

[Quotes *Bothie*, IV, 89–101: 'Him rivalling Hobbes, briefest kilted of heroes' to 'small consolement of waistcoats!'.]

Or take the description of Sir Hector's speech at the clansmen's dinner, which is rich in Homeric metaphor, as well as modern humour:

[Quotes *Bothie*, I, 88–97: 'Bid me not, grammar defying' to 'garrulous tale of Sir Hector'.]

Not, however, by such passages as these can be measured the depth and fullness of Clough's poetic nature. I have said that, in his dread of the romantic school, and his longing for that antique type of nobility in which the simpler and more homely tasks are associated with classical grace and dignity, he had borrowed much from Goethe. But his mind had been also deeply influenced by the very different poetry of Wordsworth in his strong love of a frugal, hardy and simple industry as the highest school of human character. And perhaps too, in spite of his steady preference of Aristotle to Plato, of common sense to what he thought idealism, of what is common to what is high, the deep and sometimes transcendental musings of Wordsworth's meditative mind had a charm for him of which he was almost ashamed. At all events, there is a gleam of transcendental depth and subtlety now and again in this poem, shyly—almost apologetically—put forth, and scarcely put forth but to be withdrawn. The lines in which Elspie confesses her love for Philip, the radiant poet, are couched in a very different key from that of Goethe's naturalistic school,—a different, and I think a higher key:

[Quotes *Bothie*, VII, 54–74: 'And she was silent some time' to 'And you won't understand, Mr. Philip'.]

This is a definite addition to the great doctrine of the poem, that women, like flowers, must be 'rooted in earth' to be either beautiful or useful—a definite addition and a noble addition. Here we have something of Wordsworth's conception of the poet:

> The outward shows of sky and earth,
> Of hill and valley, he has viewed,
> And impulses of deeper birth
> Have come to him in solitude.
>
> [The Poet's Epitaph]

There are 'impulses of deeper birth' struggling with the naturalism of Clough's chosen school of thought. Still, the great sea, and the wide omnipresent sunlight, are his favourite symbols of what is divine— what is broad, bright, and simple, rather than what is lofty, mysterious, and dim.

Clough always seemed to have needed external stimulus, something of excitement in the atmosphere, for his best poetic success. Thus, the siege of Rome during his residence there in 1849 was the stimulus which gave rise to his very original and striking poem, *Amours de*

Voyage, a poem brimful of the breath of his Oxford culture, of Dr. Newman's metaphysics, of classical tradition, of the political enthusiasm of the time, and of his own large, speculative humour, subtle hesitancy of brain, and rich pictorial sense. Yet so ill-satisfied was he with this striking poem, that he kept it nine years in MS., and published it apologetically at last only in an American magazine, the *Atlantic Monthly*. He himself says that what he doubted about in it was not its truth of conception, but its vigour of execution. Yet no execution could have been more perfect of the picture—a picture of inchoacy, I admit—which he intended to draw. Mr. Emerson has in some cases shown himself a fine critic; but he never made a more egregious blunder than when he found fault with Clough for not making his poem end more satisfactorily. The whole meaning and drift of it would have been spoiled if it had so ended. His idea was to draw a mind so reluctant to enter upon action, shrinking so morbidly from the effects of the 'ruinous force of the will' that even when most desirous of action it would find a hundred trivial intellectual excuses for shrinking back in spite of that desire. His own explanation of the poem is contained in the final verse:

[Quotes *Amours*, V, 217–24: 'So go forth' to 'thundered the cannon of France'.]

And it is this brain of what the author chooses to call 'feeble and restless youths born to inglorious days' that the poem is meant to delineate throughout—its speculative discontent, its passion for the abstract, its dread of being committed to a course, its nonetheless eager craving for action and for the life that can only be reached through action, its driftings and reactions; and all this is artistically contrasted with the great Roman stage on which so many great dramas have been enacted in years gone by, and whereon one great revolutionary drama was going forward at that very moment. To my mind the poem would lose half its character and meaning if the hero's incipiency of passion had been developed into anything but incipiency, if it had not faded away, just as it is represented as doing, with the first difficulties, into a restless but still half-relieved passiveness. The irony of the poem, with its background of Mazzinian and Garibaldian achievement, would have been utterly spoiled by any other conclusion. How perfect a picture of the paralysis caused by too subtly speculative a nature is there in such lines as these, for example, in which the hero declares his intention to abide by the indications of the first adverse throw of fortune:

> Great is Fate, and is best. I believe in Providence partly.
> What is ordained is right, and all that happens is ordered.
> *Ah, no, that isn't it! But yet I retain my conclusion.*
> I will go where I am led, and will not dictate to the chances.

Amours de Voyage would indeed have been spoiled, if it had ended 'prettily,' like any other novel.

The oftener I return to Clough's unfinished but striking poems, the more I am struck by something in their fresh, natural handling, and a certain lustre of sunlight on their surface, which suggests to me a modern and intellectualized Chaucer; and I think the same homely breadth and simplicity were strongly marked in his countenance. Of course, the whole essence of such genius is changed by the intellectual conditions of Clough's age, and the still higher intellectual conditions of his personal career. But the characteristic is only the more strongly marked for such striking and fundamental variations; and had he lived to fill more completely with his individual genius, and to complete, the beautiful fragments of tales which are entitled *In Mari Magno*, every one would have noticed not merely an external resemblance in structure and scheme, but a very close analogy in genius between the *Canterbury Tales* by the father of English poetry, and the series by this later representative of our academic school. This Chaucer-like love of the natural simplicities of life was probably Clough's strongest creative impulse; his mode of describing is in the same style of bold, direct, affectionate feeling for the earth and the true children of the earth; and the homely though polished pathos of his stories have again and again filled me with like haunting associations, even when the analogy was so much disguised by the different intellectual accent of our times that its secret was not easy to catch. In the following piece, there is certainly no manner of difficulty in tracing the resemblance. But though the similarity of mere style may arise from Clough's own familiarity with the poet, and with the tales whose plan he was adopting, the portrait is certainly studied from an ecclesiastical type quite foreign to Chaucer's age:

[Quotes *Mari Magno*, 'The Lawyer's First Tale', I, 57–98: 'The vicar was of bulk and thews' to 'Emilia called, was most the pet'.]

It is not the mere forms here, it is the simple, direct manner of painting which brings back a flavour of Chaucer to the memory as we read the more intellectual poet of modern days. Look, again, at Clough's feeling for woman's beauty; the mingled breadth and tenderness of his drawing, his keen sense of the healthy simplicity of true woman-liness, his constant preference for the true woman rather than the true lady, his evident bias for that which has its root in the homely earth, though it attains a beauty which earth alone could not give; it is Chaucer become conscious of the difference between his own inner mind and the taste of our modern intellectual day. Chaucer describes his ideas of feminine loveliness in the person of Blanche, wife of John of Gaunt, thus:

[Quotes *The Book of the Duchesse*, 848–65: 'I saw hir daunce so comlily' to 'on hir gan beholde'.]

And now let me take an extract from one of Clough's tales to compare with this picture of Chaucer's:

[Quotes *Mari Magno*, 'The Lawyer's Second Tale', 1–26: 'A Highland inn' to 'what follows to explain'.]

Of course the parallel must not be pushed too far, for even Chaucer, if possessed of all the new culture, and striving to harmonize it with his large, simple, healthy, human tastes, would become quite a new man. And no doubt Clough's poetry is in nature and essence intellectual. Still there is no poet of our generation whose intellectuality gives less of the effect of a thinning and refining away of life to a shadow than Clough. Such subtlety as there is in him is of a broad, sweeping, com-prehensive kind, not logical but practical; not the fine instinct with which Tennyson, for instance, follows out one by one a hundred shadowy paths of imaginative reasoning, but the wide subtlety which hovers hither and thither over one or two of the greater chasms that separate thought from action. The ground quakes under Clough's feet at points where generally it would be supposed firm; and where ordinary men's imaginative doubts begin, his scarcely reach. The effect on his poetry is to exercise his imagination in depicting not so much universal feelings as the craving of the cultivated mind for *permission* to surrender to them. In some of his most characteristic verses he asks:

[Quotes the whole of the poem beginning 'What we, when face to face we see/The Father of our souls'.]

This, like almost all Clough's poems of this class, presents the effect of a homely, simple, human beauty, half undermined by fundamental doubts—doubts suggested, indeed, only to be partially abandoned, but also to be partially maintained, as a preservative against the blind eager confidence of presumptuous faith. The massive and genial sympathy which Clough feels with the universal instincts of human nature, alike religious and social, is the first marked feature that strikes us in all his poems: then the sifting process begins of tracing them to their roots, showing how much wider is the trust placed in them in the practical conduct of modern life, than it is possible to justify intellectually; and then when he has pared these instincts down to their minimum of meaning, and we have been shown how impossible our whole life would be if they were given no greater validity than that, they are permitted, though with hesitation and a doubtful or rather hypothetical confidence, to take back something of their natural authority, now that it is fairly shown to be liable to all kinds of presumptuous error.

No doubt, this sort of large, half-genial suspense of judgment, that looks upon natural instincts with a sort of loving doubt, and yields with cautious hand a certain limited authority to human yearnings in order not wholly to lose a share in the moving forces of life, is not likely to be widely popular. With Clough this suspense of human judgment was unfortunately not supplemented by any confident belief in a divine answer to those vague yearnings, and consequently his tone is almost always at once sweet and sad. It is saturated with the deep but musical melancholy of such thoughts as the following, whose pathos shows how much more profoundly and deeply Clough thirsted for truth than many of even the most confident of those of us who believe that there is a living water at which to slake our thirst:

[Quotes 'To spend uncounted years of pain' entire.]

Yet even in poetry of this kind, which abounds in the volume, there is something of the large, hesitating melancholy that we should expect, if once a mind of homely Chaucer-like wisdom fell under a cloud of modern doubt. Instead of applying itself, like the ordinary scepticism, to particular riddles, it would touch the whole substance of life, not unkindly, with Clough's questioning finger; treat the fundamental instincts which guide us into our human relations with the same half-confidence; try to separate even in dealing with 'love', the real affinity of nature from the 'juxtaposition' of habit, and show the problem to be indeterminate with the same quaint humour. And in things divine it would state the problem as fairly, and substitute a sigh of pathetic hope for the solution, with the same sad fidelity. It may be something of a fancy, but it is at all events a fancy which touches the border of truth, if I recognize even in the type of Clough's genial scepticism something not entirely unlike the scepticism which might pervade the mind of a Chaucer, watching with the old homely shrewdness as well as the rich modern culture, the swaying tides of our theological debate, and clinging too closely itself to the human forms of beauty and goodness to come with any clear personal conviction, out of the strife.

And yet Clough's great literary powers never manifested themselves even to his most intimate friends by any outward sign at all commensurate with the profound belief they had in his genius. But if his powers did not, there was much in his character that did produce its full effect upon all who knew him. He steadily refrained from looking, even in time of severe trial, to his own interest, when what seemed to him higher interests were at issue. He never flinched from the worldly loss which his deepest convictions brought on him. Even when clouds were thick over his own head, and the ground beneath his feet seemed crumbling away, he could still bear witness to an eternal light behind the cloud, and tell others that there is solid ground to be reached in the end by the feet of all who will wait to be strong:

[Quotes 'Say not, the struggle nought availeth' entire.]

I do not think any competent judge who really studies Clough's *Remains* will doubt for a moment that he was one of the most original men of our age, and perhaps its most intellectual, and buoyant, though very far, of course, from its richest, most musical and exquisite poet. There is a very peculiar and unique attraction about what I may call the physical and almost animal buoyancy of these subtly intellectual rhythms and verses, when once the mass of the poet's mind—by no means easy to get into motion—is fairly under weigh. Mr. Matthew Arnold and Clough both represent the stream of the modern Oxford intellectual tradition in their poems, but how different is their genius. With all his intellectual precision, there is something of the boyishness, of the simplicity, of the vascular Saxon breadth of Chaucer's poetry in Clough; while Mr. Arnold's poetical ancestor is certainly no earlier than Wordsworth. There are both flesh and spirit, as well as emotion and speculation, in Clough; while, in Mr Arnold, soul and sentiment guide the emotion and the speculation. There is tenderness in both; but Clough's is the tenderness of earthly sympathy, and Mr. Arnold's the lyrical cry of Virgilian compassion. Both fill half their poems with

the most subtle intellectual meditations; but Clough leaves them all
but where they were, not even half settled, reproaching himself for
mooning over them so long; while Mr. Arnold finds some sort of a
delicate solution, or no-solution, for all of them, and sorts them with
the finest nicety. Finally, when they both reach their highest poetical
point, Mr. Arnold is found painting lucidly in a region of pure and
exquisite sentiment, Clough singing a sort of paean of buoyant and
exultant strength:

> But O blithe breeze! and O great seas,
>   Thou ne'er, that earliest parting past,
> On your wide plain they join again,
>   Together lead them home at last.
>
> One port, methought, alike they sought,
>   One purpose hold wher'er they fare,—
> O bounding breeze, O rushing seas!
>   At last, at last, unite them there!
>
> ['Qua Cursum Ventus']

40. Unsigned review, 'Arthur Hugh Clough' in the *Saturday Review*

18 September 1869, 383–5

It is difficult in the brief space of a review to do justice to a man's
memory, when he has left behind him a great deal of rather remarkable
verse, yet without winning the assured reputation of a poet, and many
thoughtful papers on a fairly wide range of subjects, without being
much of a *littérateur* or philosopher either. If this is difficult to do at all,
it is nearly impossible, while his death is still recent, to do it to the
satisfaction of those in whose hearts the personal impress of the writer
is yet strong and deep. Clough was one of those men in whom the
moral and the intellectual are so finely intermixed as to send to a

maximum their power of personal impressiveness. In this, though perhaps in little else, he resembled Sterling, like whom also he enjoyed the warm friendship of Mr. Carlyle. But Clough's power of impressing others was so absolute that it could assert itself by reticence as much as by utterance. 'I always *felt* his presence,' said one of his friends. His own line

> Mute and exuberant by turns, a fountain at intervals playing,

is said to be an exact memorial of what he was to those who were much with him. A calm judgment passed on the sum of such a man's remains, by one who never saw him, must almost inevitably disappoint those who saw and knew, and who remember.

In the arrangement of these volumes there is scarcely anything that does not deserve high praise. A brief memoir is followed by the letters and prose remains, and these make up the first volume; the verse fills the second. The memoir strikes us as uniting completeness with brevity. A man's wife, if she has the gifts of an 'honest chronicler' at all, ought to be his best biographer. The *Letters* of Lady Rachael Russell and the *Memoirs* of Mrs. Hutchinson are among the classics of this kind of literature;[1] and the unpretending account of Clough, whether actually written or only inspired and superintended by his widow, shows much of the taste and judgment which in such memorials are imperative. We cannot dismiss it without expressing genuine admiration for two contributions to it—the first from a younger sister, the close companion of Clough's boyhood; the second from Professor Conington, who (though several years his junior) belonged to the same debating society at Oxford. One of these, describing their early life at Charleston, is a model of clear and graceful narrative, just what a biographical memoir should be; to the other we shall have occasion to recur.

[A paragraph summarizing the main events of Clough's life has been omitted.]

Clough's letters are full of interest. They are not models of letter-writing, but he wrote through years of such varied and vivid and recent interest, that they form a collection well worth preserving. He writes from Rome during the siege of 1849; and from America, with

---

[1] *The Letters of Lady Rachel Russell* (1636–1723) were first published in 1773. *The Memoirs of the Life of Colonel Hutchinson*, by Mrs Lucy Hutchinson (b. 1620) were first published in 1806.

Emerson, Lowell, Longfellow, Hawthorne, Ticknor, Prescott, and Theodore Parker, all within easy reach. With Emerson he had been in Paris during the revolution of 1848, and he came back with the repute of a thoroughly *écervelé* republican, so that Mr. Matthew Arnold characteristically addressed a letter to 'Citizen Clough, Oriel Lyceum, Oxford.' Professor Child was then hard at work on his valuable and scholarlike investigations into Chaucerian scansion; and Clough, whose passion for English hexameters had thrown him much upon metre, writes freely upon that question. At Cauteretz, in the last year of his life, he met Mr. Tennyson; he walked with him down 'the valley where the waters flow,' and writes a letter which makes an extremely interesting commentary on those well-known lines.[1] Throughout the letters there occur short passages of criticism which provoke a regret that he did not more seriously and continuously take up that kind of writing, and leave behind him something more carefully and completely done than the reviews which stand among his prose remains. He writes, for example, thoughtfully and sensibly of Theodore Parker, for whose Unitarian orthodoxy, as a substitute for any other 'doxy, he had 'no particular love'; of Mr. Matthew Arnold's poems, valuing the *Scholar Gipsy* above all; of Plutarch, the Dryden translation of whom he revised for an American publisher; of Buckle's *History*, hoping his American friends are not 'Buckle-bewitched,' like all the world this side the water; and on Crabbe, about whom he truly says that 'there is no one more purely English (in the Dutch manner), no one who better represents the general result through the country of the eighteenth century.'

It is not, however, as a letter-writer that Clough comes before us in these volumes. His *Remains* present him as a serious writer and thinker on literature, or on the metaphysico-religious questions of the time, and as a writer of poems. Of his claims in this double capacity we proceed to speak. For his literary work, it will be enough to say that he seems never to have warmed to it. We have before expressed regret that he did not take up literary criticism with seriousness and vigour, for his work as it stands is clearly not his best. The *Development of English Literature from Chaucer to Wordsworth* contains some good things, in particular the just and high estimate of the mental and moral standard of the eighteenth-century literature. But even these are awkwardly expressed, and the general impression left by this, and the

1 'the valley, where *thy* waters flow': Tennyson, 'In the Valley of Canteretz'. The letter is at *PPR I*, 269.

paper on 'Wordsworth' (contrasting poorly with Professor Shairp's recent review), is thin and unsatisfactory. What his mind *was*, rather than the actual results it left on paper, is the true object of interest in Clough; and this question leads us straight to his attitude as a man of serious reflection. On this point we can fortunately be quite clear; his *Notes on the Religious Tradition* (if nothing else) make it clear; and we cannot think the mental position and experience of such a man just now either insignificant or uninstructive. Clough, then, as the final result of his mental development while at Oxford, renounced Christianity. He renounced, that is to say, its dogmatic and historic claims. Three years after Dr. Newman had resigned his Fellowship on ceasing to be in any possible harmony with the Church of England, Clough resigned his on ceasing to be a Christian. But thenceforward to the end of his life he remained sincerely attached to the moral teaching of Christianity, apart from its external embodiment. Nothing would probably have pained him more than to be deemed on these matters indifferent. This allegiance he designated as a 'falling back on the great religious tradition.' And the general inheritance of religious tradition, embodied nowhere, but traceable everywhere—in Menu, Hafiz, Confucius; in Homer and Plato; in Lucretius and Tacitus; in Hume as well as in Butler—this, and a strict adherence to duty and kindliness, supplied him through his later and married life with all he wanted of inner support.

It is, we suppose, a necessary characteristic of certain stages in national, as undoubtedly in individual, life, that this sort of mental attitude towards a great religion should attract a strong sentimental sympathy. That this is so, no one will dispute; and we are far indeed from attempting to gauge the loss or gain implied in its being so. What we are concerned in remarking is this; that Clough presents us with a case where this attitude towards Christianity can be shown to have arisen naturally out of a quality of mind having in it essentially more of weakness than of strength, and not deserving in its essence any special sympathy whatever. Professor Conington, in his interesting reminiscence of Clough,[1] records a debate in the society called the 'Decade', the subject being 'that the study of philosophy is of more value to the formation of opinion than the study of history.' This proposition Clough supported, using an argument that culminated in these words, 'What is it to me to know the fact of the battle of Marathon, or the fact of the existence of Cromwell? I have it all within me.'

---

[1] *PPR I*, 31-3.

'Not,' he explained, 'that it is of no importance to me that these things were; but it is of no importance that I should know it.' Such a proposition might conceivably be maintained from the love of paradox; but Clough was the last man to maintain it for that reason. When laid down *bonâ fide* as he laid it down, it denotes an unusual attachment to abstractions for their own sake, an exaggerated belief in the isolated independence of the human mind, and a very incomplete notion of the relations between history and the individual man. That these conditions should lead (as they led Clough) to the analogous conclusion that 'a man may know all that is important in Christianity without so much as knowing that Jesus of Nazareth ever existed,' was almost inevitable. It was natural then that he should break away more and more from any sort of alliance with dogma, and should follow the instinct described in the lines in his *Dipsychus* (lines which he was fond of quoting)—

> It seems His newer Will
> We should not think of Him at all, but turn
> And of the world that He has given us make
> What best we can.

That such intellectual conditions as have been described may have a value in certain fields of philosophical analysis is plain. But we deny that they have in themselves any claim to particular sympathy, or that they are likely to prove 'helpful' (as the phrase goes) to the present generation.

Of the poems left by Clough it would be necessary to say something more than we are about to say had not most of them been for several, and some of them for many, years before the public. The *Dipsychus* is new. It is that one of his four long poems which had no place in the earlier volume. At the risk of running counter to a probable majority of its author's admirers, we cannot but regard it as on the whole a failure. Taking up (as its name denotes) the old-world struggle between the lofty, transcendental spirit of unselfish purity, and the opposite impulses of callousness and self-interest, it deals with a trite subject in a style which does not even aim at originality. The Spirit of Evil answers to the name of Mephistopheles, and that in itself (by reason of suggested contrasts) is a pity. A semblance of movement is thrown over the poem by laying the scene at Venice, and by fixing each conflicting dialogue at some new point—the Piazza, the Lido, the Doge's Palace, St. Mark's. When we have added that the sinister spirit begins his attacks during a period of dejection, while Dipsychus is dreamily repeating the words of a powerful but repulsive ode called 'Easter Day,' with the refrain 'Christ is not risen,' enough will have been said on a poem to illustrate which nothing would be gained by a series of quotations. We should feel inclined to apply to it a phrase from the lips of Dipsychus himself, and to call it a collection 'of unripe words and rugged verse.' It will meet with a favourable reception from those who value the soul's 'tumult rather than its depth';[1] but no one who reflects on what a poet like Mr. Browning would have made of the same subject will feel disposed to call it anything more than a remarkable *tour de force*.

The *Bothie of Tober na Vuolich* remains unchanged. Say what you will to the hexameters, a pleasanter Long-Vacation pastoral than the *Bothie* never was and never will be written, and every University man who has not read it through is so far a loser. This poem, which was thrown on the world by Clough with a sort of chuckle just after he had resigned his Fellowship, was received in New England with something like enthusiasm. Among ourselves it will always, and deservedly, remain its author's best-known and most popular production. The quasi-serious moral about the equalization of different classes in society scarcely belongs to the fibre of the pastoral. That is made up of really lifelike portraits of the Oxford Tutor and his pupils, and of descriptions of Highland scenery and Highland ways only possible to a man of remarkable power, and earnestly in love with both. The excellent banter on social questions culminates when Hobbes, the enthusiastic Pugin-worshipper of the party, makes his famous proposal for a

Treatise upon *the Laws of Architectural Beauty in Application to Women*; Illustrations, of course, and a Parker's Glossary pendent, Where shall in specimen seen be the sculliony stumpy-columnar (Which to a reverent taste is perhaps the most moving of any), Rising to grace of true woman in English the Early and Later—

and so forth.

The *Amours de Voyage* is perhaps the cleverest of all the poems. It is a set of hexameter letters (with pretty, though rugged, elegiac reliefs between) describing with a very acute power of observation the growth, in spite of himself, and the ineffectual end, of a travelling attachment formed by a *dilettante* philosophical tourist. The interest is heightened by the poem having been written at Rome during the siege.

---

[1] Wordsworth, 'Laodamia': 'The gods approve/The depth, and not the tumult, of the soul.'

This power of observing and recording actual life grew on Clough, and, had he lived longer, it might have prompted a more complete poem than any he has left behind him. At any rate the series of tales called *Mari Magno*, clearly suggested by his fondness for Crabbe, and some of them written very closely after Crabbe's manner, indicate that his tendencies were working in that direction. The 'Clergyman's Second Tale' is as finely told as its moral is lofty and powerful. The scene where the penitent husband, meeting in London the woman who had beguiled him from his duty, and whose sinister life has 'run full circle,' and watching her move away as their sudden interview is broken by some passing stranger, is admirably and most impressively written:—

> He watched them in the gas-lit darkness go,
> And a voice said within him 'Even so';
> So midst the gloomy mansions where they dwell
> The lost souls walk the flaming streets of hell.

To write on the minor poems would be endless. Those on the inner life all more or less indicate the mental peculiarity of which we have spoken. The poems on 'Biblical Subjects' might, we think, just as well have been omitted. But the 'Songs in Absence,' and several of the reprints from the *Ambarvalia*, are well worth preserving. Among the former, 'Out of sight out of mind' is very charming; and of the earlier pieces, '*Quà cursum ventus*' and 'Through a glass darkly,' are relics which no reader will soon forget.

It is not difficult to understand how the author of these *Remains* should have prompted a poem like *Thyrsis*—worthy companion of *Lycidas* and *Adonais*—in a friend like Mr. Matthew Arnold. It must have been written, however, much as Andrea del Sarto may be supposed to have remembered a friend whose workmanship he could often smile at or regret, while he revered and loved his spirit. And that is the sum of the impression left by these volumes. Clough was neither great as a poetical artist, nor as a man who could furnish sure guidance to the intellect, or aid and support to the spirit. But he unswervingly maintained through life that supreme moral standard which is necessary alike for the man of creed and the man of no creed; and in literature he adhered faithfully to the sound and genuine principles of work on which alone true literary progress can be based, and for want of loyalty to which many men of greater genius than he had failed.

41. H. Sidgwick, a review in *Westminster Review*

October 1869, xcii, 363–87

'The Poems and Prose Remains of Arthur Hugh Clough', *Westminster Review*; reprinted in *Miscellaneous Essays and Addresses*, 1904, 59–90.

Henry Sidgwick (1838–1900) was a Cambridge philosopher whom G. L. Dickinson described as representing 'the Cambridge spirit [of scrupulous truth-seeking] at its best and therefore with its limitations most clearly and tragically apparent' (E. M. Forster, *Goldsworthy Lowes Dickinson*, 1934, p. 120). As Clough had done at Oxford twenty years before, he resigned his fellowship at Trinity College, Cambridge, on conscientious grounds in 1869 (the year of this essay), but his subsequent career was, unlike Clough's, not prejudiced by this. He returned to the University in 1875 to take up a 'praelectorship in moral and political philosophy' and remained there for the rest of his life, becoming an honorary Fellow of Trinity in 1881 and an ordinary Fellow in 1885. He played a prominent part in the government of the University and was a prime mover in the campaign for the admission of women as fully participating students. J. A. Symonds wrote to Sidgwick admiring this article's 'desultory' yet effective manner (*The Letters of John Addington Symonds*, II. 88–9).

These two volumes contain all that will now be given to the world of a very rare and remarkable mind. The editor has, we think, exercised a wise confidence in transgressing what is usually a safe rule in posthumous publications, and including in the volume some prose that the author had probably not composed for permanence, and some verse that is either palpably unfinished, or at any rate not stamped with the author's final approval. Clough's productive impulse was not energetic,

and only operated under favourable conditions, which the circumstances of his life but scantily afforded. Therefore the sum-total of his
remains, when all is included, does not form an unwieldy book; and
on the other hand his work is so sincere and independent that even
when the result is least interesting it does not disappoint, while his
production is always so rigidly in accordance with the inner laws of his
nature, and expresses so faithfully the working of his mind, that
nothing we have here could have been spared, without a loss of at
least biographical completeness. There is much that will hardly be
interesting, except to those who have been powerfully influenced by
the individuality of the author. But the number of such persons (as
every evidence shows), has not diminished, but largely increased during
the ten years that have elapsed since his death: the circle of interest has
gone on widening without becoming fainter, and now includes no
small portion of a younger generation, to whom especially the publication of these volumes will afford timely and welcome gratification.

The tentative and gradual process by which Clough's remains have
been published is evidence and natural result of the slow growth of
his popularity. For this there seem to have been several reasons. It is
partly due to the subject-matter of his writings. He was in a very literal
sense before his age. His point of view and habit of mind are less
singular in England in the year 1869 than they were in 1859, and much
less than they were in 1849. We are growing year by year more introspective and self-conscious: the current philosophy leads us to a close-
patient, and impartial observation and analysis of our mental pro-
cesses: and the current philosophy is partly the effect and partly the
cause of a more widespread tendency. We are growing at the same
time more unreserved and unveiled in our expression: in conversations,
in journals and books, we more and more say and write what we
actually do think and feel, and not what we intend to think or should
desire to feel. We are growing also more sceptical in the proper sense
of the word: we suspend our judgment much more than our predecessors, and much more contentedly: we see that there are many sides
to many questions: the opinions that we do hold we hold if not more
loosely, at least more at arm's length: we can imagine how they appear
to others, and can conceive ourselves not holding them. We are losing
in faith and confidence: if we are not failing in hope, our hopes at
least are becoming more indefinite; and we are gaining in impartiality
and comprehensiveness of sympathy. In each of these respects, Clough,
if he were still alive, would find himself gradually more and more at

home in the changing world. In the second place his style, at least in his longer poems, is, though without any affectation, very peculiar: at the same time he has not sufficient loudness of utterance to compel public attention. Such a style is naturally slow in making way. Even a sympathising reader has to get accustomed to its oddities before he can properly feel its beauties. Afterwards, if it has real excellence, its peculiarity becomes an additional charm. Again, the chief excellence of Clough's style lies in a very delicate and precise adaptation of form to matter, attained with felicitous freshness and singular simplicity of manner; it has little superficial brilliancy wherewith to captivate a reader who through carelessness or want of sympathy fails to apprehend the *nuance* of feeling.

To this we may perhaps add, that the tone which many of Clough's personal friends have adopted in speaking of the author and his writings has, though partly the result, been also partly the cause of the slow growth of their popularity. It was, for example, certainly a misfortune that in issuing the first posthumous edition of these poems, Mrs. Clough prefaced them with a notice by Mr. Palgrave, a critic of much merit, but quite inappreciative of his friend's peculiar genius, and whose voluble dogmatism renders his well-meant patronage particularly depressing. There is a natural disposition among personal friends to dwell upon unrealised possibilities, and exalt what a man would, could, or should have done at the expense of what he actually did; and to this in Clough's case circumstances were very favourable. In the first place he produced very little, and the habit of demanding from candidates for literary fame a certain quantum of production seems inveterate, though past experience has shown the fallacy of the demand, and we may expect it to become still more patent in the future. Indeed, if we continue as we are now doing, to extend our own literary production and our sympathy and familiarity with past and alien literature *pari passu*, the reader of the future will have so much difficulty in distributing his time among the crowd of immortal works, that he certainly will contract a dislike to the more voluminous. And in the case of poems like these, that are attractive chiefly because they are characteristical and representative, because they express in an original and appropriate manner a side of human life, a department of thought and feeling, that waited for poetical expression, voluminous production seems not only unnecessary but even dangerous. On a subjective poet continence should especially be enjoined; if he writes much he is in danger of repeating words or tune; if he tries to write much he is in danger of mistaking his faculties and forcing his inspiration.

But besides this scantiness of production, there is much in the external aspect of Clough's career which justifies the disposition to regard his life as 'wasted'—at best an interesting failure. We have before us a man always trying to solve insoluble problems, and reconcile secular antagonisms, pondering the '*uralte ewige Räthsel*'[1] of existence, at once inert and restless, finding no fixed basis for life nor elevated sphere of action, tossed from one occupation to another, and exhausting his energies in work that brought little money and no fame; a man who cannot suit himself to the world nor the world to him, who will neither heartily accept mundane conditions and pursue the objects of ordinary mankind, nor effectively reject them as a devotee of something definite; a dreamer who will not even dream pleasant dreams, a man who 'makes the worst of both worlds.'

This is no doubt a natural complaint from a practical point of view, but it ignores the fact that the source of Clough's literary originality and importance lies precisely in what unfitted him for practical success. He was overweighted with certain impulses, felt certain feelings with a too absorbing and prolonged intensity; but the impulses were noble, at least an 'infirmity of noble minds'; they are incident to most fine natures at a certain stage of their development, and generally are not repressed without a certain sense of loss and sacrifice. This phase of feeling is worthy of being worthily expressed, and it is natural that it should be so expressed by one who feels it more strongly than other men—too strongly for his own individual happiness. It is the same with other phases of feeling. Out of many poets there are few Goethes; the most are sacrificed in some sort to their poetical function, and it is but a commonplace sympathy that loudly regrets it. Those at any rate who had no personal knowledge of Clough, may recognise that this life, apparently so inharmonious, was really in the truest harmony with the work that nature gave him to do. In one sense, no doubt, that work was incomplete and fragmentary; the effort of the man who ponders insoluble problems, and spends his passion on the vain endeavour to reconcile aspirations and actualities, must necessarily be so; the incompleteness is essential, not accidental. But his expression of what he had to express is scarcely incomplete, and though we have no doubt lost something by his premature death we can hardly think that we have lost the best he had to give. His poetical utterance was

1 'age-old eternal riddles' (? source).

connected by an inner necessity with his personal experience, and he had already passed into a phase of thought and feeling which could hardly lead to artistic expression so penetrating and stirring as his earlier poems.

But we shall better discuss this question after a closer examination of his work, of what he had to express and how he expressed it.

In this examination we shall treat Clough as a poet. It is necessary to premise this, because he was a philosophic poet,—a being about whose nature and *raison d'être* the critical world is not thoroughly agreed. Philosophic poetry is often treated as if it was versified philosophy, as if its primary function was to 'convey ideas,' the only question being whether these should be conveyed with or without metre. Proceeding on this assumption, an influential sect maintains that there ought to be no philosophic poetry at all; that the 'ideas' it 'conveys' had much better seek the channel of prose. To us it seems that what poetry has to communicate is not ideas but moods and feelings; and that if a feeling reaches sufficient intensity, whatever be its specific quality, it is adapted for a poetical form, though highly intellectual moods are harder to mould to the conditions of metrical expression than others. The question is often raised, especially at the present day, when our leading poets are philosophic, whether such and such a poem—say Browning's *Christmas Eve*, or parts of *In Memoriam*—would not have been better in prose. And the question is often a fair one for discussion, but a wrong criterion is used for determining it. If such a poem is really unpoetical, it is not because it contains too much thought, but too little feeling to steep and penetrate the thought. Tried by this test, a good deal of Browning's thought-laden verse, and some of Tennyson's, will appear not truly poetical; the feeling is not adequate. Although Clough sometimes fails in this way, it may generally be said that with him the greater the contention of thought, the more intense is the feeling transfused through it. He becomes unpoetical chiefly when he becomes less eagerly intellectual, when he lapses for a moment into mild optimism, or any form of languid contentment; or when like Wordsworth he caresses a rather too trivial mood; very rarely when the depths of his mind are stirred. He is, then, preeminently a philosophic poet, communicator of moods that depend on profound and complex trains of reflection, abstract and highly refined speculations, subtle intellectual perceptions, and that cannot be felt unless these are properly apprehended. He is to a great extent a poet for thinkers; but he moves them not as a thinker, but as a poet.

We do not mean to say that Clough was not a thinker; but the term was somewhat indefinite, and in one sense he was not. His mind brooded over a few great questions, and was rather finely receptive than eagerly discursive; he did not enjoy the mere exercise of thought for its own sake. This is evidenced by the first of the volumes before us, especially the letters, which, except in the rare instances where he drops to his habitual depth of meditation, are perhaps somewhat disappointing. There is humour in them, but the vein is thin; and subtlety, perpetual subtlety, and from time to time a pleasant flow of characteristically whimsical fancy; there is also a permanent accuracy, propriety, *justesse* of observation, remarkable in compositions so carelessly thrown off; but fertility and rapid movement of ideas are wanting. They do not seem the work of a mind that ranges with pleasure and vigour over all subjects that come in its way. The critical essays, again, that have been republished, though exceedingly just, careful, and independent, and therefore always worth reading, are not very striking; with the exception of occasional passages where passionate utterance is given to some great general truth. But though he was too much of a poet to care greatly for the mere exercise of the cognitive faculties, though no one could less have adopted the 'philosopher's paradox' of Lessing, we may still call him philosophic from his passionate devotion not to search after truth, but to truth itself—absolute, exact truth. He was philosophic in his horror of illusions and deceptions of all kinds; in his perpetual watchfulness against prejudices and prepossessions; against the Idols, as Bacon calls them, of the Cave and the Theatre, as well as of the Tribe and the Market-place. He was made for a free-thinker rather than a scientific inquirer. His skill lay in balancing assertions, comparing points of view, sifting gold from dross in the intellectual products presented to him, rejecting the rhetorical, defining the vague, paring away the exaggerative, reducing theory and argument to their simplest form, their 'lowest terms.' '*Lumen siccum*,' as he calls it in one of his poems, is the object of his painful search, his eager hope, his anxious loyalty.

The intellectual function, then, which Clough naturally assumed, was scepticism of the Socratic sort—scepticism occupied about problems on which grave practical issues depended. The fundamental assumptions involved in men's habitual lines of endeavour, which determined their ends and guided the formation of their rules, he was continually endeavouring to clear from error, and fix upon a sound basis. He would not accept either false solutions or no solutions, nor, unless very reluctantly, provisional solutions. At the same time, he saw just as clearly as other men that the continued contemplation of insoluble problems is not merely unpractical, but anti-practical; and that a healthy and natural instinct forces most men, after a few years of feverish youthful agitation, resolutely to turn away from it. But with this instinct Clough's fine passion for absolute truth conflicted; if he saw two sides of a question, he must keep seeking a point of view from which they might be harmonised. In one of the most impressive of the poems classed in this edition as *Songs in Absence*, he describes his disposition

> To finger idly some old Gordian knot,
> Unskilled to sunder, and too weak to cleave;

but the reluctance to cleave knots, in the speculative sphere, does not proceed from weakness.

It is this supreme loyalty to reason, combining and conflicting with the most comprehensive and profound sympathy with other elements of human nature, that constitutes the peculiar charm of Clough's scepticism, and its peculiar adaptation to poetical expression. Towards the beliefs to which other men were led by their desires, he was as strongly, or more strongly, impelled than others; the assertions in which they formulated their hopes he would gladly have made with the same cheerful dogmatism. His yearning for the ideal he never tried to quench or satisfy with aught but its proper satisfaction; but meanwhile the claims of the real, to be accepted as real, are paramount. He clings to the 'beauty of his dreams;' but—two and two make four. It is the painfulness, and yet inevitableness of this conflict, the childlike simplicity and submissiveness with which he yields himself up to it; the patient tenacity with which he refuses to quit his hold of any of the conflicting elements; the consistency with which it is carried into every department of life; the strange mixture of sympathy and want of sympathy with his fellow-creatures that necessarily accompanies it— that makes the moods which he has expressed in verse so rare, complex, subtle, and intense.

We may classify these moods, according to a division suggested by this edition, into first, those of religious scepticism, where the philosophic impulse is in conflict with the mystical; secondly, those of ethical scepticism, where it contends with habitual active principles; thirdly, those where it is perplexed with the most clamorous and absorbing of human enthusiasms, the passion which forms the peculiar topic of poetry. It is this latter division that at once completes the consistency of Clough's scepticism, and forms its most novel, original, and least understood application. As he himself says, not only 'saint and sage,' but also 'poet's dreams,'

Divide the light in coloured streams;

the votary of truth must seek '*lumen siccum*.'

The personal history of Clough's religious scepticism has rather to be guessed than known from the records of his life that lie before us. The memoir prefixed to the volume, written with great delicacy and dignity, but with an unreserve and anxious exactness in describing his phases of thought and feeling worthy of the subject and most grateful to the reader, can tell us little on this head. Nor do the letters that lead us up to the time when he must in effect have abandoned the beliefs of his childhood at all prepare us for so deep a change. At Rugby he seems to have yielded himself entirely to the influence of Arnold, and to have embraced with zealous docility the view of life which that remarkable man impressed so strongly, for good or for evil, on his more susceptible pupils. But though somewhat over-solemn and prematurely earnest, like many Rugby boys of the time, he was saved from priggishness by his perfect simplicity. At Balliol he shows nothing of the impulsiveness, vehemence, and restlessness, the spirit of dispute and revolt, which are supposed to precede and introduce deliberate infidelity. Thrown upon Oxford at the time when the 'Newmanitish phantasm,' as he calls it, was startling and exciting Young England, he writes of the movement to his friends with a mild and sober eclecticism—a tranquil *juste-milieu* temper which would become a dean. He is candidly observant, gives measured admiration for good points, notes extravagances, suggests the proper antidotes, seems disposed, on the whole, to keep out of the atmosphere of controversy and devote himself to his studies. Nothing could give smoother promise of untroubled orthodoxy. It is true that he speaks of being 'exhausted by the vortex of philosophism;' and he must have been much more powerfully influenced by Newmanism than these letters indicate. He said afterwards, that for two years of this time he had been 'like a straw drawn up the vortex of a chimney.' His mind seems habitually to have been swayed by large, slow, deep-sea currents, the surface remaining placid, even tame; such a steady hidden movement it seems to have been that floated him away from his old moorings of belief. Gradually or suddenly the theologico-juridical, ecclesiastico-mystical dialectics that went on around him became shadowy and unreal: all his religious needs, hopes, aspirations remaining the same, a new view of the universe, with slowly accumulating force, impressed itself irresistibly on his mind, with which not only the intellectual beliefs entwined with these needs and aspirations seemed incompatible, but even these latter fundamentally incongruous. And thus began a conflict between old and new that was to last his life, the various moods of which the series of his religious poems, solemn, passionate, and ironical, accurately expresses.[1]

Perhaps the first characteristic that we notice in these is their rare reality and spontaneity. We feel that they are uttered, just as they appear, from an inner necessity; there was no choice to say them or not to say them. With some poets religious unbelief or doubt seems an abiding attitude of intellect, but only occasionally to engross the heart; their utterances have the gusty force of transitory passion, not the vitality of permanent feeling. But with Clough it is different: the whole man is in the poems—they spring from the very core of his being. The levity of some of them is as touching as the solemnity of others; it is a surface-mood, showing explored depths beneath it, in which an unrestful spirit finds momentary relief. Another characteristic is, that over the saddest cries of regret and struggles of checked aspiration is spread a certain tranquillity—not of hope, still less of despair, but a tranquillity that has something Aristotelian in it, the tranquillity of intellectual contemplation. It is curious, for example, to contrast the imperishable complaint of Alfred de Musset—

> Quand j'ai connu la vérité,
> J'ai cru que c'était une amie;

[1] A similar account is to be given of another event in his life, his abandonment of outward conformity to Anglicanism and its material appurtenances of an Oriel fellowship and tutorship. No reader of his life and writings can doubt that with him this step was necessarily involved in the change of opinions: yet many years elapsed between the two, and his biographer thinks that it was 'some half-accidental confirmation of his doubts as to the honesty and usefulness of his course' that finally led him to resignation. Such accident can surely have been but the immediate occasion, expressing the slow hidden growth of resolve. Lax subscription to articles was the way of Clough's world: and it belonged to his balanced temper to follow the way of his world for a time, not approving, but provisionally submitting and experimentalising. To do what others do till its unsatisfactoriness has been thoroughly proved, and then suddenly to refuse to do it any longer, is not exactly heroic, nor is it the way to make life pleasant; but as a *via media* between fanaticism and worldliness, it would naturally commend itself to a mind like Clough's. (Sidgwick's note.)

Quand je l'ai comprise et sentie,
J'en étais déjà dégoûté;[1]

with Clough's

It fortifies my soul to know
That, though I perish, Truth is so.

The known order of the world, even without the certainty of a
personal God, source or correlate of that order, afforded somewhat of
philosophic satisfaction, however little it could content the yearnings
of his soul. It was a sort of *terra firma*, on which he could set his feet,
while his eyes gazed with patient scrutiny into the unanswering void.
Further, we remark in these moods their balanced, complex character;
there is either a solemn reconciliation of conflicting impulses, or a
subtle and shifting suggestion of different points of view. Specimens
of the former are two hymns (as we may call them), headed '*Qui
laborat orat*,' and '*ὕμνος ἄυμνος*';[2] they attempt to reconcile the intellectual resolve to retain clear vision with religious self-abandonment.
The latter of these has a little too much intellectual subtlety and
academic antithesis; but the former is one of Clough's most perfect
productions; there is a deep pathos in the restrained passion of worship,
and the clear-cut exactness of phrase, as it belongs to the very essence
of the sentiment, enhances the dignity of the style. Somewhat similar
in feeling, but more passionate and less harmonious, is the following
fragment:—

O let me love my love unto myself alone,
And know my knowledge to the world unknown;
No witness to the vision call,
Beholding, unbeheld of all;
And worship Thee, with Thee withdrawn apart,
Whoe'er, whate'er Thou art,
Within the closest veil of mine own inmost heart.

Better it were, thou sayest, to consent:
Feast while we may, and live ere life be spent;
Close up clear eyes, and call the unstable sure,
The unlovely lovely, and the filthy pure;
In self-belyings, self-deceivings roll,
And lose in Action, Passion, Talk, the soul.

[1] The second stanza of Alfred de Musset's sonnet, 'Tristesse' (1840): 'when I knew the
Truth, I believed it was a friend; when I understood and felt it, I was already tired of it'.
[2] A hymn, yet not a hymn.

Nay, better far to mark off so much air,
And call it Heaven: place bliss and glory there;
Fix perfect homes in the unsubstantial sky,
And say, what is not, will be by and by.

Sometimes the intellectual, or as we have called it, philosophical element, shows itself in a violence of sincerity that seems reckless, but is rather, to use a German word, *rücksichtslos*;[1] it disregards other considerations, not from blind impulse but deep conviction. The tone of the poem is then that of one walking firmly over red-hot ploughshares, and attests at once the passion and the painfulness of looking facts in the face. In the fine poem called 'Easter Day' (where a full sense of the fascination of the Christian story and the belief in immortality depending on it, and of the immensity of its loss to mankind, conflicts with scientific loyalty to the modern explanation of it), the intensity of the blended feeling fuses a prosaic material into poetry very remarkably.

[Quotes 'Easter Day', ll. 27–35: 'What if the woman' to 'Christ is not risen!', and ll. 48–63: 'As circulates' to 'Christ is not risen!'.]

The complex and balanced state of Clough's moods shows itself in an irony unlike the irony of any other writer; it is so subtle, frequently fading to a mere shade, and so all-pervading. In the midst of apparently most earnest expression of any view, it surprises us with a suggestion of the impossibility that that view should be adequate; sometimes it shifts from one side of a question to the other, so that it is impossible to tell either from direct expression or ironical suggestion what the writer's decision on the whole is. In some of the later stanzas of the poem we have quoted the irony becomes very marked, as where the 'Men of Galilee' are addressed—

> Ye poor deluded youths, go home,
> Mend the old nets ye left to roam,
> Tie the split oar, patch the torn sail:
> It was indeed an 'idle tale,'
> He was not risen.

The truth is, that though Clough from time to time attempts to reconcile and settle, his deepest conviction is that all settlement is premature. We meet continually phrases like the

> Receive it not, yet leave it not,
> And wait it out, O man,

---

[1] uncompromising, unsparing.

of one of his earlier poems. To use a favourite image of his, the universe, by our present arithmetic, comes to much less than we had fondly imagined. Our arithmetic is sound, and must be trusted; in fact, it is the only arithmetic we have got. Still the disappointing nature of the result (and let us never pretend to ourselves that it is not disappointing) may be taken as some evidence of its incompleteness.

This irony assumes a peculiar tone when it is directed to vulgar, shallow, unworthy states of mind. It is not that Clough passionately repudiates these, and takes up a censorial position outside and over against them; these, too, are facts, common and important facts of humanity; *humani nihil*—not even Philistinism—*a se alienum putat*. His contempt for them is deep, but not bitter; indeed, so far from bitter that a dull pious ear may misperceive in it an unpleasing levity. His mode of treating them is to present them in extreme and bald simplicity, so that the mind recoils from them. A penetrating observer describes something like this as a part of Clough's conversational manner. 'He had a way,' says Mr. Bagehot, 'of presenting your own view to you, so that you saw what it came to, and that you did not like it.'[1] A good instance of this occurs in an unfinished poem, called 'The Shadow' (published in this edition for the first time). We quote the greater part of it, as it also exemplifies Clough's powerful, though sparingly exercised, imagination; which here, from the combination of sublimity and quaintness, reminds one of Richter, only that we have antique severity instead of romantic profuseness:—

[Quotes 'The Shadow', ll. 1–55: 'I dreamed a dream' to 'the Shadow sat all day'.]

The effect of the latter part is like that of stripping an uncomely body, familiar to us as respectably draped and costumed, and showing it without disguise or ornament. That 'the world' has never seen himself in this nakedness we feel: but we also feel that here is the world which we know. The two lines before the three last show the felicitous audacity with which Clough sometimes manages metre: nothing could more sharply give the shallowness of the mood in contrast with the solemnity of the subject than the careless glibness of the lines,

> It was a comfortable thing to think upon
> The atonement and the resurrection of the dead.

[1] Cf. p. 174 above.

The longest of the religious poems is an unfinished one called *The Mystery of the Fall*. The fundamental idea seems to be this. The legend of the Fall represents a permanent and universal element of human feeling, the religious conviction of sin, but only one element: the beliefs corresponding to it, even if intuitive consciousness is relied upon as their evidence, are not affirmed by the sum-total of valid consciousness—taking 'Sunday and work-days' together. Not only do our practical necessities and active impulses require and generate other conceptions of the universe which seem incompatible with the religious, but the latter is unsatisfying in itself: the notions of perfect creation, lapse, wrath, propitiation, though they correspond to a part of our religious experience, yet do not content our religious feeling as an adequate account of the relation of God to man. This Clough has tried to express, keeping the framework of the old legend, in dialogues between Adam, Eve, Cain, and Abel after expulsion from the garden. The transitions and blendings of the different moods are given with a close and subtle fidelity to psychological truth: and this putting of new wine into old bottles is perhaps justified by the prominence in human history of the Hebrew legend. There is no reason why Adam and his family should not be permanent machinery for serious fable, as Jove and his subordinates are for burlesque. Still the incongruity between the modern moods (and especially the perfect self-consciousness accompanying them) and the antique personages and incidents is here too whimsical: and, for poetry, the thought is too predominant, and the feeling not sufficiently intense; to some parts of the subject, as the murder of Abel, Clough's imagination is inadequate: and on the whole the result is interesting rather than successful, and we doubt whether the poem could ever have been completed so as to satisfy the author's severe self-criticism.

We take a very different view of the other unfinished long poem, *Dipsychus*. If it had received the author's final touches, a few trivialities and whimsicalities would no doubt have been pruned away: but we doubt whether the whole could have been much improved. It has certain grave defects which seem to us irremovable, and we should rank it as a work of art below either of his hexameter poems. There is not sufficient movement or evolution in it; the feeling is too purely egoistic to keep up our sympathies so long; and it is not sufficiently framed. The Venetian scenes in which the dialogue goes on, though appropriate to some of the moods, have no particular connection with the most important: whereas in *Amours de Voyage*, and still more in

The Bothie, the harmonising of external and internal presentments is admirably managed. At the same time the composition is one of great interest. The stress of feeling is so sustained, the changes and fluctuations of mood are given with such perfect propriety, the thought and expression are so bold and novel yet free from paradox, so subtle without a particle of mere ingenuity. The blank verse too in parts, though only in parts, seems to have been carefully studied, and, though a little too suggestive of Elizabethan models, to attain a really high pitch of excellence. Perhaps no other poem of Clough's has so decidedly this one 'note' of genius, that its utterances are at once individual and universal, revealing the author to the reader, and at the same time the reader to himself.

The constructive idea of the poem, which is a dialogue between a man and an attendant spirit, is taken of course from *Faust*. But Goethe (as his half-apologetic prologue hints) sacrificed something in adapting his idea to the conditions of drama: and the issues in Clough's debate are so much finer, that we feel nothing imitative in his development of the conception. The suggestions of the spirit are never clearly fiendish in themselves; with much skill their fiendishness is made to lie in their relation to the man's thoughts. The spirit, in fact, is the 'spirit of the world;' and the close of the debate is not between clear right and wrong (however plausible wrong), but between two sides of a really difficult question,—how far, in acting on society, rules and courses repugnant to the soul's ideal are to be adopted. True to himself, Clough does not decide the question; and though his sympathies are on the side of the ideal, we never know quite how far he would pronounce against the fiend.

The second part of the poem is almost too fragmentary to discuss. In it the man appears at the close of a successful career, having been attuned and attempered to the world by an immoral liaison. How far this means is justified by that end seems to us a disagreeable specialisation of the general problem of the first part, much more easy to decide. It is worked out, however, with much force. Several songs included in this poem were in the first edition published separately—by a great mistake, we cannot but think, as they have more force and beauty in their original setting; and it was a little unfair to Clough (though less than might be expected) to publish his fiend's utterances as his own.

We turn now to what we may call the amatory scepticism. This is a more proper subject of poetry, as thought here is in no danger of being too predominant over feeling; at the same time it is more novel and original, as on no subject do poets in general less allow thought to interfere with feeling. Poets, in fact, are the recognised preachers of the divinity, eternity, omnipotence of Love. It is true that with some of them fits of despair alternate with enthusiasm, and they proclaim that Love is an empty dream: but the notion of scrutinising the enthusiasm sympathetically, yet scientifically, and estimating the precise value of its claims and assertions, probably never entered into any poetic soul before Clough. Nor is it less alien to the habits of ordinary humanity. That the lover's state is a frenzy, innocuous indeed, delightful, perhaps even laudable as a part of nature's arrangements for carrying on the affairs of the world, but still a frenzy; that we all go into it and come out of it, take one view of things in general when in it and another when out of it—is what practical people accept with more or less playful or cynical acquiescence. Poets have a licence to take an opposite view—in fact we should be disappointed if they did not; but we listen to them not for truth but for pleasant illusion. It will be seen how impossible it was for Clough's nature to acquiesce in this. Goethe sings of

Den Drang nach Wahrheit und die Lust am Trug,[1]

as part of the poet's endowment. It was Clough's peculiarity, perhaps his defect, as a poet, that he had not the 'Lust am Trug.' He feels the rapture that illusion gives, he quotes more than once with sympathy

Wen Gott betrügt ist wohl betrogen,[2]

but such 'wohl' he could not himself appropriate. Nor could he serenely separate idea from fact, as his friend Emerson does in the following passage:—

And the first condition [of painting Love] is, that we must leave a too close and lingering adherence to the actual, to facts. . . . Everything is beautiful seen from the point of the intellect. But all is sour, if seen as experience. Details are always melancholy: the plan is seemly and noble. It is strange how painful is the actual world,—the painful kingdom of time and place. There dwells care and canker and fear. With thought, with the ideal, is immortal hilarity, the rose of joy.

---

[1] Goethe's *Faust*: from the '*Vorspiel auf dem Theater*' ('Prelude on the stage') spoken by the '*Dichter*' ('writer'), who says: 'Ich hatte nichts und doch genug:/Den Drang nach Wahrheit und die Lust am Trug' ('I had nothing but still I had enough:/The urge for truth and the craving for illusions'.
[2] Goethe, '*Gott, Gemüt und Welt*': 'Wen Gott betrügt der ist wohl betrogen'—'Whom God betrays is well betrayed'.

This well illustrates by contrast the fundamental mood of Clough. For his imagination at any time thus to abandon *terra firma* and console itself with cloudland would have been impossible. The fascination of the ideal was as strong for him as for other poets, but not stronger than the necessity of making it real. Hence in that period of youthful forecast and partial experience of passion, in which the finest love-fancies of most poets are woven, he perpetually feels the need of combining clear vision with exaltation. He keeps questioning Love as to what it really is, whence it comes, whither it goes: he demands a transcendent evaluation of it.

> Whence are ye, vague desires?
> Whence are ye?
>
> From seats of bliss above,
> Where angels sing of love;
> From subtle airs around,
> Or from the vulgar ground,
> Whence are ye, vague desires?
> Whence are ye?

'Is love spiritual or earthly?' is the passionate perplexity that tinges many of his songs. Or if this pearl of great price is to be found on earth, how shall we know it from its counterfeits, by what criterion discern the impulses that lead us to the true and the false? In one of the finer passages of the *Mari Magno* tales, this longing for direction is uttered.

> Beside the wishing gate which so they name,
> 'Mid northern hills to me this fancy came,
> A wish I formed, my wish I thus expressed:
> *Would I could wish my wishes all to rest,*
> *And know to wish the wish that were the best!*
> O for some winnowing wind, to the empty air
> This chaff of easy sympathies to bear
> Far off, and leave me of myself aware!
> While thus this over health deludes me still,
> So willing that I know not what I will;
> O for some friend, or more than friend, austere,
> To make me know myself and make me fear!
> O for some touch, too noble to be kind,
> To awake to life the mind within the mind!

But if love be after all only 'a wondrous animal delight' in which nature's periodic blossoming culminates, the philosophic spirit, however deep its yearning, cannot submit to it, but has to contemplate it from the outside with tender and curious sympathy. This mood tinged with playfulness inspired the charming song in which he describes how he watched

> . . . in pleasant Kensington
> A 'prentice and a maid.
> That Sunday morning's April glow,
> How should it not impart
> A stir about the veins that flow
> To feed the youthful heart?

The rapture of this sympathetic contemplation is expressed in *Amours de Voyage*.

> And as I walk on my way, I behold them, consorting and coupling;
> Faithful it seemeth and fond, very fond, very probably faithful,
> All as I go on my way, with a pleasure sincere and unmingled.
> Life is beautiful, Eustace . . .
> . . . and could we eliminate only
> This vile hungering impulse, this demon within us of craving,
> Life were beatitude, living a perfect divine satisfaction.

This leads us to the deepest issue of all—a thoroughly Platonic problem. Be this love as noble as it may, is its exaltation compatible with clear vision? Does not this individualised enthusiasm of necessity draw away from the centrality of view and feeling after which the philosophic spirit aspires? Is it not unworthy of us, for any pleasure's sake, to be tricked by its magic and take its coloured light for white?

But we are tired of reducing to prose the various phases of this subtle blending and conflict of enthusiasms. As expressed by Clough they have the perfect vitality and reality of all his moods. None of these perplexities is arbitrarily sought; the questions raised must each have been raised and decided by many human beings since self-consciousness began. If no poet has uttered them before, it is because in most men the state of mind in which they were felt is incompatible with the flow of feeling that poetry requires. Clough's nature was, perhaps, deficient in passion, but it had a superabundant tenderness and susceptibility to personal influence, which made him retain the full feeling of personal relations while giving free scope to his sceptical intellect.

In one of the two long hexameter poems published in his lifetime, *Amours de Voyage*, Clough has given a dramatic embodiment to the motives that we have been analysing. The poem is skilfully composed.

Thoroughly apprehending the aversion which practical humanity feels for these perplexities, he somewhat exaggerates the egotism of the hero of the piece to whom he attributes them, handles him with much irony throughout, and inflicts a severe but appropriate Nemesis at the close. The caricature in Claude is so marked that we are not surprised that Clough, the least egotistical of men, was indignant when a friend appeared to take the poem as an account of the author's own experiences. 'I assure you,' he writes, 'that it is extremely not so.' Still this attitude of the author could not reconcile the public to a hero who (as the motto has it) *doutait de tout, même de l'amour*. That the poem never attained the success of *The Bothie* we are not surprised. It has not the unique presentations of external nature which give such a charm to the earlier poem: it wants also the buoyant and vivacious humour which is so exuberant in *The Bothie*, and of which the fountain in Clough's later years seems almost to have dried up. But it shows greater skill in blending and harmonising different threads of a narrative, and a subtler management of the evolution of moods; it has a deeper psychological interest, and in its best passages a rarer, more original imagination. The '*amour*' is very closely interwoven with the incidents of the French siege of Rome (of which, by the way, Clough's letters give us interesting details), so that the two series of events together elicit a complete and consistent self-revelation of the hero. The amative dubitations turn principally on two points—the immense issues that depend on amative selection compared with the arbitrary casual manner in which circumstances determine it, and the imperious claim of passion for a concentration of interest which to the innermost, most self-conscious, self is profoundly impossible. These play into one another in the following very characteristic passage:—

[Quotes *Amours de Voyage*, iii, 107–16: 'Juxtaposition, in fine' to 'the light of our knowledge!' and 123–36: 'But for the steady fore-sense' to 'the victual that He has provided.'

(The lines italicised are:
But for assurance within of a limitless ocean divine, o'er
Whose great tranquil depths unconscious the wind-tost surface
Breaks into ripples of trouble that come and change and endure
(not, —)]

The three lines that we have italicised seem to us almost perfect specimens of the English hexameter, showing the extreme flexibility which the metre has in Clough's hands, and his only, and none of the over-accentuation which neither he nor any one else can generally avoid. Very opposite opinions have been delivered as to the merits of this hexameter. Some most appreciative readers of the poems declare that they read them continually under protest; that no interest in the subject and no habit can make the metre tolerable. Mr. Arnold, however, on this subject an especially Rhadamanthine critic, considers the success of Clough's experiment to be so decided as to form an important contribution to the question (which has occupied a most disproportionate amount of human intellect in our time), How Homer is to be translated? We do not take either view. We think Clough's metre, as he uses it, felicitous; but we do not think that this proves anything as to the appropriateness of the hexameter for translating Homer, or for any other application of 'the grand style.' Clough has not *naturalised* the metre. He has given it ease, but not simplicity; he has not tried to give it simplicity, and therefore he has succeeded with it. All English hexameters written quite *au sérieux* seem to us to fail; the line ought to be unconscious of being a hexameter, and yet never is. But Clough's line is, and is meant to be, conscious of being a hexameter: it is always suggestive of and allusive to the ancient serious hexameters, with a faint but a deliberate air of burlesque, a wink implying that the bard is singing academically to an academical audience, and catering for their artificial tastes in versification. This academic flavour suits each poem in a different way. It harmonises with the Oxonian studies of *The Bothie*; and here, indeed, the faint burlesque inseparable from the metre becomes from time to time mock-heroic. In *Amours de Voyage*, it suits the over-culture, artificial refinement of the hero's mind: he is, we may say, in his abnormal difficulties of action and emotion, a scholastic or academic personage. In short the metre seems to belong to a style full of characteristic self-conscious humour such as Clough has sustained through each of the poems; and we cannot analyse its effect separately. Clough we know thought differently; but we are forced to regard this as one instance out of many where a poet takes a wrong view of his own work. His experiment of translating Homer into similar hexameters is nearly as much a failure as Mr. Arnold's, or any other; and his still bolder experiment of writing hexameters by quantity and not accent results, in spite of the singular care and even power with which it is executed, in a mere monstrosity.

We consider then that it was a happy instinct that led him to the metre of *The Bothie*. In more ordinary metres he often shows a want of mastery over the technicalities of verse-writing. He has no fertility of rhymes, he is monotonous, he does not avoid sing-song, he wearies us with excessive, almost puerile, iterations and antitheses. It is very remarkable, therefore, how in this new metre, self-chosen, he rises to the occasion, how inventive he is of varied movements, felicitous phrases, and pleasant artifices of language, how emphatically yet easily the sound is adapted to the sense, in a way which no metre but blank verse in the hands of a master could rival. Another evidence of the peculiar fitness of this instrument for his thought is the amount that he can pack without effort into his lines; as *e.g.* in the following description of one of the members of the Oxford reading-party:—

> Author forgotten and silent of currentest phrase and fancies,
> Mute and exuberant by turns, a fountain at intervals playing,
> Mute and abstracted, or strong and abundant as rain in the tropics;
> Studious; careless of dress; inobservant; by smooth persuasions
> Lately decoyed into kilt on example of Hope and the Piper;
> Hope an Antinous mere, Hyperion of calves the Piper.

It is hard to imagine so much said so shortly in any other style.

The flexibility of the metre aids in bringing out another great excellence of these poems; the ease and completeness with which character is exhibited. There is not one of the personages of *The Bothie*, or even of *Amours de Voyage*, where the sketching is much slighter, whose individuality is not as thoroughly impressed upon us as if they had been delineated in a three-volume novel by Mr. Trollope. We are made to understand by most happily selected touches, and delicately illustrative phrases, not only what they are in themselves, but precisely how they affect one another. It becomes as impossible for us to attribute a remembered remark to the wrong person as it would be in a play of Shakespeare. To say that Clough's dramatic faculty was strong might convey a wrong impression, as we imagine that he was quite devoid of the power of representing a scene of vivid action; but the power of forming distinct conceptions of character, and expressing them with the few touches that poetry allows, is one of the gifts for displaying which we may regret that he had not ampler scope.

The descriptions of natural scenery in *The Bothie* form probably the best-known and most popular part of Clough's poetry. In this, as in some of his most important poetical characteristics, he may be called, in spite of great differences, a true disciple of Wordsworth. His admiration for the latter appears to have been always strongly marked; and one of the more interesting of the prose remains now published is an essay on Wordsworth, perhaps somewhat meagre, but showing profound appreciation, together with the critical propriety and exactness of statement characteristic of Clough. His simplicity, sincerity, gravity, are all Wordsworthian; but especially his attitude towards nature. Through a manner of description quite different we trace the rapt receptive mood, the unaffected self-abandonment, the anxious fidelity of reproduction, which Wordsworth has taught to many disciples, but to no other poet so fully.

In the essay referred to we find a view of Wordsworth's poetical merits, which to many persons will appear paradoxical, but which seems to us perfectly true, and applicable to some extent to Clough himself. He says that Wordsworth, the famous prefaces notwithstanding,—

'really derives from his style and his diction his chief and special charm'; . . . he bestowed 'infinite toil and labour upon his poetic style'; 'in the nice and exquisite felicities of poetic diction he specially surpassed his contemporaries'; and 'his scrupulous and painstaking spirit, in this particular, constitutes one of his special virtues as a poet. . . . He has not . . . the vigour and heartiness of Scott, or the force and the sweep and the fervour of Byron. . . . But that permanent beauty of expression, that harmony between thought and word, which is the condition of "*immortal* verse," they did not, I think—and Wordsworth did—take pains to attain. There is hardly anything in Byron and Scott which in another generation people will not think they can say over again quite as well, and more agreeably and familiarly for themselves; there is nothing which, it will be plain, has, in Scott or Byron's way of putting it, attained the one form which of all others truly belongs to it; which any new attempt will, at the very utmost, merely successfully repeat. For poetry, like science, has its final precision; and there are expressions of poetic knowledge which can no more be re-written than could the elements of geometry. There are pieces of poetic language which, try as men will, they will simply have to recur to, and confess that it has been done before them.'

And he goes on to say that 'people talk about style as if it were a mere accessory, the unneeded but pleasing ornament, the mere put-on dress of the substantial being, who without it is much the same as with it.' Whereas really 'some of the highest truths are only expressible to us by style, only appreciable as indicated by manner.'[1]

With all this we agree: but it seems to us that two conditions are necessary for the success in style spoken of, and that Clough has only given one. In order to attain it, a man must be conscious of very definite characteristic moods, and must have confidence in them, take

[1] Lecture on Wordsworth: see *SPW*, 107–22.

an interest in and value their definite characteristics; then in expressing them he must work with a patient, single-minded effort to adapt
the expression to the mood, caring always for the latter more than for
the former. This was certainly the manner of Clough's composition,
and hence many of his poetic utterances have, as he phrases it, 'final
precision.' We do not mean to compare their effect to Wordsworth's.
Clough has none of the prophetic dignity of his master, of the latter's
organ-music he has not even an echo: and he far surpasses him in
subtlety. There is a peculiar combination of simplicity and subtlety in
his best things, the simplicity being as it were the final result and outcome of the subtlety, so that the presence of the latter is felt, and not
distinctly recognised, which we find in no other poet except Goethe.
It is this combination that fits him for his peculiar function of rendering
conscious the feelings that pass half unconsciously through ordinary
minds, without seriously modifying them. There is a pretty instance
of this in an idyllic song which we will quote. Most of the song is rather
commonplace; a peasant-girl driving she-goats homeward thinks
alternately of the scene, and of her absent lover. Suddenly we are surprised with this very Cloughian sentiment.

> Or may it be that I shall find my mate,
> And he returning see himself too late?
> *For work we must, and what we see, we see,*
> *And God he knows, and what must be, must be,*
> When sweethearts wander far away from me.

The excellence of the lines that we have italicised we should describe
paradoxically by saying that their naïveté is at once perfect, and
as naïveté, impossible.

On the other hand, if Clough has many of Wordsworth's excellences,
he certainly has his full share of the cognate defects. It is natural, perhaps, to the man who values the individuality of his thought and
feeling so much as to spend great care on its expression, to want the
power of discriminating between those parts of it that are, and those
which are not worth expressing. Certainly Clough has not, any more
than his master, the selective faculty that leads to the sustained elevation and distinction which we expect from a great poet, and which the
adoption of a simple manner renders peculiarly indispensable. Commonplace thought and feeling in strikingly simple language does not
make, perhaps, more really worthless poetry than commonplace
thought and feeling in ornate language; but its worthlessness is more

patent. There is this one advantage, that the critic is not forced to dwell upon it: no one's taste is perverted, except perhaps in the first charm of the poet's novelty. No one now pretends to admire the dulness and twaddle in Wordsworth; and in Clough even more than in Wordsworth the expression rises and falls with the matter: the dullest and most trivial things are the worst put. We will only say that the genius of twaddle, which often hovers near his muse, makes its presence especially felt in his last poems, the *Mari Magno* tales. These must, of course, be judged as unfinished productions; but no retouching could have enabled them to rank very high as poetry. They are easy, pleasant, even edifying reading, and they essentially want effectiveness. They are written in obvious emulation of Crabbe; and in a natural and faithful homeliness of style, which occasionally becomes a transparent medium for a most impressive tenderness, they certainly rival Crabbe; but their general level is much lower. The charm of Crabbe, when he is not tender, lies in the combination of unobtrusive dignity, and a certain rustic raciness and pregnancy, with a fair share of the artificial point and wit that properly belong to the Popian measure. Clough has nothing of this; and though in the best passages his characteristic fineness of apprehension makes amends, on the dead levels of narration the style is much inferior to Crabbe's: its blankness is glaring. In the first tale especially the genius of twaddle reigns supreme; it reminds us of—we will not say the worst, for it has no bad taste, but—the second-rate portions of Coventry Patmore.

The inferiority of these poems is due, as we before hinted, to a deeper cause than a temporary defect of vigour or a mistaken experiment of style. It is evident that we have here Clough without his peculiar inspiration—his talent, we may say, but not his genius. As an artist he is noteworthy—his production has many high qualities, viewed as technically as possible; it is not, however, as a mere artist, but as an utterer of peculiar yet representative moods, that he has the power to excite our deepest interest. But these moods are the moods, in the main, of youth; and when Clough, after a period of more than usually prolonged adolescence, finally adopted the adult attitude towards life, they ceased to dominate his habitual thought and feeling. Not that any abrupt change shows itself in him. There were two tempers singularly entwined in him throughout: his letters for the most part present a striking contrast to the contemporary poems. In the latter we find chiefly absorbing effort after an ideally clear vision, a perfect solution of problems: in the former mild practical wisdom, serene submission to the imperfections of life, cheerful acquiescence in 'the best under the circumstances.' And this quieter tone naturally grew upon him. Not that he could ever separate speculation from practice, or in either sphere settle down into smooth commonplace: but he grew tired of turning over the web of commonplace notions and rules, and showing their seamy side: he set himself rather to solve and settle instead of raising and exposing difficulties. At the same time the sincerity which had led him to emphasise his passionate perplexities, still kept him from exaggerating his triumph over them: he attains no fervour of confident hope, nor expansion of complacent optimism: he walks in the twilight, having adapted his eyes to it somewhat, but he does not mistake it for dawn. Whether in such twilight he would ever have seemed to see with sufficient clearness to impel him to utter his vision to the world, is doubtful: at any rate the utterance would, we imagine, have taken a prosaic and not a poetical form. He was looking at life steadily till he could see it whole: aspiring, as he says in an early poem, to

> . . . bring some worthy thing
> For waiting souls to see.

But the very loftiness of this aspiration, and the severity with which he would have judged his own claims to be a teacher, incline us to think that he would never have uttered the final outcome of his life's thought. What he wished to do for the world no one has yet done: we have scarcely reason to believe that he could have done it: and he would have been content to do nothing less. His provisional views, the temporary substitutes for 'demonstrated faith' by which he was content to walk, he would hardly have cared to publish. That they would, however, have been interesting, we can see from the only fragment of them that the editor has been able to give us—a paper on 'The Religious Tradition.' From this, as it illustrates a different side of Clough's mind to that on which we have been led chiefly to dwell, we will conclude by quoting some extracts:—

The more a man feels the value, the true import, of the moral and religious teaching which passes amongst us by the name of Christianity, the more will he hesitate to base it upon those foundations which, as a scholar, he feels to be unstable. Manuscripts are doubtful, records may be unauthentic, criticism is feeble, historical facts must be left uncertain. Even in like manner my own personal experience is most limited, perhaps even most delusive; what have I seen, what do I know? Nor is my personal judgment a thing which I feel any great satisfaction in trusting. My reasoning powers are weak; my memory doubtful and confused; my conscience, it may be, callous or vitiated.

. . . I see not what other alternative any sane and humble-minded man can have but to throw himself upon the great religious tradition. But I see not either how any upright and strict dealer with himself—how any man not merely a slave to spiritual appetites, affections and wants—any man of intellectual as well as moral honesty—and without the former the latter is but a vain thing—I see not how anyone who will not tell lies to himself, can dare to affirm that the narrative of the four Gospels is an essential integral part of that tradition. I do not see that it is a great and noble thing . . . to go about proclaiming that Mark is inconsistent with Luke . . . it is no new gospel to tell us that the old one is of dubious authenticity. I do not see either . . . that it can be lawful for me, for the sake of the moral guidance and the spiritual comfort, to ignore all scientific or historic doubts, or if pressed with them to the utmost, to take refuge in Romish infallibility . . .

Where then, since neither in Rationalism nor in Rome is our refuge,—where then shall we seek for the Religious Tradition?

Everywhere; but above all in our own work: in life, in action, in submission, so far as action goes, in service, in experience, in patience, in confidence. I would scarcely have any man dare to say that he has found it, till that moment when death removes his power of telling it. Let no young man presume to talk to us vainly and confidently about it. Ignorant, as said Aristotle, of the real actions of life, and ready to follow all impressions and passions, he is hardly fitted as yet even to listen to practical directions couched in the language of religion. But this apart—everywhere . . . among all who have really tried to order their lives by the highest action of the reasonable and spiritual will.

42. From an unsigned review in *Putnam's Magazine*

December 1869, iv, 752–4

Putnam's was an American magazine which published a few of Clough's poems and his 'Letters of Parepidemus' in 1853–4.

. . . he who would be a just critic must take up Time into his mind; must have for his point of view the far future; must bring his intellect into the few broad lines of thought into which the movement of the age is to concentrate itself at last, and which are to be prolonged to other ages. At least he must aim at this; and the nearer he can come to it the greater his success. True criticism has for its best feature the sense for what is abiding, what is immortal; detects this and honors it, and so does for the day the work of time. It is certainly a rare article. Was it ever rarer than now? This is often called an age of criticism; but is it not rather an age of impatient and shallow judgments? It produces abundantly, and in part greatly, but does not know its own greatness, nor divide wheat and chaff. In recent American literature there are enough and able strictures on many things in government, in society, and in books; but where is there a contribution of note to that form of culture which makes each mind a test of truth, informing it with the principles by which societies and books live and die?

Perhaps there has been nothing of this kind lately more important than the *Remains* of Arthur Hugh Clough, which his wife has just edited so tastefully for Macmillan and Co., of London. When an author has been dead nine years, it seems late to introduce him; but it is a fact that Mr. Clough has had no fair introduction to the American or even the English public until this charming monument appeared. As for direct criticism, the book contains less of it than it provokes; except a few of his essays here reprinted, with two charming 'Letters of Parepidemus,' first published in *Putnam's Monthly* in 1853, there is hardly anything formal in this line. Yet the tone of the man is so high, partakes so much of that which is of no age or nation, but of humanity, that the genuine enjoyment of it is a good help to forming a literary judgment, a *werdende Einsicht*.[1] Clough's was a poorly husbanded mind. His powers, gathering up early and concentrated on a worthy purpose, would surely have achieved work among the best, and, indeed, none but a mind capable of this can be a true judge of others' work. The critic may not be an actual producer, but he must have the capacity which, rightly trained, could have done the thing he judges. Yet, to go to the bottom of the thought at once, has not every man this capacity entire? Is not humanity as a whole in each one—the undeveloped Homer, Bacon, Washington, folded up in germ and hidden away in the depths of each? Well, not denying this, it is safe to say that, as the wing must be feathered before it can fly, the intelligence must be brought out of the rudimentary form into consciousness and cultivation before it can appreciate. Clough's strong passion was hatred for the rudiments of literary organs in himself, and desire for finish, for perfectness, that every writing might be a living form aptly embodying exact truth of thought.

He was a poet, too; but in poetry as well as criticism he was out of tune with his times, and is only growing into popularity with the next generation. His love and reverence for Tennyson were profound, perhaps just because they differed so widely. Tennyson's best art has never been the delight of the multitude; but a poem by him is not only a perfect work of art, it is a battalion of phrases, an army of thoughts, from which stragglers find their way through all literature. Those 'jewels, five words long,' make most of his popularity. But Clough is rarely quotable. He has one thing to say; his poem is the way to say it; and he struggles to make it mean just that, and nothing besides. No fine words or thoughts divert his attention, or arrest him for a moment. Homer did much the same, and Dante; but their greater genius blazed out sideways also in immortal gleams of beauty, because they could not help it. The greatest of all poets is the most quoted, having said the best and wisest things; but his greatness is shown far more in wholes than in parts, and would not seem less to those who have caught a real sight of it, if all the pretty sayings commonly known were left out. We are not comparing Clough with these men; in him not only all the pretty sayings are left out, but all else, except indications of the severe and high ideal he was growing toward. He has left but one complete poem which can make a very intense impression—his 'Easter Day in Naples'; a bold utterance of the warfare in his mind

---

[1] 'A developing insight.'

between traditional faith and its sweet associations, on one side, and the skeptical culture of the times on the other. It is a struggle to save the chief symbol of his religion, while reason, though trying in vain to wrest it from him, quite changes its meaning. Even this fine poem lacks, the author plainly felt its lack, of just the perfect touch which signals greatness; but as long as the unending war of faith and fate, of the ideal and the actual, shall be waged with the weapons that are now clashing in it, with the creeds and the doubts of these times, so long will men find their unrest soothed by the expression such lines as these give it:

[Quotes 'Easter Day', ll. 64–94: 'Is he not risen, and shall we not rise?' to 'Christ is not risen' and 'Easter Day', II, ll. 5–7: 'But in a later hour' to 'whatever hath been said' and 18–25: 'Though he be dead' to 'Christ is yet risen'.]

LATER ESTIMATES

(to 1920)

43. Two Comments by Edward Dowden

1874, 1877

From *Fragments of Old Letters E. D. to E. D.W., 1869–1892* (1914), 94–5, and from 'The Transcendental Movement and Literature', *Contemporary Review*, xxx, July 1877 (esp. 309, 315–16), reprinted in *Studies in Literature* (1887) (esp. 68, 78–80).

Edward Dowden (1843–1913) was in 1867 appointed to the Chair of English Literature, Trinity College, Dublin, which he held until his death. He was best known for his psychological studies of Shakespeare and of several of the nineteenth-century sages.

From *Fragments from Old Letters*, 15 May 1874:
. . . If I have time I'll give a lecture on A. H. Clough—or two—with whom I am now a good deal in sympathy.

He knew very fully the Ascension-tide truth, 'Unto your life's Jerusalem return', and, without any of Carlyle's mystical worship of work for work's sake, felt in a very practical way how there was a spiritual life running on through all level and bare parts of life (while he didn't the less feel the gain of the moments of higher vision and rarer insight). The men in College *now* are less fortunate than *we* were ten years ago. Browning, Wordsworth, Clough were more beneficent influences than Swinburne, Morris, and Rossetti.

From *Studies in Literature*:
. . . The writings of one who came under the influence of Mr. Carlyle, and who was a friend of Emerson, may serve here to illustrate the

difficulties into which religious sentiment, theistic and pantheistic, was brought by doubts with reference to the basis of theology forced upon the intellects of men. That which gives to the poetry of Clough an interest almost unique is his susceptibility to ideas, impressions, and emotions which are antagonistic to one another, which he could not harmonize, yet none of which he would deny. Shelley, when he wrote, was always under the influence of a single intense feeling urging him to song. Clough wrote almost always with the consciousness of two or more conflicting feelings. If he is in the mood for an ideal flight, you may be sure the most prosaic of demons is at his elbow about to remind him that feet and not wings are the locomotive instruments of a human creature. When he is most devout he becomes the object of the most vigorous assaults of the tempter. Now in the friendliest spirit he approaches science, as she utters her oracles, and in a moment he is forced away to attend to the scarce-heard whisper of some inward monitor who may be very God.

This susceptibility to various cross and counter influences, which must have caused some of the sorrow of Clough's life as a man, is the source of the special virtue of his work as a poet. He will suppress no part of himself to the advantage of any other part. If he and his perceptions of truth are not a harmonious whole, he will not falsify things by forcing upon his nature a factitious unity. Standing towards modern science is a trustful and friendly attitude, he yet could not accept it as a complete account of the facts so long as certain inner voices were audible, into accord with which scientific doctrine had not been brought. A pupil of Dr. Arnold, he found some comfort in dealing with his doubts in the manner recommended by Teufelsdrockh, *Do the duty that lies nearest to thee*:[1] but he remained aware that such a method for the solution of doubts is personal, not absolute. Clough's poetry may be said to be true, upon the whole, to the transcendental lobe of his brain; his prose, had he continued to write prose, would probably have given expression to his enquiring intellect, and to the generous practical tendencies which impelled him in the direction of the social world. There were times when the Mary in Clough's heart tried energetically to transform herself into a Martha, rose up troubled herself about many things, and declared that it was well to do so; but always a moment came when she went back to sit at the Master's feet, and chose the good part:

---

[1] 'Do the duty which lies nearest thee': *Sartor Resartus*, bk. II, ch. 9.

[Quotes *Dipsychus*, Scene IV, 83–8: 'O let me love my love' to 'mine own inmost heart'.]

Within Clough's nature contended the spiritual instincts and intuitions, an intellect compelled to sceptical doubts by the tendencies of his time, and a will bent upon disinterested practical activity. The low worldliness, cynicism, mammon-worship, ignoble prudence, and paltering with conscience of our age were all apparent to him, but could not touch and stain his soul. The Evil Spirit of his Faust-like poem, *Dipsychus*, is this low worldliness, this ignoble prudence, this cynicism, the demon of a *saeculum realisticum*, who draws down men to hell.[1]

44. [Bishop Arthur T. Lyttelton], 'The Poetry of Doubt'—Arnold and Clough, article in *Church Quarterly Review* vi

April 1878, 117–39

This article was reprinted in *Modern Poets of Faith, Doubt and Paganism* (London, 1904), 91–104.

Arthur T. Lyttelton (1852–1903), Suffragan Bishop of Southampton, was a liberal in politics and a tolerant high churchman.

We would contrast with Mr. Arnold's tone of thought, with his hopes, his sympathies, and his beliefs, not one of the more definitely Christian poets such as Mr. Tennyson or Mr. Browning, nor one whose irreligion is as definite, such as Mr. Swinburne; but one whom Mr. Arnold would, we suppose, claim as a sympathiser in thought, and who was, indeed,

---

[1] To illustrate what has been said of Clough, the reader may refer to his review of Newman's *The Soul*, his poems 'The New Sinai', 'Qui Laborat Orat' and *Dipsychus*. (Dowden's note.)

much in the same perplexity and doubt, his friend, Arthur Hugh Clough.

He was one of those whose whole life was coloured by the impressions received at Oxford during the stirring years 1837–42. Not one whose faith was raised and fortified by the discussions and the personal influences of the time, but one who, as he himself expressed it, was 'like a straw drawn up the draught of a chimney' and afterwards left floating in the air without much of definite guidance or impulse. On first reading Clough's poems we seem to be in an atmosphere of doubt and of little else. Two of his longer poems are entirely occupied with the vacillations of mind which beset those who are starting on life's journey, and can see little before them but an uncertain road and a lowering sky. To one of these he has prefixed the motto 'Il doutait de tout, même de l'amour,' while the name of the other, Dipsychus, expresses the state of division and wavering which seems to be the lot of 'feeble and restless youths born to inglorious days.' And the poet's characteristic humour, which is hardly absent from any of his poems, is not exactly a straightforward perception and enjoyment of the incongruities of life, with a consciousness all the while of the preponderating serious realities, but an irony, benevolent and natural, yet at times almost inscrutable, which makes the two sides of life seem inextricably confused. Most of his poems are concerned with the uprooting of old opinions, and share to the full the uncertainty that has invaded all provinces of thought; and his humorous irony tends to increase the appearance of utter confusion in which the world is lying. This causes the difficulty of really getting to the root of his meaning; he is not essentially dramatic, like Mr. Browning, for he seldom hides himself behind the mask of another character; but the genial irony of his humour eludes at times any firm apprehension. Read such poems as the Amours de Voyage, and especially the section beginning—

Juxtaposition, in fine; and what is juxtaposition—

or the song of the spirit in Dipsychus—

There is no God, the wicked saith—

or the verses headed, Wen Gott betrügt, ist wohl betrogen, and the difficulty of disentangling the lines, so to speak, of Clough's thought will be evident. The humour is apparent on the surface, but it is not so easy to discover how deep it goes.

Clough, then, seems to be essentially the poet of doubt; more so, at first sight, than Mr. Arnold himself. It pervades his poems, and we do not find that, like Mr. Arnold, he seeks a refuge in the calm strength and certainty of Nature, there to find the endurance so sorely needed; but he rather regards Nature as a background to the mixed and confused drama of human life, which it cannot explain nor greatly relieve. His poems are mostly of purely human interest; even those which are speculative derive their impulse from the bearing of speculation on life and duty; and to fly from mankind to seek a higher teaching or a calmer security in Nature would be foreign to Clough's instincts. Nature, indeed, is to him, as to Shakespeare or Chaucer (with whom Mr. Hutton has well compared him) an unfailing source of delight, but it is the childlike, unreflecting delight of an earlier period, something of the same kind of feeling as that which he describes in the *Piper* of the reading-party, who

> Went, in his life and the sunshine rejoicing, to Nuneham and Godstowe;
> What were the claims of degree to those of life and the sunshine?

Life and the sunshine pervade Clough's poems, but he finds no deep lessons in the external beauty that he describes so well, nor does he dwell on Nature for its own sake, but rather as the setting and accompaniment of human action. He can, with genuine truth, feel that

> Life is beautiful, Eustace, entrancing, enchanting to look at;
> As are the streets of a city we pace while the carriage is changing,
> As a chamber filled in with harmonious exquisite pictures.

But it is human life that he means, and the thought is inspired by what he sees in the streets of Rome, not in the solitudes of Nature. Still, the very unselfconsciousness of his love of Nature makes the feeling all the healthier and happier; there is much of the breeziness of a Scotch moor, or of the open sea, in his poems. It is a strong contrast after Mr. Arnold's cool English scenery, the river bank with its lapping wavelets and the trailing wild-flowers washed by the waters, to come upon Clough's glimpses of the burns descending to the 'great still sea,' and to feel the keen air of the salt breezes. In his two finest lyrics the chief image is taken from the sea, in the boundless expanse of which he seems to get a special inspiration, while his verse often reminds one of the freedom and motion of the waves. But we do not turn to Clough for an insight into the hidden meanings of Nature, nor for a portrayal of the calm and easily overlooked beauties of the world, as we turn to

Wordsworth or to Mr. Arnold. What, then, is the special interest of
Clough as a poet?

We have said that he seems to be the poet of doubt, and in this he
apparently resembles Mr. Arnold. But it is not only in their view of
Nature that the two Oxford poets differ; it is impossible to read them
without being struck by the essentially different way in which the
same intellectual and spiritual facts come before them. And this is
especially noticeable in regard to the absorbing question of the certainty of religious truth. Mr. Arnold, as we have seen, is chiefly interested in it as affecting his own consciousness, and regrets the old faiths,
and has no very joyous expectation of the future, because he is self-
centred. With Clough, all this is changed. There is no restless longing
for a rest, which is only attainable by means of a sort of stoical endurance, but a strong, buoyant, and somewhat proud confidence in a final
truth, and a determination to abide its appearance. Mr. Arnold and
Clough are both waiting for what the future shall bring forth; but,
unlike the former, Clough waits for it in cheerful hope, not without
sympathy for the past, but convinced that the ultimate manifestation
will be vouchsafed to man in the future. Thus the different characteristics of the two poets are best illustrated by the differing modes in
which they treat an almost identical subject. Both have written short
poems on the subject of the final victory of good over evil, light over
darkness; but the whole tone is entirely distinct. With Mr. Arnold the
central idea is that of the individual soldier baffled and at last overcome
in the struggle, and falling with a sort of sullen confidence in the final
victory, which, however, seems to afford but little consolation in the
prospect:

> Creep into thy narrow bed,
> Creep, and let no more be said.
> Vain thy onset! all stands fast!
> Thou thyself must break at last.

> Let the long contention cease!
> Geese are swans, and swans are geese.
> Let them have it how they will!
> Thou art tired; best be still.

> They out-talked thee, hissed thee, tore thee?
> Better men fared thus before thee!
> Fired their ringing shot and passed,
> Hotly charged—and broke at last.

Charge once more, then, and be dumb!
Let the victors, when they come,
When the forts of folly fall,
Find thy body by the wall.[1]

In Clough's poem the individual, far from being the centre, is depicted as the only hindrance to the success of the whole cause; the strife is conceived as almost ended already, and the despondent fighter is rebuked:

Say not, the struggle nought availeth,
The labour and the wounds are vain,
The enemy faints not, nor faileth,
And as things have been they remain.

If hopes were dupes, fears may be liars;
It may be, in yon smoke concealed,
Your comrades chase e'en now the fliers,
And, but for you, possess the field.

For while the tired waves, vainly breaking,
Seem here no painful inch to gain,
Far back, through creeks and inlets making,
Comes silent, flooding in, the main.

And not by eastern windows only,
When daylight comes, comes in the light,
In front, the sun climbs slow, how slowly,
But westward, look, the land is bright.

Nothing can be finer than the two images by which he expresses the character of the struggle; the third stanza brings before us at once the whole scene of an incoming tide, with that peculiar sense of the vastness and openness of the sea which distinguishes Clough. The contrast of the whole with the bitter and sarcastic resignation of Mr. Arnold's poem; the different conceptions of the struggle itself; in the one a confused, smoke-enshrouded contest, but in the open field, in the other desperate charges against strongly held forts; the buoyant hope of victory in the one, and the careless, hardly mentioned belief in it in the other; all these points afford us some insight into the very distinct characteristics of the two sceptical poets. The difference goes beyond the mere superficial treatment of a subject in a few stanzas; it pervades

[1] 'The Last Word.'

all their poems. And the fundamental distinction that underlies this superficial unlikeness will, we think, be found to be that while it is doubtful whether Mr. Arnold really holds to or is possessed by the idea of anything external to himself, in Clough's poems numberless passages express not only his unshaken trust in God, but the great influence which his trust has on all his nature, upon every thought and emotion. And this is the more remarkable because he cannot define Him or even conceive Him:

> I will not prate of 'thus' and 'so,'
> And be profane with 'yes' and 'no;'
> Enough that in our soul and heart
> Thou, whatsoe'er Thou may'st be, art.

With a feeling which, to him at least, may have seemed to deserve in some measure our Lord's blessing on 'those who have not seen, and yet have believed,' he can exclaim:

> Be Thou but there—in soul and heart,
> I will not ask to feel Thou art.

It is evident that this attitude in regard to truth is very different from Mr. Arnold's emotional and subjective estimate of it. And it is an attitude which, though it must be called one of suspense, must still be distinguished from scepticism; for though Clough rejects all definitions of God that have yet been promulgated, he does not take pride in believing in an indefinite Being, whose only attribute is to be unknowable, but his faith is in a God whom hitherto man has been unable rightly to conceive, but who assuredly will reveal Himself to us; and till He does so the poet can wait in patient confidence:

> No God, no Truth, receive it ne'er—
> Believe it ne'er—O Man!
> But turn not then to seek again
> What first the ill began;
> No God, it saith; ah, wait in faith
> God's self-completing plan;
> Receive it not, but leave it not,
> And wait it out, O Man!

The whole of this poem, the 'New Sinai', is well worth studying, as a development of Clough's religious philosophy. God, he says, has already rebuked idolatry and polytheism by the declaration, 'I am One'; He will hereafter rebuke both the new idolatries and 'the atheistic systems dark,' which have, like 'baby thoughts,' dogged the growing man. Our duty is to wait, not in a forced endurance, but in the belief that

> Some lofty part, than which the heart
>   Adopt no nobler can,
> Thou shalt receive, thou shalt believe,
>   And thou shalt do, O Man!

The human soul, then, with Clough, is not the centre of the universe, to which all truth must be brought, the object for which all truth exists, but rather one of the attendants at the shrine of truth, of small interest compared with the paramount claims of some Being external to us, who is Truth and Light. To this fact he clings, and here, diametrically opposed to Mr. Arnold, he finds relief from the confused turmoil of modern doubt and speculation:

> It fortifies my soul to know
> That though I perish, Truth is so;
> That, howsoe'er I stray and range,
> Whate'er I do, Thou dost not change.
> I steadier step when I recall
> That, if I slip, Thou dost not fall.

If we bear in mind Clough's conviction that truth is something greater than his soul, and that there may be all the difference in the world between truth and his confused apprehension of it, we shall the better understand his relation to Christianity as a possible form of truth. Though he cannot accept the historical facts of the Gospel, yet he is in no hurry to turn away and seek for a new religion. He is earnest in pleading for a humbler attitude of mind, and his complaint against the world is not that its scepticism has perturbed his soul's calm, but that in its hurry and carelessness it may have passed by some essential truth, and therefore he adjures his brother-men to pause:

> The souls of now two thousand years
> Have laid up here their toils and fears,
> And all the earnings of their pain—
> Ah, yet consider it again.

But though Clough's religious attitude is, at first sight, one of intellectual suspense, yet he does not hold truth to be perceptible to the intellect alone, or, at least, he is inclined to follow without reluctance the leadings of the emotions, even where the head cannot justify the

conclusions of the heart. So in the wonderfully terse and thoughtful
lines headed 'Through a glass darkly,' after suggesting as an alternative,
which we know, from his whole tone of mind, he would have rejected
with disdain, that we may

> for assurance' sake,
> Some arbitrary judgment take,
> And wilfully pronounce it clear,
> For this or that 'tis we are here,

he declares that the hope which is given to us constrains in a manner
our intellect:

> Ah yet, when all is thought and said,
> The heart still overrules the head;
> Still what we hope we must believe,
> And what is given us receive;
>
> Must still believe, for still we hope
> That in a world of larger scope,
> What here is faithfully begun
> Will be completed, not undone.
>
> My child, we still must think, when we
> That ampler life together see,
> Some true result will yet appear
> Of what we are, together, here.

The close of these verses leads us to a further result of Clough's
firm trust in some external reality—namely, his longing for 'faithful'
work upon earth, his belief that genuine labour in the cause of good
will have its fruit, either here or elsewhere; and if not, why, still it is
work, and action is our duty. Even his hesitating heroes, who cannot
for themselves decide on any course of action, can see the beauty of
definite work, and he pronounces his decision for deeds done in behalf
of something not ourselves, rather than for self-culture in words which
he puts in the mouth of Dipsychus:

> Ah, not for profit, not for fame,
> And not for pleasure's giddy dream,
> And not for piping empty reeds,
> And not for colouring idle dust;
> If live we positively must,
> God's name be blest for noble deeds.

This, too, is the moral of the *Bothie of Tober-na-Vuolich*: that the beauty of life comes from its reality, that is, from the reality of the work which we can do on earth. But this is held without attacking culture in the one-sided way which is so common. What he rejects is the false culture which proceeds on the assumption that the object of life is to perfect oneself without regard to the work which has to be done. Some are meant for beauty, others for 'subduing the earth and their spirit,' and both should do their work. In spite of the longing for simplicity of life, in spite of the superficial flavour of Rousseau in this poem, it is obvious that Clough is far from rejecting either education or civilization. The beauty of Elspie's nature could only be really seen by one who, like Philip, had 'the knowledge of self, and wisely instructed feeling.' The very form of the poem, the buoyant refinement which the irregular hexameters suggest, the free Scotch life with the accompaniment of academic study and speculation, combine to give us the impression of a mind subtle yet curiously simple, vigorous, though apparently distracted by speculative hesitation. And though the abundant humour of the poem makes it not easy to be sure how far Clough was speaking his own opinions through the mouths of his *dramatis personæ*, yet both in this and in his other two long poems, *Dipsychus* and *Amours de Voyage*, we can hardly doubt that the poet has himself experienced the difficulties and questionings which he depicts. And if this be so it is remarkable how Clough, through all this wavering and cloudiness, never really looses his stand on the firm earth. In most of his speculative poems he brings us back at the close to the solid reality of life and duty, which in the earlier part he has been refining away. He does not solve the problems, but he is certain that there is a solution; and it matters not much whether he individually has the solution or not:

> . . . And as limited beings
> Scarcely can hope to attain upon earth to an Actual Abstract,
> Leaving to God contemplation, to His hands knowledge confiding,
> Sure that in us if it perish, in Him it abideth and dies not,
> Let us in His sight accomplish our petty particular doings.

So, confident of this, he can afford to lose himself, as it would seem, in the subtle speculations of his poems, such as those which he well describes in 'The Questioning Spirit', for they end with the thought:

> I know not, I will do my duty.

After apparently sharing fully in the doubts, and sympathising with

them, he seldom fails, reverting to his secure standpoint, to rebuke
the anxious intellect, and to point to that which, after all said, is unwavering and abiding. Take, for example, the fine conclusion of 'The
Stream of Life':[1]

> O end to which our currents tend,
>   Inevitable sea,
> To which we flow, what do we know,
>   What shall we guess of thee?
>
> A roar we hear upon thy shore,
>   As we our course fulfil;
> Scarce we divine a sun will shine
>   And be above us still.

Timid unbelief could hardly be more simple and forcibly rebuked;
and yet by the very form of the rebuke, 'scarce we divine,' the poet
shows that he enters into the feeling, that he sympathises with the
mind which is confused by the roar of the waves, though at the same
time he knows and must point out that the sun is 'above us still.' For
a similar return from the uncertain quagmire of sceptical rationalism
to the firm ground of hope and trust, take 'Epi-Straussium,' in which
he accepts the worst that criticism can do, and then points to the Sun
of Truth which still illumines the building, even though it has risen
too high for the 'pictured panes.'

The contrast between Clough and Mr. Arnold can be carried further
than the broad differences as to truth and duty. In Mr. Arnold's view
of human relations we find the inevitable hopelessness which we
believe to be the result of the self-centred attitude of his mind:

> . . . we leave behind—
> As, chartered by some unknown Powers,
> We stem across the sea by night—
> The joys which were not for our use designed,
> The friends to whom we had no natural right,
> The homes that were not destined to be ours.[2]

Clough, too, imagines separation of friends; he also represents life
as a voyage; but what a difference in the tone! What a buoyant motion
in the very measure, as of a great ship leaping forward before a strong
wind!—

> But, O blithe breeze! and O great seas,
>   Though ne'er, that earliest parting past,

[1] i.e. 'O Stream, descending to the Sea.'   [2] Arnold, 'Human Life?'

> On your wide plain they join again,
> Together lead them home at last.
>
> One port, methought, alike they sought,
> One purpose hold where'er they fare,—
> O bounding breeze, O rushing seas!
> At last, at last unite them there!

His thoughts instinctively turn, after he has felt the parting, to the final goal; the tone is that of joyful hope, while Mr. Arnold ends with calm sadness, looking at the present separation and loss, and at nothing beyond.

But perhaps the strongest contrast—and with this we will conclude— is to be found in their respective treatment of love. Mr. Arnold's we have seen; we have seen him resisting it, reluctantly giving way to the fascination, and wrenching his soul back to its loneliness once more. To Clough it is far more of an interest than it is to his fellow-poet. Many of his poems are occupied with the discussion of love in various aspects; and though this subject cannot escape from his subtle mind without undergoing, like all others, a process of refining away, yet generally in the end he reverts to an extremely simple, and not conventional, but natural position, and at times raises the mingled selfishness and self-renunciation of love into a higher sphere by means of a lofty conception of duty, in the performance of which united lives are of more avail than solitary:

> Yet in the eye of life's all-seeing sun
> We shall behold a something we have done,
> Shall of the work together we have wrought,
> Beyond our aspiration and our thought,
> Some not unworthy issue yet receive;
> For love is fellow-service, I believe.

Here we will conclude our examination of the deeper characteristics of these two poets. We have refrained as much as possible from criticising, in the more technical sense; our office has been to explain and to analyse, not to judge. No doubt, analysis and explanation involve, to a certain extent, criticism also; but we have endeavoured to refrain, when dealing with men who are undoubtedly poets, and therefore have claims on our reverence, from that special function of modern criticism which consists in a fine perception of blemishes rather than beauties, which delights to tell its hearers not what the poet says, but what he does not say. As poetry, we will not criticise these writings;

as containing schemes of life, we will only add, in conclusion, that Mr. Arnold stands self-condemned. From the general tone of his poems it is obvious that the sadness pervading the world remains in himself, in spite of the proud self-absorption which he extols as the remedy; and from one pathetic passage it would seem that he has at times a sense of the inconsistency between his professed object and his method, between the Pantheistic absorption into Nature at which he aims, and the studied self-culture and isolation in which he would live:

> But mind—but thought—
> If these have been the master part of us,
> Where will *they* find their parent element?
> What will receive *them*, who will call *them* home?
> But we shall still be in them, and they in us—
> And we shall be the strangers of the world,
> And they will be our lords, as they are now;
> And keep us prisoners of our consciousness,
> And never let us clasp and feel the All
> But through their forms, and modes, and stifling veils.
> And we shall be unsatisfied as now;
> And we shall feel the agony of thirst,
> The ineffable longing for the life of life
> Baffled for ever; and still thought and mind
> Will hurry us with them on their homeless march,
> Over the unallied unopening earth,
> Over the unrecognising sea.[1]

Self-culture cannot give us a religion, not even the Religion of Pantheism. And when we turn to Clough, we find that it is precisely in proportion as he feels himself able to cling to something external to him that he is hopeful, energetic, and religious. Would it not therefore seem that if these poets be representatives of our age, no teaching can satisfy it but that which will give it something external and objective wherein to rest; that no merely emotional, introspective religion will lose the chains which bind us, for they are the chains of self; but that now, as of old, it is only the Truth that can make us free?

[1] 'Empedoles on Etna,' Act II, 345–61.

45. Clough and Arnold: from an unsigned review, 'Matthew Arnold's Poems', in the *Nation*

31 October 1878

Matthew Arnold is more widely known in this country [i.e. America] as the critic and the liberal thinker than as the poet; yet, to our mind, his poetry is more valuable than his prose, and it is to him and Clough that the men of the future will come who desire to find the clearest poetic expression of the sentiment and reflection of the most cultivated and thoughtful men of our generation. They are both called the poets of doubt; but, apart from this characteristic of them, there are in Clough a simplicity of narration, a thrust of wit, and, throughout, a graceful manliness which make him dear to many who have never known the shadow of scepticism; and likewise there are in Arnold a vividness in picturesque description, a penetrative imagination, a moral ardor, a sensitiveness to all that is charming in this world—individual powers and qualities whose results in poetic work are delightful apart from the restless and regretful spirit which infects all his writing. . . .

46. Samuel Waddington, from *Arthur Hugh Clough*

1883, Introduction, 3–21

In his Preface to the 'first volume devoted to the criticism and study of Clough' (some copies appeared in 1882), Waddington states, 'I have more especially availed myself of the notices, reviews and other fugitive papers respecting him, which have been published during the last quarter of a century.' As Hutton argues in the next item, Waddington is relatively weak on the critical side—the extract given below being the best he can offer. He is primarily concerned with the Life and the content of the poems, but he wisely warns readers to guard against premature disappointment with the latter by reading them 'whole', not dipping merely.

. . . it seems probable, seeing that the minds of men are differently constituted, and variously influenced by imagination and reason, by thought and emotion, that there will ever be found in our midst these two schools holding opposite views respecting the province and proper sphere of poetry. The one delights, and will always continue to delight, in the form, the manner, the music, the metaphor, the graceful phrase, the uncommon, the well-chosen or, perhaps, archaic term, and all the thousand-and-one adjuncts that go to form the dress in which the poet clothes his thought,—or, alas, in some instances conceals his want of thought. The other school also delights in all these things;—it rejoices in the harmonious arrangement of words, and in the subtle felicity of expression;—it loves

the light that never was on sea or land;[1]

but these, these alone, these unaccompanied by any deep 'under-song of sense,' are not sufficient for it, and it asks, 'Is not the body more than raiment, and the soul of more importance than the body?'

[1] Wordsworth, 'Elegiac Stanzas Suggested by a Picture of Peele Castle in a Storm'.

Why dost thou pine within and suffer dearth,
Painting thy outer walls so costly gay?[1]

Or, in the words of Isaac Barrow, it exclaims: 'If it is true that nothing has for you any relish except painted comfits and unmeaning trifles, that not even wisdom will please you, unless without its peculiar flavour, nor truth, unless seasoned with a jest, then in an unlucky hour have I been assigned as your purveyor, neither born nor bred in such a frivolous confectionery.'

Such, roughly and briefly stated, are the two opposite views that are held by the respective partisans and upholders of the especial value in poetry of form and manner, on the one hand, and of thought and subject-matter, on the other:—but it is in the latter rather than the former of these schools that the poet who is the subject of these pages has for the most part found his disciples and admirers. Those who cherish, and find pleasure in studying the writings of Clough—and we believe that their number, both in this country and in America, is much larger than is usually supposed—admire him, not for the smoothness of his numbers, or the melody of his verse, but for the nobility of character, the subtlety of thought, and the sincere earnestness and zeal in the pursuit of both truth and truthfulness, that are marked in no uncertain letters upon all his compositions, whether in prose or verse. As regards the question, however, respecting the province of poetry, to which reference has already been made, it will be well before proceeding to the study of the poet's own writings that some insight should, if possible, be obtained into what were the opinions which he himself held on this subject. With this view the following interesting extract is quoted from a paper published by him in the *North American Review* for July, 1853,[2] in which he reviewed and compared the respective poems of the late Alexander Smith and Mr. Matthew Arnold. He writes:—

We have before us, we may say, the latest disciple of the school of Keats, who was indeed no well of English undefiled, though doubtless the fountain-head of a true poetic stream. Alexander Smith is young enough to free himself from his present manner, which does not seem his simple and natural own. He has given us so to say, his *Endymion*; it is certainly as imperfect, and as mere a promise of something wholly different, as was that of the master he has followed. We are not sorry, in the meantime, that this *Endymion* is not upon Mount Latmos. The natural man does pant within us after *flumina silvasque*;

[1] Shakespeare, Sonnet 146 ('Painting thy *outward* walls').
[2] 'Recent English Poetry', SPW, 143–71; PPR I, 360–1.

yet really, and truth to tell, is it not, upon the whole, an easy matter to sit under a green tree by a purling brook, and indite pleasing stanzas on the beauties of nature and fresh air? Or is it, we incline to ask, so very great an exploit to wander out into the pleasant field of Greek or Latin mythology, and reproduce, with more or less of modern adaptation,

the shadows

Faded and pale, yet immortal, of Faunus, the Nymphs, and the Graces?[1] Studies of the literature of any distant age or country; all the imitations and *quasi*-translations which help to bring together into a single focus the scattered rays of human intelligence; poems after classical models, poems from Oriental sources, and the like, have undoubtedly a great literary value. Yet there is no question, it is plain and patent enough, that people much prefer *Vanity Fair* and *Bleak House*. Why so? Is it simply because we have grown prudent and prosaic, and should not welcome, as our fathers did, the Marmions and the Rokebys, the Childe Harolds and the Corsairs? Or is it, that to be widely popular, to gain the ear of multitudes, to shake the hearts of men, poetry should deal, more than at present it usually does, with general wants, ordinary feelings, the obvious rather than the rare facts of human nature? Could it not attempt to convert into beauty and thankfulness, or at least into some form and shape, some feeling, at any rate, of content—the actual, palpable things with which our every-day life is concerned; introduce into business and weary task-work a character and a soul of purpose and reality; intimate to us relations which, in our unchosen, peremptorily-appointed posts, in our grievously narrow and limited spheres of action, we still, in and through all, retain to some central, celestial fact? Could it not console us with a sense of significance, if not of dignity, in that often dirty, or at least dingy, work which it is the lot of so many of us to have to do, and which some one or other, after all, must do? Might it not divinely condescend to all infirmities; be in all points tempted as we are; exclude nothing, least of all guilt and distress, from its wide fraternization; not content elsewhere, but seek also to deal with what may be better elsewhere, but seek also to deal with what *is* here? We could each one of us, alas! be so much that somehow we find we are not; we have all of us fallen away from so much that we still long to call ours. Cannot the Divine Song in some way indicate to us our unity, though from a great way off, with those happier things; inform us, and prove to us, that though we are what we are, we may yet, in some way, even in our abasement, even by and through our daily work, be related to the purer existence.

Thus writes, and very wisely, the poet himself,—and it is both surprising and instructive to note, as the eye passes along the eloquent and impassioned sentences, how closely the sense, the gist of the whole passage, approximates to those words of Keats, . . . that the great

[1] *Amours*, III, 225–6.

end and aim of poetry should be 'to soothe the cares and lift the thoughts of man.'[1] The very fact that two poets, such as were Keats and Clough, whose compositions are in many respects so very dissimilar,—who in seeking a field in which the poetic genius might work and develop its powers to advantage, turned their backs upon each other, and parted at the very threshold,—who travelled, or seemed to travel, on their respective paths in quest of apparently very different objects of desire,—that these two poets should nevertheless agree on this important subject, and should hold like views respecting the fundamental principle of what should be the great end of poetry, is, to say the very least of it, instructive, and a matter which should not be overlooked by our youthful bards and modern reviewers.

There have recently been various theories propounded respecting what may best serve as a true definition of 'poetry;'—and while Mr. Matthew Arnold tells us that it is the *criticism* of life, Mr. Alfred Austin intimates that it is nothing of the kind, but that it is the transfiguration or imaginative *representation* of life. Possibly there is much truth in both of these theories, and yet, after all may we not say in the words of Wordsworth,—

> Dear child of Nature, let them rail!
> —There is a nest in a green dale,
> A harbour and a hold,
> Where thou . . . shalt see
> Thy own delightful days, and be
> A light to young and old.[2]

And may not these lines, also, serve in a measure to indicate one phase at least of what poetry either is, or ought to be? But so long as the term is widely and variously employed, as it is at present, it is manifestly a waste of time to try and include under one definition its manifold and various meanings. Originally it would appear to have meant rhythmical compositions, or creations, of any kind or character; and a century ago it would have been considered applicable to what we should now only deem to be correctly described as 'verse:'—while it would not have been held to be an appropriate term for any composition in prose, even if written by such imaginative or emotional writers as Thomas Carlyle and Mr. Ruskin.

The 'poetry of life' is plainly far removed from the poetry (if there

---

[1] 'Sleep and Poetry'.
[2] 'To a Young Lady', ll. 1–6 (ll. 4–5 are actually: 'Where thou, a Wife and Friend, shalt see/Thy own heart-stirring days, and be').

be any) in Pope's *Essay on Man*, or Samuel Butler's *Hudibras*:—while the poetry that Wordsworth could find in 'a primrose by a river's brim,' or in his favourite, 'the lesser celandine,' is an entirely different thing from that which inspires some of Mr. Matthew Arnold's philosophic, didactic, and yet very beautiful sermons-in-sonnets, such as are his 'East London,' 'The Better Part,' and 'Worldly Place.' But let us once more refer on this subject to the paper by Clough in the *North American Review* where he writes:—

You have been reading Burns, and you take up Cowper. You feel at home, how strangely! in both of them. Can both be the true thing? and if so, in what new form can we express the relation, the harmony, between them? Are we to try and reconcile them, or judge between them? May we escape from all the difficulty by a mere quotation, and pronounce with the shepherd of Virgil,

> 'Non nostrum inter vos tantas componere lites
> Et vitulâ tu dignus, et hoc.'[1]

Will you be content, O reader, to plod in German manner over miles of a straight road that seems to lead somewhere, with the prospect of arriving at last at some point where it will divide at equal angles, and lead equally into two opposite directions, where you may therefore safely pause, and thankfully set up your rest, and adore in sacred doubt the Supreme Bifurcation?[2]

But now let us consider a moment what is the conclusion at which we are arriving,—what is the end and aim of these introductory observations. Is it to set up, and adore the poetic Supreme Bifurcation, as the poet himself humorously designates the point where the pathways of two schools of poetry divide? Is it to show that the wonder-working process of Evolution has in its literary progress created at various points of divergence new and distinct species of poetry? Is it to indicate that whereas one school, or species, will more especially serve 'to soothe the cares,' another will rather 'lift the thoughts,' of Man? Is it to urge that both of these schools are good in their way, and to be esteemed for their own particular merits? Is it to prove that of Clough and Keats, as of Cowper and Burns, it may justly be said,

> Et vitulâ tu dignus, et hic?

Or, lastly, is it to point out that it is hardly wise in literature—any more than it is in religion—to confine the growing, the ever-increasing

---

[1] 'It is beyond us to judge such a high dispute! Both are deserving ...' (Virgil, *Eclogues* III, 108-9).
[2] *PPR I*, 376; *SPW*, 162.

world of thought, and truth, and sympathy, by any narrow exclusive dogma, or definition, that may at the time best fit in with our own opinions and predilections?

Yes—these, taken together, constitute the goal to which our observations tend, for in writing of a poet, such as Clough, who is far removed from the sphere in which the new poets that have arisen during the last fifteen or twenty years are moving, it would seem necessary to point out *in limine* that it does not follow that one is right, and the other wrong, when two poets choose very different methods, and compose poems on opposite principles. There is, after all, much of fashion in these matters, and in addition there is the influence which the events of the period, the religious and political movements of the times, must always have upon the poet's work. It is to this that Mr. Stopford Brooke refers when he writes:—

Keats marks the exhaustion of the impulse which began with Burns and Cowper. There was now no longer in England any large wave of public thought or feeling such as could awaken poetry. We have then, arising after his death, a number of pretty little poems, having no inward fire, no idea, no marked character. They might be written by any versifier at any time, and express pleasant indifferent thought in pleasant verse. But with the Reform agitation, and the new religious agitation at Oxford which was of the same date, a new excitement or a new form of the old, came on England, and with it a new tribe of poets arose, among whom we live. The elements of their poetry were also new, though their germs were sown in the previous poetry. It took up the theological, sceptical, social, and political questions which disturbed England. It gave itself to metaphysics and to analysis of human character. It carried the love of natural scenery into almost every county in England, and described the whole land. Some of its best writers are Robert Browning and his wife, Matthew Arnold, and Arthur Hugh Clough.[1]

Of these four only two, unfortunately, are still left with us to work and use their influence in our midst, at a time when their influence is especially needed, and when the school of purely *Decorative Poetry* (to use the late Mr. Bayard Taylor's phrase) which addresses itself to the eye and ear, rather than to the heart and brain, is beginning to somewhat weary its readers. Of Browning and Clough it is especially true that they are 'thinkers' rather than 'singers,' and the following which has been written respecting the former is also true of the latter:

He as a singer has been surpassed by many inferior men. We had almost said he seldom sings. But he is a poet for all that, and sings sweetly too, when he

[1] *English Literature from* A.D. 670 *to* A.D. 1832 (1876), ch. VIII.

pleases. But he is chiefly dear to the age as a feeler and a thinker; he is also dear because knowing all, and having been racked with its doubts, and stretched upon the mental torture-wheels of his time, he does not despair.

It is possible that Mr. M. Arnold when he recently defined poetry as the 'criticism of life,' was thinking more especially of these two poets, Browning and Clough, these spiritual analysts of the social body, that unveil the conventional shams of the world, that show us life as it really is, and do not hesitate to criticize our most cherished dogmas of duty and religion. But there is another, and far wider, definition of poetry, given, we believe, by John Stuart Mill, that it is, 'Thought coloured by emotion, expressed in metre:'[1]—and if we accept this as approximately true, then may we accept, also, Clough's compositions as true poetry, for in them we find the most subtle 'thought' accompanied by the most deep and impressive emotion, which is none the less deep and impressive because it is held under restraint, and bears the calm demeanour of discipline. Those, who, on bygone Sabbath afternoons, when the shades of approaching darkness began to deepen the gloom of the grand old Abbey, have listened in past years to the touching eloquence and the calm yet impressive language of Arthur Penrhyn Stanley, will recognize at once the same spiritual fervour,—the same earnest, yet restrained, zeal and emotion—in the poems of Clough and the sermons of the late Dean. And, indeed, are not these in a measure but different pipes of the same organ-stop,—are they not fragrant flowers gathered from the same holy garden,—the work and wisdom of two scholars that had been nurtured and trained under the fostering care of one and the same master, that great and good man the late Dr. Arnold? Thought, coloured by emotion, yet subject to discipline;—sincere earnestness in the pursuit of Truth coloured by charity towards the holders of opposite views and opinions; a desire to impart wider views and a larger sympathy to the various sects of society with their petty shibboleths and narrow party-spirit;—such, truly, were the feelings and the aims that inspired the spiritual fervour of both poet and priest; and such is the didactic purpose which we find to be present, though not objectionably obtruded, in most of the poems and prose writings of Clough.

[1] Not, I think, an exact quotation: in his *Autobiography* (1873) Mill speaks of Wordsworth's poems as expressing 'not mere outward beauty, but states of feeling, and of thought coloured by feeling, under the excitement of beauty' (World's Classics Edn., p. 125); in his essays 'What is Poetry' and 'Two Kinds of Poetry' (1833) Mill had stressed primacy of feeling in the poet.

A didactic purpose? Yes,—for when a great truth has taken possession of the heart,—when an eternal verity (as Carlyle would have said) hath entered into and overpowered the spirit of the man,— then, and then only, out of the fullness of the heart the mouth speaketh, and teacheth whether it will or not. Then, and then only, the poet uttereth such impassioned poems, as 'The world is too much with us, late and soon,' as Hood's 'Bridge of Sighs,' or Mrs. Browning's 'Cry of the Children.' But we have already discussed this subject above, and we will not refer to it further, beyond stating that the effect produced by a man who is in earnest will always be greater than that produced by one who is only playing his part; and that the character of the worker will, in some way or other, be mirrored in the works that he produces.

Believe me (were the words of Sir Frederick Leighton on a recent occasion), believe me, whatever of dignity, whatever of strength we have within us, will dignify and will make strong the labours of our hands; whatever littleness degrades our spirit will lessen them and drag them down. Whatever noble fire is in our hearts will burn also in our work, whatever purity is ours will chasten and exalt it; for as we are, so our work is, and what we sow in our lives, that, beyond a doubt, we shall reap for good or for ill in the strengthening or defacing of whatever gifts have fallen to our lot.

In the following pages the reader will have before him the history of the life, and description of the character, of one whom we, for our part, believe to have been a very pure, and noble, and good man; he will also have an account and study of his poems and other writings, and he will thus have an opportunity of judging for himself how very true in this instance are the words we have here quoted. It has been said, and with much truth, that 'Clough lived his poem;'[1] and his life and poetry are alike free from any impurity, from any folly or unfaithfulness; in neither will the reader come upon any 'deathless traces of a dreadful history,' and they who have an appetite for—a hungering after—stories of crime, of desertion and death;—of poems composed in the dreamy interregnum of sober moments in lives of delirious intemperance, whether produced by alcohol or opium,—must seek their unwholesome food elsewhere: they will not even meet with any epistolary compositions unworthy to have been written by a man of true nobility of character, by a man of a sane and thorough manliness. And if Sir Frederick Leighton be right, as we think he unquestionably is, that 'as we are, so our work is;' and that 'whatever purity is ours will

[1] Cf. Palgrave above, p. 118.

chasten and exalt it,' then may we look for, and expect with no fear
of disappointment, a loftier spirituality, a higher tone, and a nobler
purpose in the poetry of Clough than in that of the majority of our
English poets. We say, in his words, 'we could each one of us be so
much that somehow we find we are not; we have all of us fallen away
from so much that we still long to call ours; cannot the Divine Song
in some way indicate to us our unity, though from a great way off,
with these happier things?' And we reply that such a song is in a
measure to be found in the poetry of many bards who have indicated,
who have shown to us our relationship to a purer existence and a
happier state. In the poems of Goethe and Schiller, and no less in those
of our own Spenser and Wordsworth, is such a Divine Song to be
traced, such an echo, as it were, from a more heavenly shore,—a
musical cadence of angels' voices freed from our earthly bonds, our
weakness, and our worldliness, and, alas! our human worldly-holiness.
And not only in these, but in many others of our English poets, is such
a strain to be found, and in none is it more marked than in the poetry
of Clough; indeed, as might be expected, it is the main feature of his
verse; it is the light illuminating, more or less brightly, nearly the
whole of his compositions.

The following elegiac lines, which form part of one of his earlier
poems, illustrate to some extent the general tone and tenor of his
poetry, and with them we will conclude these introductory observations.

> Go from the east to the west, as the sun and the stars direct thee,
>   Go with the girdle of man, go and encompass the earth.
> Not for the gain of the gold; for the getting, the hoarding, the having,
>   But for the joy of the deed; but for the Duty to do.
> Go with the spiritual life, the higher volition and action,
>   With the great girdle of God, go and encompass the earth.
>
> Go with the sun and the stars, and yet evermore in thy spirit
>   Say to thyself: It is good: yet is there better than it.
> This that I see is not all, and this that I do is but little;
>   Nevertheless it is good, though there is better than it.
>   [from 'Hope evermore and believe, O man']

47. R. H. Hutton, 'The Unpopularity of Clough', review in the *Spectator*

25 November 1882, lv

This review of Samuel Waddington's *Arthur Hugh Clough: A Monograph* was reprinted in *Brief Literary Criticism*, ed. E. M. Roscoe (London, 1906), 304–15.

The appearance of Mr. Waddington's admiring and sympathetic 'monograph' on Clough—why call, by the way, a publication of this kind a monograph, which properly means a study of something artificially separated from its natural context?—affords us a good opportunity of asking why Clough is not better known than he is in modern English literature; why his fame is not greater, and his often magnificent verse more familiar to modern ears. In Mr. Haweis's hasty and scrappy book on the 'American Humourists', Mr. Haweis scoffs parenthetically at the present American Minister's 'curious notion that Clough was, after all, the great poet of the age' (*American Humourists*, p. 83);[1] and even one of Clough's most intimate friends, Mr. F. T. Palgrave, has lent some sort of authority to Mr. Haweis's scoff, by the remark—to us as amazing as it appears to some good critics candid,—that 'one feels a doubt whether in verse, he [Clough] chose the right vehicle, the truly natural mode of utterance.' We can only say, in reply, that Clough seems to us never to touch verse without finding strength, never to attempt to speak in prose without losing it, and becoming half-inarticulate. But there clearly must be some reason or quasi-reason in a view which a whole generation of lovers of poetry have not disproved, but to some extent verified, by the relative neglect in which, during a time when verse has secured an immense amount of attention, Clough's stirring and often elevating poetry has been left. Mr. Waddington, we are sorry to see, does not address himself to this question, and throws but little light on it. And with all his genuine

[1] 'present American Minister': J. R. Lowell, American Ambassador to Great Britain 1880–4; for Lowell's opinion of Clough, see Introduction, *passim*.

appreciation of Clough, his study is wanting in the strong outlines and massiveness of effect which might have done something to secure for Clough the public esteem which he will certainly one day secure. Mr. Waddington is too discursive, and does not bring the great features of his subject into sufficiently strong relief. His essay might increase the vogue of a public favourite, but will hardly win popularity for one who has never yet emerged from the comparative obscurity of a singer delightful to the few, though his name even is hardly recognised by the many.

For our own parts, though we should not assert that Clough is the great poet of our age, we should agree heartily with Mr. Lowell that he will in future generations rank among the highest of our time, and that especially he will be ranked with Matthew Arnold, as having found a voice for this self-questioning age—a voice of greater range and richness even, and of a deeper pathos, though of less exquisite sweetness and 'lucidity' of utterance, than Matthew Arnold's own—a voice that oftener breaks, perhaps, in the effort to express what is beyond it, but one also that attempts, and often achieves, still deeper and more heart-stirring strains. Clough had not Mr. Arnold's happy art of interweaving delicate fancies with thoughts and emotions. Poems like 'The Scholar Gipsy' and 'Thyrsis', like 'Tristram and Iseult', 'The Sick King of Bokhara' and the stanzas on 'The Author of "Obermann"', were out of his reach. And, no doubt, it is precisely poems of this kind, into which, across the bright web of rich and stimulating fancy, Mr. Arnold has woven lines of exquisitely drawn and thoroughly modern thought and feeling, that have gained for Mr. Arnold his increasing, though not as yet overwhelming, popularity. Clough had nothing of this fanciful art. He was realist to the bottom of his soul, and yet, though realist, he looked at all the questions of the day from the thinker's point of view, and not from the people's point of view. He did not frame his pictures, as his friend does, in golden margins of felicitous fancy. He left them almost without a frame, or, at any rate, with no other frame than that furnished by the plain outline of his story. This might but have increased his popularity, had Clough's subjects been like Burns's subjects, the common joys and sorrows of the human heart. But it was not so. His subjects, for the most part, have a semi-scholastic ring, but do not embody those elaborate artistic effects which soften a scholastic ring to the ear of the people. He was a self-questioner, who did not cast over his questionings that spirit of imaginative illusion which, in Mr. Arnold's poetry, sometimes makes even self-questionings sound like the music of a distant and brighter sphere. Clough's poetry is full of direct, home-thrusting questioning—concerning character in the making, faith in the making, love in the making; and powerful as it is, this analytic poetry no doubt needs more than any kind of poetry, for its immediate popularity, the glamour which Mr. Arnold's artistic framing throws round it.

Nor is this the only difference. The charm of Clough's humour, the strength of his delineation is so great that, if the only difference between him and Matthew Arnold were the difference between a plain and an attractive setting, that advantage of Mr. Arnold's might, we think, have been counterbalanced by the deeper pathos of Clough's pictures, and the stronger lines in which he draws. But there is another difference. Matthew Arnold, negative as the outcome of his thought too frequently is, never leaves you in any kind of doubt as to what he means. His lines are always sharply chiselled. He is dogmatic even in his denials of dogma. Lucid and confident to the last degree, he never leaves the mind without a very sharply-marked impression of a clear thought. And even where that thought is not popular—even where it is the reverse of popular—such sharp, distinct lines, gracefully graven, are likely to gain more readers and admirers, than lines of freer sweep, but more uncertain drift. Compare, for instance, some of Mr. Arnold's finest lines on the dearth of true revealing poets, with some of Mr. Clough's finest on the same subject. Mr. Arnold, after bewailing the loss of Goethe and Wordsworth, turns to the hermit of the Alps, M.de Senancour (his 'Obermann'), and addresses him thus:

[Quotes 'Stanzas in Memory of the Author of "Obermann"', ll. 81–104: 'And then we turn' to 'renounced his own'.]

Now hear Clough, on the same subject:

[Quotes 'Come, poet, come!' entire.]

One feels the difference at once between the picture of the lucid insight of solitary renunciation, and the ardent invocation addressed to a new teacher of a dimly-anticipated lesson. The one poet is distinct, the other vague, and though the more distinct teaching is the less hopeful, it sinks more easily into the reader's mind. Yet, for our parts, we find a richer music in the vague hope of Clough, than even in the sweet sad despondency of Arnold.

Further, Clough not only sings finely of the immature stage of

322

moral character, but of the immature stage of faith, and the immature stage of love. He studies both in the making—admitting it to be a riddle how that making will end. Here, for instance, is a fine poem on faith in the making, which will be popular one day, as describing a stage which many will then have passed through, but which has not found its popularity yet:

[Quotes 'What we, when face to face we see' entire.]

And here, once more, is a curiously subtle passage on love 'in the making', which must wait, we suppose, for its popularity till the human heart understands itself better, and is franker with itself, but which will have its popularity then. It is from *The Bothie of Tober-na-Vuolich*, the most buoyant and humorous poem of the higher kind produced in England during the present century. The enthusiast of the poem is descanting on the beauty which physical labour adds to the charm of women:

[Quotes *The Bothie*, ll. 31–106: 'Well then, said Hewson, resuming;' to 'with the fork in the garden uprooting potatoes'.]

That is not a picture of love, but a picture of the initial stages of love, and of that which often prevents love from ripening. Nor can such pictures be popular while the mind shrinks from looking in the face the poor beginnings of his own highest powers. One day, however, Clough will vindicate the justice of Mr. Lowell's judgement on him, though that day may not be yet. Arnold will, perhaps, grow to even greater popularity, before the growth of Clough's popularity begins. But begin it will, and wax, too, to a point as high, perhaps, as Arnold's ever will be, for Clough's rapture and exultation, when they reach their highest points, are beyond the rapture and exultation of Arnold, though his music is less carefully modulated, and his pictures less exquisitely framed.

48. R. H. Hutton, 'Amiel and Clough' in *Spectator*

9 January 1886, lix, 42–3

The *Journal Intime* of Henri Frédéric Amiel (1821–81), published posthumously, became one of the most discussed 'confessional works' of the nineteenth century. Mrs Humphry Ward's translation, to which Hutton refers, had been published in 1885. Matthew Arnold came to this celebrated work with some reluctance, he tells us—he shrunk, no doubt, from the excessive contemporary enthusiasm for it—and his essay, 'Amiel', did not appear until September 1887 (*Macmillan's Magazine*); he makes no reference to the parallel that might be drawn with Clough.

Mrs. Humphrey Ward, in the interesting introduction which she has prefixed to her beautiful translation of *Amiel's Journal*, indicates, though not as distinctly as we should have been disposed to do, the close analogy between Amiel's dread of practical life and Clough's dread of practical life. And there certainly was a close analogy, as well as a wide difference, between their views. Amiel, it is clear, never did anything at all equal to his powers, through a jealous regard for his own intellectual independence. He could not bear to commit himself to any practical course which would mortgage, as it were, his intellectual freedom. 'The life of thought alone,' he wrote, 'seems to me to have enough elasticity and immensity, to be free enough from the irreparable; practical life makes me afraid.' And yet he knew that a certain amount of practical life was essential even to a true intellectual life, only he was anxious to reduce that practical life to a minimum, in order that the intellectual life might remain as free as possible. Clough, too, had the greatest distrust of the practical ties into which he felt that the tenderness of his nature would bring him. The whole drift of his *Amours de Voyage* was to show that fidelity to the intellectual vision is inconsistent with the class of connections into which the sentiments of a tender heart bring men; and not only inconsistent with

324

them, but so superior to them, that sooner or later the intellect would assert its independence and break through the dreams to which, under the influence of feeling, men submit themselves. The difference between the two men's views was in substance this,—Amiel rather condemned himself for his fastidious assertion of intellectual freedom, and held that had his character been stronger, he would have embarked more boldly on practical life, and would have made a better use of his talents in consequence; Clough, on the contrary, rather condemned himself for the weakness which allowed him to drift into the closer human ties. He speaks of them as more or less unreal, as more or less illusions, out of which he must some day recover, and return to the assertion of his old intellectual freedom. Amiel reproached himself for not trusting his instincts more, and for living the self-conscious life so much; Clough reproached himself for letting his instincts dispose of him so much, and for not resisting the illusions into which his instincts betrayed him. It is very curious to compare the different modes in which the Genevan student of Hegelian philosophy and the English student of Greek thought, writing at very nearly the same time, express the same profound terror of embarrassing themselves by all sorts of ties with the narrownesses and imperfections of the human lot. In Amiel's case, however, in spite of the moral self-reproach with which he viewed his intellectual fastidiousness, it was undoubtedly in great measure the contagion of Hegelian Pantheism which made him fancy that he could identify himself with the universal soul of things; and, on the other hand, it was the timidity of an excessive moral sensitiveness which made it intolerable to him to enter into the very heart of practical life, with the fear before his eyes that he might create for himself a lifelong regret by taking an irreparable false step. This, he seems to say, was the reason why he never married, just as it was in part the reason why Clough, in the *Amours de Voyage*, makes his hero reproach himself for his desire to marry. Amiel felt that to enter into a relation of which he had the highest ideal, and then to find it far below his ideal, would entail on him a shame and a remorse which he would simply be unable to endure. And at the very close of his life, he writes, with much less than his usual feeling of self-reproach, a sort of defence of his own detachment from the world. He declares that to have done anything voluntarily which should bring upon him an inner shame, would have been unendurable to him.

I think (he says) I fear shame worse than death. Tacitus said, 'Omnia serviliter pro dominatione.' My tendency is just the contrary. Even when it is voluntary, dependence is a burden to me. I should blush to find myself determined by interest, submitting to constraint, or becoming the slave of any will whatever. To me, vanity is slavery, self-love degrading, and utilitarianism meanness. I detest the ambition which makes you the liege man of something or some one. I desire simply to be my own master. If I had health, I should be the freest man I know. Although perhaps a little hardness of heart would be desirable to make me still more independent. . . . I only desire what I am able for; and in this way I run my head against no wall, I cease even to be conscious of the boundaries which enslave me. I take care to wish for rather less than is in my power, that I may not even be reminded of the obstacles in my way. Renunciation is the safeguard of dignity. Let us strip ourselves, if we would not be stripped.

There you have the moral secret of Amiel's pride, without the self-blame with which he usually accompanied it. His pride was due partly to a moral dread of incurring responsibilities he could not bear,—'responsibility,' as he said, 'is my invisible nightmare,'—and partly to the dread of appearing ridiculous and contemptible to himself if he should find himself unequal to them. That reminds us very much of the spirit which Cardinal Newman, as a young man,—before he entered on his great Tractarian mission,—rebuked in himself:—

> Time was, I shrank from what was right
> From fear of what was wrong;
> I would not brave the sacred fight
> Because the foe was strong.
>
> But now I cast that finer sense
> And sorer shame aside;
> Such dread of sin was indolence,
> Such aim at Heaven was pride.[1]

Amiel's feeling is absolutely described in these lines, though the keen censure cast upon it by Dr. Newman was probably not reflected,—at least in the latter part of his career,—in Amiel's own conscience. But, as we have already hinted, there was doubtless another and a more intellectual strand in the feeling,—the deep impression that by binding himself in a number of complex relations to only half-known or utterly unknown human beings,—to persons who might disappoint him bitterly, and to children unborn who might turn out anything but the beings to whom he could sustain the close tie of fatherhood,—he should fritter away the power of reverie in which he took such

---

[1] Newman, 'Sensitiveness' (1833), printed in *Lyra Apostolica* (1836) and *Verses on Various Occasions* (1880).

delight. Under the spell of some of the more ambitious German philosophies, he fancied that he could identify himself with the soul of things; and this dreaming power he valued, as it seems to us, much beyond its real worth, if indeed that worth were real at all:—

My privilege is to be the spectator of my own life-drama, to be fully conscious of the tragi-comedy of my own destiny, and, more than that, to be in the secret of the tragi-comic itself—that is to say, to be unable to take my illusions seriously, to see myself, so to speak, from the theatre on the stage, or to be like a man looking from beyond the tomb into existence. I feel myself forced to feign a particular interest in my individual part, while all the time I am living in the confidence of the poet who is playing with all these agents which seem so important, and knows all that they are ignorant of. It is a strange position, and one which becomes painful as soon as grief obliges me to betake myself once more to my own little *rôle*, binding me closely to it, and warning me that I am going too far in imagining myself, because of my conversations with the poet, dispensed from taking up again my modest part of valet in the piece.—Shakespeare must have experienced this feeling often, and Hamlet, I think, must express it somewhere. It is a *Doppelgängerei*, quite German in character, and which explains the disgust with reality, and the repugnance to public life, so common among the thinkers of Germany. There is, as it were, a degradation, a Gnostic fall in thus folding one's wings and going back again into the vulgar shell of one's own individuality. Without grief, which is the string of this venturesome kite, man would soar too quickly and too high, and the chosen souls would be lost for the race, like balloons which, save for gravitation, would never return from the empyrean.

This passage gives the intellectual facet of the moral feeling at the root of Amiel's 'finer sense' and 'sorer shame,'—the moral feeling which made him shrink back from all sorts of practical responsibility, lest he should undertake what was beyond him, or lose his complete detachment from the narrowness of life. The two feelings together— the love of reverie in the larger sense, and the dread of responsibility,— sealed up his life almost hermetically within his own bosom, and made him a stranger to the world. He longed to free himself from the narrow shell of his own individuality, and consequently dreaded accepting duties and obligations which would have made that individuality more definite and more oppressive. And yet Amiel felt himself tied down to this narrower life by one string which he could not ignore. When he felt the touch of grief,—which, as Mrs. Browning says, is something more than love, since 'grief, indeed, is love, and grief beside,'—then he was aware that he was hemmed within the conditions of a distinct individual lot, that he was seeking something which he

327

could not obtain, while yet he could not suppress, or even wish to suppress, his desire to obtain it. Grief brought home to him the strict limits of his individuality as nothing else brought them home. He could deny himself the more intimate ties of life, but he could not deny himself grief for the severance of such ties as he had. He could not soar above his own individual nature when his heart was bleeding. Then he felt that it was not for him to look at his own life with an impartial imagination, as he would look at any other person's, or as Shakespeare might have looked at one of the characters he had created; for then he felt that throb of anguish which he could not evade by any soaring on imaginative wings, however lofty and free the flight. His intellect was held captive by his griefs,—otherwise, as he said, he might have almost lost his individuality in the ecstasy of reverie.

Clough's attitude of mind towards these practical ties, of which he, too, dreaded the constraining power, was very different. He evidently regarded the intellectual life as the true life, and the life of ordinary man as more or less a condescension to conditions within which his nature could never suffer itself to be long confined. He looked on at the actual experience of his sensitive and tender nature with a little amusement and a good deal of contempt. This is how he makes his hero lecture himself, for instance, when he finds himself gradually falling in love:—

[Quotes *Amours de Voyage*, Canto I, 228–52: 'Yes, I am going,—I feel' to 'whose salt wave I have tasted'.]

Evidently, to Clough's mind, 'the great massy strengths of abstraction' were the levels on which only he could tread firmly, while all the experiences he was destined to undergo in the region of feeling were a sort of illusion, a sort of dream. To Amiel, grief was the cord which kept him from soaring into aimless reverie. To Clough, thought was the rope which kept him from sinking into the enchantments of a world of illusions. He trusted his thoughts, not his feelings. Clough's feelings charmed him away from the life of thought, and thought brought him home again to the real and solid. Amiel's thoughts charmed him away from the life of feeling, and his feelings brought him home again to the real and solid.

Was either of them right? We should say not. Thought undoubtedly does correct, and correct with most salutary inexorability, the illusions of feeling. And, again, feeling does correct, and correct with equally salutary inexorability, the day-dreams of thought. The man who habitually distrusts his feelings is just as certain to live in a world of illusion as the man who habitually distrusts his thoughts. But undoubtedly Amiel, who allowed the illusion of imaginative reverie and intellectual freedom to govern his career much more absolutely than Clough allowed his faith in 'the massy strengths of abstraction' to govern his career, made the greater mistake of the two. Had Amiel not been so sedulous to ward off the pressure of responsibilities to which he did not feel fully equal, he might doubtless have made mistakes, and entered into relations which he would have found painful to him and a shock to his ideal. But the truth is that those relations which are not all that we desire them to be in human life, which are not ideal relations, are of the very essence of the discipline of the will and of the affections, and no man ever yet escaped them, without escaping one of the most useful experiences of human life. Amiel, like Clough, was far too much afraid of hampering the free play of his intellect. No man ever yet did a great work for the world, without hampering the free play of his intellect. And yet it is no paradox to say that no man ever yet had the highest command of his intellect who had not times without number hampered its free play, in order that he might enter the more deeply into the deeper relations of the human heart.

49. Unsigned review in the *Saturday Review*

7 July 1888, 25–6

Like No. 50, this review was occasioned by the publication of the new edition of *The Poems and Prose Remains* (see headnote, p. 335).

The appearance of a new and enlarged edition of the poems of Clough, with the memoir and pretty full selections from his scanty prose writings in a companion volume, both of convenient size, gives a very good opportunity for surveying briefly the work of a man who has been very variously judged, but who, it is pretty evident, has been something of an influence lately. Clough, who has been called by a limping lampooner 'the father of all such as take an interest in *Robert Elsmere*,' and who was to some extent the prototype of Robert Elsmere himself, has always been greatly *prôné* by a certain not uninfluential clique of University wits. But it is, we confess, with something like surprise that we see from a note in this edition that it is the twelfth of his poems that has appeared since his death, and that by far the larger number of these reprints are of quite recent issue. Four editions sufficed, it would seem, for the consumption of the first fifteen years; but from 1877 to the present year, both inclusive, only three years have passed without a fresh impression. This is a fact which, take it how we may, is not to be neglected. A volume of poems by a dead man, not recently dead, and on subjects for the most part of no apparent general interest, without any particular graces of form or anything that can be called strong poetic inspiration, does not go through eight editions in eleven years, half a generation after its author's life is closed, without corresponding to some definite, if passing, appetite, taste, disease, or whatever *libentius audit*, of the day and time.

The thing is the more remarkable that the most careful reading of Clough (and we have taken pains on this occasion to read or re-read him as a whole) fails to show him to an impartial critic as a man of very great, or even of great, power in any one direction. Something has been said of his verse already, and this something can be easily and not tediously amplified into a sufficient judgment. It is essentially the verse of a clever and thoroughly well-educated man, not unpoetically minded, and with strong velleities towards poetry, but without any special, and certainly without the least original, poetical faculty either of conception or execution. The *Bothie of Tober-na-Vuolich*, independently of its composition in the ugly, shambling *pastiche* of a hexameter which had such an inexplicable interest for the men of the middle of this century, is little more than a common-place mixture of University 'gup,' as they would say in India, and of the misty Radicalism of 1849. The famous bathing-pool piece, so constantly quoted, is no doubt a good, indeed a fine, piece of description; but there the poetical value of the thing pretty well begins and ceases. *Amours de Voyage* takes up the hexameter again, and applies it with certainly not greater success to that kind of novel in verse which (though some practitioners of distinction, such as the late Mrs. Browning and the living Lord Lytton, have favoured it) is not a good kind, and Clough's is not good in its kind. The tales of *Mari Magno* are, for the most part, written in verse pedestrian below the level of the worst part of *The Angel in the House*, and not above *Doctor Syntax*. *Dipsychus*, the last of the larger poems, stands no doubt a little higher. It is, except *Manfred*, the most distinct in conception of the numerous imitations of *Faust*; but the first part is monotonous, except for its inequality, and there is such a mere fragment of the second that it is impossible to judge how Clough would have succeeded in a more complicated and ambitious venture. The poem, however, contains his most powerful work, except 'Easter Day,' from which *Dipsychus* in a manner takes its start, and a very few shorter pieces, such as 'Quâ Cursum Ventus' (the finest stanzas of which are known to all from their quotation in *Tom Brown*), and the smart 'Latest Decalogue,' which shows that, if Clough had had a healthier mind, he might have been more considerable as a satirist than he ever could have been as a serious poet. We anticipate the indignant interruption of Cloughomaniacs, to the effect that it is the thought, not the expression, that they admire; but we shall come to that presently. Meanwhile, we may complete our own criticism by observing that Clough is always an echo. Longfellow, Tennyson, Browning, Matthew Arnold, Emerson, ring by turns on the ear trained to detect such ringing; and his letters contain the very best bit of imitated Carlylese we know, with hardly the exception of the *jeux d'esprit* of Mr. Alexander and Dr. Stirling.

But this last, of course, is intentional parody; the poetical echoes clearly are not.

In prose proper Clough cuts even a less distinguished figure. His letters are very interesting, but not by any means as the letters of a great man are. They convey their matter pleasantly, and the matter (such as the Paris Revolution of '48 and the Siege of Rome, at both of which Clough was present) is often good in itself. Moreover, they contain many unconscious and, therefore, half-ludicrous and half-pathetic glimpses of the fatal priggishness which Arnold impressed on his pupils, and which characterized the whole of what has been called the Rugby-Balliol set, to a very recent period, if not to the present day. Out of letters his prose work is very small indeed. He rather prided himself on his inability to write upon subjects selected for him, or to select subjects for himself, which inability ended in his leaving by way of an *opus magnum* nothing but a patching-up of old translations of Plutarch. One or two papers in English literature, here reprinted, are very sound in general view, as well as carefully and well written. But they are infinitesimal in bulk, of little distinction in expression, and showing neither any very fixed principles in criticism nor any wide knowledge of literature beyond the school classics and English itself. None of Clough's prose is either in originality or in expression beyond what may be called good Fellowship-essay standard, and whether of that standard or any other, there is exceedingly little.

It is clear therefore that, putting aside altogether the mere clique interest above referred to, which has been long exhausted or at a low ebb, it must be something different from literary accomplishment which is admired in Clough; and, arguing from facts instead of to them, there is no doubt whatever that this is the case. Clough, as has been hinted jestingly above, was almost the first to formulate, if not to feel, that irreligious religiosity which was the rebound of the Tractarian movement at home and the neo-Catholic movement abroad, and which has produced Amiels and Robert Elsmeres and other doleful creatures in fact or in fiction. He gave *éclat* to it by his resignation of his fellowship, and he lived on it in the literary sense all the rest of his life. With regard to the resignation, Clough himself, to do him justice, makes very little fuss, and though we desire to do every credit to his unquestioned rectitude, no very great fuss need have been made by any one. The fellowship would have expired of itself in a few months; he was avowedly sick to death of his Oxford duties, and anxious to get rid of them, and he was not only (unlike some friends of his who are dead, and one or two who are alive) too honest a man to take orders without believing, but also, belief apart, he evidently disliked the notion of a clergyman's life. His emancipation, no doubt, threw him loose on the world; but not more than if he had made a love match. He was very soon picked up and made comfortable with a Government appointment, and even before this, and before his short appointment as head of University Hall, he was so far from being in any straits for subsistence that he could spend the best part of two years either in foreign travel or in staying comfortably at home and writing the *Bothie*. This is not very severe mortification for conscience' sake. However, he had behaved like a gentleman, and not like certain deans, vice-chancellors, and so forth, and he had an ample reward in reputation not alone among persons of his own kidney.

That kidney is, we regret to say, the kidney of 'second-rate sensitive minds,' as a famous title has it, and we fear that the popularity of Clough just now shows that second-rate, or anything down to hundredth-rate minds, which would like to seem sensitive, are uncommonly plentiful with us. It was as natural to Clough to maunder about faith and the soul as it is to some people to maunder about their livers and to others to maunder about their salvation. In all his writing, prose and verse, on the subject, no valid objection to Christianity is ever once formulated. He allows over and over again that it satisfies him morally in the widest sense. In a remarkable document, the most important by far of his prose work, which is supposed to express his very latest thoughts, he makes further admissions in the orthodox sense, and, what is more, he makes strictures on his fellows the undogmatic religionists which are quite destructive of any form of rationalism. If he was not orthodox, we fear the reason must be sought in three things—that he was morbidly sensitive; that his intellect, thought acute, was far from robust; and that he was deeply tainted with the priggish bumptiousness aforesaid, the bumptiousness which insists that everything must be made clear to *it*. He says somewhere that 'he must not sin against his own soul by perverting his reason.'[1]

---

[1] Cf. 'Notes on the Religious Tradition':
I do not see . . . that it can be lawful for me, for the sake of the moral guidance and the spiritual comfort, to ignore all scientific or historic doubts, or if pressed with them to the utmost, to take refuge in Romish infallibility, and, to avoid sacrificing the four Gospels, consent to accept the legends of the saints and the tales of modern miracles.
I believe that I may without any such perversion of my reason, without any such mortal sin against my own soul, which is identical with reason, and against the Supreme Giver of that soul and reason, still abide by the real Religious Tradition.

(*PPR I*, 422; *SPW*, 290)

He might as well have said that it is sinning against a foot-rule to acknowledge the existence of the Infinite. Of his bumptiousness there are many proofs here. When he tells his sister that 'he does not care a straw' about missing his first, he talks, even for a clever disappointed boy of twenty-two, intolerable nonsense. If it was not true, he was a silly prig for saying it; and, if it was true, he was a sillier for thinking so. Years afterwards, when he was a man of nearly thirty, he says that some think him at times almost a Puseyite; but 'he could be provoked to send out a flood of lava boiling hot amidst their flowery ecclesiastical fields and parterres.' This is having a good conceit of oneself, and also 'talking book,' with a vengeance.

To a man of this kind Christianity is necessarily unsatisfactory, exactly because of its very highest qualities. He measures Christ by Clough, finds that the measure is not long enough, and is at once sure that there must be something wrong—as, indeed, no doubt there was, though not in the direction he thought. But being, with all his vanity, an honest and in a way devout creature, he expresses his discomfort in his *Dipsychus* and his 'Easter-Day,' and all his other little introspective moanings and groanings. It does not appear, to do him justice, that—like his friend, and in many ways magnified double, the late Mr. Matthew Arnold—he ever patronized religion, or was ever quite satisfied with the state of things in which he found himself. But, with this difference, he was very much Mr. Arnold's 'moon.' He was vastly his inferior in poetical and critical faculty and in power of work; his inferior also immensely in appreciation of the joy of living, in wit, and in flexibility.

But these very inferiorities, it would seem, give him an additional attraction for the other second-rate sensitive minds, the other morbid egotists who, a hundred years ago, would have been Calvinists, either certain of their salvation or certain of their damnation, who are now dogmatic unreligionists or undogmatic religionists, and who never at any time could either acquiesce in simple and humble faith or rise to the serener and saner conception of philosophical Christianity.

50. Coventry Patmore, 'Arthur Hugh Clough', a review in *St. James's Gazette*

10 August 1888, 7

This review was reprinted in *Principle of Art* (London, 1889), 106–12.

Patmore (1823–96) was a poet influenced by the Pre-Raphaelites; his *The Angel in the House*, a long sentimental poem celebrating wedded love was issued in parts during the 1850s and became one of the most popular poems in Victorian England. He entered the Roman Catholic Church in 1862.

This is a review of two volumes published in 1888, *Poems of Arthur Hugh Clough*, New & Revised Edition (London: Macmillan) and *Prose Remains of Arthur Hugh Clough*, with a Selection from his Letters and a Memoir edited by his wife (London: Macmillan). The contents of these volumes were virtually identical with those of the similar publications of 1869, with these exceptions: the *Rugby Magazine* poem 'Thoughts of Home' ('I watched them from the window') has been dropped from the *Poems* and there is no memoir; the 'Review of Mr. Newman's *The Soul*' has been left out of the *Prose*. This new version of the *Poems* was printed seven times, the last occasion being in 1909. After this date, there was no more comprehensive edition of the poems attempted until 1951.

Arthur Hugh Clough, though he cannot take rank high among artists, whether in prose or verse, who have acquired a classic position by the production of works which are the flowering in beauty and repose of a unique individuality, is not for a moment to be confused with the great crowd of writers who, however excellent they may have been in their lines, have never obtained a hearing through the noble and preponderating interest of personal character. Clough worshipped Truth with more than the passion of a lover, and his writings are, for the most part, the tragic records of a life-long devotion to a mistress who steadily refused his embraces; but as it is greatly better to have loved without attaining than to have attained without loving, so Clough's ardent and unrewarded stumblings in the dark towards his adored though unseen divinity are greatly more attractive and edifying to those who have shared, successfully or not, the same passion, than is that complacent fruition of her smiles which she often accords to those who are contented to be no more than her speaking acquaintances. Regarded from a purely intellectual point of view, Clough's utterances on religion, duty, etc., are little better than the commonplaces which in these days pass through the mind and more or less affect the feelings of almost every intelligent and educated youth before he is twenty years of age; but there are commonplaces which cease to be such, and become indefinitely interesting, in proportion as they are animated by moral ardour and passion. Speech may work good by warming as well as by enlightening; and if Clough's writings teach no new truth, they may inflame the love of truth, which is perhaps as great a service. Though he professes that he can nowhere see light where light is most necessary and longed for, his mind is utterly opposed to the negative type; and he exactly exemplifies the class of believer whom Richard Hooker endeavours to comfort, in his great sermon on 'the perpetuity of faith in the elect,'[1] by the reminder that a longing to believe is implicit faith, and that we cannot sorrow for the lack of that which we interiorly hold to be non-existent. A question that must suggest itself to most readers of the two volumes before us is, What is the use and justification of these endless and tautological lamentations over the fact—as Clough conceived it to be—that, for such as him at least, 'Christ is not risen'? The reply is, that the responsibility of the publication of so much that is profoundly passionate but far from profoundly intellectual scepticism was not his. With the exception of some not very significant critical essays, the volume of prose consists of letters, which were of course not meant for the public; and the greater part of the poetry remained to the day of Clough's death in his desk, and would probably never have left it, with his consent, unless to be put in the fire.

Those who recognize in the *Bothie* Clough's almost solitary claim to literary eminence must somewhat wonder at the considerable

[1] 'A learned and comfortable Sermon of the Certainty and Perpetuity of Faith in the Elect; especially of the Prophet Habbakuk's Faith' (Oxford, 1612), by Richard Hooker (1554?-1600).

figure he stands for in the estimation of the present generation. The fact is that Clough, like James Spedding, was personally far more impressive than his works; and the singularly strong effect produced among his friends by the extreme simplicity and shy kindliness of his life and manners, and the at once repellent and alluring severity of his truthfulness, gave his character a consequence beyond that of his writings with all who knew him though ever so slightly; and the halo of this sanctity hangs, through the report of his friends, about all that he has done and renders cold criticism of it almost impossible. The absurdly bad portrait which stands at the beginning of the volume of verse does not give the slightest suggestion of the manly force, feminine shyness and sweetness, and boyish candour which made the countenance of Clough the true mirror of his soul, and a never-to-be-forgotten impression in the minds of all who had once seen it. No one who knew Clough can so separate his personality from his writings as to be able to criticize them fairly as literature; no one who has not known him can understand their value as the outcome of character.

The impressionable and feminine element, which is manifest in all genius, but which in truly effective genius is always subordinate to power of intellect, had in Clough's mind the preponderance. The masculine power of intellect consists scarcely so much in the ability to see truth, as in the tenacity of spirit which cleaves to and assimilates the truth when it is found and which steadfastly refuses to be blown about by every wind of doctrine and feeling. The reiterated theme of Clough's poetry is that the only way of forgetting certain problems now, and of securing their solution hereafter, is to do faithfully our nearest duty. This is no new teaching: it is that of every religion and all philosophy. But Clough had no power of trusting patiently to the promise, 'Do my commandments and you shall know of the doctrine.' This was the ruin of what might otherwise have been a fine poetic faculty. A 'Problem' will not sing even in the process of solution, much less while it is only a hopeless and irritating 'Pons.' Clough was curiously attracted by Emerson, of whom he spoke as the only great contemporary American. Now Emerson, at his very best, never approached greatness. He was at highest only a brilliant metaphysical epigrammatist. But a religion without a dogma, and with only one commandment, 'Thou shalt neither think nor do anything that is customary,' had great attractions for Clough; to whom it never seems to have occurred that the vast mass of mankind, for whose moral and religious welfare he felt so keenly, has not and never can have a

337

religion of speechless aspirations and incommunicable feelings, and that to teach men to despise custom is to cut the immense majority of them adrift from all moral restraint. The promise that we shall all be priests and kings seems scarcely to be for this world. At all events we are as far from its fulfilment now as we were two thousand years ago; and we shall not be brought nearer to it by any such outpourings of sarcastic discontent as go to the making of such poems as the tedious Mephistophelian drama called *Dipsychus*, which Clough had the good sense not to publish, though it is included with many others of equally doubtful value in posthumous editions of his works. This class of his poems possesses, indeed, a lively interest for a great many people of our own time, who are in the painful state of moral and religious ferment which these verses represent; but it is a mere accident of the time that there is any considerable audience for such utterances, and in a generation or two it is probable that most men will feel surprise that there could ever have been a public who found poetry in this sort of matter.

The *Bothie of Tober-na-Vuolich* is the only considerable poem of Clough's in which he seems, for a time, to have got out of his slough of introspection and doubt and to have breathed the healthy air of nature and common humanity. In spite of many artistic short-comings, this poem is so healthy, human, and original, that it can scarcely fail to survive when a good deal of far more fashionable verse shall have disappeared from men's memories. The one infallible note of a true poet—the power of expressing himself in rhythmical movements of subtilty and sweetness which baffle analysis—is also distinctly manifest in passages of the *Bothie*, passages the music of which was, we fancy, lingering in the ear of Tennyson when he wrote certain parts of *Maud*. The originality of this idyl is beyond question. It is not in the least like any other poem, and an occasionally ostentatious touch of the manner of *Herman and Dorothea* seems to render this originality all the more conspicuous in the main. Another note of poetical power, scarcely less questionable than is that of sweetness and subtilty of rhythm, is the warm and pure breath of womanhood which is exhaled from the love-passages of this poem. Clough seems to have felt, in the presence of a simple and amiable woman, a mystery of life which acted for a time as the rebuke and speechless solution of all doubts and intellectual distresses. These passages in the *Bothie*, and, in a less degree, some others in the *Amours de Voyage*, stand, in the disturbed course of Clough's ordinary verse, like the deep, pure, and sky-reflecting pools which occasionally appear in the course of a restless mountain river.

51. Lionel Johnson, from an unsigned review of Matthew Arnold's *Poetical Works* in the *Academy*

10 January 1891, xxxix, 31–2

This review was reprinted in Johnson's *Post Liminium* (ed. Thomas Whittemore), 1911, 296.

Lionel Johnson (1867–1902), minor poet and critic, was one of Yeats's 'Tragic Generation', a member, with Yeats himself, Dowson and others of the Rhymers' Club of the 'nineties. Like all of his fellow Rhymers, Johnson was strongly in reaction against most of the great Victorians, blaming them for importing into poetry 'impurities' such as politics, religion, philosophy etc.

Johnson praises the lofty humanism and universal appeal of Arnold's meditative poems which, he goes on, 'are more than records of a transitory emotion, the phase and habit of an age. Such a description would apply to Clough: his mournful, homesick, desultory poems are indeed touched with decay, because they are composed without care, in no wide spirit of contemplation; reading them we do not think of 'Sophocles by the Aegean,'[1] nor of the *lacrimae rerum*. . . .[2]

[1] From Arnold's 'Dover Beach'.
[2] *Sunt lacrimae rerum et mentem mortalia tangunt:* 'There are tears for all things and human sufferings touch the heart' (Virgil, *Aeneid* I, 462).

339

52. A. C. Swinburne, from 'Social Verse', the *Forum*

October 1891, 169-85

Reprinted in *Studies in Prose and Poetry* (London, 1894), 84–109, and in *Complete Works*, ed. Edmund Gosse and Thomas J. Wise, London, 1926, XV, 264–88.

Algernon Charles Swinburne (1837–1909), who had in his early years admired the great Victorians, Tennyson, Browning and Arnold, later grew increasingly critical of them for their lack of passion, of the pagan touch. It was inevitable that one who had sung so feelingly of 'the raptures and roses of vice' should have been severe upon Clough also. The effect of this brilliant and, no doubt, very damaging fragment may be gauged by Saintsbury's implicit reference to it in his *A History of Nineteenth Century Literature* (see No. 53). Swinburne was reviewing an anthology of social and occasional verse edited by Locker-Lampson.

. . . Even more out of place [than C. S. Calverley] in such good company [i.e. such as Peacock, Byron, Thackeray] is the weary and wearisome laureate of Oxonicules and Bostonicules, Mr. Lowell's realized ideal and chosen representative of English poetry at its highest in the generation of Tennyson and Browning; whose message to his generation may be summed up as follows:

> We've got no faith, and we don't know what to do:
> To think one can't believe a creed because it isn't true!

Literary history will hardly care to remember or to register the fact that there was a bad poet named Clough, whom his friends found it useless to puff: for the public, if dull, has not quite such a skull as belongs to believers in Clough.

> Et certamen erat, Corydon cum Thyrside, parvum.[1]

---

[1] Cf. Virgil, *Eclogues* VII, 16: '*et certamen erat, Corydon cum Thyrside, magnum*'. Arnold's elegy upon Clough was entitled 'Thyrsis'.

53. George Saintsbury, from *A History of Nineteenth Century Literature*

1896, 316–17

George Saintsbury (1845–1933) was one of the trio of historical critics, the others being Sir Edmund Gosse and Sir Arthur Quiller-Couch, who dominated the English literary world in their casually critical way during the late Victorian and Edwardian periods. Saintsbury's numerous books included the first short critical study of Matthew Arnold (1899).

Clough has been called by persons of distinction a 'bad poet'; but this was only a joke, and, with all respect to those who made it, a rather bad joke. The author of 'Qua Cursum Ventus,' of the marvellous picture of the advancing tide in 'Say not the struggle,' and of not a few other things, was certainly no bad poet, though it would not be uncritical to call him a thin one. . . .

It is not necessary to be biassed by Matthew Arnold's musical epicede of Thyrsis in order to admit, nor should any bias against his theological views and his rather restless character be sufficient to induce anyone to deny, a distinct vein of poetry in Clough. His earliest and most popular considerable work, *The Bothie of Tober-na-Vuolich* . . . is written in hexameters which do not, like Kingsley's,[1] escape the curse of that 'pestilent heresy'; and the later *Amours de Voyage* and *Dipsychus*, though there are fine passages in both, bring him very close to the Spasmodic school, of which in fact he was an unattached and more cultivated member, with fancies directed rather to religiosity than to strict literature. *Ambarvalia* had preceded the *Bothie*, and other things followed. On the whole, Clough is one of the most unsatisfactory products of that well-known form of nineteenth century scepticism which has neither the strength to believe nor the courage to disbelieve 'and have done with it.' He hankers and looks back, his 'two souls' are always warring with each other, and though the clash

[1] Charles Kingsley, *Andromeda* (1858).

and conflict sometimes bring out fine things (as in the two pieces above cited and the still finer poem at Naples with the refrain 'Christ is not risen'), though his 'Latest Decalogue' has satirical merit, and some of his country poems, written without undercurrent of thought, are fresh and genial, he is on the whole a failure. But he is a failure of a considerable poet, and some fragments of success chequer him.

54. J. M. Robertson, 'Clough', *New Essays Towards a Critical Method*

1897

In the essay with which he opens his book John Mackinnon Robertson (1856–1933) declares his intention to make a contribution to the systematizing or 'scientizing' of 'The Theory and Practice of Criticism'. He finds the influential criticism of Taine and Ste Beuve unduly subjective: he praises instead, while showing the bias of each, Hennequin's *La Critique Scientifique* (1888) and Renouvier's *La Critique Philosophique* (1889). Nevertheless, recognizing that subjectivity is inevitable and valuable, in critics as in writers, he exhorts the critic above all to know himself and to aim, as objectively as he can, to 'confess' openly to the reader his own temperamental characteristics and bias in thought and feeling. The critic, as Arnold and Lowell had done, can best approach just estimates by applying comparative standards and widening his outlook into as many fields as he can. The all-round criticism may then comprise an 'Aesthetic Analysis', a 'Psychologic Analysis', and a 'Sociological Analysis'.

Robertson notes in his Preface that in his study of Clough, 'which claims for him a status and a kind of recognition that have not latterly been given him, I have attempted to relate the criticism of the writing, as is fitting, to a view of the organism and surroundings of the writer.' He also notes that his essay was actually written in 1887.

The essay has been printed entire here, with its lengthy survey of English novelists, because the whole is relevant to the particular comments on Clough and is also an unusual attempt in Victorian criticism at comparative judgment.

To some readers of the various appreciative criticisms which have been passed upon Arthur Hugh Clough, it must have seemed odd that the friendly writers should have so little to say of the poet's measure of success in a pursuit which bulked largely in his artistic work—the writing, in the verse form, of what is none the less analytic fiction. Setting aside the *Mari Magno: or, Tales on Board*, which are also character studies, about half his verse is made up simply of *The Bothie of Tober-na-Vuolich* and *Amours de Voyage*; and to the critic of fiction the latter production cannot well fail to be at least interesting, while the former is known to have interested a good many readers who would not profess to be specially critical. So silent, however, has criticism been on the subject, that there is probably an air of extravagance about an attempt to show that Clough was a great and original artist in fiction.

When, in 1848-9, Clough wrote his *Bothie* and *Amours*,[1] the leading English novelists were Lytton, Thackeray, and Dickens; and of these the last, being at work on *David Copperfield* (1849), had yet to write *Little Dorrit*, *Great Expectations*, the *Tale of Two Cities*, *Bleak House*, and *Our Mutual Friend*; while Thackeray was but beginning to produce his masterpieces, *Vanity Fair* dating from 1846-8, and *Pendennis* from 1849-50.[2] Charlotte Brontë had conquered fame by *Jane Eyre*; but *Shirley* only appeared in 1849, and *Villette* was not to come till 1853. George Eliot, again, had not yet dreamt of fiction; and across the Atlantic Hawthorne had thus far produced only his short tales; so that English fiction, on the whole, might be said to have reached only the beginnings of its greatest development. Such a division is, of course, arbitrary, just as, though in a much greater degree, it is arbitrary to make divisions between Dark Ages, Middle Ages, and Modern Times; but when simply put forward for what it is worth, it may serve usefully to emphasise the fact that before the time in question English novelists had done very little in the direction of what is coming to be recognised as the main work of the modern novel, the serious, analytical presentment of normal types of character. The terms here used must be taken as strictly definitive; or, rather, they had better be themselves defined to prevent misconception; and this can best be done by first noting the limitations of the art of the earlier novelists. It will probably not now be generally disputed that, while Defoe once for

[1] The latter seems to have been completed in 1849, though not published till 1857-8. It was then a pecuniary success, which the *Bothie* had not been. 'In a commercial point of view, the publications of the *Amours* has been a great event to me. This is the first money I ever received for verse-making, and it is really a very handsome sum.' Letter in *Prose Remains*, ed. 1888, p. 245. (Robertson's note.)

[2] *Vanity Fair* was published serially from January 1847 to July 1848, and *Pendennis* from November 1848 to December 1850.

all gave English prose fiction a bias to circumstantial verisimilitude; and while Richardson, with all his limitations, gave the lead in the direction of a true analysis of character; Jane Austen was practically the first English novelist to attain real success in the rendering of normal life—that is to say, the first who gives us no impression of inadequacy within the limits of her undertaking. Richardson is far too much occupied with his thin-spun psychologising to hit off with any vividness the objective totality of his personages as it might conceivably appear to a keen onlooker; for ever pulling the strings, he never seems to get a view of his own drama; and thus the very freshness of method which gave his letter-writing characters, with their serious conformity to the literary conventions of the time, such a hold on the interest of his contemporaries, is for us to-day the great bar to the assimilation of his work. Fielding, again, is unquestionably at his best where his types are neither serious nor normal—that is, where he is giving us *genre* studies, an Adams, a Squire Western, a woman of the people, a sketch in satire, or an effect in comedy. Tom Jones is only inferentially real, and Sophia never becomes more than a suggestion, like Amelia, of a type of young lady which Fielding adored. As for Goldsmith, the general truth of suggestion, the value of the lighter detail, in *The Vicar of Wakefield* is not more obvious than the conventionality of much of the framework and much of the posing; while Scott, finally, hardly once contrives to give true vitality to a character which does not depend for its effect on novelty. There is none the less genius in his projection of the fresh types, as Davie Deans, Cuddie Headrigg, Monkbarns, the Bailie, Dandie Dinmont, and the rest; or in the skill with which the action of Jeanie Deans is made to enshrine her in our memory; but the fact remains that his normal personages, those hypothetically interesting figures round whom his really observed characters are grouped, are the merest 'walking gentlemen' and gentlewomen. As to this there was no real doubt among competent readers in his own time; his fame, in so far as it did not depend on the gratitude of ordinary novel-readers for a fresh kind of excitement, being based on the general sense of the felicity with which he drew what were nominally his minor personages. No reader could, in the nature of things, imagine Captain Brown, or Waverley, or Mr. Francis Osbaldistone, anything like as vividly as he did even Counsellor Pleydell or Saunders Mucklebackit; and while the wizard's young ladies are a little more thinkable than his heroes, Diana being admittedly a substantial success, their society is far indeed from having any such fascination for the reader of to-day as it had for the 'male of their species' with whom their chivalrous creator provided them. But Jane Austen, as no one saw better than Scott, achieved just such a success in drawing the people of the English upper-middle and middle-upper classes as he had done with the types he had observed in the Scotch peasantry. Here, in a young woman's novels, were people such as every reader met every day, somehow made as real as Borderers and Highlanders; more persistently real, as it happened, by virtue of the writer's general method; and somewhat inexplicably entertaining by virtue of one's very perception that there was nothing irresistibly entertaining in these same people in actual life. It was the triumph of pure art: the commonplace had been made immortal by sheer felicity of reproduction. Not that the new comer at once attained her due classic authority. While the few good readers—who included, let us remember, not only Scott, but, in the next generation, the much-maligned Macaulay —felt that there was here something quite new in fiction, something not attained to by Miss Burney any more than by Richardson, yet the habit of finding the truer touches of novelists mainly in their grotesques, or ostensible comedy-types, was of such long standing that readers still had a tendency to esteem Jane Austen, even as they did Fielding and Smollett, for her more emphasised studies, which were, by the conditions of her art-world, her fools; and the very perfection of her fools tended somewhat to strengthen the bias. Hence, when George Eliot much later sought to present people of all grades of mind, she could still be met by a criticism which found her Mrs. Poysers and Aunt Gleggs admirable but thought her less piquant studies little worth having in comparison.

In Jane Austen, then, we might almost say, we have the first of the moderns in fiction. He, or she, who does not delight in her cannot be credited with a true taste; or, let us say (remembering Charlotte Brontë's inappreciation), is one-sidedly developed. This being duly premised, a devout admirer may with a clear conscience go on to say that Jane Austen left unattempted the application of the naturalist method to normal character in its relation to the deeper issues of life. Her art played on the normal in individual experience as well as on the normal in individuality: she drew not only the people who belong to the ordinary drawing-room, but the drawing-room section of their inner life, so to say; and some will probably have it, with Mr. Harrison, that these were her fixed limits. As I must not overload a note on Clough with a study of Jane Austen, I will not here discuss the matter, but simply posit the fact that her performance was defined as has been said; and that when she had done there was still left to be achieved in fiction that adequate study of not only the weightier natures, but the more intellectual sides of these, which later thinking tends to demand from the professed student of character. Not less certain is it, however, that before the middle of the century the further step had not been fully taken. Setting aside the Marryats and Levers, who never turned to the intellectual side of things at all, we are bound to decide that Lytton lacks truth, and that Dickens, whatever may be thought of his later work, had certainly not so far mastered the serious side of life in his earlier period as to yield a product which will satisfy a cultured reader to-day. But did even Thackeray fully succeed in his earlier work, or in his later, in giving us such an artistic treatment of the intellectual life as can be said worthily to complement his pictures of the simply social life? I cannot better indicate the precise issue involved than by asking how far, say, *Pendennis* now satisfies us as a sketch of a young man with a deep intellectual experience, and how far Thackeray now impresses us as a man able to describe or transcribe such an experience. It implies no touch of detraction from the praise due to Thackeray's consummate and incomparable talent, to say that at this particular point he falls short; that his scope did not permit him to reach those sides of mental life at which he has ineffectually hinted in *Pendennis* (and this is the conclusion pointed to by the later work in *Philip*); or, alternatively, that on this as on one or two other points he wrote down to the standards of the British parlour of his time.

If, then, British fiction in 1848–9 was on the whole thus imperfectly intellectual, so much the more would be the merit of any man who at one stride attained the higher level; and this achievement it is that I venture to claim for Clough, in respect of these two works of his which are in form hexameter poems, but are in essence works of narrative, analytical, psychological fiction. Little read as they still are in proportion to their merits, I will rather assume them to be known to my readers than recapitulate their contents, as the mere telling of their simple stories would reveal nothing of their charm and power, which can only be gathered from a deliberate perusal. What really needs to be pressed is the relation that such works bear to the contemporary novel, and the faculty for fiction to which they testify. In the criticism of Clough's own generation one finds indeed some tribute to the power of the character-sketching in both the *Bothie* and the *Amours*; but—and this is the special point—no clear perception that just this merit, in the circumstances, took the two works out of the list of poetic successes and placed them high among the fictional, where alone could any analogous art be found, and where, further, it would be hard to find anything equally subtle in the same line. Doubtless it was the simple fact of Clough's having written in hexameters that stood mainly in the way of the proper classification; and it will be necessary to consider what that fact substantially amounts to.

What seems to me to have been done by those who say that Clough proved we could have good English poetry in hexameters is: having found that a work in hexameters may be entirely successful in its art, to assume that it is therefore first-rate hexameter verse. Now, the literary question raised by Clough's hexameters is rather too complex to be so simply disposed of. It includes, to begin with, the old question as to what the technical 'values' of poetry really are; and on this there is need to guard against obscuring the issue by discussing the kind of impression we get from those classic poets to whom the hexameter was native. Asking rather what are the constituent elements of our own best poetry, we find that they may be resolved into effects of cadence, consonance, and concentrated and charming verbal expression; that without these the verse form has no value, whatever be its metre; and that no metrical form, as such, gives the least permanent security for their presence. It almost follows from this that true poetic values, unalloyed by effects which are not such as to justify the verse form, can only be had from short poems—that all lengthy works in verse inevitably involve much inferior performance, and that such works must rely for their acceptance on the reader's pleasure in the successful passages inducing him to tolerate the others. For a variety of reasons, I believe that Clough quite felt all this, at least in his younger days; and I accordingly do not believe that in writing the *Bothie* and the *Amours* he was aiming at strictly poetical effects at all.[1] This opinion has been ere now expressed; Mr. Swinburne having suggested in his essay on Mr. Arnold's poems, that Clough meant his hexameters to be regarded as 'graduated prose' and not as poetry;[2] on which Professor Masson rejoins to the effect that such a view is quite out of

[1] The source of his impulse is noteworthy: 'Will you convey to Mr. Longfellow,' he writes to Emerson in 1849, 'the fact that it was a reading of his "Evangeline," aloud to my mother and sister, which, coming after a reperusal of the *Iliad*, occasioned this outbreak of hexameters?' (*PPR I*, 136). (R's note.)

[2] Swinburne, 'Matthew Arnold's New Poems' (1867), *Essays and Studies* (1875), p. 164: 'Mr. Clough's . . . are admirable studies in grad uated prose, full of fine soundand effect.'

the question. But if, instead of saying anything about 'graduated prose,' a phrase which simply raises the further question why Clough did *not* write graduated prose pure and simple, if that were the kind of effect he wanted—if rather we say that he aimed at an effect which was not poetic, I think we should be stating the plain truth. On the face of the matter, very much of the *Bothie* and of the *Amours* is humorous; in fact, humour, buoyant in the first and sombre and subtle in the second, pervades the whole conception of the two works; which is as much as to say that they are not to be classed as poetry proper, if indeed they are to be called poetry at all. I am, however, sufficiently conscious of the psychological difficulties of the problem to prefer waiving the last challenge, and simply to say that where verse is humorous its effects, granting them to have certain analogies with those strictly poetic, certain properties which clearly belong to the verse form, are nevertheless of a distinctly different order from those others. This may seem at bottom a truism, but on the acceptance of it there depends such a point of practice as the deciding not to give the same name to horse and ass because both are cattle for riding. Humorous verse has undoubtedly this quality in common with beautiful verse, that when it is quite successful we return to it on the sheer strength of the fascination of the words, in their kind; and such charm over us is assuredly a special credential of the finest verse. It is the words, and the order of the words, that make the poetry; not the idea as it might be paraphrased in any prose form, however accurately. Well, one cannot help being repeatedly charmed with those lines of Peacock's:

> The mountain sheep are sweeter,
> But the valley sheep are fatter;
> We therefore deemed it meeter
> To carry off the latter—

for their happy fusion of rhyme and humour, which would be utterly lost in a prose statement; whereas it is just a fusion of rhyme and beauty that perpetually captures us in the lines:

> Music that gentlier on the spirit lies
> Than tired eyelids upon tired eyes;[1]

and a charm of pure quintessential beauty of choice expression, absolutely dependent upon phrase and cadence, that conquers memory in those of Arnold's:

[1] Tennyson, 'The Lotos-Eaters'.

As the pale waste widens around him,
As the banks fade dimmer away,
As the stars come out, and the night-wind
Brings up the stream
Murmurs and scents of the infinite sea.[1]

But since the 'rhythmical creation of beauty,' to use Poe's phrase,[2] has thus so inexpressibly different an effect from that of the rhythmical creation of amusement, an effect so much more different from the latter than from that of fairly elevated prose, one hardly cares to give the name of poetry to both. I would finally say, then, that Clough wrote in hexameters because there was a certain artistic effect he was able to get from hexameters, which served his purpose, but which he never regarded as the same in kind with that which he aimed at in his finer rhymed poetry. And this particular artistic effect, accruing to the hexameter as he handled it, was not, as I take it, a strictly metrical or cadencial effect at all, but one of delicately humorous parody—so delicate that while the humour was often effusive it could be refined away at need till it put no check on a perfectly serious intonation and purpose. Clough, in short, wrote in hexameters not because he thought that special metre, *quâ* metre, tractable to serious verse, but because the hexameter was the metre of Homer and Virgil to begin with, and thus afforded endless opportunities for jests of style that would appeal to academic readers; and because further there was no blank measure in which pungency and piquancy could be better maintained at less cost of enforced dignity. He had thus the two resources of parody of classic manner and parody of rhythm in general; a combination, I suppose, the more difficult to analyse and describe truly because it is so unique. For the rest, it is needless to renew the other dispute as to whether Clough's verses were true hexameters after all. Mr. Swinburne says not; and Poe, to judge from his assaults on Longfellow's attempts, would probably extend his ban to Clough's. As to the latter, it may perhaps be agreed that, deliberate quaintness apart, they are 'about as good as they make 'em,' as the youth of London say; and no more needs to be granted.[3] Clough's own opinion on the subject is difficult to gather; the only clues being this brief 'Note' on the back of the title-page of the first edition of the *Bothie*:

[1] Arnold, 'The Future'.
[2] From 'The Poetic Principle' (1848: 1850).
[3] Mr. Arnold considered (Lectures *On Translating Homer*, p. 79) that 'Mr. Clough's hexameters are excessively, needlessly rough.' The *tu quoque* cannot be foregone. Mr. Arnold's own hexameters are insupportable—neither classic nor English. (R's note.)

The reader is warned to expect every kind of irregularity in these modern hexameters; 'spondaic'[1] lines, so called, are almost the rule; and a word will often require to be transferred by the voice from the end of one line to the beginning of the next;

and some passages in the first of his *Letters of Parepidemus*, as this:

Homer's rounded line, and Virgil's smooth verse, were both of them (after more puzzling about it than the matter deserves, I have convinced myself) totally unlike those lengthy, straggling, irregular, uncertain slips of *prose mesurée* which we find it so hard to measure, so easy to read in half a dozen ways, without any assurance of the right one, and which, since the days of Voss, the Gothic nations consider analogous to classic hexameter.[2]

it may be added that his careful translations from Homer in hexameter, though extremely interesting, do not make good English verse; while his other *Essays in Classical Metres* are entirely afflictive.

There will still be put by some, perhaps, the further question, Why did Clough write in verse at all if his purpose was to any extent serious fiction? I would say, on that, that he happened at a particular period to be steeped in Greek verse, and at the same time overflowing with 'criticism of life' as he saw it around him; and that he found in these works of his the fittest expression possible for him at the moment. It so happened that he could write elastically and spontaneously at the given time in the given manner; the manner being in itself a stimulus peculiarly fit in his case. He seems never to have written prose with any such facility as is shown in the *Bothie*, which would appear to have taken only somewhere about a month in the writing: his prose essays are mostly laboured and ineffectual; heavily packed with culled passages of Latin verse; never seeming to kindle all along the line, or to be written because of a clear sense of something to say. They never write themselves: they are composed; and smack of Carlyle and I know not how many other intellectual fashions of his young days. But in the *Bothie* we seem to have the exuberance of a holiday-making undergraduate with the keen judgments, the wide observation, and the musings, of the ripening man. Hence, an artistic success without parallel in its kind. There is, I venture to say, no piece of fiction in the language, within similar compass, which can compare with this for

---

[1] I do not quite understand what Clough here meant by 'spondaic.' Surely Poe was right in deciding that the ancient hexameter was spondaic, and that English hexameters fail just for lack of spondees. Clough's hexameters are just about as trochaic and dactyllic as other people's. (R's note.)

[2] *PPR I*, 397.

quantity and quality, in its combination of truth, force, and variety of character-drawing, truth of environment, depth of suggestion, and range of association and sympathy. No English writer has yet appeared who has shown the skill to pack such a picture and commentary as that of the opening banquet-scene into anything like the same space of prose. Told in prose at the same length, indeed, the multifold description and episode would have an air of crowding, of willed terseness, such as we have in Flaubert's *Salammbô*; whereas the verse, with all its load of significance, seems positively to loiter by the way, in the mock-Homeric and Miltonic iterations of epithets and dallyings with phrases and descriptions. It seems to be written for the sheer humour of the thing; and yet Thackeray could not have better have turned the humour to the account of the portraiture. Admiring notice has been taken by Mr. W. M. Rossetti of one line which conveys a whole story:

> Pipers five or six, among them *the young one, the drunkard*

—a touch even more simply effective now than it was in the first edition, where the epithet 'drunken' came again in the line further on, about the small piper nodding to Lindsay; but the section is full of similarly weighty strokes. The tutor, 'the grave man, nicknamed Adam,' so admirably exhibited by a series of incidental, effortless dramatic touches as the story goes on, is already permanently outlined by that phrase and the lines on his dress; the 'shrewd ever-ciphering factor' is as it were henceforth identifiable; the whole cast of character of each of the students seems to be known definitely once for all; even the *attaché* and the Guardsman are individualised by an imperceptible touch; the Marquis of Ayr gesticulates before us; and Sir Hector, in particular, is at once photographed and permanently revealed by a few lines of burlesque comment and the incomparable report of his toast-speech on *The Strangers*, the entire creation being accomplished in a sort of unconscious addendum to the scholar's smiling apostrophe:

> Bid me not, grammar-defying, repeat from grammar-defiers
> Long constructions strange and plusquam-Thucydidean.

—the last epithet a paragraph in itself.[1] There lacks nothing to indicate the entire Highland environment; and with the all-round allusion

---

[1] The general reader will perhaps excuse an elucidatory reference to a choice sample of Anglo-Thucydidese in the footnote on page 300 of Marsh and Smith's *Student's Manual of the English Language*. (R's note.)

there is thrown in one entirely sufficient vignette of the students'
living-place and bathing-place:

> Where over a ledge of granite
> Into a granite basin the amber torrent descended,
> Only a step from the cottage, the road and the larches between them.

So matchlessly vivid is it all that one could almost swear it a faithful
transcript from actual fact; but the chances are that the total opening
section, like the piece as a whole, is an artistic combination of various
recollections and various fancies. In the first edition the 'pastoral' is
thus dedicated: 'My long-vacation pupils will I hope allow me to
inscribe this trifle to them, and will not, I trust, be displeased if in a
fiction, purely fiction, they are here and there reminded of times we
enjoyed together.' It could be wished that some of these pupils had
put on record, for the enlightenment of future critics, some note as
to the element of traceable fact in the artistic whole.

The easily evolving story of the *Bothie* is so steadily pregnant from
first to last that to touch on all its good points would be to make a
commentary much longer than the book; and it must suffice me here
to touch on one or two points only before turning to the *Amours de
Voyage*. One is, the success with which Clough has given us, in Hewson, a type of hot-headed young enthusiast, in such a way as to secure
abundant sympathy and full understanding, without for a moment
turning him into a hero and challenging our homage. Where before
had anything of the kind been done? I cannot recall a youthful Radical
in English fiction who is not either intellectually magnified, or handled
with a hostile animus, or thrust down our throats. In Clough there is
no such malpractice: the lad is treated with absolute insight and absolute kindliness, yet without a shade of flattery, and becomes for us,
enthusiast as he is, as absolutely real as Sir Hector, or as any observed
personage in any novel; and how much fictional skill went to doing
this can only be indicated by suggesting a comparison of Hewson
with any other imagined young democrat the reader can think of,
Felix Holt included. Another noteworthy feature is the presentment of
the girl Elspie Mackaye, a study which may be suspected of idealism,
but which is yet wonderfully true, as those who have known the
Highlands at all widely or intimately can testify. Elspie is perhaps
specifically the Highland girl of a fine type as one sees her in vacation-
time; but, granting that, she is charmingly well drawn; and the proportion of idealisation is, it may be said without hesitation, much

353

below that infused in Dorothea Brooke or Maggie Tulliver, not to speak of Myra and Romola. It may be doubted, indeed, if she is not to the full as true as Ethel Newcome. Now, this again constitutes a great success, when it is considered how lightly, how dramatically, Clough has laid his touches on. Girls of the people we have had in abundance in more recent fiction; but one so estimable and yet so little idealised, or one drawn with such strong simplicity, it will not be easy to call to mind; and I can think of nothing so good of earlier date.

A power to paint women of another type might very safely have been inferred from the sketch of Elspie in the *Bothie*; but the *Amours de Voyage* furnishes the decisive proof. Having the encouragement of the judgment of most of his readers to consider the *Bothie* a success, Clough made his next attempt at fiction an essay in hexameters likewise; this time, however, so obviously disclaiming a poetic purpose, by throwing his story into the form of letters, that the fact of its not having been generally dealt with as a novel is a little surprising. The power of the character studies in the *Amours*, as in the *Bothie*, has not been overlooked; but what has been awanting is the distinct recognition that in both works the versifier has surpassed the existing prose fiction on its own ground. For the whole work of these Italian letters is no less fine, if less brilliant in form, than that of the earlier composition; the quieter tone being in fact the outcome of the greater subtlety of the study. What he attempted in this case was a study of the mind of a cultured and original Englishman in Rome, as acted upon on the one hand by the historic associations of the city and the contemporary problems connected with that history, and on the other by his intercourse with the inevitable person of the other sex, with whom he gradually falls in love, though the affair, so far as the story goes, comes to nothing. Told in its scanty detail, the narrative is about as slight as a fiction could well be; but it is just the investing of such a plot with permanent interest that makes the work the masterpiece it is. As in the earlier piece, the workmanship is perfect nearly all round. There is no inadequacy. The commentary on Rome and its history; the sketch of the acquaintances whose appearance on the scene begins the story; the man's self-criticism and self-satire; the woman's reticent self-revelation; the prattle of the sister; the interludes on the Roman political situation; the chimes of half-elevated song that seem to lend themselves subtly to the note of passion, at first obscure, afterwards swelling to something of a lyric strain, only to die away finally in the minor— it is all masterly, as perfect as it is original. We shall not see just such another performance. Hexameter stories in imitation of Clough would be by many degrees more unsatisfactory than imitations of Whitman, for the simple reason that his work is so infinitely more difficult to equal; but it seems to me to-day, looking first at Clough's work and then at the developments fiction has taken and is taking in Russia, France, and America, that here in England this merely privately famous man of the schools had curiously anticipated later tendencies and achievements by a whole generation. All that is most characteristic of the best new work—the graded half-tints, the simple drawing, the avoidance of glare and melodrama, the search for the essential interest of the normal—all of it belongs to these experiments in hexameters. There has been no equally good portraiture of feminine character *in minimis* and in whole before or since. But, what is more, Clough had really philosophised his fiction in a style quite beyond the faculty of all but one or two of the moderns; contriving to make an intellectual man both ideally impressive and artistically true; a rare feat in the novel, where the anatomy of the higher grades of mind has hitherto been attempted with so little real success. The forceful simplicity of the unpretentious drawing of Claude can be best appreciated when contrasted with the labour bestowed on Daniel Deronda—and the result. Clough's work has the masculine weight and precision that in Turguénief makes a short story live in the reader's mind like a great experience. Much tolerable workmanship will be forgotten before this.

There is, indeed, an air of paradox in saying that one of the ablest performances in modern fiction, which at its best is above all things naturalistic, is one cast in the artificial form of letters in verse; and certainly the phenomenon is fitted to make us very careful how we theorise about right and wrong in art forms. Say what we will about hexameters, it is clear that these verse-novels of Clough's are 'idealised' work as beside prose realism: so far as treatment goes, the method is obviously not that of naturalist fiction. In fact, Clough is at times not careful to preserve verisimilitude even within his artistic limits; as when he makes one of Mary Trevellyn's letters to Miss Roper[1] begin thus:

> You are at Lucca baths, you tell me, to stay for the summer;
> Florence was quite too hot; you can't move further at present.
> Will you not come, do you think, before the summer is over?

Since the letter could obviously have been made to read in a less

[1] Canto v. 3.

impossible manner and yet convey all the facts required, the work-manship here must be pronounced faulty. But, making allowance for such faults of detail, which belong to inexperience in an uncommon method, what could be more essentially naturalistic than the whole presentment of the women's cast of mind and way of taking things? It is singular how perfectly the contents of actual letters are suggested in Clough's hexameters; so scrupulously sunk to the strictly prosaic level, wherever necessary, as to stop just short of the flavour of bur-lesque. Lines which in themselves are absolutely *banal*, conveying epistolary phrases also *banal* in themselves, yet curiously retain just the needful artistic value for the suggestion of a girl's femininely veiled emotions and hopes and fears; the commonplace letter becomes alive for us by its burden of narrative implication, very much as it would in a novel as realistic as sifted prose could make it. Indeed we may search a hundred prose novels in vain for such delicate fidelity of suggestion. The touches in the portrait are as refined as any of Mr. Henry James; and yet how much more real is the lady than some of that artist's presentments!

But no less essentially true, on the other hand, does the painting remain when it rises above the common-place into sheer poetry, as in these fine lines[1] in which Claude comments on the failure of the Italian rising:

> Whither depart the souls of the brave that die in the battle,
> Die in the lost, lost fight, for the cause that perishes with them?
> Are they upborne from the field on the slumberous pinions of angels
> Unto a far-off home, where the weary rest from their labour,
> And the deep wounds are healed, and the bitter and burning moisture
> Wiped from the generous eyes? or do they linger unhappy,
> Pining, and haunting the grave of their bygone hope and endeavour?

If there were any danger of this apostrophe lessening our sense of the reality of the sceptical, critical young Englishman, unrestfully musing at Rome, it would be sufficiently averted by the unflinching fall of key and pitch that follows:

> All declamation, alas! though I talk, I care not for home nor
> Italy; feebly and faintly, and but with the lips can lament the
> Wreck of the Lombard youth, and the victory of the oppressor.
> Whither depart the brave?—God knows; I certainly do not.

The snatch of poetry, equally with the half-real half-affected cynicism, and with the general mordant criticism on Rome and hu-

[1] Canto v. 6.

manity and its ways, is part of the presentation of the young man's mind; a true product of the century in its restless analysis of its instincts. Nothing in the story is more dramatically convincing than the hero's passage from the analytical mood to that of charmed surrender to the feminine attraction he had just been analysing. Half-way, we have this:—

Allah is great, no doubt, and Juxtaposition his prophet.
Ah, but the women, alas! they don't look at it in that way.
Juxtaposition is great;—but, my friend, I fear me, the maiden
Hardly would thank or acknowledge the lover that sought to obtain her,
Not as the thing he would wish, but the thing he must even put up with . . .
Ah, ye feminine souls, so loving, and so exacting,
Since we cannot escape, must we even submit to deceive you?
Since, so cruel is truth, sincerity shocks and revolts you,
Will you have us your slaves to lie to you, flatter and—leave you?

The girl indeed did not 'look at it that way;' the one sex being as faithfully reproduced as the other. Her first judgment is perfectly 'observed':

> I do not like him much, though I do not dislike being with him.
> He is what people call, I suppose, a superior man, and
> Certainly seems so to me; but I think he is terribly selfish.

Later we learn from the silly sister that

> Mary allows she was wrong about Mr. Claude *being selfish;*
> He was *most* useful and kind on the terrible thirtieth of April.

And in a postscript:

> Mary has seen thus far.—I am really so angry, Louisa—
> Quite out of patience, my dearest! What can the man be intending?
> I am quite tired; and Mary, who might bring him to in a moment,
> Lets him go on as he likes, and neither will help nor dismiss him.

He indeed did not make rapid progress, for before the doctrine of Juxtaposition we had this:

> I am in love, you declare. I think not so; yet I grant you
> It is a pleasure indeed to converse with this girl. Oh, rare gift,
> Rare felicity, this! she can talk in a rational way, can
> Speak upon subjects that really are matters of mind and of thinking
> Yet in perfection retain her simplicity. . . .
> No, though she talk, it is music; her fingers desert not the keys; 'tis
> Song, though you hear in the song the articulate vocables sounded,

Syllabled singly and sweetly the words of melodious meaning.
I am in love, you say; I do not think so, exactly.

And still the woman is woman, as in this postscript to a letter of the silly sister:

> . . . All I can say for myself is, alas! that he rather repels me.
> There! I think him agreeable, but also a little repulsive.
> So be content, dear Louisa; for one satisfactory marriage
> Surely will do in one year for the family you would establish;
> Neither Susan nor I shall afford you the joy of a second.

To which the silly sister adds a post-postscript:

> Mr. Claude, you must know, is behaving a little bit better;
> He and Papa are great friends; but he really is too *shilly-shally*,
> So unlike George! Yet I hope that the matter is going on fairly.
> I shall, however, get George, before he goes, to say something.
> Dearest Louise, how delightful to bring young people together!

And yet again the girl, after a 'let us say nothing further about it' as to a deviation of Mr. Claude from the agreed-on travelling plan of the party, half opens her heart thus:

> Yes, my dear Miss Roper, I certainly called him repulsive;
> So I think him, but cannot be sure I have used the expression
> Quite as your pupil should; yet he does most truly repel me.
> Was it to you I made use of the word? or who was it told you?
> Yes, repulsive; observe, it is but when he talks of ideas
> That he is quite unaffected, and free, and expansive, and easy;
> I could pronounce him simply a cold intellectual being.—
> When does he make advances?—He thinks that women should woo him;
> Yet, if a girl should do so, would be but alarmed and disgusted.
> She that should love him must look for small love in return; like the ivy,
> On the stone wall, must expect but a rigid and niggard support, and
> E'en to get that must go searching all round with her humble embraces.

And he too had his reasons:

> Is it my fault, as it is my misfortune, my ways are not her ways?
> Is it my fault that my habits and ways are dissimilar wholly?
> 'Tis not her fault; 'tis her nature, her virtue, to misapprehend them;
> 'Tis not her fault; 'tis her beautiful nature not ever to know me.
> Hopeless it seems—yet I cannot, though hopeless, determine to leave it;
> She goes—therefore I go; she moves—I move, not to lose her.

And then comes the swerving aside, the result of the silly sister's George having said

> Something to Mr. Claude about what they call his attentions;

and Mary's postscripts multiply, and Miss Roper explains, and Mr. Claude eagerly decides to follow and propose; and the travellers journey at cross purposes and never meet; and the foiled lover, half content to accept the decision of Fate, decides to winter in Egypt, while the now heart-sore Mary returns with her party to England. There is something peculiarly modern in this ending that is no ending; something indefinitely in advance, technically speaking, of the symmetrical *dénouements* of previous fiction; something artistically in advance of much good fiction of our own time. Alike artistically and philosophically the whole is closed by one of the half-lyric strains which begin and end the cantos:

> So go forth to the world, to the good report and the evil!
> Go, little book! thy tale, is it not evil and good?
> Go, and if strangers revile, pass quietly by without answer.
> Go, and if curious friends ask of thy rearing and age,
> Say 'I am flitting about many years from brain unto brain o
> Feeble and restless youths born to inglorious days:
> But,' so finish the word, 'I was writ in a Roman chamber,
> When from Janiculan heights thundered the cannon of France.'

The end is thus fittingly on the plane of idealist art; and yet who will say that the whole has not been as rigorously true a presentment of the literal life as the most determined naturalist could achieve? It is English naturalism, certainly: Clough, whose 'name is handed down in William Arnold's *Rules of Football* as the best goal-keeper on record',[1] was substantially English in his tastes. But all the same he had here succeeded in putting into an unlikely enough and ostensibly idealist art-form a piece of character fiction more essentially naturalistic than anything produced anywhere up to his time; nay, more deeply so than anything done in the forty years since, for he had contrived to handle a man's philosophy and a woman's emotions in a love-story with equal ease and verisimilitude, and to give his tale in hexameters a philosophic ripeness without a tinge of pedantry. The critical lesson is the old one that there are no rules for geniuses; that, as it has been put afresh by a gifted though faulty fictionist of our own day, Mr. Moore, 'art is eternal; that it is only the artist that changes; and that

---

[1] *PPR I.* 'Memoir', 11.

the two great divisions—the only possible divisions—are, those who have talent, and those who have no talent.'[1]

For most men verisimilitude in fiction and drama will be best attainable by the most strictly natural media; but Shakspere, again, could put more reality into blank verse dialogue than the Nashes and Lylys could put into prose; and there is no calculating the capacity of an original faculty to innovate in method, or to lead captive the captivity of form. And I do not scruple to risk derision by thus mentioning Clough in the same breath with Shakspere, being satisfied that he had some measure of Shakspere's endowment; though the scanty recognition of it among his countrymen promises small acceptance for such a view.

It may well be that it is the smallness of Clough's product that has hindered the recognition of his real greatness; mere volume counting for so much in the impression made on the world even by fine work; and it may be too that his comparative failure in serious poetry has affected the general attitude toward his whole remains. I say comparative failure; for his poetry well-nigh makes up by its deep intellectual interest for its lack of the true poetic charm. *Dipsychus* and the rest of it is indeed better worth reading than a good deal of verse of much wider vogue.[2] It has not, however, truly caught either the trained or the untrained ear; and this, with the habit of treating his hexameters as being equally with the rest essays in the poetic art, goes far to account for the limited character of his reputation. Then his *Mari Magno: or, Tales on Board* must have helped to subdue the critical tone in his regard, for here, there can be no doubt, the artistic failure is as complete as the earlier success. To account for it, we must fall back on the accounts we have of Clough's mental constitution—the

[1] *Confessions of a Young Man*, p. 121.

[2] Mr. Lowell has twice spoken very highly of Clough's poetic merit, but with significant differences of expression. One passage runs:—'Clough, whose poetry will one of these days, perhaps, be found to have been the *best utterance in verse* of this generation' (Essay 'On a Certain Condescension in Foreigners,' *My Study Windows*, 6th ed., p. 56). The other is,

We have a foreboding that Clough, imperfect as he was in many respects, and dying before he had subdued his sensitive temperament to the sterner requirements of his art, will be thought a hundred years hence to have been the *truest expression in verse* of the *moral and intellectual tendencies*, the doubt and struggle towards settled convictions, *of the period in which he lived*.

(Essay on 'Swinburne's Tragedies,' *ibid.* p. 157.)

The latter verdict will doubtless hold good of Clough's total product, but it in effect gives up the point of his strictly poetic success. (R's note.) Cf. Introduction, p. 12.

slowness of his mind to set to work at all times, and the conditions of his health in his later years. He had written his good things under the two strong impulses of physical vigour and Italian travel; and in the absence of similarly happy conditions he produced nothing more that could be ranked beside them. In the *Mari Magno* we have an all too decisive test of the fitness of rhymed verse as a vehicle for narrative that aims at being serious without being archaic; and a proof of Clough's wisdom in choosing the hexameter even where his purpose was not tinged with humour. In that, the freedom of the medium allowed him to be serious and impressive when he wanted; in the rhymed pentameter, applied to fictional purpose, verisimilitude was far harder to reach; and even the simple seriousness that was all he now had in his mind is continually turned to absurdity by the pitfalls of the rhyme. When a man gravely writes in the couplet measure of 'A beauteous woman at the table d'hôte;' and tells how, on board ship, he

> amid a dream
> Of England, knew the letting-off of steam—

artistic charm is over and done with. The couplet, like the hexameter, might have been used humorously; but for a sober, matter-of-fact tale, as Crabbe had sufficiently shown, it is the fatallest of all metrical conveyances.

And yet in these hopeless verses are contained two tales which, in their structure and detail, still betray the mind of a born fictionist; a mind which sees characters instantaneously as organic wholes, and has no more difficulty in presenting them with all their specific differences than a good portraitist has in giving the lines of different faces. We are told that Clough had a wonderful eye for scenery, remembering the hang and lie of roads and hills, streams and valleys, in a fashion that surprised his friends. He had just such a faculty for discriminating character. The slightly-sketched tale-tellers in the *Mari Magno* are like drawings by Keene; and through the racking couplets the people of the stories, especially of the second, keep their form and colour with the same steadiness that is seen in the hexameter novels. The old curious felicity of indicating a character by a few touches is not gone; and the reader, when he can forget the versification, seems to have gained some new knowledge of life from the few pages he has turned over. The people are 'observed:' we feel that we have been reading transcripts from actual private histories. And we can understand how

361

different from ordinary biographical eulogy is Professor Shairp's reminiscence, à propos of Clough's unsuccessful try for a Balliol Fellowship in 1842: 'I remember one of [the examiners] telling me at the time that a character of Saul which Clough wrote in that examination was, I think he said, the best and most original thing he had ever seen written in any examination.' Why, with this genius for a great art, Clough did so little in it, and never seemed even to realise clearly where his genius lay—this is a question the answering of which raises divers points as to his total idiosyncrasy, his training, and his intellectual environment.

Something has to be allowed for a constitutional lack of productive energy, otherwise definable as intellectual fastidiousness, the physical side of which is perhaps to be looked for by the clue of the paralysis which finally struck him down after a fever. Of his character as seen in childhood his sister testifies: 'One trait I distinctly remember, that he would always do things from his own choice, and not merely copy what others were doing.' And again: 'Arthur even then was too fastidious to take off his shoes and stockings and paddle about as we did.'[1] The child was father to the man. Nor was native fastidiousness the only force at work. In his prime he gives, in a letter to a friend, this account of his hard schooling:

I may, perhaps, be idle now; but when I was a boy, between fourteen and twenty-two throughout, I may say, you don't know how much regular drudgery I went through. Holidays after holidays, when I was at school, after a week or so of recreation, which very rarely came in an enjoyable form to me, the whole remaining five or six weeks I used to give to regular work at fixed hours. That wasn't so very easy for a schoolboy spending holidays, not at home, but with uncles, aunts, and cousins. All this and whatever work, less rigorous though pretty regular, that has followed since during the last ten years has been, so far as external results go, perhaps a mere blank and waste; nothing very tangible has come of it; but still it is some justification to me for being less strict with myself now. Certainly, as a boy, I had less of boyish enjoyment of any kind whatsoever, either at home or at school, than nine-tenths of boys, at any rate of boys who go to school, college, and the like; certainly, even as a man I think I have earned myself some title to live for some little interval, I do not say in enjoyment, but without immediate devotion to particular objects, on matters as it were of business.[2]

And to that picture of destructive education he adds another touch in the 'Passage on Oxford Studies' extracted in the *Prose Remains*, de-

[1] Memoir in *PPR I*, 4, 16.   [2] *PPR I*, 173-4.

scribing the sickness of heart that overtook him on going to the university, at the prospect of endless classics: 'An infinite lassitude and impatience, which I saw reflected in the faces of others, quickly began to infect me.' Such a youthful experience must have told on the adult man, laming the springs of creative energy and dispiriting the abnormal genius.[1] But it is with a sense of fresh exasperation that one thinks of such a faculty being further weakened for practical performance by the effeminate ecclesiastical atmosphere of the Oxford of the Newman epoch, when currents of febrile mysticism and timorous scepticism drew young men this way and that; not one in a hundred of those affected being able to attain a stable and virile philosophy. Clough himself said afterwards that for two years he had been 'like a straw drawn up the draught of a chimney' by the Newman movement; and it would not be going too far to say that if he were not one of those 'wrecks' declared by Mr. Gladstone to have been 'strewn on every shore' by the academic tempest in question, he was at least left less seaworthy for life. It has become a little difficult to think either of the mystics or of the half-hearted sceptics as men of high intellectual power: it seems a trifle strange in these days that one such as Clough, having once realised the force of the rational criticism of the popular creed, should be unable robustly to readjust his life to the sane theory of things. But so it was. The character-student suffered as much from the disintegration of his inherited faith as did any hectic disciple of them all; and when he found he could be neither Catholic nor Protestant he seemed to lapse into a sense of intellectual homelessness. The English universities, in which the nation's best educational endowments are turned mainly to the account of training men to preach to the illiterate or the unquestioning the religious system of the Dark Ages, seem to unfit men systematically for any independent appraisement or application of their natural powers. The reigning theory of things in these venerable halls—at least till just the other day—was that a scholar, having undergone the venerable curriculum, is to be a clergyman or a barrister, or possibly a doctor, or alternatively a private gentleman or politician or ornamental man of business, agreeably conscious, through a gentlemanly middle life, of once having studied the classics. Thackeray only took to literature for sheer need of money; Lytton is almost our only other novelist who had an academic preparation, and as an artist he gained little enough by it, though one

---

[1] At Oxford, according to Clough, who was, however, probably exaggerating, the verdict on the *Bothie* was that it was 'indecent and profane, immoral and (!) communistic.'

can see that the same preparation can be very valuable in many ways, apart from the mere instruction it nominally implies. Spencer, Grote, Mill, and Lewes—not to speak of Gibbon—almost seem to owe their power of working on original lines to the accident of missing the university stamp; Darwin, Huxley, and Tyndall, to judge by results, need never have entered a college door. Even the late Professor Balfour remains a promise of possibilities.

But this by the way. The relevant facts for us here are that Clough, missing what seemed his natural career as a priest, had yet been so permeated by the ecclesiastical and university view of human activity as to be in a measure unfitted to apply his powers in any other way. He could not settle down peacefully in intercourse with men who had definitively turned their backs on an impossible faith: there is evidence that he found such men uncongenial in their decided rationalism, as they doubtless found him in his melancholy retrospectiveness. One feels that just twenty years earlier the same Clough could have quietly found his way into the clerical grooves, like many another man of potential genius, leaving no literary legacy of any importance to his countrymen, and living to face alike Strauss and Newman with the sheathing prejudices of profession and habit. In fine, we may say that he stood in religion and philosophy as he did in his fiction—between two widely-different generations; sundered from the past, but slow to begin to face the future. But whereas his religion had been a profound prepossession, the removal of which taxed his whole moral nature and left him lamed with the struggle, his spontaneous and hardly purposive excursion into the field of intellectual art yielded a remarkable result, suggestive no less of the manifold intellectual forces that lie cramped or latent around us, than of the power of certain institutions and conventions to keep them down.

It is not fitting, however, that the last word on such a personality as Clough's should be a suggestion of frustration. Frustration, after all, is a matter of comparison, and whatever impression he may make on later readers, he was to his own generation, which in that way could best judge him, an impressive and not a weak figure. Let us remember him by the words of one whose name will live with his longer than these comments:

[Quotes Arnold's *On Translating Homer: Last Words*: 'I mention him because' to 'naturalness, buoyant rapidity', and 'But that in him' to 'literary life'. See p. 107.]

Homeric simplicity is perhaps not the description which would suggest itself to most men; but whatever words can serve the literary memory of the author of *The Bothie of Tober-na-Vuolich* and *Amours de Voyage* will be ungrudgingly allowed by those who can appreciate the singular independence of his work.

55. Unsigned article, 'Clough and his Defender' in the *Academy*

2 October 1897

In a recent review of Mr. John Mackinnon Robertson's volume, *New Essays towards a Critical Method*, an allusion was made to the somewhat curious appreciation of Arthur Hugh Clough's verse which it contains. Clough's reputation might be thought to have so waned and dwindled during the last twenty years among all classes of readers that it might seem by this time to have well-nigh reached its vanishing point. As a member of a famous group of Rugby men, he is held by many to have been thrust into a position of eminence which his work never really merited, and the charm of his personality seems, during his life, and even after his death, to have enlisted for him the rather undiscriminating admiration of a powerful circle, especially among Oxford men, who exerted themselves to thrust him down the throats of an undiscerning public. But the cult of Clough has died entirely in the Oxford of to-day, and if it lingers at all among men of letters, it seldom makes itself heard. By most of us Clough, particularly Clough the poet, has been weighed in the balance and found wanting. One or two of his lyrics in the Arnold manner are occasionally quoted, and one may admire the dexterity and adroitness of *The Latest Decalogue*. But *The Bothie of Tober-na-Vuolich* (which we cannot pronounce) and the *Amours de Voyage* (which we cannot read) are dead past recall.

This, we say, was, or so we thought, the general opinion. The *Bothie*, as we all know, is not poetry, or anything at all like poetry—it is burdened with a detestable metre. No one, we imagine, at this time of day defends the classical hexameter as a possible form in English verse, and it is exceptionally tiresome reading. Mr. Robertson, however, holds a different opinion. He does not, of course, defend the *Bothie* or the *Amours de Voyage* as poetry. That, we imagine, is past the capacity of even the most tolerant or the most eccentric critic. He therefore throws them overboard as poems, and proceeds to eulogise them as prose! Let us quote his own words in order to be sure to do him justice.

[Quotes Robertson, 'I do not believe that, in writing the *Bothie*' to 'we should be stating the plain truth', see above, pp. 348-9.]

We confess that all this certainly does incline us to 'raise the further question' why Clough did *not* write prose, graduated or otherwise, if the effect he aimed at was not a poetic one. And without troubling to go into the question of what Clough had or had not in his mind in the years 1848 and 1849, a question which obviously admits of no sort of final solution, we may say at once that the important point to us is that the effect which he *did* achieve was certainly not poetic. But Mr. Robertson's contention raises, to our thinking, the much more interesting question whether it is any defence of a poem to say that it makes excellent prose fiction. In fact, when you have settled in your own mind that a poem is not a poem, is there any ground left on which you can defend it? Mr. Robertson maintains that there is; that analysis of character, truthful observation, depth of suggestion, and the rest suffice to raise Clough's detestable hexameters into the region if not of great poets at least of great masters of fiction. The theory is an ingenious one, but in our opinion somewhat dangerous. It is a little like praising a picture while admitting that it is abominably painted, a thing which is seldom done at least by the critical.

But it is evident that Clough's hexameters do not offend Mr. Robertson in the way, or at least to the extent, that they offend many people. He quotes, apparently without a shudder, even with enjoyment, such lines as these:

Allah is great no doubt, and juxtaposition his prophet.
Ah, but the women, alas! they don't look at it in that way.
Juxtaposition is great; but, my friend, I fear me, the maiden
Hardly would think or acknowledge the love that sought to obtain her,
Not as the thing he would wish, but the thing he must even put up with. . . .
Ah, ye feminine souls, so loving, and so exacting,

Since we cannot escape, must we even submit to deceive you?
Since, so cruel is truth, sincerity shocks and revolts you,
Will you have us your slaves to lie to you, flatter, and—leave you?

And this again we choose from his selections at random. The others
are quite as bad.

I do not like him much, though I do not dislike being with him,
He is what people call, I suppose, a superior man, and
Certainly seems so to me; but I think he is terribly selfish.

It is certainly as well that Mr. Robertson did not take up the cudgels
for this on poetic grounds. But is it legitimate even as prose? Will it
stand the great test? Can one read it?

That seems to us to be the crucial point with regard to Clough.
Can anyone with an ear of even ordinary sensitiveness read stuff of this
kind for any length of time with patience? Can he read it without
actual suffering? We think not. We quite admit that in all long narrative poems, from Homer downwards, there will always be found
passages here and there deficient in interest, deficient in charm, unsatisfactory in rhythm. The hand of the potter will shake now and
then. But mere doggerel is unpardonable, and this stuff is mere
doggerel. Mr. Robertson says it is amusing doggerel. That is a matter
of taste, and on a question of humour it is impossible to dogmatise.
We fail to find it amusing. It may be urged that in satirical verse and
in humorous verse poetical excellence is often sacrificed, and that
effects, especially in satire, are often produced by means that would be
entirely unpermissible in lyric or even in heroic verse. This is true
enough, but satire, too, has its rules and its limitations, and, as long as
it employs metre at all, must reckon with metre for its effects. The
success of Juvenal, the success of Johnson, the success of *Hudibras*, is
achieved by means of the verse, and not in spite of it. Mr. Robertson,
however, would have us believe that the splendours of the *Bothie*
and the *Amours* exist in spite of their metrical form. Indeed, we gather
that he would have been only too glad—as also should we—if Clough
had written them in honest homely prose. He does not venture to
defend the hexameter form even for analytical fiction. He merely
recognises, in Clough's case, what he calls its necessity. We, unfortunately, recognise nothing of the kind. In our view Clough was the
victim of a fatal delusion with regard to classical hexameters in believing that they could be successfully employed in English. It may
have been partly what Mr. Robertson calls 'the exuberance of the

holiday-making undergraduate,' which caused him to attempt to employ the metre of Homer and Virgil in English poetry, but it must also have implied a certain defective sensibility to sound and rhythm not to have promptly abandoned the experiment.

It is inconceivable that anyone of real poetic instinct and feeling should have found the hexameters of the *Bothie* either impressive or amusing. Mr. Robertson says that Clough probably did not think hexameters, *quâ* hexameters, 'tractable to *serious* (English) verse.' Our contention is that he ought not to have considered them tractable to English verse at all, and that if he did so originally, the *Bothie*, and the rest, not to mention Longfellow's *Evangeline*, should have sufficed to undeceive him. If his sense of rhythm was not strong enough to save him from so unwise an adventure, his sense of humour—Mr. Robertson declares that he had a sense of humour—should have been strong enough for the purpose. Altogether we are afraid that the zeal of his new defender will not avail to put Clough once more upon the pedestal. In the words of Swift—

His kind of wit is out of date.[1]

And so is his kind of verse.

56. E. Forster, from a letter replying to the above, in the *Academy*

20 October 1897, 331

In the *Academy* of October 2 your reviewer writes an article on Arthur Hugh Clough, which, as a life-long admirer and careful student of that poet, I should much like to supplement.

The writer states it as his opinion that the reputation of Clough has reached its vanishing point, and that 'his kind of wit,' as well as his 'kind of verse,' is out of date.

[1] 'Verses on the Death of Dr. Swift'.

This may be so, perhaps, with regard to some of his poems, especially those to which the writer confines himself. The *Bothie* is, undoubtedly, laborious reading, and the *Amours de Voyage* are as bad, if not worse. But it is not for the sake of these, or even 'one or two lyrics in the Arnold manner,' that I venture to think the name of Clough will be still long remembered.

One of our critics wrote some years ago: 'Clough was the poet of devout scepticism, as Arnold was the poet of devout unbelief.' Whether this judgment be true or not, it is pre-eminently as a religious poet that Clough takes his place among the earlier writers of the century. The author of *Dipsychus* and *Poems on Life and Duty* may surely claim an equal rank with Matthew Arnold. It must be allowed he had not the same happy turn for metre and rhythm as his friend, but he possessed what in Arnold is so often wanting—a keen sense of humour. It would be hard to name any poet—unless it be Heine—in which the pathetic and the ludicrous, the tragedy and comedy, are so inextricably mingled. Where shall we find, for instance, such a felicitous summary of the problems of life as in the utterance of the Spirit in *Dipsychus*:

> This world is very odd, we see,
> We do not comprehend it;
> But in one fact we all agree,
> God won't, and we can't mend it.

The actual sum total of his philosophy—as deduced from his poems —may not amount to very much. As he says, his desire was rather

> Oh, let me love my love unto myself alone,
> And know my knowledge to the world unknown.

Yet in his negative teaching he is often very daring in his expression. If the author of 'Obermann' considered it 'a gratifying marvel' that the Archbishop should invite him once a year to dinner, what is to be said for the writer of 'Easter Day,' with its persistent refrain:

> Christ is not risen—No!
> He lies and moulders low?

In all those minds on whom the problems of the day still press un-solved and apparently insoluble, A. H. Clough yet holds an honoured place. We may regret that he should ever have written the *Bothie*— which we agree with your reviewer in not being able to pronounce— but we can well forgive the error for the sake of the many fine poems he wrote—*not* in hexameters!

57. Stopford A. Brooke, part of 'Arthur Hugh Clough' from *Four Poets: A Study of Clough, Arnold, Rossetti and Morris*

1908, 26–47

Stopford Augustus Brooke was educated at Trinity College, Dublin, and ordained in 1857. He left the Anglican Church in 1880 and became a celebrated chapel minister. His *Primer of English Literature* (1876), which was very favourably noticed by Matthew Arnold (see *Mixed Essays*, 1879), was Brooke's best known work.

Writing to Viscount Bryce in September 1908, after the publication of *Four Poets*, Stopford Brooke summed up his view of Clough as follows:

> I have always liked Clough better than others who have expressed surprise that I wrote about him at all. That fine, sub-gentle, surface-dabbling spirit of his does not belong to the modern poets who must run glittering 'in the open sunlight or they are unblest.' He did not ask himself why he wrote, but just wrote out of his soul which was always roving through little woods of thought where pleasant streams made a quiet noise; and he didn't care a withered leaf what the world thought of him.
>
> (Quoted in Lawrence Pearsall Jacks, *Life and Letters of Stopford Brooke*, London 1917, II, 644.)

Thus Clough is with Shakespeare at last, warbling 'his native woodnotes wild' . . .

Of all the poets who played on England as on a harp, Clough was one of the most personal. He was even more personal than Arnold, who could detach himself at times from himself. But Clough was never self-detached in his poetry, even when he tried to be so. He contemplated his soul and its sensitive and bewildered workings incessantly, and saw in them the image of that which was going on in the soul of the younger men in England. Sometimes he is intensely part of the spiritual strife he is conscious of, because he is so conscious of it in himself; sometimes he watches it from without, as a Press correspondent might the battle he describes; sometimes, in the course of a single poem, he flits from the inside to the outside position, or from the outside to the inside; but always it is the greater image of his own soul that he watches in the struggle of the whole; always he is intimately close to the trouble or calm, the wondering or the anchoring of the eager, restless, searching, drifting being within, whom he did not wish to be himself. No one is more intimate, more close, more true to this inward life. It is this which makes him so interesting and so much a favourite with those who like him. They see a man in much the same condition as they are, or have been, themselves; they feel that he has been quite true to himself in it, and has done his very best to tell the truth—and to read true things said truly is always a keen, if sometimes a sorrowful pleasure. Moreover, no obscurity, no vagueness, troubles the reader. We are conscious that he has striven with all his might to render the matter in question into the most lucid form he can; and few have put remote and involved matters of the soul into such simple words as Clough.

Again, we see, through all the confused trouble he describes, and in spite of all the wavering and uncertainty, that he has one clear aim—that of getting out of the storm, if possible, into some bright light and quiet air. He does not like the confusion and the questioning, and the trouble, but desires to be quit of them, if this can be done truthfully. He will not shut his eyes to any difficulty, nor retire to his tent while the battle is going on, nor pretend there is no confusion, for the sake of light and sweetness. Truth to himself first—then he will be fit to see the Truth itself, if it be possible. But it is his aim, his hope, his impassioned desire, even in despair, to see it at last. That Truth *is*, he believes; and he sets himself to work his way to it through the tangled forest of life.

> It fortifies my soul to know
> That, though I perish, Truth is so:
> That, howsoe'er I stray and range,
> Whate'er I do, Thou dost not change.
> I steadier step when I recall
> That, if I slip, Thou dost not fall.

To a certain degree then, he was above scepticism. He did not think

371

it a fine condition; the last thing he imagined was that there was any reason for being proud of it; nevertheless he would not move one inch out of it till his reason and conscience together told him he might leave this or that question behind. The only thing he knew was that there was a clear solution to be found somewhere, sometime, in the Truth itself. Even the star of that knowledge was sometimes overwhelmed in clouds. He kept his head and heart however; he was finally master in his soul. He moved amid the disorganised army of his thoughts and emotions, like a great captain who sees and knows the troubled state of his army, and the desperate and broken ground over which it has to advance; who visits every regiment and knows the wants of each; who has entered every tent, who is aware of the fears, doubts, failures and despairs of every man—but who is determined to lead the army on, because he knows that, far away, there is a safe and quiet resting-place—soft grass and clear streams within a fortified defence—where he can camp them at last, order them, and restore their spirit. Sometimes he is all but hopeless; whence he has brought the armies of his soul he cannot tell; whither they are going he cannot tell; all is doubt and trouble; but again, there are hours of rest when the place whither he is going and its far off light are clear; at times he feels a proud joy in the fighting forwards; at times nothing lives but exhaustion, yet he never thinks of surrender. Here is a poem which puts this life of his into clear, gentle, but impassioned form.

[Quotes 'Where lies the land to which the ship would go'.]

Whence and whither our ship came, and goes, and the ship of all humanity, we cannot know, though we may hope to know. We live by faith, not knowledge. Sometimes the battle is illuminated and rejoiced by sudden outflamings of faith; again, it is darkened by absolute despair. Faith in God rushes up one day through the crust of doubt and drowns every sceptical thought; the next day, there is no God. Christ is not risen; the day after He is risen. There is no rest, no clear heaven, no knowledge of whence and whither—nothing but tossing to and fro. Even when he falls back on duty, a voice in his heart tells him it is not enough. He must find the unknown Perfect his soul desires.

At last, he is enraged with his condition. Life is slipping away in overthinking, in this way and that dividing the swift mind. The soul, while he is young, is growing old in a diseased confusion. Is this life, he asks, this the end of our stay on earth?

PERCHE PENSA? PENSANDO S'INVECCHIA[1]

To spend uncounted years of pain,
Again, again and yet again,
In working out in heart and brain
    The problem of our being here;
To gather facts from far and near,
Upon the mind to hold them clear,
And, knowing more may yet appear,
    Unto one's latest breath to fear
The premature result to draw—
Is this the object, end and law,
    And purpose of our being here?

There are those who are not troubled by any such questions, simple
folk who believe and have peace, and Clough praises their life and
thinks them true and happy; at moments he can feel with them, but
not for long. There are others who find peace and power to live and
work by giving up all questions of this kind as hampering life and
useless for good. But Clough was not of that temper, and could not
enter its region. He did his duty, but a tender intensity of passion urged
him beyond it to find the rest in perfection. He was the image and the
expression of thousands who lived in that disturbed time, when criticism and science set the battle in array against the set theology. It is
the image and the expression, even now, after the battle has raged for
sixty years, of the condition of a number of persons who are impassioned to find a faith by which they can live, who desire to believe
but are unable, who are equally unable to find peace in unbelief. Thus
moving, like a Hamlet, through the strifes of theology and religion,
he resembles Hamlet in another way. When the Prince is suddenly
flung into the storm of action, he takes momentarily a fierce part in
it, and enjoys it, till overthinking again seizes on him. Clough repeats
this in his life, and his poetry is touched with it.

These are the causes of the pleasure with which we read Clough's
earlier poetry—its clear image of a certain type of men and women in a
spiritually troubled time, its close contact with and intimate expression
of the constantly debating soul, its truthfulness, its sanity amid scepticism, its statement of all sides of the matter in hand, its personal
humanity, and its sympathy with man, its self-mastery and its clear
aim. There is also plenty of good matter of thought and of emotion
worthily controlled—great things in poetry, provided they are expressed poetically. But the poetry itself is not of a high quality; its

[1] Title supplied by 1869 editors.

373

level is only a third of the way towards greatness; it is imaginative, but the imagination in it never soars and never is on fire, never at a white heat; on the contrary, its play is gentle, soft, touched, like an autumn evening when summer has just died, with tender, clear brooding light. The greater number of these poems are such as a man who lived in a constant atmosphere of trouble and battle might write, when, wearied with the strife, he enjoyed an hour of forgetful rest after trouble, and of sheathing of the sword after battle; and I do not know of any other poet of whom this may be said so truly. In that he is alone—that is the distinction of these early poems. And this clear, soft, brooding note is just as clearly struck in the poems which have nothing to do with the trouble of the soul, but with matter of the affections. I quote this little idyll: how grave it is, and tender; what an evening light rests upon it; not the light of Italy, but of the northern sky among the mountains. What self-control breathes in it; what a quiet heart, quiet, not by the absence of passion, but by self-restraint, and by that on which Clough so often dwelt and which subdued his poetry so often—by the sense of the inevitable, of a fate which, hemming us in on every side, imposes on us its will, and ignores our struggle and our pain;

[Quotes 'Les Vaches', 'The skies have sunk, and hid the upper snow'; under the 1862 title, 'Ite Domum Saturae, Venit Hesperus'.]

There may be, he thinks, inevitable partings, however true men and women be to one another. Life moves us to an end of which we know nothing, which we cannot master.

This is a favourite motive of his, as indeed it was of Matthew Arnold. They must have discussed it a hundred times at Oxford. We may exercise our will on circumstance, but it is of no avail. We try, and try again and yet again, but a little thing, of which we take no note, turns us from the goal. At last we grow wearied of being baffled, and give up the thing we desired; and then in the hour when we have released ourselves from pursuing, we wonder, as we look back, whether we really cared for the thing we pursued, or whether the person we pursued cared for us. A series of slight pressures of circumstance on a dreamy and sensitive soul drifts the will away from its desired goal, and each of the drifts is accepted. Clough must have felt that this was the position of a part of his soul, perhaps with regard to matters of thought, certainly so far as the affections were concerned; or, if that is assuming too much, he must at least have sympathized keenly with this position in others. At any rate, he knew all about it. It is a frequent motive in his poems, and one whole poem, the *Amours de Voyage*, is a careful study of this matter of the heart. Clough seems to take a personal delight in the slow, subtle, close drawing, week by week, of the wavering, wandering, changeful drifting of the heart of the hero, in love, into pursuit, and out of love—never one moment's resolution, never an hour of grip on circumstance, never one bold effort to clench the throat of Fate. Many are involved in similar circumstances, and have a similar temper; and the result in the poem is the exact result of a soul in that condition. And it seemed, I suppose, to Clough that it would be well to paint their condition, to show its folly, its evil and its end. 'Go, little book' he says—

> Go, and if curious friends ask of thy rearing and age,
> Say, 'I am flitting about many years from brain unto brain of
> Feeble and restless youths born to inglorious days.'

Of course, we need not believe in the inevitableness of the position, nor indeed did Clough finally. When he recorded it, he recorded what he had felt and known in himself, but he had passed out of it. Only, what he had then attained—for I think he speaks of himself—'that happiness was to be found in knowledge, that faith passed, and love passed, but that knowledge abided'[1]—was not, it seems, a much better position. Knowledge, to be sure, is a good thing, but it is a foundation for life which is always shifting. Its abiding is only for a short time, and its professors have to relay their foundations. And in the moral realm, in the conduct of life, to say nothing of the spiritual realm, knowledge, or what passes for knowledge, is frightfully insecure, and is attended with one fatal comrade, with pride in itself.

This is always true: 'Knowledge puffeth up, but Love edifieth';[2] and if I may judge from the bulk of his poetry, Clough came to that at last. As to this insistence on fate, on the inevitable in circumstance, it is not an image of true life. Man is not master of the whole of fate, for he is not able to see all, but a great deal of what he thinks inevitable is in his hands. If he cannot climb over obstacles, he can get round them; that is, if he have courage, and chose to exercise his will; to be what he was made to be—a cause in the universe. Fate, as they call it, seems herself to remove the obstruction, if we take her gaily and

---

[1] *Amours de Voyage*, V, 198: 'Faith, I think, does pass, and Love; but knowledge abideth'.

[2] *First Epistle of Paul to the Corinthians*, viii. 1: 'Knowledge puffeth up, but charity edifieth'.

boldly. If we march up to the barrier, we find it to be mere cloud through which we go easily to the other side. It is always wise to disbelieve in obstacles.

If the gentleman in the *Amours de Voyage*, when he found that he had just missed his love at Florence, had not waited to analyse his feelings, and then arrived too late at the next town where she had been, and then paused to analyse again his sensations, and then was the victim of a mis-directed letter, and then gave up his pursuit; had he knit his heart into any resolution, instead of saying 'Whither am I borne,' he would easily have found the girl, and found his happiness. Fate? nine-tenths of fate are in our own hands, but we let the other tenth master us, and then fate fills the nine-tenths which was in our power with her own sombre self. This is our punishment, and we deserve it.

Well, it is a good thing to have the whole matter laid before us with such remarkable closeness and veracity as Clough has done in this poem. Its hero is a characteristic type: cultivated, retiring, disliking society. He has been thrown in the past, like Clough, into a world of jarring strife and noise, of mental and spiritual disturbance. Sensitive, refined till he thrills at a touch, angry with the circumstances of life which call him to act—when action, which forces him into contact with vulgar reality out of philosophic dreams, is as repugnant to him as it was to Hamlet 'a cursed spite' of fate—he welcomes any change, any chance, which takes him out of the world of strife and effort. This also was the case with Clough himself, from whom the hero of the poem is partly drawn.

He was wearied with the strife within; he sought the world without; he welcomed the chance of employment elsewhere. He left Oxford, and afterwards went to America. There he gathered pupils around him at Cambridge, and wrote for the reviews. The things he wrote were not of any high quality; they have not even subtlety; they have no distinction. Uncontent still, he came back, his friends having found him a place in the Education Office, to England. And then, his career being decided for him, and his drifting boat anchored by another hand than his own, he settled down to the prim ways, and regular work, and consistent routine of a government office, with its pleasant holidays. And then, too, he married, and loved his wife, his children and his home; and gathered love around him, and found that love *did* abide and edify. His humour was set free from sorrow. The questions which had so deeply perplexed him were still subjects of careful thought, but they tormented him no more. He passed, we are told, 'from the speculative to the constructive phase of thought,' and would have, had he lived, expressed his matured conceptions of life in a more substantial way. He was happy and useful. He was always oppressed with the 'sadness of the world, and the great difficulties of modern social life,'[1] but he turned his mind steadily, in this atmosphere of love and happiness, and with the deep experience they gave him, to help towards this solution. I wish he had had time to record in poetry his conclusions, but office work is a great disintegrator of poetic creation, and very little was done, and that not good as poetry, before the blind Fury came with the abhorred shears, and slit the thin-spun life.

He was only forty-three years old. The tales published under the title of *Mari magno* were written during the last holidays of his life, while he searched for health, and the last of them when he was dying. They are for the most part concerned with the question of marriage: its true end, its trials, fitness for it, and other matters. They have their own interest, but their main interest, like that of all the poems, is Clough's revelation of his character. He was, with that sensitive nature of his, a reserved man; but when he wrote poetry, the unconscious disclosure of his soul—the piece of human nature he knew best, and in which he was most interested—was so fine and accurate and all the more attractive because it was done unawares—that it fascinates even those readers who do not think highly of the poetry.

There is, however, another element in it which has its own fascination. This is the ceaseless change of mood within one atmosphere, like the ceaseless change of cloud scenery in a day of the same kind of weather from morning to evening. We never can tell what is coming in a poem, what the next verse will bring out, what new turn will be given to the main matter. Moreover, from day to day his mood varied. He might be sarcastic on Monday, depressed on Tuesday, gently humorous with life on Wednesday, despairing on Thursday, joyous with hope and strong in fortitude on Friday, idyllic on Saturday, sceptical on Sunday morning, religious on Sunday evening, and subtle, delicate and tender every day. This has its own attraction for certain people, and those who like him, like him dearly.

Then, he had an excellent, light-flitting, kindly humour. Sometimes it was broad enough, as in that poem about money, written in Venice, in the character of a vulgar rich man, two verses of which I quote.

---

[1] The quotations in this paragraph are from Mrs Clough's 'Memoir', *PPR I*, 45, 48.

[Quotes *Dipsychus*, IV, 130-40: 'As I sat at the café' to 'so pleasant' etc.]

Sometimes his humour touches lightly and softly the comfortable, thoughtless life, as in these two verses on the gondola—

> Afloat; we move. Delicious! Ah!
> What else is like the gondola?
> This level floor of liquid glass
> Begins beneath us swift to pass.
> It goes as though it went alone
> By some impulsion of its own.
> How light it moves, how softly! Ah,
> Were all things like the gondola!
>
> With no more motion than should bear
> A freshness to the languid air;
> With no more effort than exprest
> The need and naturalness of rest,
> Which we beneath a grateful shade,
> Should take on peaceful pillows laid.
> How light we move, how softly! Ah,
> Were life but as the gondola!
>
> So live, nor need to call to mind
> Our slaving brother here behind![1]

Sometimes it is a humorous mock at his own want of decision and force, as in that poem which wonders how Columbus could ever have conceived, or, rather, ever have carried out his conception of a world beyond the apparent infinity of waters. 'How in God's name did Columbus get over?' is the first line of the poem, and it ends by insisting that no one who had guessed that there was a world beyond the great waters would ever have gone sailing on, and that he himself could never have done it. ''Tis a pure madness, a pure wonder to me.' The *Bothie* also is full of quaint, observant humour. All the Oxford elements of his day are there; liked, even loved, but held up to gentle, subtle ridicule, delicately touched, but touched home. Oxford's young enthusiasm is pictured in the pupils, its quiet temper in the tutor, its dress, its ways of talk, the beginning of its æstheticism, its hereditary self-satisfaction, its variety of youthful intellect, its high sense of honour and morality, its manliness, its noisy athleticism, its sense that

[1] Cf. *Poems* (1951), *Dipsychus*, IV, 3-36.

Oxford is, on the whole, though a doubt may now and then intrude, the mother, and the father, too, of the intellectual universe; and its reading-parties, with a tutor, the incubator of statesmen, poets, philosophers, radical emigrants, and conservative squires, all fitted to replenish the earth and subdue it, to counsel and lead the world.

The poem, written in broken-boned hexameters, belongs to his early time. It is his longest effort. Four young men, with a grave tutor, form a reading party in the Highlands. They go to a sporting function at the Laird's, and Philip Hewson, the radical and revolutionist of the party, in whom Clough, no doubt, sketched his own opinions at this time, meets there a Highland girl, the daughter of a small farmer near Braemar. The farmer invited Hewson to visit him if he should come that way. He falls in love with the girl, begs her to marry him, and sends for the tutor to guarantee his character. The girl refuses at first; their stations in life are different. She will be, she thinks, in his way. The farmer doubts on the same grounds. Will his daughter be happy? But Philip does not desire to live in this burdened, denaturalized England; his opinions (and they may represent a dream of Clough's) lead him to a freer life, close to Mother Earth, in a new land. Will she come with him, taking a plough, a tool-box, a few books, pictures, and £500 to New Zealand? The tutor thinks he could not do better; the girl is charming, intelligent, a true-hearted woman; both are in love, love based on mutual reverence; and Philip is a hard worker, who will put all his theories to the test in an eager life in a fresh country. So they marry; and Clough, whom the social subject of marriage engaged all his life, airs his views in tender converse between Philip and Elsie, mixed, as is always the case in his work, with a certain high reasonableness, to which their love gives beauty.

There is a true love of Nature, especially of Scottish scenery, in the poem. Clough loved the mountains. Wales and the Highlands were dear to him. He wandered alone, meditating, among the glens; it was his great pleasure to have his contemplation broken by Nature's sudden shocks of mild surprise, and to weave what he saw into what he thought. His friend, Frank Palgrave, who wrote a gentle, distinguished memoir of him, said that his mind was 'haunted like a passion' by the loveliness of poetry and scenery; that by his 'acceptance in the natural landscape, he had inherited a double portion of the spirit of Wordsworth. He loved Nature, not only for its earthly sake, but for the divine and the eternal interfused with it.' This seems too strongly said, out it is the judgment of a friend. Clough may have loved Nature as much as

379

Wordsworth, but he had not Wordsworth's power of expressing his love. His descriptions are ill-composed; the spiritual passion he felt slightly appears in them. In the *Bothie*, the halting metre mangles the description; indeed, here, as in the whole of his poetry, the execution lags behind the conception. Art had not thrown her mantle over this man; the language does not enhance or uplift the thought; it rather depresses and lowers it; and, though we always understand him, which is a blessed gift to us, considering what we suffer from others, we wish that the clearness of the poem had been accompanied by a finer composition and workmanship. Palgrave even goes so far as to say that 'one feels a doubt whether in verse he chose the right vehicle, the truly natural mode of utterance.' If that means that Clough would have perhaps done better to write in prose, I am sure, though it sounds bold to say so, that the critic is wrong. I have been surprised by the inferiority of Clough's prose to his poetry. His prose does not rise beyond the level of the ordinary review; his soul is not living in it. On the contrary, in his poetry, though it does want art, and does not seek for it, there is a spirit always moving—a delicate, fantastic, changing spirit; a humanity, with a touch here of Ariel, and there of Puck; a subtle sound and breathing such as one hears in lonely woods and knows not whence it comes, and a melody of verse which his friend Matthew Arnold never arrived at; and these qualities prove, as I think, that prose was not the true vehicle of his thought, and that poetry was. I cannot conceive that even the mocking arguments of the Fiend in *Dipsychus* would be half as well expressed in prose. There is a short prose dialogue at the end of that poem. To read it and compare it with the poetry is proof enough of this. As to the impassioned utterances of the soul in *Dipsychus* struggling to hold its immortal birthright against the tempter who cries: 'Claim the world; it is at your feet'—some passages of which are quite remarkable in spiritual, I do not mean religious, poetry—they would be impossible in prose. Prose could not reach their feeling, nor the delicate interlacing of their thinking. It is in describing the half-tones of the spirit's life as well as of the life of the heart, in touching with the delicate finger the dim, delicate regrets and hopes and fears which flit before us like moths in twilight, in following with soft and subtle tread the fine spun threads of a web of thought, in recording the to and fro questions and answers of our twofold self within, and passing from one to another, each different as light and darkness—with distinctive power and pleasure in the play—it is in these remote, unsailed-on seas of feeling and contemplation that Clough's best work is done, and very few have done the same kind of work so well. The best of this kind is written in the region of the spirit, but he loved also to write, as we have seen, of remote regions of the affections, where Destiny, as it were, played her part in bringing together, and in dividing, lovers and friends; and the pathetic quiet, the still submission to the parting, and the silent, sorrowful hope that Destiny may again unite those she has divided, are as simply told as they are tenderly felt. Here is a poem which uses a common occurrence—one of his favourite methods —to enshrine a sad, and not too common an experience in life.

[Quotes 'Qua Cursum Ventus'.]

I may have quoted more of this poetry than is in proportion in a short essay, but I feel that Clough has been too much neglected; and the reading of the whole of this intimate history of a soul, struggling to light in a time of great spiritual trouble, is likely to be of use to many who, in our changed circumstances, are going through a similar kind of trouble, and for similar reasons, to that which Clough endured.

The trouble did not last all his life. He attained a harbour of peace, when he took life by the right handles. The inward storm retreated over the mountains, and at eventide there was a clear quiet. Had he lived, he might have made music for us out of the peace as soft and clear as his earlier music was sad and harsh, and yet, in the harshness, tender. When he was less within his own soul—that ill-fortuned dwelling for us—and moved in and out among men, his hopes for man, his faith in God, his love of natural humanity, revived, and with them came restoration of the calm he had lost. Even in 1849, about the year he left Oxford, where self-contemplation has her natural seat for those who care for it, he had begun to look beyond his inner soul to humanity, and to think that if he did not get on, others might; if truth did not dawn on him, it might have risen on others; that in the world there might be fighters who had won the field, though he had been put to flight; that his strife might have unconsciously helped them to their victory; that the struggle, though so dark and despairing, was not without its good;—and he used concerning this more hopeful thought a noble image in the poem I now quote. What the image suggested became true as the years of the century went on. It is even truer now. We have a closer, more faithful grasp on truth than Clough could have; we have a diviner and a clearer hope. And what the last verse says was realised also, one is glad to think, in his own life.

[Quotes 'Say not, the struggle nought availeth'.]

These happier, more hopeful words belong to 1849. He died in 1860 [1861]. A kinder, gentler, more delicate soul has rarely lived among us. The Tennyson children used to call him the Angel-child. His fantastical spirit, his finer thought which would have liked to have danced on life's common way, the Ariel in him, would seem to have fitted him for fairyland, were it not that the sore trouble of the world, and the mystery of God's way with it, were, in that tempest-tossed time, too much for him. He was forced to enter the battle with eyes which saw too many things at the same time. The confusion might have overwhelmed him, but the other side of his nature came to his help. His lightheartedness, it is true, departed, save at happy intervals, but he never allowed its absence to injure his association with his friends. And then, to meet his distress, he had great allies within— profound love of and belief in truthfulness, no self-deceit ever touched his soul; a set and honest manliness, a rooted scorn of the temptations and the base things of the world; a great love of freedom and a deep sympathy with men who strove for it; a soul which honoured the ideals and the vital causes of humanity; a love of natural life and a longing to see the divine in it; a fresh delight in the sweetness and beauty of earth and sky and sea; and a humility which touched with its grace all whom he met. His sarcasm, which grew out of the bitterness of his struggle, out of his silent, passionate, tormented inner life, bit only on himself, and spared the world; and when it fell on the world's follies, it was so mixed with happy humour that it half-healed the wound it gave. He had his martyrdom, but he was martyred for us, and the blood of these martyrs is the seed of that invisible Church which rises yearly, beyond all our creeds and scepticisms, into fuller weight and power.

His literary position is rather a solitary one. He has no parents and no children. I seem, however, to trace in some of his religious poems the poetic influence of Keble. What is plain is: that he stands between the absence of art in poetry which marked men like Bailey and Alexander Smith—in their long, uncomposed, intemperate, and self-conscious poems—and a man like Matthew Arnold, who made a study of his art, who was excessively conscious of being an artist, who worked out a theory of his art on the bed of which, like Procrustes, he strained out or shortened his poems; who rarely, therefore, was spontaneous; who questioned his emotion till it grew cold instead of yielding to the angels of impulse whose wings brushed his shoulder, and whose celestial colours glimmered before his eyes. Arnold's art was too conscious of itself to be great art, but he forced the lesser poets of his time to study and practise their art with conscientious care. In our own time we have had somewhat too much of the art of poetry pursued as if it were a science. In many ways it has passed into the artificial; but also since his time no poet has dared to neglect it, dared to write without care and study of what has been done in the past by the great masters. But he did this more by his art-criticism in prose than by art-example in his poetry. He was an artist in poetry more by study than by nature.

Clough wrote side by side with Arnold, but was not influenced by Arnold's demand for artistic excellence. He wrote what came to him with all the carelessness, but without the natural genius, of Walter Scott. He did not obey, though he knew, what noble art demanded. Yet, he reached a higher place among the poets than his natural gift, alone, would have given him. And he owed this, I think, to the steady, informing, temperance-insisting culture of a great university. He was a scholar and had studied and loved the Greek and Roman models of what high poetry is. He might—since he had no poetic genius, only a gentle and charming talent—have been enslaved by a scientific art, a slavery from which genius saves a man, and have become one of the literary prigs of poetry who prate of art but cannot practise it; who gain the whole world of a clique's applause and lose their soul as poets. He was saved from this by the strength of the passion with which he wrote, by his truthfulness which did not condescend to modify his ideas and by his love of clearness. But though he had this one artistic merit of clearness, he was, unlike a true artist, indifferent to beauty of form, to excellence, to delicate choice and arrangement of words and music. He spent no trouble on his work. His poetry, therefore, with all its personal charm, remains in the porch, not in the temple, of the Muses. . . .

58. 'Arthur Hugh Clough', article in the *Contemporary Review*

February 1914, cv, 285–8

This article was occasioned by the publication of Charles Whibley's apologetic Introduction to *Poems of Arthur Hugh Clough* (London, 1913). The tone of this Introduction is well conveyed by the extract from it which the reviewer cites in his article. Whibley devotes much space to a discussion of Clough's use of the hexameter which, on the whole, he finds unsatisfactory.

The critical estimation of the great Victorian poets is taking a new phase. We are now beginning to regard them as the poets of a past age, and to estimate their place in literature without any of the disturbing elements due to the influence of their personalities on their own generation. Browning, Tennyson, Clough, and Arnold form a group by themselves, a group that set their souls to the same problems, each according to the measure of his gifts. This group of stars has during the last few years been to some extent obscured by passing clouds. The dazzling personal influence has passed away, and new schools of some merit, but of no particular note, have occupied the more limited attention that is to-day available for the art of poesy. These current writers, who supply incapacity for form and absence of scholarship by vigour that is not unattractive and coarseness that vainly calls itself virile, have not really taken the place of the mighty men of the Victorian era, and this fact makes probable an early return to the poetic art of that period. Mr. Charles Whibley's essay on Clough, prefixed to the new edition of that poet's works, is a sign of the return movement. That we have a final estimate of the poet before us is difficult to believe, but Mr. Whibley's brilliant critical faculty has placed before the public an issue as to the disputable position of the poet that is of extraordinary value. The present writer believes, Mr. Whibley does not believe, that Clough was a great poet. It will be of interest to consider the case. Mr. Whibley writes as follows:—

He had not the detachment of the artist. He was not content to aim at the perfection of his work. He could make no just separation of the man and poet. He did but attempt to teach in song what he learned in suffering. The suffering, to him at least, was very real, and the consequence of this reality is that in thought and feeling his verses are profoundly sincere. He had certain opinions which he wished to express, certain arguments to justify, and he thought that poetry was the best vehicle for these arguments and opinions. He was not a great poet, because uppermost in him was the spirit of criticism. He suppressed his evident talent of observation, that he might discuss in metre the vexed questions of the moment. And though he was ever intent to criticise life, he was no stern critic of his own poetry. . . . the reason that he sometimes failed in the making of his verses was, I think, that the need of expression was too active in him. His thoughts clamoured so loudly for utterance that he could not control them, and, instead of a great poet, he became, so to say, the mouthpiece of his own doubting age. In other words, he was so faithful to the 'movements' of his time, that he appears already somewhat antiquated and out of fashion.

Now, this critical passage is not convincing, because admitting, as we may well admit, the truth of the statements of fact, they do not bear the deductions. Every word written might be applied to Shakespeare, who certainly had not 'the detachment of the artist,' aimed at no perfection of work, never separated the man from the poet, was essentially a realist, a man of opinions, a critic of life whose thoughts clamoured for utterance, the mouthpiece of his age, its hopes and fears and movements. If these qualities rule a man out of immortality, Shakespeare is as much ruled out as Clough, and many an eighteenth-century critic would have ruled out each impartially. Now, it is not claimed that Clough stands in the company of Dante, Chaucer, Shakespeare, and Milton, but he had in wonderful measure the very qualities that give the touch of immortality to these four great poets; the sense of reality, the critical mind, the human fellowship, the power to subordinate art to creation, the flood of thought. The detachment of the artist from life is the prime note of decadence in art. On these grounds we should believe that there is at any rate the likelihood that Clough will be esteemed a great poet. But, of course, the conditions which have been essential to the greatness of other poets need not necessarily produce greatness. We merely assert that the qualities that Mr. Whibley pronounces to be proofs of mediocrity are, in fact, conditions precedent of greatness.

When we turn to the actual work that Clough gave us in the twenty years in which spasmodically he devoted his great powers to poetry, we seem to see an artist that never fully realised those powers. Born in 1819, dead in 1861, he was only approaching his maturity when he fell on silence. Shakespeare's greatest work, the greatest work of Chaucer and Milton, were produced after the fortieth year was passed, and it is just to believe that Clough had before him possibilities far greater than his actual achievement. The fact that his work pictures with intense reality the religious doubts that affected so many of that age is of immense value. Probably no other poet has so vividly expressed the troubles of the soul, and for all his doubts again and again he comes to the sound conclusion that it is not the mind, it is not philosophy, that will settle those questions:—

> Ah yet, when all is thought and said,
> The heart still overrules the head;
> Still what we hope we must believe,
> And what is given us receive;
>
> Must still believe, for still we hope
> That in a world of larger scope,
> What here is faithfully begun
> Will be completed, not undone.

The bitter irony of that unfinished poem, 'The Shadow', and of 'The Latest Decalogue', shows that Clough felt intensely the unrealities of the Churches and of life in his day. But of the essential necessity of faith and of the simple majesty of the Christian hope he had, as his 'Easter Day' shows, no doubt. Had he lived as long as Shakespeare he would have come to the untroubled outlook on religion of that greatest of poets. As it was he reached the stage of *All Is Well:*—

> In spite of dreams, in spite of thought,
> 'Tis not in vain, and not for nought,
> The wind it blows, the ship it goes.
> Though where and whither, no one knows.

But if Clough's religious and didactic poems give us a unique insight into a soul, his marvellous swiftness of thought and sense of speed and power of brilliant narrative are shown in *The Bothie of Tober-na-Vuolich* and *Amours de Voyage*. The old quarrel as to Clough's 'outbreak of hexameters' is a fruitless one. We agree that 'his lines may be called hexameters only by courtesy.' Call the line what you like, for its purpose it is extraordinarily effective, and we do not believe for a minute that in writing with such ease and speed and force he was fighting 'a hopeless battle against the genius of his language.' The true hexameter cannot be introduced, but this line used by Clough justifies itself. Mr. Whibley admits that it has 'the merit of colour and rapidity'; while it has this merit the result certainly does not lack thought, *nuance*, humour. The line will not condemn Clough as a poet, for when all is said these poems are as enjoyable to-day, as fresh, rapid, and full of colour as when first written. The same can be said for few of the narrative poems of his contemporaries, if we except Browning. That Clough was only just coming into his own when he wrote during the months of travel in search of the health that was never to be found, his *Mari Magno, or Tales on Board*, is plain enough. He did not live to revise the tales, but, unrevised as they are, they attract the reader in the way that Chaucer attracts. Let the general reader, good easy soul, read these narrative poems, and he will revel in them. In some ways they are wonderful, full of movement, life, and truth, the care of the great artist, ever chary of the unnecessary word, ever touching in the under-tones, visible in every line. Had Clough lived, he might well have been among the greatest of our poets. As it is, he is a great poet, whose work will be still alive when the large mass of nineteenth-century poetry will be as dead as the paper it is printed on.

59. Martha Hale Shackford, 'The Clough Centenary: His *Dipsychus*', in *Sewanee Review*

October 1919, xxvii, 401–10

If Clough's centenary year was marked by little noteworthy remembrance in England, the Americans remained, as always, faithful with this first serious attempt to evaluate *Dipsychus*. Martha Hale Shackford was a lecturer at Wellesley College, Massachusetts. Her commentary on the life, though it adds nothing new, has been retained for comparison in tone with the Victorian treatments of the subject.

An English poet with special interest for Americans is Arthur Hugh Clough, born in 1819, who spent several years of his childhood in America and in later years had many American friends. One of the most finely sensitive thinkers of the Victorian Age, Clough had traits that we admire especially: flexibility and shrewdness of intelligence joined with an invincible idealism. The friend of Lowell, Emerson, Norton, Agassiz, and others, he was respected, here, for his scholarship and loved for his personal charm. During one year, 1852, when he was living in Cambridge he became an affectionate interpreter of American character, and when he went back to England he was distinctly a medium of better understanding of our ideals and purposes. Even in death he has an American associate, for he lies near Theodore Parker in that beautiful Protestant cemetery in Florence, where purple fleurs-de-lis, roses, and tapering green cypress trees surround him with silence.

The general reader knows Clough as the author of several short poems which voice the spiritual unrest and aspiration of his day, but his position as a poet is not as clearly established as is that of his friend Matthew Arnold. A few people read Clough's long vacation pastoral, *The Bothie of Tober-na-Vuolich*; fewer read the charming descriptions of Italy in *Amours de Voyage* (first published in America); fewer still read his most thoroughly characteristic long poem—the unfinished *Dipsychus*.

388

Essentially a man of his epoch yet deeply critical of it, Clough must be studied as a citizen of the Victorian Age. That age was dominated by a rapidly increasing industrialism and a more and more autocratic science. Men were absorbed in mechanical matters, in physical laws; railways, steamboats, telegraph lines, mills, and merchandise seemed nearer and more real than questions of faith and truth. It is true that there were great reforms in this period,—slavery in the colonies was abolished, the corn laws were repealed, factory acts were passed, the Catholics emancipated, and steady slow progress in civic betterment was made. But as regards the average man, life was so full of material things that he had scant time for things spiritual. The mood of the age is fairly enough represented in the philosophy of such a man as Huxley, who wrote as late as 1870 in his essay on Descartes' *Discourse*,

I protest that if some great Power would agree to make me always think what is true and do what is right, on condition of being turned into a sort of clock and wound up every morning before I got out of bed, I should instantly close with the offer. The only freedom I care about is the freedom to do right; the freedom to do wrong I am ready to part with on the cheapest terms to any one who will take it of me.

He would forfeit man's most precious possession,—the need to struggle for his virtue. It is incredible that a thinking man would be willing to abrogate all his rights in the experience which comes from making moral decisions. Life lived automatically would be hideously childish, a travesty, a preposterous anti-climax. Clough had none of this tendency to shirk the moral issue, he had none of the superstitious reverence for virtue by mechanics not by choice. And the very source of Clough's power as a poet lies in his eternal protest against spiritual ease and smugness.

The great stumbling-block to the enjoyment of Clough's poetry is the fact that he was perhaps the most ironical poet of the whole nineteenth century. The literal-minded reader is baffled by a style which is subtle, based upon the desire to ridicule false, meretricious ideas by gravely seeming to champion these ideas. In 'The Latest Decalogue' Clough lashes iniquity with a potent vigor, but he does it indirectly, professing to accept standards which we know are abhorrent to him. Yet who can fail to understand his meaning in—

Honour thy parents; that is, all
From whom advancement may befall?

389

Again, Clough has much of the spirit of mysticism shared by Plato and Thomas à Kempis. He was absorbed in a world beyond the senses, and he knew that much of our spiritual knowledge must be gained not by reason but by that instinctive, contemplative reverie known as illumination. His poem,—

> Oh Thou whose image in the shrine
> Of human spirits dwells divine;—

is the best illustration of his mystical mood. Unlike such mystics as Vaughan or Blake or Tagore he lacked the impulse to express his mysticism in verse that has the objectively pictorial appeals of beauty. He leaves too much to implication, he makes a greater appeal to the reader's thought than to his imagination.

It has been said too many times that Clough was the poet of hopeless doubt, that he provokes pessimism and despair. Clough did doubt; he sought rational proof to support faith; he wore himself out in purely intellectual debate, but his true attitude is shown, most unequivocally, in the short poem that is best known of all his works:—

> It fortifies my soul to know
> That, though I perish, Truth is so;
> That, howso'er I stray and range,
> Whate'er I do, Thou dost not change.
> I steadier step when I recall
> That, if I slip, Thou dost not fall.

Before discussing his poetry, it is necessary to study the poet's life, in order to understand how completely his conduct exemplified his ideals. Clough was from boyhood profoundly sensitive to the appeals of moral beauty. From his mother of symbolic name, Anne Perfect, he inherited and learned a deep seriousness of attitude, and the circumstances of his early life, his separation from his family when he was at school in England, ripened a tendency already sharply defined. As the most distinguished pupil of Dr. Arnold's school at Rugby, he showed not only gifts of sheer intellectual power but also, impressively, a nature intensely scrupulous in conduct, earnestly searching out those truths which bear on man's mysterious relation to God. Without being, or seeming, a prig, actually a champion runner and a lover of sport, Clough was a favorite at school. More than his distinction in scholarship his individual attractiveness and charm won him affection and a leader's place. He carried off all the academic honors, and when he left, Rugby lost a presence recognized by all as 'touched to fine issues.'

At Oxford his power was recognized speedily and his friends learned to respect his stimulating analyses of truth. Living at Balliol at the time when Newman was at the height of his power and influence, when Oxford reverberated to the footsteps of pilgrims toward the higher life, Clough's vivid nature was quick to respond to the deepest aspirations of those young men who so sincerely endeavoured to overthrow apathy and institute the *vita activa* in religion. The Tractarian Movement swept on its way, ending with Newman's entrance into the Roman Catholic Church. Clough, eager at the beginning, became more and more troubled as he saw what began as a movement for reform turn into a debate about dogma and authority. So absorbed was he in the thoughts aroused by this controversy, so driven to analysis and speculation regarding fundamental religious beliefs, that he rather ignored the routine duties of his college work and failed to win the honors his friends expected him to receive. He took an inconspicuous B.A., but he won in 1842 a fellowship at Oriel, the last competition in which, it is said, Newman was one of the examiners. Of course at Oriel he came even more closely into the atmosphere of Newman's group, and his ferment of thought continued,—his endless reading, questioning, debating. His duties he performed with great success, but at the very height of his usefulness he made the decision which seemed to him necessitated by honor of conscience,—he resigned his fellowship on the ground chiefly that he could no longer subscribe to the thirty-nine articles: in short, that he was not in sympathy with Oxford's conservative and sectarian attitude towards religion.

In those days everyone who entered the university had to subscribe to the thirty-nine articles of religion as set forth by the English Church. Few thought twice about the matter, regarding it as a mere tradition to be humored, but Clough, with his intense intellectual honesty, could not take the matter conventionally. The scrupulousness of his action is the more remarkable because he did not deny any of the articles, he merely found it impossible to affirm them satisfactorily; so without making a show, or seeming to demand sympathy, he quietly renounced the deepest hopes and satisfactions of his life, gave up his tutorship and his fellowship and left Oxford.

Such quiet heroism is seldom appreciated, and Clough was regarded not as a hero but as a problem. To-day we see more clearly how nobly he acted in refusing to be a hypocrite, to receive benefits while he was conscious of uneasy doubts and incomplete loyalty. His renunciation involved the loss of almost all the associations and the friendships he valued. Detaching himself from the place that he loved he became the resident of a world crude, hard, difficult to a man of fine sensibility and a lover of old-established customs and traditions. The Oxford world represented fullness and depth of life. The stateliness of the old gray buildings, the quiet beauty of green quad and of gently flowing river, the sound of mellow chimes coming across the soft air, the almost visible and audible tradition of the place had appealed to him with keenest power. To go away, to feel that sense of loneliness and longing, embittered always by a sense of estrangement due to misunderstanding on the part of his friends tested the very fiber of his spiritual life. Most of all he missed the zest and stimulus of his friendships there, the interchange of ideas, the pursuit of knowledge, the daily contact with men of like tastes and energies. To give up these was essential tragedy.

Soon after leaving Oxford Clough was in Paris with Ralph Waldo Emerson, an event of profound suggestiveness but of scant record for those who would like to know the nature of their conversations. In 1849 he was in Rome, returning in the autumn of that year to become Head of University Hall of University College, London. In 1850 he visited Venice where he received the impulse to begin *Dipsychus* in the latter part of that year. His journey to America in 1852, his arduous work in England at the Education Office, his duties as secretary to a commission for examining scientific military schools on the continent broke down his health, and after a vain journey in search of restoration he came to Florence, where malarial fever, followed by paralysis, ended his life, in 1861.

In approaching the unfinished drama, *Dipsychus*, the reader should bear in mind the fact that it is the most satiric of all of Clough's poems. It is the reverse side of his own life, the negative aspect of his positive action. It presents in loosely dramatic scenes the spiritual irresolution of the typical young Oxford man who, visiting Venice and delighting in all the shimmering beauty of the city, fascinated by the gay life, is, however, continually debating whether the appeal of the easy and conventional is the appeal of materialism or of good, honest common sense. The higher and the lower natures are in constant interplay, the remonstrant voice of the aspiring, mystical mood of Dipsychus is answered by the satiric Spirit of conformity, the spirit of *laissez-faire* in the world of moral duty, until Dipsychus gives himself over to the care of the Mephisto within himself.

The scene opens in the Piazza at Venice, while Dipsychus, pondering once again the problem of the resurrection, is interrupted, taunted by the Spirit calling attention to the sights and sounds nearby, far more significant than empty musings about religion. So the semi-drama continues, in and about Venice. There are charming pictures of the city, suggested by a vivid line or phrase; all the easy comfort, the picturesque attractiveness is made clear; and yet, always, there is the undercurrent of speculation. The questions Dipsychus is asking, 'Is there really evidence to hold us to the truths taught in the Bible? And if the Bible is true, is the teaching sufficient for the needs of the yearning human soul? Does philosophy, being more distinctly based on reason, prove a satisfactory substitute for religion? Are Berkeley and Kant right?—is sensuous experience only an illusion? is thought the only reality? If philosophers prove too abstract, are the poets and artists better guides to living? and, in the last analysis, are we so ringed around by necessity that we have no choice at all? Does the iron law of life compel us to conform? Or, divinest of dreams, has the individual perfect liberty, the power and the right to live his own life, in a sanctity of spirit gained from perfect communion between the Creator and the created? Are the old familiar friends, after all, eternally true?—do faith, hope, love, lead us on to duty, positive, courageous, constructive action?' By every implication Clough asserts his belief in a sort of Pragmatism:—

> Yet if we must live, as would seem,
> These peremptory heats to claim,
> Ah, not for profit, not for fame,
> And not for pleasure's giddy dream,
> And not for piping empty reeds,
> And not for colouring idle dust;
> If live we positively must,
> God's name be blest for noble deeds.

As a Critique of Pure Worldliness *Dipsychus* is most successful; as a work of art it fails. Readers complain that it is too casual, too disconcerting, a medley of blank verse and of various stanzas; that it moves not logically but chronologically. All of this is true. There are too many influences operative in *Dipsychus*,—reminiscences of the plot of *Faust*, suggestions of the manner of Alfred de Musset's *Les Nuits*, direct obligations to the Socratic dialectic, and much that is due to the satiric habit of Lord Byron.

From the literary point of view it is as a satire that *Dipsychus* is most interesting, and it should be judged as a satire on character.

Many people make the mistake of censuring it because it has not the dramatic unity of Ben Jonson's satiric comedies, or because it does not lead inexorably onward as does Swift's *Argument Against Abolishing Christianity*, or because it has not the sustained tone of such formal satire as Dryden's terrible *Mac Flecknoe* with its—

> Trust nature, do not labour to be dull.

Clough, it seems, is closest in method and in purpose to Byron. Of course the difference between Byron, as a man, and Clough needs no discussion. It is the moral fastidiousness and uncompromising idealism of Clough which makes him so memorable a person. But Clough enjoyed Byron's satires, was impressed by his attack on Cant and Hypocrisy, and delighted, in an almost undergraduate fashion, in Byron's tricks, his jaunty, adroit manipulation of puns, antitheses, double rhymes, even *doubles entendres*, and anticlimax.

A specimen from Byron will refresh the reader's memory of the finer side of his satires upon hypocrisy:—

> But *'carpe diem,'* Juan, *'carpe, carpe!'*
> To-morrow sees another race as gay,
> And Transient and devour'd by the same harpy.
> 'Life's a poor player,' then 'play out the play,
> Ye villains!' and above all keep a sharp eye
> Much less on what you do than what you say:
> Be hypocritical, be cautious, be
> Not what you *seem*, but always what you *see*.

Similarly, Clough inveighs against the Victorian snobbery and love of social position:—

> 'Good manners,' said our great aunts, 'next to piety:'
> And so my friend, hurrah for good society.

This cynicism is carried further by Clough, in order to picture the conventional tone of average religious life of that day:—

> Why, as to feelings of devotion
> I interdict all vague emotion;
> But if you will, for once and all
> Compound with ancient Juvenal.
> *Orandum est,* one perfect prayer
> For *savoir-vivre* and *savoir-faire*.

The satire varies, there is playful jesting at Oxford's faith in athletics as the cure-all:—

But you with this one bathe, no doubt,
Have solved all questions in and out.

Men's futile and cowardly evasions of direct action are noted:—

Yet as for you,
You'll hardly have the courage to die outright,
You'll somehow halve even it.

More cynical is the picture of the fate of the man who really desires
to take his part in active service:—

We ask action,
And dream of arms and conflicts; and string up
All self-devotion's muscles; and are set
To fold up papers.

The whimsical verses that follow express a very profound truth,
part of Clough's creed:—

Our gaieties, our luxuries,
Our pleasures and our glee,
Mere insolence and wantonness,
Alas! they feel to me.

How shall I laugh and sing and dance?
My very heart recoils,
While here to give my mirth a chance
A hungry brother toils.

The joy that does not spring from joy
Which I in others see,
How can I venture to employ,
Or find it joy for me?

The very best of the satire comes in the stanzas that occur as a sort of
chorus; these are so consummately ironical that they delude many
readers into the belief that Clough approves of accepting a compromise, whereas, in truth, they are almost savagely contemptuous of the
man who yields placidly to custom and comfort. There is not, in
nineteenth-century English poetry, a more effective example of pure
irony than the lines that follow; but irony is usually misunderstood or
distrusted by the majority of readers, who do not like enigmas. For
those who enjoy paradox, antithesis, feigned cynicism, the play of

concealed weapons, Clough offers examples of keenest sort; this is one of his masterpieces:—

> Submit, submit!
> 'Tis common sense, and human wit
> Can claim no higher name than it.
> Submit, submit!
> Devotion, and ideas, and love,
> And beauty claim their place above;
> But saint and sage and poet's dreams
> Divide the light in coloured streams,
> Which this alone gives all combined,
> The *siccum lumen* of the mind
> Called common sense: and no high wit
> Gives better counsel than does it.
> Submit, submit!

Translate this into its opposite: 'Aspire, aspire, follow ideals, and avoid the cheap compromises dictated by prudence and common sense,' and we have the philosophy of Clough clearly before us. Every one of these stanzas, to be understood, must be read perversely; and it will ring with passionate exhortation to keep up the good fight against 'the power of this world.'

For each of us *Dipsychus* has a special sting; we see ourselves as in a mirror, and we are brought into the presence of a good man's withering scorn of our futile evasions and cowardice in meeting life. The placid citizen who goes out each morning, thinking,—

> Men's business wits, the only sane things,
> These and compliance are the main things,

will learn from Clough that there are 'higher, holier things than these.' This poet believed in the individual's duty, in the individual's obligation to take a vigorous part in life. His collected poems bear witness, on almost every page, to this faith. He believed that man must progress, not by shambling along following the habit of the world, forever adapting himself to existing conditions, but by resolute, fearless scrutiny of the world, followed by determined positive action in an effort to change conditions for the better.

60. James Insley Osborne, from
Arthur Hugh Clough

1920, Conclusion 187–91

Clough was even less fortunate in his second English biographer than in his first, so far as criticism was concerned. The extract given below fairly summarizes the content of the book, which is handled with considerable generosity by MacDowall in his review in *The Times Literary Supplement* (see the next item).

The respect in which Clough was most consistently of the nineteenth century is that all of the settings he uses are nineteenth-century settings. His long narrative poems are all of them about people of his own time; and so are the stories that his lyrics suggest—for a lyric always suggests a story of some sort as its background. Tennyson and Browning and Arnold took much of their material, most of it indeed, from the past, and often from the traditions of other nations than their own. But Clough's criticism of life is invariably of the life of Britons of his day and generation. This is a real peculiarity. Its importance is lessened, but by no means destroyed, by remembering what modern poems *Idylls of the King* and *Empedocles on Etna* and *The Statue and the Bust* are, and how English, in spite of their foreign or antique subject matter. Clough found human life enough in the world about him without going far afield for it. His mind, indeed, however powerful, had not the intrepidity for travelling. It was still finding plenty to feed on in the home pasture when it ceased its activities.

It is not to be denied that the problems Clough worked at are also all of them nineteenth-century problems, though it might be urged that the nineteenth century made its own nearly all problems of all times. And it was the most universal and timeless of these problems that interested Clough. The nature of friendship and love and marriage and parenthood, the service of God and fellow service—he examines directly these large and eternal things, and not merely abnormal or unusual instances of them, or aspects of them considered to

397

be new. He was not the man to care much whether his works were up-to-date or not and whether they were novel or not. Pettiness of all sorts, over-valuation of little things, was what he hated most, and he was singularly successful in avoiding it. Differentiating a vast number of aspects of a thing, and arranging them, perhaps chronologically, is the kind of thing he called 'fiddle-faddling': just as the people who find profit and delight in that kind of juggling find 'fiddle-faddling' Clough's disposition to sit for ever on large problems he could not solve instead of deserting them for little problems that he could solve. But others than philosophers of the pigeon-holing school may fairly object to this disposition of Clough's. And it is certainly a respect in which he was not typical of his age.

Archbishop Whately said of Clough that he had no following: meaning, specifically, that his defection carried out of the Church no other men than himself. This is true, and may be taken as showing on Clough's part either sense and consideration or a lack of courage. To call his refusal to proselytize good sense is perhaps to be reminded of the great chapter in which Dean Swift so satisfactorily proves that all revolutions and discoveries in human thought are varieties of madness; and calling it lack of courage, one may remember Emerson's dictum that 'there is a certain headiness in all action,' and that courage is willingness to act. If Clough had been willing, early in his life, to set limits to his thinking, to pick a direction and a road and to keep the road and pay no attention to byways, however highly recommended—if he had been willing to do this, he might have added a new form of protest against the Church to the other fine enthusiasms of his day, and might have ridden off on it and cut a figure. But before he could mount for his ride and gallop off to become another Great Victorian, it was necessary that he should tell himself that he had settled problems which he felt that he had not settled, and this for better and for worse he was unable to do.

In a world in which a man's chances of accomplishing anything memorable are small, it may appear graceless to be asking so insistently why this man did not accomplish more, instead of marvelling that he accomplished so much as he did. New, though perhaps small, editions of Clough have been appearing at rather short intervals ever since his death. He wrote and he is read. Public taste, on the whole, seems to be moving in his direction rather than away from him, so that he will probably continue to find readers. And so long as he finds them they will probably, even though they like him, keep on finding him something of a failure, and speculating on why he failed. Lack of determination, inadequate opportunity, limited comprehension—here are the causes of failure; but Clough had a strong and steady will, the best of training and of friends, a wealth of good sense. More careful examination will show, perhaps, that the determination was too content to remain determination instead of removing the need for itself, that the training, though splendid for the usual boy, was of the wrong kind for at least one boy, and that a disproportionate share of the good sense rested on merely vicarious experience. But behind these suppositions will lurk a presentiment of some unescapable limitation in the man's physical nature. He was not sufficiently sensuous. He did the best he could with a nervous system that was simply not finely enough organized, not delicate enough, to delight and gloriously to succeed in creative effort.

61. A. S. McDowall on Osborne's *Arthur Hugh Clough* in *The Times Literary Supplement*

4 March 1920, 153

The spell which Clough threw over his contemporaries has become a memory, and yet his poems are by no means dead. It ought to be possible, therefore, to survey them candidly, and this acute and interesting book is a great help towards doing so. It disabuses one of the idea that Clough is out of date because he wrote about 'problems.' As a conscientious intellectual he could not help doing that, but his musings are not of the single type which they have often been supposed to be. Nothing ages so quickly for new generations as the religious perplexities of the old, and it is unlucky for Clough that a simplifying legend has labelled him the poet of doubt. With the emphatic notes of 'Easter Day' in our mind, or the more subtle avowals of poems like '*ὕμνος ἄυμνος*,' it is rather hard not to yield to this impression. But it is scarcely true of the first or last current of his poetry; nor does it represent the ruling one, except for a time. What preoccupies him most is the relation of feeling to action, and the purity or falsity of both. As his difficulties came largely from his intellectual nature, he puts them in a speculative way. And as the conscience and the intellect in him were equally exigent he is bound to raise the final query about 'the purpose of our being here.' But, as Mr. Osborne reminds us, he deals more and more with these matters on their human and universal side. 'The nature of friendship and love and marriage and parenthood, the service of God and fellow-service'— these are the problems to which he continually comes back. He is facing immediate questions, whether mental or practical, and this necessity determines his imaginative form.

Whatever may be thought of Clough's quality as an artist, there is much in his comment which is not easily brushed aside. No other English poet has so anatomized the idea of duty, or the possibilities of acting truly, or even (Hamlet always excepted) the possibility of acting at all. Idealist though he was, no one has faced more honestly the perplexities of love and marriage. If Matthew Arnold's view of poetry as a criticism of life applies to anyone, it certainly applies to Clough. In spite of this, his position as a poet is more uncertain than that of many who have had less interesting things to say. The final reason of that, no doubt, is the one Mr. Osborne puts succinctly in the last words of his book. 'He did the best he could with a nervous system that was simply not finely enough organized, not delicate enough, to delight and gloriously to succeed in creative effort.' Yet even this is hardly the whole of the matter. Strange as it may be to say it of anyone so persevering, we are not at all sure that as a poet he did the best he could. Serious, even over-serious, as he was about so many things, did he take poetry seriously enough? He could not live by it, and he did not live for it; only partially does he serve the Muse. The occupations of his life lay elsewhere, like Arnold's; yet Arnold, one feels, surmounted the difficulty as Clough did not. Arnold never gives us the feeling that he is writing poetry as an amateur, but Clough, with all his earnestness, gives this fairly often. It may be too much to expect a man to live for the pleasure of posterity, and Clough was too modest to calculate on a second life with the immortals. But, knowing what he had to say, and guessing at finer possibilities behind, we are tempted to grudge the honest work which he gave to other things than poetry.

From this point of view it is hard not to treat his conscience as a personal enemy. It invades him like a grey shadow, inhibiting the æsthetic faculties. From the beginning we see it urgent for the lion's share, and stipulating that his happier moments shall not be wasted on the 'trifler, Poesy.' Much, if not all, of the responsibility for this can be transferred to Rugby and its Headmaster, who strung Clough's moral sensibility to so extreme a pitch. Mr. Osborne is no doubt right in thinking that this tension, and the reactions from it, affected Clough far more deeply than the seething Tractarianism of Oxford. The early poems express the mood and yet provide relief from it, in their shy and tentative simplicity. Mainly Wordsworthian exercises, as Mr. Osborne calls them, they still have a charm and promise which were never quite fulfilled. The paths are not yet closed. But the dilemma of innocence and worldliness, which was the simplest and most touching form of Clough's moral problem, appears plainly in 'The Higher Courage,'[1] and was to have long echoes in *Dipsychus*. There seems to be more in the former poem than the revolt from willing and desire to remain undecided which his critic finds. Behind Clough's mental probings is a feeling very like that yearning for a lost candour, that recoils to the first vision of the soul, which Vaughan has once for all expressed:—

> Some men a forward motion love,
> But I by backward steps would move.[2]

If Clough had never gathered up his self-communings into one complete and poignant expression, we should have had, for this side of him, only the shorter introspective poems—sensitive records of the fluctuations of his soul, full of true though reticent emotion, yet inviting a wish that the thoughts which returned so often should be fused in a more coherent form. The prompting came to do this, and yielded *Dipsychus*. Tastes have differed about that poem. To Mr. Osborne it seems the most honest and thoughtful of Clough's long poems; the best of them, for anyone who wants to understand him, but by no means the best in point of art. It was written in a dark hour, and the poet is still entangled in some wisps of the cloud. But his distress has made him less deliberate; and out of it, as Mr. Osborne reminds us, he plucks a new and precious gift—the gift of irony. Hence come those deft interjections of Dipsychus's other self, which are the salt and sparkle of the poem, and almost the only relief to that

---

[1] I.e. 'Come back again my olden heart'.
[2] Vaughan, 'The Retreat'.

long soliloquy of introspection which is staged so oddly in the fairest city of Europe. Mr. Osborne would gladly have had it otherwise. But when he says that a good train of narrative might have satisfied all objections, and that never did a work of art stand in greater need of a story, he makes us feel unregenerately that we would rather have the hazardous performance as it stands than a more conventional achievement. The execution wavers; we are vague at moments as to whether the hero is deciding to live like plain people, or to live ambitiously, or to drop into an easy sin. *Agir, c'est nuire.*[1] Clough gives his various readings of that thought, and his emotion cannot be gainsaid. Perhaps it was well that one drama of the mind should have clung so resolutely to mental scenery, and it was rare that an Englishman should choose that way to write it.

It is possible—Mr. Osborne himself has an inkling of it—that *Dipsychus* may carry farther in the end than the *Bothie* and *Amours de Voyage*, which take the fancy more obviously. The *Bothie* is acquiring an exquisitely Early Victorian bloom; it has almost become a document. This may do it no harm; it makes a wider appeal than the spell of Oxford. But the fate of the *Bothie* and *Amours de Voyage* must turn on the value of Clough's response to the world outside him—the world of man and nature. Here, in the glimpses of moor and tumbling stream throughout the *Bothie* and the Roman landscape of the other poem, are those 'sights and sounds of the country' which were held dear by him. Here are his reflections on character and the general life, sane and penetrating, advancing beyond his time to ours when he speaks of women and of society. And here, not least, is a genial sense of humour. There is the stuff of novels and stories in these poems; *Amours de Voyage* might be an early Henry James, and it has its likenesses to Swinburne's excursion into prose fiction. All this is enough to make poetry which can be read with real interest and amusement, perhaps even with delight; but it is not enough to make great poetry. The hexameter tells against it, not so much from any metrical uncouthness as because it wakes the suspicion that Clough does not mean to go too far. It was disarming of him to choose this form for the *Bothie* and so forestall the charge of donnishness. But his second choice of it suggests the line of least resistance. He has gained in experience and decision by the time he comes to *Mari Magno*; he is close, now, to a synthesis of reason, love and duty. But this late work, which he

_____
[1] 'To act is to err' (source untraced).

never had the chance to go over, stands as a fragment, in a form still too curt and narrow to express his feeling adequately.

It is tiresome, however, to hunt for missing excellences. If there is a defect in Mr. Osborne's book, it is that he seems less inclined to dwell on the positive qualities of Clough's poetry than on its shortcomings. The plan of the book accounts partly for this, as it is not primarily a discussion of the poems, but takes them as they come in a psychological and critical study of Clough's life. There it is masterly; the analysis is searching, but there is sympathy as well as justice in the author's intuition. He notices how every one who writes of Clough's poetry quickly begins talking of the man, and it is as natural to end as to begin there. Do we really wish that Clough had been different? Mr. Osborne allows that his character is a fine one; and it is not certain how far he could have been changed as a poet. In the end he almost persuades us that his defects are qualities. We give up asking for the keen sense of beauty which he did not possess. We make terms with the encroaching conscience, recognizing how much of his flavour is due just to that. The unprofessional nature of his poetry has, at any rate, one advantage: no one who feels him uncongenial is obliged to try to read him. Those who do read him allow for his shyness and his inhibitions, and find something real beneath them—a fidelity of thought and feeling which is uncommon and wears well.

Select Bibliography

GOLLIN, RICHARD M., HOUGHTON, WALTER E., and TIMKO, MICHAEL, *Arthur Hugh Clough, a Descriptive Catalogue*, The New York Public Library, 1968. A comprehensive annotated bibliography divided into three parts: Poetry, Prose, Biography and Criticism. The critical section lists 500 items.

ARMSTRONG, ISOBEL, *Arthur Hugh Clough*, London, 1962. A pamphlet in the British Council's 'Writers and Their Work' series.

CHORLEY, KATHARINE, *Arthur Hugh Clough: the Uncommitted Mind*, Oxford, 1962. A thoroughgoing attempt to explain Clough's 'failure' in terms of his psychological defects.

GOODE, JOHN and HARDY, BARBARA, *Major Victorian Poets: Reconsiderations*, Routledge & Kegan Paul, 1969. Two important essays in revaluation.

HOUGHTON, WALTER E., *The Poetry of Clough: an Essay in Revaluation*, New Haven, 1963. The fullest critical study of Clough to date.

LEVY, GOLDIE, *Arthur Hugh Clough: 1819–1861*, London, 1938. A full, but non-critical, biographical study.

LOWRY, H. F., *The Letters of Matthew Arnold to Arthur Hugh Clough*, Oxford, 1932. Includes a valuable introduction.

THORPE, MICHAEL, Introduction to *A Choice of Clough's Verse*, Faber and Faber, 1969. A plea for revaluation.

TIMKO, MICHAEL, *Innocent Victorian: the Satiric Poetry of Arthur Hugh Clough*, Ohio University Press, 1966. Stressing Clough's 'positive naturalism' or 'moral realism', Timko seeks to counter the myth of failure by demonstrating the constructive nature of the satirical poetry.

VEYRIRAS, PAUL, *Arthur Hugh Clough (1819–1861)*, Paris, 1964 (published 1965). A detailed study of the man and the 'milieu'.

WILLIAMS, DAVID, *Too Quick Despairer: A Life of Arthur Hugh Clough*, Rupert Hart-Davis, 1969.

Index

II. ARTHUR HUGH CLOUGH: WRITINGS

III. GENERAL

2/79

AP 20 79

THE CRITICAL HERITAGE SERIES

GENERAL EDITOR: B. C. SOUTHAM

Volumes published and forthcoming

Continued